THE ARDEN CRITICAL COMPANIONS

GENERAL EDITORS
Andrew Hadfield and Paul Hammond

ADVISORY BOARD
*MacDonald P. Jackson, Katherine Duncan-Jones, David Scott Kastan,
Patricia Parker, Lois Potter, Phyllis Rackin, Bruce R. Smith
Brian Vickers, and Blair Worden*

Shakespeare and Renaissance Europe
ed. Andrew Hadfield and Paul Hammond

Shakespeare and Renaissance Politics *Andrew Hadfield*

Shakespeare and the Victorians *Adrian Poole*

Shakespeare and Comedy *Robert Maslen*

Shakespeare and Music *David Lindley*

Shakespeare and Elizabethan Popular Culture
ed. Stuart Gillespie and Neil Rhodes

Shakespeare and Law *Andrew Zurcher*

Shakespeare and Religion *Alison Shell*

Shakespeare and the Medieval World *Helen Cooper*

Shakespeare and his Texts *Tom Lockwood*

THE ARDEN CRITICAL COMPANIONS

SHAKESPEARE
AND RELIGION

ALISON SHELL

Bloomsbury Arden Shakespeare
An imprint of Bloomsbury Publishing Plc

B L O O M S B U R Y
LONDON • NEW DELHI • NEW YORK • SYDNEY

Bloomsbury Arden Shakespeare

An imprint of Bloomsbury Publishing Plc

Imprint previously known as Arden Shakespeare

50 Bedford Square	1385 Broadway
London	New York
WC1B 3DP	NY 10018
UK	USA

www.bloomsbury.com

**BLOOMSBURY, THE ARDEN SHAKESPEARE and the
Diana logo are trademarks of Bloomsbury Publishing Plc**

First published in 2010, paperback edition first published 2015

British Library Cataloguing-in-Publication Data
A catalogue record for this book is available from the British Library.

ISBN: HB: 978-1-9042-7170-3
PB: 978-1-4725-6817-5
ePDF: 978-1-4081-4360-5
ePUB: 978-1-4081-4361-2

Library of Congress Cataloging-in-Publication Data
A catalog record for this book is available from the Library of Congress.

Printed and bound in India

CONTENTS

TEXTUAL NOTE

In quoting from early-modern texts, expansions of abbreviations are shown in square brackets, with the exception of 'n' and 'm', which have been silently expanded; u/v and i/j have been silently normalized.

All biblical references come from Lloyd E. Berry (ed.), *The Geneva Bible: A Facsimile of the 1560 Edition* (1969: repr. Peabody, Mass.: Hendrickson, 2007).

Except where otherwise indicated, the following editions have been used for quotations from Shakespeare's works:

All's Well That Ends Well. Ed. Susan Snyder. Oxford: Oxford University Press, 1993.

Antony and Cleopatra. Ed. Michael Neill. Oxford: Oxford University Press, 1994.

As You Like It. Ed. Juliet Dusinberre. Arden Shakespeare, Third Series. London: Thomson, 2006.

Cymbeline. Ed. Martin Butler. Cambridge: Cambridge University Press, 2005.

Hamlet Second Quarto Text. Ed. Ann Thompson and Neil Taylor. Arden Shakespeare, Third Series. London: Thomson, 2006.

Henry IV: Part One. Ed. David Bevington. Oxford: Oxford University Press, 1987, repr. 1998.

Henry IV: Part Two. Ed. René Weis. Oxford: Oxford University Press, 1997.

Henry V. Ed. Gary Taylor. 1982: repr. Oxford: Oxford University Press, 1998.

Henry VI. Part III. Ed. John D. Cox and Eric Rasmussen. Arden Shakespeare, Third Series. London: Thomson, 2001.

Julius Caesar. Ed. David Daniell. Arden Shakespeare, Third Series. Nelson: Walton-on-Thames, 1998.

King Lear. Ed. Jay L. Halio. Cambridge: Cambridge University Press, 1992.

King Richard II. Ed. Andrew Gurr. Cambridge: Cambridge University Press, 1990.

Macbeth. Ed. A.R. Braunmuller. Cambridge: Cambridge University Press, 1997.

Measure for Measure. Ed. N.W. Bawcutt. 1991: repr. Oxford: Oxford University Press, 2008.

A Midsummer Night's Dream. Ed. Peter Holland. Oxford: Oxford University Press, 1994.

Much Ado About Nothing. Ed. Claire McEachern. Arden Shakespeare, Third Series. London: Thomson, 2006.

Othello. Ed. E.A.J. Honigmann. Arden Shakespeare, Third Series. Walton-on-Thames: Nelson, 1997.

Richard III. Ed. Pat Baldwin and Tom Baldwin. Cambridge: Cambridge University Press, 2000.

Romeo and Juliet. Ed. Jill L. Levenson. Oxford: Oxford University Press, 2000.

Sonnets. Ed. Katherine Duncan-Jones. Arden Shakespeare, Third Series. London: Thomson, 1997, repr. 1998.

The Tempest. Ed. Stephen Orgel. Oxford: Oxford University Press, 1987, repr. 2008.

Titus Andronicus. Ed. Jonathan Bate. Arden Shakespeare, Third Series. 1995: repr. London: Arden, 2003.

Twelfth Night. Ed. Keir Elam. Arden Shakespeare, Third Series. London: Thomson, 2008.

The Two Gentlemen of Verona. Ed. William C. Carroll. Arden Shakespeare, Third Series. London: Thomson, 2004.

(with John Fletcher) *The Two Noble Kinsmen*. Ed. Lois Potter. Arden Shakespeare, Third Series. London: Arden, 1997.

'Venus and Adonis.' In *Shakespeare's Poems*, ed. Katherine Duncan-Jones and Henry Woudhuysen. Arden Shakespeare, Third Series. London: Arden, 2007.

The Winter's Tale. Ed. Susan Snyder and Deborah T. Curren-Aquino. Cambridge: Cambridge University Press, 2007.

ACKNOWLEDGEMENTS

This book was researched during two periods of research leave granted by Durham University, and the first draft was completed during a term's leave funded by the Arts and Humanities Research Council. To both institutions, I would like to record my thanks.

My series editors, Andrew Hadfield and Paul Hammond, were discerning readers of the book, generous with their scholarship and impeccably patient on the many occasions that deadlines slipped. Blair Worden's comments as reader for the press were supportive and well targeted. During the publication process, Charlotte Loveridge, Margaret Bartley, Anna Brewer, Jennifer Key and Neil Dowden were a pleasure to work with.

I could not have negotiated a 300-mile commute and a number of family-related difficulties over the last five years without Arnold Hunt, whose support and close engagement with the project has been just as crucial in scholarly matters. Petra Hunt, who has been very patient with her mother's preoccupation and is just starting to like Shakespeare, has made it all worthwhile. In trying to inspire her, I have been conscious of all that my mother, Jean Shell, did to pass on her own love of Shakespeare and literature to me. To her, to my father, Stephen Shell (a great reader-aloud), and to my parents-in-law, Bryan and Fiona Hunt, I am grateful for more than I can say.

The following individuals and repositories have been especially crucial to my efforts: the staff of the British Library rare books and manuscripts sections, and of Durham University Library; Mairi Macdonald at the Shakespeare Study Centre; Brother James Hodkinson, S.J., and Anna Edwards, at the Jesuit archives in Mount Street; Bro. Ninian Arbuckle, at the Franciscan Province in Forest Hill. I am deeply grateful to the following individuals for engaging in useful discussion, and in many cases supplying references or reading portions of the book: Robert Bearman, Susan Brigden, Colin Burrow, Alison Chapman, Helen Cooper, John D. Cox, Brian Cummings, Peter Davidson, Michael Dobson,

Frances Dolan, Susan Doran, Eamon Duffy, Katherine Duncan-Jones, Paul Edmondson, Alison Findlay, Tom Freeman, Eva Griffith, Beatrice Groves, Hannibal Hamlin, Canon Michael Hampel, Joan Osark Holmer, Lisa Hopkins, Phebe Jensen, David Scott Kastan, John Kerrigan, Peter Lake, Rhodri Lewis, Laurie Maguire, Judith Maltby, Arthur Marotti, Thomas M. McCoog, S.J., Donald Measham, Robert Miola, Susannah Brietz Monta, Nicholas Moschovakis, Molly Murray, Diane Purkiss, Debora Kuller Shuger, Nigel Smith, Tiffany Stern, Jane Stevenson, Richard Strier, Dennis Taylor, Gary Taylor, Stanley Wells, Martin Wiggins, Michael Wood, Gillian Woods, and all those who helped to refine the content of this book through engaging with it at conference presentations. Among my once and future colleagues at University College London, I would especially like to thank Helen Hackett, whose detailed comments on Chapter 2 of this work were invaluable, Gerard Kilroy, René Weis and Henry Woudhuysen.

This book goes to press in my last few months as a member of the English department at Durham University. I have been exceptionally fortunate in the heads of department that have overseen the long gestation of this book, Michael O'Neill, Patricia Waugh and Stephen Regan. My medieval and early-modern colleagues within the department have been stimulating sources of advice: Robert Carver, the late Robin Dix, Mandy Green, John McKinnell, Barbara Ravelhofer, Corinne Saunders, Gillian Skinner, Richard Sugg. It is to them, to all my dear past and present colleagues at Durham, and to the students that I taught when I was there, that I would like to dedicate this book.

ABBREVIATIONS

ARCR   Allison, A.F., and D.M. Rogers (comp.). *The Contemporary Printed Literature of the English Counter-Reformation between 1558–1640. Volume II. Works in English.* Aldershot: Scolar, 1994

EEBO   *Early English Books Online*

Lewis and Short   Lewis, Charlton T., and Charles Short. *A Latin Dictionary.* 1879. This edn, Oxford: Clarendon, 1980

ODNB   *Oxford Dictionary of National Biography* (online)

OED   *Oxford English Dictionary* (online)

STC   A.W. Pollard and G.R. Redgrave (comp.). *A Short-Title Catalogue of Books Printed in England, Scotland & Ireland, and of English Books Printed Abroad, 1475–1640.* Second edition, rev. W.A. Jackson, F.S. Ferguson and Katharine F. Pantzer. 3 vols. London: Bibliographical Society, 1976–9

Wells and Taylor   Wells, Stanley, and Gary Taylor (general eds). *The Oxford Shakespeare: The Complete Works.* Second edition. Oxford: Clarendon, 2005

ILLUSTRATIONS

INTRODUCTION

Holy Trinity Church, Stratford-upon-Avon, is Shakespeare's church. There he was baptised, there he is buried, and there a monument to him was erected after his death. Every year, on the Saturday closest to St George's Day, a procession of townsfolk comes to lay flowers on his grave, and a service giving thanks for his life and work is held the day after.[1] Throughout the year, tourists make pilgrimages to the building on his account. But the church has many other points of interest, including a fine set of medieval misericords: ledges on wooden tip-up seats designed to give some relief to tired clergy during the singing of church services, taking their name from the Latin for 'mercy', *misericordia*.[2] With their elaborate, often frivolous carving, they permitted relaxation from the rigours of Christianity in more than one way. Much of the imagery on the Stratford misericords is pagan: a harpy straight out of classical literature, and a green man, a fertility symbol associated with pre-Christian beliefs. Much is broadly humorous or even satirical: one misericord consists of three grimacing masks, a second features a termagant wife beating her husband with a saucepan, while a third shows a couple of monkeys pretending to be doctors, gravely inspecting a flask of urine. The badge of the earls of Warwick, a bear and ragged staff, appears on a fourth. Like Shakespeare's body of work, these carvings pay homage to secular hierarchies and to non-Christian mythology, but most of all to everyday life. Like it, they exist within a Christian framework, but taken out of context, draw one's attention away from religion.

Much has been written about the immanence of the sacred in the medieval era, and much of it is sentimental. But it remains true that medieval England was a time and place where everyday life was widely depicted in church, and post-Reformation England was not. The fear of idolatry and impure religion so characteristic of Protestant thought had varied effects, and even during the fiercest periods of the Reformation, it would be simplistic to see all Protestants as hostile to artistic creation. But in Shakespeare's England, the kind of artistic licence allowed to the misericord carvers would have had to find a place outside church, and any aspect of worship not strictly utilitarian would have had to be justified in the face of hostile critique. These rigours and cautions have developed a strange afterlife in the kind of polemical discourse, now so familiar in the English-speaking world, which perceives all religious belief and practice as life-denying. In the current climate, mainstream churches would be perceived as shirking their evangelical obligation if they portrayed human endeavour as tainted, or the arts as a distraction from worship. In the twenty-first century, the Church of England – to which Shakespeare apparently subscribed – places a high value on the arts. Creative artists are perceived as participating in God's work, and often enough, Shakespeare is invoked as the supreme artist. Like the anonymous carvers of the misericords in the church he knew best, he is seen as celebrating the infinite diversity of creation: a notion which, as we shall see, is explored in the literary theory and emblematics of the Renaissance, and which may therefore have shaped his authorial ambitions. His drama and poetry is often thought of as embodying an incarnational aesthetic, and read for edification – more than any of his contemporaries' religious writings, even though he has much less to say about God than they do.

Any study of Shakespeare and religion must confront a paradox. Shakespeare's writing has been seen both as profoundly religious, giving everyday human life a sacramental quality, and as profoundly secular, foreshadowing the kind of humanism that sees no necessity for God. Perhaps, as a paradox should, this describes the same phenomenon in two ways. Both characterizations recognize Shakespeare's high doctrine of the audience; both acknowledge that part of his

dramatic sophistication is to depict human particularity while implying a transcendent, portentous quality in the human condition. This
latter quality has proved uniquely attractive to would-be allegorists,
and several overtly religious readings of Shakespeare have taken the
allegorical path: from G. Wilson Knight, arraigned by fellow Shakespeareans for seeing Christ-figures everywhere, to Clare Asquith's recent
Shadowplay, which sees Shakespeare's writing as encoding Catholic
rebellion within Protestant England.[3] The following study describes a
rather different Shakespeare: one whose language is saturated in religious discourse and whose dramaturgy is highly attentive to religious
precedent, but whose invariable practice is to subordinate religious
matter to the particular aesthetic demands of the work in hand.[4] For
him, as for few of his contemporaries, the Judaeo-Christian story is
something less than a master narrative.

The rest of this introduction will survey the broad religious climate
that Shakespeare and his first audiences knew, while in Chapter 2 of this
study, the possible beliefs of Shakespeare, his family and his associates
will be looked at in more detail. But before moving away from Holy
Trinity Church, one more misericord demands our attention: a con-
torted figure, probably a tumbler, which has had its head defaced at some
point. One can speculate – the evidence permits nothing more – that it
may have fallen foul of an iconoclast who disapproved of entertainers

FIGURE I   A misericord in Holy Trinity Church, Stratford, John Cheal
© Inspired Images 2010. By kind permission of Vicar and Churchwardens
at Holy Trinity Church, Stratford.

being depicted in God's house.[5] Whether or not this is the real reason for the damage, those of Shakespeare's contemporaries who saw Shakespeare's writing as inimical to religious practice might well have sympathized with such an act. This book bears witness to them, as they contemplate Shakespeare's work and find in it the unpleasant side to nature, creativity and fiction.

How, then, are we to characterize the religious landscape of England during Shakespeare's lifetime?[6] It was almost completely a Christian world, an emphasis the present study will reflect; even London contained only a few Jews and Muslims, though notions of them had an enormous imaginative importance which fed into Shakespeare's characterization of Shylock and Othello.[7] Architecturally and socially, the church was the prime focus for a community; through events in the church year, and such sacraments and rites of passage as baptisms, marriages and funerals, its services shaped day-to-day experience and governed the life cycle.[8] Christian presuppositions and Christian language pervaded oral, written and printed discourse, not always to pious effect. To take one example among many in Shakespeare's work: when the pages in *As You Like It* have sung a song, and Touchstone says to them 'God b'wi' you, and God mend your voices' (5.3.46–7), this is nothing more than a leave-taking seasoned with mild abuse. But it illustrates the linguistic embeddedness of Christian blessing, characterizes Touchstone as someone who does not mind taking the name of God in vain and identifies the professional theatre as an institution willing to dramatize this: all points which would have made some of Shakespeare's contemporaries uneasy.[9]

Tudor England was, after all, a time when religious change occurred at an unpredecented and bewildering rate. Shakespeare lived under two monarchs, Elizabeth I and James VI/I, at a time when England's official religion finally changed from Catholic to Protestant. In 1564, the year of his birth, Elizabeth I had been on the throne for six years. She and her advisors had already set about re-Protestantizing a nation which had been restored to Catholicism for five years under Mary I, harking back to the previous reign of Edward VI, but shaping a distinctive religious consensus which, in some respects, has lasted to this day. Though English people have never all been committed to the Church of England, it remains England's established church at the time of writing. Elizabeth I's personal religious views have given rise to much debate, but seem to have been Lutheran rather than Calvinist in character, especially in relation to church furnishings: Calvinists took a harder line on images and ornamentation than Lutherans, and Elizabeth kept a crucifix in her private chapel in contravention of the Church of England's official, Calvinist-inflected position on images. James VI/I, a monarch unusually interested in theology, brought some personal emphases to a broadly Calvinist position: in particular, a fascination with ecumenism and a commitment to working out the full implications of his position at the head of the Church of England.[10] Elizabeth's studied reticence and James's affirmation of the king's sacral authority can both be seen as stratagems to unite England's church, and certainly the period of Shakespeare's lifetime was one of comparative religious stability so far as the views of the monarch were concerned. But it was also one where the confessional switchbacks of the earlier Tudor period had not been forgotten, and where the Church of England was beset with fierce internal debate, while also having to see off challenges from outside.

The most obvious of these came from the Catholic church.[11] Pope Pius V's excommunication of Elizabeth in 1570 turned every Catholic into a potential threat, from the government's point of view. The Elizabethan Act of Supremacy (1559), requiring an oath of loyalty from all office-holders and graduates, served – like the Oath of Allegiance later ordered by James VI/I – to divide England's Catholic community, at home and in exile abroad; some emphasized loyalty to the monarch and questioned the pope's ability to intervene in state affairs, others believed that no loyalty could conscientiously be given to a heretic.[12] While some Catholic individuals could enjoy a surprising amount of freedom, others were persecuted. To be a Catholic priest in England was punishable by death, while the notion that Catholics were politically dangerous lay behind the severe penalties incurred by recusants, those who absented themselves from Church of England services. Yet the Church of England was structured in countless ways by its Catholic past, not least architecturally; church services continued to take place in medieval buildings where, often enough, a surprising number of statues, stained glass windows and wall paintings had survived the waves of iconoclasm under Henry VIII and Edward VI.[13] Even in absence or partial obliteration, Catholic matter was eloquent. Abbey ruins or defaced rood-lofts could be interpreted in the approved manner as denoting a religion purged of superstitious accretion, but read against the grain, they could engender nostalgia. Shakespeare has been read, and with reason, as showing something of this nostalgia himself: a point which will be more fully explored in Chapter 2. But if so, this does not mean he was a Catholic; many of an antiquarian bent, or with an imaginative sympathy for the past, were capable of experiencing wistfulness for the old religion without wishing to put back the clock.

Given how many medieval religious artefacts were destroyed in Tudor England's successive bouts of iconoclasm, it is hard not to see late sixteenth- and early seventeenth-century England as a time of cultural impoverishment, as far as the religious experience of ordinary people went. Yet looking at the improved availability of scripture, exactly the opposite seems true. While there was wide familiarity with Bible stories and scriptural messages in medieval England, detailed text-based knowledge of the Bible was unachievable on a wide scale until the advent of printing. For that matter, it remained beyond many English people thereafter. But thanks to the importation of books from the Continent and the development of an indigenous print culture, England's population became markedly more literate over the early-modern era, and literacy was increasingly stressed as a desirable quality for the Christian. Much of this might have happened without the change in religion; the relationship between Protestantism and print, though close, has often been exaggerated.[14] Still, it remains true that making the Scriptures available in the vernacular was one of the reformers' main aims, and throughout the sixteenth century, most attempts to translate the Bible into English came from those of reformist sympathies. In literature from all denominations, the Scriptures would have been quoted, paraphrased and interpreted; religious titles have recently been estimated to comprise around half the total output of material printed between 1475 and 1640, the period covered by the *Short-Title Catalogue*.[15]

The increasing unfamiliarity of Judaeo-Christian scripture and tradition, in a world where so many students of Shakespeare have been brought up in other faiths or none, has prompted his recent editors to gloss references that their predecessors assumed were common knowledge. This in turn has highlighted the sheer density of Shakespeare's biblical allusiveness, and the question of which Bible translations he encountered and used: not always an easy one to answer, since translators frequently borrowed from each other, and allusions metamorphose as part of the imaginative process.[16] But scholars have tended to agree that Shakespeare refers most to the Geneva Bible, and may well have owned a copy. Readily available from the mid-1570s and published in a variety of formats, this was the likeliest of the Bible translations to be in private ownership, though some potential readers would have objected to it on theological grounds; its marginal notes were theologically directive and often anti-Catholic in tone, betraying its genesis among the English Protestants living in exile on the Continent during Mary I's reign. Echoes of the so-called Bishops' Bible, derived from the Great Bible authorized for the Church of England's use under Henry VIII, have also been detected in Shakespeare's work: not surprisingly, since it was publicly available in places of worship and would have been an obvious source of texts for sermons.

Though players and preachers were often at loggerheads in this period – a point which will be returned to in Chapter 1 – contemporary sermons and plays have a good deal in common. Both genres exploited the affect of scripture as well as its authority; both demanded a wide and detailed scriptural recall from their better-informed audience members. More generally, both played to the special relationship between scripture, the Christian believer and oral means of communication: necessarily so, at a time when most sermons and many plays never saw print. But this common ground should not lead one to underestimate the differences in motive. While a preacher would have taxed his audience's memories for evangelistic and didactic reasons, the biblical allusions in the work of professional playwrights like Shakespeare tend to be deployed in the service of generalized moralism, or of simple ornamentation, or as a way of fastening their own work more firmly in the minds of the auditors. It is no surprise that the books of the

Bible that Shakespeare alludes to most often – the gospel of St Matthew and the Psalms – are among those which were most familiar. Psalms would have been particularly well known as a regular part of worship in the Church of England.[17] Singing the metrical psalms by Thomas Sternhold and John Hopkins provided a rare opportunity for active congregational participation in services, and the psalter at the back of the Prayer Book featured prominently in morning and evening prayer. No book of the Bible would have been repeated more in a liturgical context, and as with any piece of poetry, alluding to one verse could have brought the whole poem to mind. Shakespeare sometimes seems to be exploiting this. Where Bolingbroke declares before the duel at the beginning of *Richard II*, 'Strong as a tower in hope, I cry amen' (1.3.102), the striking image would immediately have recalled Psalm 61:3: 'For thou hast bene mine hope, and a strong tower against the enemie.' But in the context of Richard's fall and Bolingbroke's rise, the psalm's continued expression of hope, ending 'Thou shalt give the King a long life: his yeres shalbe as manie ages' (61:6), might have given the allusion a latent irony for the attentive auditor.

The same psalm goes on: '[The king] shal dwell before God for ever: . . . So wil I alway sing praise unto thy Name in performing daiely my vowes' (61:7–8). Monarchy is a constant theme of the Psalms, and their liturgical use in Elizabethan and Jacobean England would have reinforced a sense that the monarch's headship of the Church was God-given. The Church's homilies, one of which would have been read on every Sunday and holy day on occasions when sermons were not being preached, similarly purveyed the message that to be a good Christian was to be a loyal subject.[18] So did the Prayer Book itself, by the sheer fact of its existence. The 1552 Prayer Book of Edward VI, slightly revised, was imposed upon the Church of England by the Act of Uniformity passed during the first year of Elizabeth I's reign, and retained by James VI/I with minor adjustments; familiar for several decades by the time Shakespeare began writing, it remained a constant point of reference throughout his career, with an authority and numinousness second only to the Scriptures.[19] The Prayer Book, like most liturgical writing, derived its authority from a bricolage of ancient sources, and the fact that it was based on medieval service books was one reason why Puritans came to dislike it as insufficiently reformed.[20] Yet to Catholic readers, what it excluded would have been equally painful.

Shakespeare's liturgical and scriptural frame of reference may have something to tell us about his religious sympathies, though no firm consensus on this topic has yet been reached: the poignant use Shakespeare makes of Catholic liturgical material might seem to indicate leanings towards the old religion, while the fact that he seems to have deployed the Protestant Bishops' Bible and the Geneva Bible more than the Catholic Douai/Rheims New Testament might be held to point in the other direction.[21] But on the whole, Shakespeare's dense religious allusiveness tells us less about his own convictions than about the culture he grew up in, and the references he expected his audience to notice. In England as elsewhere in Europe, print and the Reformation brought about, in different and interconnected ways, a highly text-based awareness of the Christian faith, and the alertness to biblical allusion and religious matter of an average London audience member in Shakespeare's time can hardly have been surpassed in the history of theatre. But audiences were not homogeneous, nor a completely representative cross-section of London's population in Elizabethan and early Stuart England; as Chapter 1 of this study argues, one must especially remember those who stayed away from the theatre for principled reasons. In terms of Shakespeare's broader reception history, too, confessional and ideological diversity must be kept in mind. Shakespeare is, for a writer of his time, unusually assimilable to secularizing and agnostic world-views, but there is no straightforward trajectory away from religious to agnostic response in Shakespeare studies. In particular, the long tradition of explicitly Christian readings continues, and publications on him from religious presses, not always noticed or fully credited by the mainstream academy, continue in a path traversed by so many of Shakespeare's earlier critics.[22]

But given that Shakespeare's religious beliefs are probably irrecoverable, what of his religious practices? During his working life, the demands of rehearsing and performing plays would have made it difficult to attend morning and evening prayer on weekdays.[23] But the majority of English people submitted to the legal requirement to go to church on Sundays and holy days, and given the lack of evidence to the contrary, it seems likely that Shakespeare was among them.[24] Some would have gone because of the penalties for not going, others because it was the custom, others because they keenly assented to the Church of England's tenets. Of those who conformed reluctantly, some would have been Catholics who, for various reasons, felt unable to risk fining, imprisonment or sequestration of their estates, and some would have been those whom historians have variously referred to as 'Puritans', 'the godly' or 'the hotter sort of Protestants'. Where church-papists would, if possible, have attended illicit Masses or alternative forms of Catholic worship, Puritans supplemented their statutory attendance at church in other ways, especially in cases where they felt the ministry of the parish priest was inadequate.[25] Typically they would have attended sermons outside their own parish, a practice known as 'sermon-gadding', and conducted Bible study at home.

Basic to Puritanism was the notion that, while the English church was reformed, it had not gone far enough: that its church government and ceremony still retained elements of popery, while its pastors were often too lax in imposing Christian morality on their flock. But while the Puritan urge to seek out godly associates and distance oneself from the wider community could make for anti-establishment feeling and even separatism, one should not underestimate the number of high-ranking clergy with Puritan sympathies at this date.[26] Theologically there would have been considerable common ground between them and other clergy, since for much of Shakespeare's working life, the Church of England was, in effect, a Calvinist church. But as Chapter 4 of this study will explore, Calvinism was not monolithic, especially with regard to such topics as predestination. 'High' Calvinism, which maintained that God had decreed the salvation or damnation of individual souls from the beginning of time, proved to be a doctrine too severe for unproblematic dissemination at grass-roots level; towards the end of Shakespeare's working life, the backlash against high Calvinism was making itself felt in both theological and imaginative arenas. Moderate Calvinists ameliorated and de-emphasized the topic

INTRODUCTION 11

of predestination, and the period also saw early signs of Arminianism, a version of Protestantism that argued for the role of human free will in the process of salvation, which was to become dominant in the established church in the late 1620s and 1630s.[27] As will be argued below, playwrights too expressed horror at dictates mimicking those of the Calvinist God, using the rhetorical manipulation of emotion which, rather than theological argument, was their stock-in-trade.

Intellectual subtlety is not the same thing as emotional elaboration; the process of creating character can sometimes demand crude material. As already suggested, the drama of Shakespeare's time caricatured representatives of non-Christian religions in a way which carries over from other imaginative discourse, fictional and non-fictional. Inter-denominational polemic, of which the age was so full, frequently found its way into drama, and Shakespeare himself makes use of polemical texts and attitudes on more than one occasion.[28] His treatment of Puritanism, which one can describe as showing a qualified lack of sympathy, will be discussed further in Chapter 1. He also absorbed material hostile to Catholicism: in *King Lear*, he famously exploits Samuel Harsnet's polemical account of Catholic exorcisms, *A Declaration of Egregious Popish Impostures* (1st edn 1603), for the names of demons imagined by Edgar in his disguise as Tom O'Bedlam.[29] In *Macbeth*, the Porter's speech contains topical references to the Jesuit priest Henry Garnet executed in the aftermath of the Gunpowder Plot.[30] Sometimes references to religious controversy can crop up in passing, suggested by nothing more than a word or two. When, in *All's Well that Ends Well*, Lafeu comments on Helena's healing of the king, 'They say miracles are past' (2.3.1), this throwaway remark evokes Protestant denigration of Catholic miracle in a way which invests Helena with a saintly aura, but also reminds us that her achievement is explicable in natural terms. At other times, religio-polemical discourse is deployed to deliberately anachronistic effect. In *Titus Andronicus*, a story set in ancient Rome, Aaron the Moor characterizes Lucius, Titus's son, as observing 'twenty popish tricks and ceremonies' (5.1.76): an insult which is softened by the wrongdoing and overt atheism of its speaker.[31] As this might suggest, Shakespeare draws on anti-popery less than many of his contemporaries; the plays where he uses contemporary Catholic settings peopled by nuns and friars – *Measure for Measure, Romeo and Juliet, Much Ado About Nothing* – convey a more neutral attitude to the faith than those of than a contemporary like John Webster, whose vision of a corrupt popish world permeates *The White Devil* and *The Duchess of Malfi*. Yet in his *King John*, which dramatizes an English monarch's stand against papal control, Shakespeare tones down the anti-Catholicism typical of other dramatizations but does not entirely erode it. A recent commentator, Jean-Christophe Mayer, has seen Shakespeare as 'anatomizing' polemic in the play, mimicking its operations rather than taking sides himself.[32]

In Shakespeare's time as now, disagreements occasioned by opposing truth-claims sometimes got in the way of neighbourly charity, but at other times were bypassed in the name of it.[33] Questions of how far tolerance should extend, or whether one should compromise at all on matters of faith, were ones which the social outworkings of the Reformation made of day-to-day relevance; given their potential to create tension and conflict, they were bound to affect drama too. One of the few things on which most scholars can agree is Shakespeare's interest in dramatizing differing points of view – most conspicuously in the mid-period tragicomedies which some still like to call 'problem plays' – and setting up situations which evoke diverse, fluid reactions from audiences. Ideas of truth as complicated, dialogic or hidden to mortals can give rise to scepticism; this study concurs with many past ones in seeing scepticism as a mental posture very well suited to dialogue and drama, and identifying an affinity between it and Shakespeare's work.[34] There is no necessary connection between scepticism and godlessness; as Richard Popkin and others have remarked, much sceptical enquiry at this date has fideistic underpinnings, and in an uncertain world, the church and revealed religion could be seen as an anchor. Yet where the habit of enquiry turned in more heterodox directions, both it and drama could be seen as fostering atheism. Two of Shakespeare's contemporaries, Thomas Kyd and Christopher Marlowe, were perceived as atheistical in their time – something which may or may not tell us anything about their actual views, but speaks volumes about how dramatists as a group could be seen.[35] Looking at Marlowe's work in particular, the charge is not entirely baseless, and it chimes in with elements in Shakespeare's writing too, though as far as we know Shakespeare was never accused of atheism. A play like *King Lear* may not exactly be an atheist's tragedy, but it contains elements which have consistently, and with reason, been read as atheistical.[36] After all, atheism as a rhetorical stance, deliberately constructed to invite disapproval and refutation, would have been nothing new to Shakespeare; the character of Aaron, cited above, illustrates one way in which he made use of it. Straw men can sometimes come alive, and imaginative constructs model the real world.

At this date, the notion of atheism had more to do with religious heterodoxy than outright disbelief in a supernatural order. Asserting that hell is a fable in the presence of a devil, Marlowe's Dr Faustus could be termed an atheist with an exceptional eagerness to embrace the occult – at the beginning of the play, at least. Notoriously, the tragedy ends with a warning to the wise 'only to wonder at unlawful things / Whose deepness does entice such forward wits / To practice more than heavenly power permits'.[37] Whether this warning straightforwardly evokes Genesis's condemnation of curiosity, or is a figleaf for less didactic and more subversive purposes, has been much debated. But either way, the body of the action offers the imaginative auditor an opportunity to try on a magician's cloak.[38] Shakespeare's work offers no character so obviously provocative as Faustus, but Prospero, who comes closest, is in some respects more subversive still. His actions certainly invite us to reflect that magic powers may be abused, but his cessation of magic *per se* is more the ending of a particular phase in his life than a passing from darkness to light, and the practice of magic is not explicitly condemned. The difference is partly to do with location: where *Dr Faustus* is grounded in latter-day Christian Wittenberg, Prospero's island offers a heterocosm: a discrete imaginative world custom-built for a particular play, where cosmology is symbiotically related to narrative and structure. It is no coincidence that the lines which glance at the possibility that magicians may be damned – 'And my ending is despair / Unless I be relieved by prayer' (5.1.333–334) – are spoken by Prospero as part of the epilogue, as he prepares to travel back to Christian Europe, and as the audience is gently tipped back into the outside world. Where the setting is less eclectic than in

The Tempest, or more heavily inflected by Christian notions of divine vengeance, characters who illicitly seek out the supernatural tend, like Faustus, to get their come-uppance: to some extent with the conjurers in *Henry VI: 1*, and most obviously with *Macbeth*, where the protagonist's wary collusion with supernatural powers owes so much to Marlowe.

With Macbeth's witches we enter the *demi-monde* of folk religion. In the Elizabethan and Jacobean eras, the supernatural powers of witches were believed in by many educated individuals: most illustriously, and with some relevance to *Macbeth*, James VI/I.[39] But it was by no means an undisputed area of belief. As John D. Cox has pointed out, suspicion as an antecedent of fully-fledged scepticism can be traced in the way that thinkers such as Reginald Scot attacked credulity concerning phenomena marginal to Christian theology, such as the witch's powers and the existence of ghosts.[40] On the imaginative front, a nod to demystification could serve, if anything, to point up supernatural thrills. Plays like *Hamlet* or *Julius Caesar* debate the existence and correct interpretation of ghosts and portents, forestalling audience members' attempts to rationalise, and reaffirming the existence of the uncanny within the confines of drama. But if ghosts and witches belong to tragedy, fairies inhabit comedy, and there is a decorum to this; belief in fairies was so much associated with women, children and the unlearned that the question of their existence and efficacy was, compared to ghosts and witches, less of an intellectual crux at the time Shakespeare was writing.[41] The idea that fairies might appear to both witches and innocent parties was admittedly distrusted as a way of making demonism seem harmless. Testifying to contact with fairies was often a feature of witch trials, and Shakespeare's fairy allusions are at their edgiest where they point up a kinship with witchery, as in *All's Well That Ends Well*;[42] since Helena is a woman, her healing arts potentially invite charges of witchcraft that, as Regina Buccola has explored, are moderated and deflected by associating her with faery motifs.[43] But from the later sixteenth century onwards, fairy belief declined in plausibility and thus became more easily separable from demonic forces of other kinds.[44] Though the spectacle of credulity is evoked by the fairy masquerade in *The Merry Wives of*

Windsor, it is an obvious pretence and no metaphysical questions accompany it; in *A Midsummer Night's Dream*, Shakespeare's most sustained exercise in popular paganism, fairies can be given comic treatment because they are almost as safely dead as the classical gods.

A Midsummer Night's Dream, on one level the most un-Christian of plays, does nevertheless illustrate issues which impact on the Christianity of Shakespeare's time and after. Combining Britain's indigenous faery traditions with figures from classical mythology such as Theseus and Hippolyta, and – as will be argued below – traces of medieval Catholicism, it is highly syncretic; there is something postmodernist about its individualistic, pick-and-mix attitude to belief. Heterocosms of this kind are common in English Renaissance drama, perhaps reaching their apogee in Tudor and Stuart court masques; whether read against Christianity or explicitly including elements of it, they demonstrate how playwrights and poets were freer than purveyors of non-fiction to identify similarities between different belief-systems and religious practices. For the latter, learning from the ancients was not a problem, but worshipping like the ancients was – which is why comparative religion, like so many other intellectual developments, has roots in polemic. The early-seventeenth-century Protestant commentator John Boys is one of thousands who illustrate this, invoking the Koran and pagan goddess-worship to argue that the Catholic position on Marian veneration is idolatrous.[45] As the seventeenth century moved into the eighteenth, thinkers like John Toland were to turn the similarities between religions into a general condemnation of priestcraft.[46] But if Enlightenment hostilities of this kind can be seen as prefiguring modern-day comparative religion, so too can the friendlier and more ludic comparisons of poets and playwrights. While these were neither intended nor received as serious contributions to religious debate, they would have helped to make inter-faith comparisons possible, and an intuition of this may partly explain the nervousness of antitheatricalists.[47] In the context of their time, playwrights' imaginative linkages contrast strikingly with a theological world where divisions, even within Christianity itself, were more often accentuated than bridged; defending their faith, both Protestants and Counter-Reformation Catholics tended to emphasize the ways in which their version of

Christianity was set apart from other denominations, let alone other religions.

NOTE 1

For Catholics, the position was complicated still further by the differences between England's old faith and Counter-Reformation Catholicism: often less a matter of practice than of polemicized self-consciousness. The sympathetic recollection of medieval religion seems to have been possible for both Catholics and conformists, and does not necessarily betoken sympathy for the new Catholicism warier of schism and heresy, and galvanized by a sense of mission. Looking again at *A Midsummer Night's Dream*, one can recognize pro-Catholic overtones of the former kind, where the epilogue describes the liturgical practice of asperging: 'With this field-dew consecrate / Every fairy take his gait / And each several chamber bless / Through this palace with sweet peace' (5.1.406–409).[48] The lines certainly exploit Catholic nostalgia, but like Robert Herrick's faery verses in the next generation, they remind the audience that to link Catholics and fairies is to draw on the association of popery with superstition. While this plays to the prejudices of conformists with an imaginative or antiquarian bent, it would have thoroughly displeased anyone whose allegiance to Catholicism went further than nostalgia.[49] Here as elsewhere, Shakespeare cannot be seen as someone with much time for the imaginative utilitarianism typical of English Counter-Reformation writing: a topic which will be more fully explored in Chapter 2. Yet he is sympathetically alive to the traces of a religious past which so many of his original audience would have remembered, or known about from the reminiscences of an older generation. And since one must not overstate the differences between pre- and post-Reformation England, there is no denying the exuberant use Shakespeare makes of medieval festive traditions with their roots in the liturgical calendar. Even if religious drama *per se* had been comprehensively discouraged by the time Shakespeare began writing, the performance of secular drama was linked at many points to a festival calendar which had strong elements of continuity with that used in medieval England.[50]

Shakespeare's debt to medieval religious drama did not end there.[51] Biographers have even speculated that he might have seen some productions in his younger days, especially given that Stratford-upon-Avon was so near Coventry with its famous mystery-play cycles.[52] The wider fact of medieval Catholicism also permeates those history plays set in medieval England, sometimes to surprising effect. While the speakers' range of reference is mostly in keeping with their times, there are many moments where a post-Reformation conditionality appears. In *Richard III*, for instance, Queen Elizabeth apostrophizes her sons, the dead Princes in the Tower: 'If yet your gentle souls fly in the air / And be not fixed in doom perpetual, / Hover about me with your airy wings' (4.4.11–13). To Catholics, purgatory interposed between death and the 'doom perpetual' of heaven – hell seems an unlikely option for these young and innocent victims, and the word 'doom' should surely be taken in its neutral rather than its negative sense.[53] Here, the significance of purgatory to the distraught Queen is that, as a middle state for the soul, it was popularly interpreted as allowing the return of spirits to earth in circumstances such as murder. The Queen's speech is poignantly appropriate for a bereaved mother, conditionality and all, but her acknowledgement that the logic of the afterlife may prevent such an encounter taking place would not have been lost on a listener alert to such things. In fact the princes' ghosts do later appear, as part of the vengeful parade that curses Richard on the eve of the battle of Bosworth. The providentialist significance of the occasion, and the sheer theatrical potency of the ghosts' presence on stage, is perhaps striking enough to make their ontological status unimportant. Yet it is significant that a common Protestant explanation of ghosts, as demonic apparitions, is not appropriate here.[54] While ghosts are everywhere in Elizabethan and Jacobean drama, so too are warnings about where they might come from, and the act of believing in them at all – not least, as commented above, in Shakespeare's own work. Thus, imaginative narratives referring to a real Catholic past may have acted as one of the environments where otherwise sceptical audience-members submitted to having their credulity stretched.

The romance mode, with its multiple interconnections to that same past, was another. 'It is required / You do awake your faith' (5.3.94–95), Paulina famously adjures Leontes in *The Winter's Tale*, as they come to see Hermione's statue; and when the statue comes to life, the play's characters are obliged to accept improbability.[55] Shakespeare's late tragicomedies have recently come into the critical limelight as his most triumphant exploitations of the interrelationship between theatricality and the miraculous, and this scene has attracted particular attention, with some critics going so far as to see it as a pro-Catholic statement.[56] Hermione's living statue certainly carries overtones of Catholicism's wonder-working images, and even though the dramatized events are improbable rather than miraculous, it is hard not to view the scene in the context of contemporary Catholic/Protestant debates about the use of statues within worship. Contentions of this kind need to be qualified by an awareness that post-Reformation Catholicism, while affirming the existence and efficacy of miracles in general, could adopt a highly critical attitude towards particular events claimed as miraculous; within Protestantism, on the other hand, the idea of miracles was often denigrated as popish, but notions of God's providence continued to provide an alternative – and sometimes remarkably similar – explanatory framework for wondrous happenings.[57] Thus, where the theatre mimics supernatural and incarnational promises, these resonate not just with Catholicism but all Christianity, complicating the seeming opposition between religious truth and theatrical falsity, and using the spiritual authority of Christianity to glorify the theatrical medium. Hence, the scene prompts a number of questions: Is Shakespeare using theatre to affirm miracle in a way that enhances Christian belief? – Is he evoking a sense of wonder that is religious but not specifically Christian? – Or is he transferring the numinous potential of religion to theatre? None of these contentions are easily dismissible, but the debate is not yet over. Previous critics entering this particular arena have been most helpful where they have read Shakespeare back against the religious culture of his time, drawing attention to the strong element of theatricality in sermons, liturgical acts of worship, and other occasions explicitly directed towards religious ends in a way that the professional drama of Shakespeare's time was not.[58]

As the above account suggests, views on Shakespeare's religious self-positioning have shifted in recent years. It was once common to refer to his work as elevated beyond religion; though the inspiration he drew from the religious issues of his era has been increasingly recognized, it remains very easy to detach his writing from them. The picture painted of Shakespeare below is of a writer supremely interested in exploiting past and present religions for intellectual and emotional effect, including the Church of England Christianity to which he probably subscribed; it also describes someone whose prime motivation, judging by his work, was not religious but literary and dramatic. This is not, of course, to deny the many points of intersection between Christianity, literature and drama. In Shakespeare's work alone, the theme of forgiveness – to take one instance among many – has an immense shaping power. More broadly, religions foster artists, aesthetic and religious discourses both engage with notions of truth and beauty, and the high view of human creativity taken in much twentieth- and twenty-first-century Christian theology has roots in the humanistic tradition Shakespeare knew.[59]

But where religion and aesthetics start pulling apart is where a creative artist, without necessarily forswearing religious matter, sees religion not as something that artistic endeavour should serve, but as raw material like anything else. Shakespeare's writing draws upon Christianity, but does not concede to it, or to any of the other religions he uses. All are subsumed to the specific demands of the aesthetic artifact, raising the earthly creator to a position where he jockeys for position with God – or, as some would see it, is made into a god himself. For many unbelievers, art has been and continues to be a substitute for religion; some creative artists, Shakespeare among them, have seriously been called divine; and Harold Bloom's *Shakespeare: The Invention of the Human* (1998) shows veneration alive and well in our own time: 'Bardolatry, the worship of Shakespeare, ought to be even more a secular religion than it already is. The plays remain the outward limit of human achievement: aesthetically, cognitively, in certain ways morally, even spiritually.'[60] One cannot say Shakespeare explicitly demands this tribute of his votaries, but he has often received it, and his *modus operandi* helps to suggest why.

There are good historical reasons why the discipline of English studies has tended to attract those who distrust ideological and religious dogma. But, precisely for that reason, one should not succumb uncritically to single-author cults either. In Shakespeare's case, while one can see this happening and be aware of the personal self-aggrandisement involved, one can also interpret it as benign; his work compels, but on the whole, compels towards tolerance and the acknowledgement of multiple viewpoints. Yet by the same token it has power to displease, even among those whose job it is to read and appreciate imaginative literature; in recent years, Gary Taylor's critique of Shakespeare as ideologically evasive has made this point.[61] He is not the first to do so, as this study will show; one of its main aims is to identify the ways in which Shakespeare's work could have failed to please contemporaries with a keen interest in religious issues or – which is not necessarily the same thing – a deeply devotional sensibility. In Shakespeare's time as now, someone's pleasure in a creative work cannot be separated from an awareness of how that work promotes, denigrates, draws upon or ignores particular ideologies, belief-systems or ethical standards. It follows that for those whose sensibilities are informed by particular ideological, ethical or religious criteria, works which depart from those criteria are aesthetically deficient: a case which can be put both by philistines, and by commentators as sophisticated as St Augustine. For those among Shakespeare's contemporaries whose aesthetic sensibilities recoiled from any source of pleasure they identified as immoral, Shakespeare's works were less caviar to the general than foie gras to a vegan.

Chapters 1 and 2 of this study recover the views of those who took an unenthusiastic view of Shakespeare, both in himself and as representative of particular literary priorities. Chapter 1 discusses antitheatricalism, an attitude strongly – and not altogether unreasonably – associated with Puritanism, both in Shakespeare's time and now. Chapter 2 supplements this by describing the utilitarian poetics typical of the English Counter-Reformation, and how Shakespeare fell foul of these. Chapter 3 moves on to examine how Shakespeare exploited the tropes of popular religiously inspired moralism in his writing, with particular attention to how repentance is treated, while Chapter 4 reads some of Shakespeare's plots against the theological debates surrounding the issue of predestination in late-sixteenth- and early-seventeenth-century England. The conclusion considers how the classical god Terminus, visible in the final tragicomedies, emblematizes two ideas: how an author can compete with a god, and how even a god can be seen as deferring to the author. Here, as so often in early modern Europe, imaginative familiarity with the classical pantheon could have a profoundly secularizing effect. The irony is that, for Shakespeare's generation of playwrights in England, classical religious language in drama was often a way of deferring to the notion that the Christian God could not be represented on stage without profanity; there is a kind of piety so sensitive to inappropriateness that it blocks imaginative Christian discourse altogether, and obliges writers to explore secular alternatives.

But Shakespeare has more often been compared to another minor classical deity: the sea-god Proteus, proverbial as a shape-changer. In Renaissance metaphor and iconography, Proteus's appearances are frequent and appropriately versatile. He could symbolize unformed primordial matter, the generative principle or the diversity of creation, and accordingly features in neoplatonic theory. He could take on connotations relevant to natural philosophy or humanism, such as the investigation of nature or the multifarious achievements of mankind.[62] Possessing prophetic powers, he could stand for the prophet or seer, and as a guardian of sea-creatures, he could easily be linked to the shepherd-poets of pastoral.[63] Within rhetoric, he could evoke the ideal of copiousness or emblematize the evasiveness of truth within literature.[64] As all this implies, he was a figure who invited moralistic and judgemental interpretations; at one moment he might personify delight in the endless play of imaginative possibilities, and at another, deceit, disguise and evasiveness. In the classical sources, Proteus morphs as a way to avoid answering questions: as Vergil puts it, 'But when you hold him in the grasp of hands and fetters, then various forms and the features of wild beasts will frustrate you'.[65] As Stephen Batman remarked, 'Some thincke that by Proteus the dyvers affections, of mans mynde are signified',[66] which suggests why actors, whose job was, in Hamlet's words, 'to hold as 'twere the mirror up to nature' (3.2.21–22), were especially likely to incur criticism for proteanism.[67] Gary Taylor's criticism of Shakespeare has a kind of antecedent here. Given the long tradition of seeing Shakespeare as the pre-eminent poet of things as they are, calling him protean has usually been a prelude to praising him; but the figure is a double-edged one, and the more pejorative associations are also relevant.

Accusations of personal untrustworthiness and unaccountability were especially damaging when religious questions were involved, and not surprisingly, the figure of Proteus was one of many points where classical mythology and Christian polemic interlocked. Both Catholics and Protestants referred to him. John Bridges accused papists of sowing discord while boasting of unity: 'Thus these fellowes jarre alwayes amonge them selves, and in all their doctrines, fal into . . . points of discorde, . . . as the Proverbe is, *Quo teneam vultus mutantem Prothea nodo?*'[68] Conversely, heresy is described as *Proteo mutabiliorem* (more mutable than Proteus) in a play put on in the early seventeenth century at the English Catholic college in Valladolid.[69] But Tudor England was a time when many changed religious shape more than once, and even a more settled orthodoxy could have a protean quality. The Thirty-Nine Articles, drawn up in Elizabeth I's reign as a way of codifying the Church of England's belief and practice, have been called 'minimal in their requirements' by a recent commentator, and their compilers' practical concern to maximize agreement has, throughout the history of Anglicanism, proved a standing invitation to creativity.[70] Some individuals, such as the notorious turncoat Andrew Perne, went down in history as real-life Proteuses.[71] Others would have noted the advantages of mental flexibility, and we are surely to include Shakespeare among these.

Shakespeare was interested in Proteus from the beginning of his career. In *Henry VI: 3*, the future Richard III describes himself as able to 'change shapes with Proteus for advantages, / And set the murderous Machiavel to school' (3.2.192–193).[72] A character is called after Proteus in another early play, *The Two Gentlemen of Verona*, appropriately enough given his inconstancy in personal relationships. The play turns on the fact that Proteus's pursuit of Silvia represents a double betrayal: of his friend Valentine, who has been courting her, and of his own sweetheart Julia.[73] If this points towards a schematic quality in the characterization, this is not an unfair assessment of what may have been Shakespeare's first play. But to say that a play is allegorically driven is not necessarily an adverse criticism, and where

FIGURE 2   Image of Proteus, from Andrea Alciati, *Emblematum liber*. Lyon, 1550. By permission of Glasgow University Library (Sp Coll S.M. Add 265).

Proteus's character lifts into complexity, this is not a departure from allegory but a systematic working-out of his name's implications. Proteus stands for creativity as well as inconstancy and deceit, and it is no coincidence that he is given the play's best lyrical moments. One such, a ravishing hymn to the power of poetry, occurs in Act 3.2:

> Say that upon the altar of her beauty
> You sacrifice your tears, your sighs, your heart.
> Write till your ink be dry, and with your tears
> Moist it again, and frame some feeling line
> That may discover such integrity;
> For Orpheus' lute was strung with poets' sinews,
> Whose golden touch could soften steel and stones,
> Make tigers tame and huge leviathans
> Forsake unsounded deeps to dance on sands.
>
> (3.2.72–80)

As Proteus uses the word, integrity is seen as nothing more than a perfectly achieved poetic construct. But, unavoidably, it has moral resonances too. In the context of the scene, the notion of discovering integrity is particularly ironic, since Proteus is playing false on several fronts at once: frustrating Valentine's chances with Silvia, purporting to give advice to another suitor of Silvia's while furthering his own case, and straying further from Julia all the while. Julia is presented as his polar opposite, indignantly repudiating her waiting-woman's suggestions that his protestations of love may be false: 'His words are bonds, his oaths are oracles, / His love sincere, his thoughts immaculate, / His tears pure messengers sent from his heart' (2.7.75–77). As an assessment of Proteus this is laughably inept, but it shows her own innocence and idealism.

The first of Shakespeare's cross-dressing heroines, Julia sets off in male disguise to find Proteus, and when Proteus serenades Silvia in a later scene, she is listening. The Host comments on her sad demeanour:

> HOST: I perceive you delight not in music.
> JULIA: Not a whit, when it jars so.
> HOST: Hark, what fine change is in the music!

JULIA: Ay, that change is the spite.
HOST: You would have them always play but one thing?
JULIA: I would always have one play but one thing.

$$(4.2.64–69)^{74}$$

To Julia, the aesthetic sophistication of the music is nothing more than a painful reminder of Proteus's falsity. Thus, an audience's delight in the lyrical uplift of the song 'Who is Silvia?' is checked on ethical grounds; the betrayed Julia takes no pleasure in the music, and sympathizing with her has the effect of moving the discussion onto a more abstract plane. Thanks to the ambiguity of the word 'one', the remark, 'I would always have one play but one thing', is interpretable on several levels. With Proteus as referent, Julia's remark is a personal one, with poignantly bawdy overtones; but it can also be read as a general injunction to constancy, one which acknowledges that faithfulness can and should work against the enjoyment of variety. Shakespeare was never to dramatize the link between poetry, deceit and the limits of pleasure so explicitly again; *The Two Gentlemen of Verona* preserves evidence of a turn not taken.

At the play's denouement, Proteus's attempted rape of Silvia is witnessed by Valentine, causing Proteus to apologize and repent:

My shame and guilt confounds me.
Forgive me, Valentine; if hearty sorrow
Be a sufficient ransom for offence,
I tender't here. I do as truly suffer
As e'er I did commit.
VALENTINE: Then I am paid,
And once again I do receive thee honest.
Who by repentance is not satisfied
Is nor of heaven nor earth, for these are pleased;
By penitence th'Eternal's wrath's appeased.

$$(5.4.73–81)$$

This is as explicit a dramatization of contrition and forgiveness as any in Shakespeare's work. But while good enough for Valentine – who, in the play's most disturbing moment, appears to offer Silvia to Proteus forthwith – it is exceedingly brief, and has often been seen as unconvincing.[75] Hence, it heralds one of the questions which pervades this study: why, when Shakespeare's drama so often turns on issues of forgiveness, so little explicit attention is given to repentance. Where possible, it takes place off stage. Where it is voiced, the speakers are laconic. In either case, it is treated in a manner which does not implicate the audience in the abjection of the character: a world away from the active penitential involvement solicited by so many of Shakespeare's immediate dramatic predecessors.

A crux for this book.

In *The Two Gentlemen of Verona*, repentance is Proteus's last change, as far as we know, and as he oscillates to a standstill, the play concludes. Exemplary lives allow for improvement but not for wild switchbacks, and it is not surprising that the figure of Proteus crops up more in polemic than in devotional writing. Polemic tends to identify change in religion as a source of weakness, but religious autobiography and devotional writing tend in another direction, thanks to the notion of metanoia. It is hard to read far in either medieval and early modern literature without coming across the notion of literature as a tool of metanoia: a word which will sometimes be used throughout this study in preference to 'conversion'. While the two terms overlap considerably, 'conversion' tends to imply the transference between denominations or faiths as well as the process which 'metanoia' describes, the Christian endeavour of repenting and turning towards God. Many of Shakespeare's precursors, contemporaries and successors felt all literature worthless which did not urge this course upon the reader, and the engraved title-page of Walter Montagu's devotional work *Miscellanea Spiritualia* (1st edn 1648) sums up this attitude. On the left-hand side is a fashionable gallant labelled 'Perversus'; on the right, a penitent sinner labelled 'Conversus'; an angel leaning down from heaven brandishes a flaming sword and scourge towards the former, while proffering the latter a flaming heart, symbolic of devotion to God.

'We are made a spectacle to the World, to Angels, and to Men, saith Saint Paul, the Mirror and Patern of all Penitents and Converts, as if he had been obliged to summon all Creatures as Spectators to the prize of the high calling of God, which he was running for', writes Montagu in his prefatory address to the book.[76] Montagu was a convert himself, and his advocacy of metanoia or penitence would not have been without denominational implications, but he rightly distinguishes it from conversion. In an environment such as early-modern England,

FIGURE 3   Walter Montagu, *Miscellanea Spiritualia, or Devout Essayes*, 1648.
© The British Library Board E. 519.

where changes in one's religious belief and practice had conspicuous public consequences, both would have provided dramas to rival theatrical productions; in 1635, Montagu's own conversion to Catholicism transfixed the English court far more than his prolix pastoral drama *The Shepherd's Paradise* had done.[77] Montagu goes on to describe notorious public conversions, such as his own, as the 'Theatre of St Paul'. The passage quoted above contains not one, but two metaphors from Paul's Epistles: the first playing up the notion of quasi-theatrical spectacle, and the second, placed in dialogue with the first, reminding us that competitive sport is a spectacle too. Plays have spectators, but the theatre of conversion ideally goes further, impelling the spectator to become an actor themselves, or an athlete in the personal and strenuous pursuit of God. Montagu's passage disengages the link between theatre and illusion; converts and penitents stand or run as themselves, leaving the staging of unreal dramas to the perverted, left-hand world.

Shakespeare's dramatic and poetic corpus, which gives such high importance to the feigning of identity and the power of the imagination, could hardly be more different from these religiously inflected notions. His writing foregrounds the creative activity of the author, in which actors and audience are invited to participate; Montagu, together with many other authors of this date whose priorities were consciously religious, was working to a Christian script which he believed to be pre-existent and overarchingly authoritative, and thus concerns himself more with how audiences and actors should behave, and what spectacles should be presented to them. The difference is less a standoff between truth and falsity, more one of truth being sought in two utterly different ways – which may be why metanoia and conversion tend to take place offstage in Shakespeare's plays, where they happen at all. It may be no coincidence that the play where he most explicitly dramatizes penitence, *The Winter's Tale*, is also an apologia for the power of theatrical illusion.[78]

But Shakespeare is still a writer whose achievement is celebrated in an Anglican service every year. While apparently sidelining the power of the Christian God in whom all but a very few of his audience would have believed, he has also been read as gloriously testifying to that

God's power. His reputation for being spiritually inspirational, often enough in a Christian context, would have astounded those of his contemporaries whose opinions this study seeks to recover. But so far, his is the last word; his writing has long since, and to an incalculable extent, helped the idea of improving literature become less exclusivist than theirs. Advocates of Shakespeare's high spiritual stature, whether they speak from a Christian or non-Christian standpoint, could reply to rigorist critics using the words of his contemporary John Donne, whose work, unlike Shakespeare's, is nowhere detachable from religion. Donne is describing a passage from the Book of Job: 'It is the word of a naturall man; and the holy Ghost having canonized it, sanctified it, by inserting it into the booke of God, it is the word of God too. Saint Paul cites sometimes the words of secular Poets; and approves them; and then the words of those Poets, become the word of God; . . . therefore when we speake to godly men, we are sure to be believed, for God says it; if we were to speake to naturall men onely, we might be believed . . . '[79] The dichotomy between godly and natural readers is one that can inform our view of Shakespeare, the writer who not only dominates the non-biblical canon, but who, more than any other, has yielded a secular scripture.[80]

Chapter One

ANTITHEATRICALISM
IN SHAKESPEARE'S AGE

INTRODUCTION

L ooking at Shakespeare's career in relation to the religious and
literary culture of his time presents one with a paradox: that
Elizabethan London of the late 1580s and early 1590s, where Shakespeare's first surviving plays were performed and printed, was one of
the most antitheatrical climates that England has ever known.[1] From
the late 1570s, both clerical and lay commentators had intervened in
a debate, conducted through pamphlets, sermons and other non-
dramatic literature as well as plays themselves, as to whether theatre
was allowable or not, and if it was, which kinds of theatre were best.
This chapter will be giving an account of the case against the theatre,
and trying in particular to assess what features of Shakespeare's
drama might have been found offensive by antitheatricalists. Damned
both for profane references to sacred topics and for ignoring sacred
topics altogether, playwrights and players were seen as operating within
an intrinsically corrupt medium, with criticism of the professional
theatre swelling loudest of all. The first part of this chapter will be
sketching the outlines of the religious case against the theatre, while
the second will be focusing on how Shakespeare's plays might have
looked to an antitheatrical commentator.

Controversy addressed such issues as the legitimacy of intermixing
good behavioural examples with bad, and the staging of swearing,
obscenity and lasciviousness; whether one could represent divine things
on stage without profaning them; and conversely, what the implications

were of staging pagan matter. At their most theoretical, writers interrogated topics such as idolatry and the moral status of representation; at their most practical, they considered whether theatres were desirable within cities.[2] Theatres were seen as a resort for whores, pickpockets and gamblers, and they drew people away from church services, especially when players performed on the Sabbath.[3] Attendance at them courted plague, which in turn could be seen as manifesting God's anger.[4] London's flourishing dramatic culture is proof that not everyone attended to the antitheatricalists. But we will never know how many Londoners did not go to the theatre because of their strictures, and we do know that these turned the simple act of going to a play into one that had to be morally and religiously justified. The high-profile pamphlet controversy which Shakespeare would have encountered in his earlier playwriting years was succeeded, later in his active life, by a steady drip of hostile references to drama within sermons and moralistic literature; in Charles I's reign, the debate gained a new lease of life with William Prynne's *Histrio-Mastix* (1633), an antitheatrical treatise which did much to bring about the closure of London's theatres in 1642. Shakespeare did not live to read *Histrio-Mastix*, but it is in a tradition which he would have known.

But why should the debate have arisen when it did? As Jonas Barish has commented, antitheatrical attacks often occur at times when the theatre is flourishing, and this was certainly the case within Elizabethan England:[5] London's first purpose-built commercial theatre, the Red Lion, had opened in 1567, to be followed by others.[6] Antitheatricalism, then, was in part a conservative response to a powerful new medium which seemed ripe for abuse – one can compare the backlash against television in its early days. In part too, it betokens the divided and often inflammatory religious atmosphere of a time when the Puritan movement was growing in importance, and Catholics were suffering a high level of persecution. Commentators in the debate come from several styles of churchmanship, and it is hardly surprising that – as will be discussed below – many points at debate relate insistently back to theological differences.

PURITANISM AND ANTITHEATRICALISM

Who were the antitheatricalists? Until recently, the answer would
simply have been 'Puritans', and suitably qualified, the notion still has
something to commend it. But Puritans were not alone in being
antitheatrical. Several elements of the case against players could be
wielded by Catholics, Protestants and those with a more secular moralistic agenda, as well as by those who were merely concerned with
the social problems posed by rogues and vagabonds; it is very common
to see playgoing listed with other evidence of dissipation like whores
and card-playing. The general accusation that attending plays was a
waste of time could be used to remind readers of how they would have
to give an account of every misspent second to God.[7] The quest to
define Puritanism has proved irresistible to scholars, but three things
agreed on by most commentators are particularly relevant to this
study: a feeling that the reformed church in England needed to strive
towards further purification; an emphasis on inward spirituality; and
an oppositional stance, stemming from a belief that those saved by
God were a minority whose Christian way of living was obvious to all.
They could have subscribed to all the standard moralistic condemnations of the stage; besides, their frequent willingness to sacrifice
social cohesion wherever they felt it undermined personal religious
integrity led to a suspicion of communal festivity *per se*, which would
have been an added reason to speak against the theatre. Generalized
antitheatrical diatribes in sermons or religious tracts frequently come
from those of Puritan sympathies; as ever, the balance of evidence
favours the male clerisy, but the biography of Margaret Duck, who
lived in London near the Blackfriars theatre, gives us a vignette of a
laywoman who boycotted plays.

> . . . notwithstanding the many opportunities she had to see
> Playes, to which the neighbourhood and vicinity of the Play-house
> there, and the frequent throngs of Gentlewomen which prest
> thither, might have been forcible and prevailing invitations, she
> could never while she lived there, nor all the time of her being
> in London, be induc'd to see any; and being sometimes advised

by her dearest friend, to go thither as other Gentlewomen did, to avoid too much retirednesse, she answered, 'tis hard to say whether with more discretion or religion, She liked it not, and next to Gods house, she could best spend her time in her own.[8]

Playwrights rose to the implied challenge. During and after Shakespeare's time there was a pronounced tradition of mocking Puritans on stage, Shakespeare himself being responsible for some of the period's best-known comic and satirical creations in this vein. Art may often have modelled life, with Puritans valorizing the playwrights' stereotypes by playing up to them.[9] While dramatic representations of Puritanism tended to foster its association with joylessness and censure, it has been argued that Falstaff – who started life named after the Lollard and proto-Protestant martyr Sir John Oldcastle – recalls stereotypes of Puritans whose emphasis on personal interpretation of the Scriptures led them to lawless and lustful extremes: a useful reminder that some anti-Puritan criticism characterized Puritans not as suspicious of partying, but as only too prone to it.[10] While hypocrisy does not feature strongly among Falstaff's array of vices, Angelo in *Measure for Measure*, who begins the play as morally 'precise' (1.3.50) and attempts to maintain a pious façade even when he degenerates into a lust-driven, manipulative tyrant, epitomizes the common suspicion that all Puritans were hypocrites; Malvolio in *Twelfth Night*, ostentatiously holding himself aloof from the other characters, typifies the equally frequent accusation that they were anti-social. But the jibe famously levelled at him, 'Dost thou think because thou art virtuous there shall be no more cakes and ale?' (2.3.112–113), comes from Sir Toby Belch at his rowdiest, and reminds the audience that anti-social behaviour comes in more than one form; as the play proceeds, Malvolio is mocked, but so too are his onstage mockers. A sermon by Robert Sanderson contains an admonition as even-handed as Shakespeare's, condemning both Puritans – 'our Brethren, and their Lay-followers, [who] by their uncouth and somtimes ridiculous behaviour [have] . . . given prophane persons too much advantage to play upon them' – and the 'loose persons . . . that make it their sport upon their Ale-benches to rayle and scoffe at Puritanes'.[11] The passage is a reminder that

plays would have formed a continuum with other forms of anti-
Puritan scoffing. Sanderson's condemnation of Puritanism on the one
hand and low life on the other is a means of defining himself as a
morally upright, mainstream member of the Church of England, and
the passage is an aside in an argument that the church should retain
some ceremonial. But drama offers considerably fewer handles, and
the fact that Shakespeare's anti-Puritanism has been so much
discussed is a sign of how few clues he gives his readers and audiences
about his beliefs.

As this implies, the relationship between antitheatrical discourse
and the stage's hostility to Puritans is strong. But as many recent
critics have argued, it is also complex, and to see all antitheatricalism
as emanating from Puritans would be reductive:[12] some Puritans, such
as Thomas Middleton, were prolific and successful playwrights, and
the antitheatricalist Stephen Gosson attacked Puritans as vehemently
as plays.[13] A more recent fashion has been to pose a distinction
between Catholic theatricality as expressed in liturgical contexts, and
Protestant condemnation of ceremony, identifying the latter attitude
as lying behind attacks on the theatre. But there are two problems
with this: first, it ignores the fact that many Protestants, especially in
the Lutheran tradition, retained a good deal of religious ceremonial,
and second, it erodes the distinction between what happened inside
and outside church. The reformed tradition could be very friendly
towards religious drama, and some reformers were even dramatists
themselves: John Foxe's apocalyptic drama *Christus Triumphans* (1556)
puts Christ on stage in a way which, not many years later, would have
been impossible in English Protestant theatre.[14] The Continental
reformer Theodore Beza, who wrote a play on the story of Abraham
and Isaac which was translated into English, believed that drama was
acceptable as long as it was derived from the Scriptures: the exact
opposite, as will become clear, of what came to prevail in the England
of Shakespeare's time.[15] Protestants employed drama in polemical
contexts too. In England under Henry VIII, the first English reformers
made considerable use of drama as an evangelizing tool – something
which, in fact, predates sustained attempts to suppress the mystery
cycles.[16] The ex-Carthusian monk John Bale appropriated the genre of

morality play to criticize the kind of religion which had given it birth, and early in Elizabeth's reign, the Catholic writer Thomas Dorman accused players of popularizing the new religion.[17] Thus, in England as elsewhere on the Continent, there was nothing inevitable about the association of Protestantism and antitheatricalism. However, England saw a pronounced difference between generations of reformers, and the expression of this difference can only be helped by bringing the association between Puritans and antitheatricalism carefully back into play.[18]

Antitheatrical reflections can be found in sermons, advice manuals, biographies and moral treatises; it is important to see antitheatrical pamphlets in relation to these other genres, especially as they now seem so negative and hectoring when read on their own. This is partly because of their stylistic antecedents in classical satirists such as Horace and – especially – Juvenal, as well as the writings of church fathers who were themselves drawing on satirical models. Despite its moral energy, the satirical and exhortatory mode of these texts downplays the antitheatricalists' best argument, how playgoing could detract from the joys of religion.[19] Accentuating the negative, they call it perverse to take more pleasure in profane matter than in the word of God, and attribute that perverseness to general human depravity, individual reprobation, or Satan at work. Sometimes, though, they go further, and become conscious of their own capacity to be enthralled. The seductiveness of the theatre was, after all, why it was dangerous in the first place: to quote Stephen Gosson again, 'Cooks did never show more craft in their junkets to vanquish the taste, nor painters in shadows to allure the eye, then poets in theatres to wound the conscience. There set they abroach strange consorts of melody, to tickle the ear; costly apparel, to flatter the sight; effeminate gesture, to ravish the sense; and wanton speech, to whet desire to inordinate lust.'[20] This language forced the comparison of theatres to brothels, a standard criticism which Gervase Babington expands in his explanation of why plays are most pernicious to audience members when mounted privately. 'If they be dangerous on the day time, more daungerous on the night certainely: if on a stage, & in open courtes, much more in chambers and private houses. For there are manie roomes beside that, where the play is, & peradventure the strangenes of the place & lacke of light to guide them, causeth errour in their way . . . '[21]

THE ANTITHEATRICALISTS

This suggests one answer to a question running through this chapter: given the obvious attractions of the theatre, what did antitheatricalists dislike about it, and what were they afraid of? Antitheatrical discourse resolves itself into several strands: some more self-interested, or more obviously a rhetorical exercise, than others. Looking only at the debate as set out in antitheatricalist pamphlets, one might be forgiven for thinking it a little stagey.[22] But the sustained reiteration of concerns about playgoing in sermons and religious tracts, well after the more famous pamphlet-exchanges had run their course, implies that the issue continued to be of intense pastoral relevance to many clergymen. In the 1620s, for instance, Thomas Taylor sees playgoing as evidence of spiritual backsliding: 'How many have wee observed so strict in their course, that they could endure no sinne . . . Now they see many of the same things to bee more indifferent . . . Nay they are growne so strong, as their stomacks (like Ostriches) can digest Othes, Playes, profane and wanton speeches, in themselves and others.'[23] Preachers' condemnations of plays, like those of other antitheatricalists, can often seem extremely vague, but there are good reasons for this. They would, after all, have faced the amateur censor's usual dilemma: to see or read something rumoured to be offensive is potentially upsetting for oneself and helps to encourage the producers, but not to see or read it means that one has to condemn without the evidence. Too much detail about contemporary drama might have seemed suspicious to a congregation, whereas one could hardly go wrong sticking to generalized awful warnings about the theatre, and indictments of it from the church fathers. As will be argued below, it is not hard to find material in Shakespeare and other playwrights which would have raised religious hackles, but this does not necessarily mean that preachers knew it was there.

Other factors may be at work too. Given the often-reiterated complaint that parishioners who should have been going to church were instead sneaking off to the theatre, it seems clear that many clerical commentators had a sense of being in professional competition with the players.[24] Even the layman Anthony Munday, writing an antitheatrical pamphlet during his temporary alienation from the theatre, aligns himself with this group in suggesting a ban on Sunday plays.[25] As Munday's career suggests, antitheatricalists often had personal reasons to dislike the theatre. The unsuccessful playwright Stephen Gosson may have turned to antitheatrical commentary out of personal disappointment, though William Rankins went in the other direction, moving from antitheatrical commentary to playwriting.[26] Financial incentives could sometimes have operated, since both Rankins and Munday may have been paid to write against the theatre.[27] From the purely literary point of view, antitheatricalism would have operated within the wider tradition of the palinode: a recantation of one's previous writing which often took the form of a generalized farewell to poetry.[28] Shakespeare nods to this within Prospero's famous speech in *The Tempest*, 'Our revels now are ended': 'And, like the baseless fabric of this vision, / The cloud-capped towers, the gorgeous palaces, / The solemn temples, the great globe itself, / Yes, all which it inherit, shall dissolve, / And, like this insubstantial pageant faded, / Leave not a rack behind' (4.1.148, 151–156). Since the actors and theatrical props in question are magical and fugitive, the whole scene has a paradoxical quality, giving flesh to the notion that theatre is an illusion. Phrases such as 'baseless fabric' and 'insubstantial pageant' bear this out, and could easily come from an antitheatricalist's arsenal. In context, they exude a nostalgic yearning that would have been foreign to an antitheatricalist – Prospero is, after all, preparing to relinquish his magical powers – but remain a conventional reminder of worldly vanity; part of the scene's subtlety is to show Prospero preparing for old age and death by making these exemplary reflections his own.

If this passage gives us a glimpse of Shakespeare borrowing from contemporary moralistic discourse, there were times when moralists repaid the compliment. Despite the strong antitheatrical bias of so many sermons, one should not assume that all preachers were that way inclined, and scholars' analysis of commonplace-books has thrown up occasional instances of clergy who drew on the drama of Shakespeare and his contemporaries to embellish sermons. Two well-known examples from around Shakespeare's time are Thomas Adams, who quoted from Webster's *The White Devil*, and the Oxford cleric Nicholas Richardson who used an image of a tethered bird from *Romeo and Juliet* in a sermon first preached in 1620, to illustrate God's love for his saints: ' 'Tis almost morning. I would have thee gone – / And yet no farther than a wanton's bird, / That lets it hop a little from his hand, / Like a poor prisoner in his twisted gyves, / And with a silk thread plucks it back again, / So loving-jealous of his liberty' (2.1.221–226).[29] The commonplace-book compiler who gives us this information also notes other dramatic passages, probably for use in his own sermons, but, suggestively, gives the titles of some plays in code.[30] Nothing better emblematizes what could be a profound ambivalence to the theatre, even among preachers who enjoyed drama and borrowed from it.

HYPOCRISY AND DRAMATIC REPRESENTATION

Antitheatricalists were aligning themselves with a long ecclesiastical tradition. As a glance at the sidenotes of most antitheatrical pamphlets reveals, the early church had a habit of condemning the theatre, with the church father Tertullian's diatribe *De Spectaculis* among those most frequently cited.[31] The association made by St Augustine between acting and idol-worship had epitomized antitheatrical sentiment throughout the Middle Ages, and continued authoritative in the Renaissance; another church father whom both Protestants and Catholics would have respected, he fitted the mood of an age when the act of representation, whether in art or drama, was so open to question and censure.[32] Given that the dramatic medium depends on pretending to be what one is not, it invites accusations of hypocrisy that would have resonated with contemporary religious anxieties. While medieval Christianity had a well-developed notion of hypocrisy, it would characteristically have condemned as a hypocrite someone whose actions were visibly incompatible with his or her professed religion. But the Reformation complicated matters, because of the Protestant belief that conformity to Christian practice was no guarantee of salvation. If you could not be sure whether you yourself, let alone your next-door neighbours in the pew, were living the Christian religion or merely acting it, the notion of hypocrisy was bound to become more alarming than hitherto.

Players at least were honest hypocrites, not pretending not to pretend; but because their profession undermined any simple relationship between being and seeming, they were easy targets. Even their manner of publicizing themselves could be rendered suspect by accusations of hypocrisy. Referring to Christ's injunction in the Sermon on the Mount, 'Therefore when thou givest thine almes, thou shalt not make a trumpet to be blowen before thee, as the hypocrites do in the Synagogues and in the stretes, to be praised of men' (Matthew 6:2), William Burton commented:

Our Saviours purpose is to illustrate his precept by an example of counterfeits and players, who do all their feats of purpose to be seene of men: to which end, they have a stage erected, that men may see them, making proclamation, that whosoever come to such a place, at such an houre, shal see such a mans players, that is, such a mans hypocrites make a play, that is, play the hypocrites by counterfeiting and shewing diverse mens actions and diverse mens persons . . .[33]

The Sermon on the Mount implies a distinction between the hypocrites' meritorious actions and the inappropriate publicity they are seeking; as it goes on to comment, popular admiration is what they are principally concerned with, and it is, therefore, all the reward they can expect. But the verse, like the rest of the Sermon of the Mount, problematizes any wider definition of hypocrisy as not being what one seems; in verses 16–17 of the same chapter, for instance, Christ condemns the hypocrites who 'loke . . . sowre' when they fast, and praises those who anoint their heads and wash their faces so that their fasting is only obvious to God. Hence, if one does not want to appear better than one is, or to get maximum credit for one's good deeds, this can sometimes in itself force a distinction between outward and inward appearance. This is where Burton's tirade goes well beyond what the Gospel actually says, illustrating how hypocrisy to the antitheatricalist is not an attempt to appear better than one is, but other than one is. Burton certainly condemns the player who 'counterfeiteth the King, and yet is no King, but a base fellow' and admits with rough humour that 'some play the rogues part, and are rogues indeede' (p. 37), but argues that players are hypocrites either way: first, because they represent persons other than themselves, second, because they seek publicity for so doing. His exegesis wildly distorts the Gospels, but is very revealing on the topic of antitheatrical prejudice.

Anti-popery systematized notions of hypocrisy with its claim that the visible Catholic church, which proclaimed itself as true, was a snare and a delusion. In particular, the Catholic Mass, where bread and wine were said to become the body and blood of Christ through the process of transubstantiation, was seen as nothing more than a stage-play, while the liturgical formality and ceremonial grandeur of Catholicism made broader comparisons with the theatre easy to sustain.[34] Thus Catholics, like players, often served as the occasion for a wider debate on the status and validity of representation. Yet where the picture starts getting more complicated is that many Catholics would have sympathized with the concerns articulated by Protestant antitheatricalists.[35] While the Council of Trent made no specific pronouncements on theatre, Michael A. Zampelli has recently argued that the post-Tridentine Catholic world was more hospitable to antitheatrical sentiment than ever before.[36] This may have had an effect even on underground Catholicism in England. A manuscript which survives in the Folger Shakespeare Library testifies to an abortive attempt in 1618 on the part of William Harrison, Archpriest of England, to prevent Catholic clerics going to the theatre.[37] The fact that this does not seem to have worked is telling in itself. But as supplemented by a protest against the prohibition by the secular priest Thomas Leke, and a rejoinder to the protest by Harrison's assistant John Colleton, it gives us some idea of Catholic theatregoing habits, albeit not uncontradictory. Leke remarks, 'We knowe that most of the principal Catholicks about London doe goe to playes', while Colleton responds, 'The Catholicks that use to playes are the young of both sexes, and neither matron, nor grave, or sage man is there seen'.

While declaring that the prohibition was directly aimed at specific offenders, including Leke himself, Colleton's statement reveals that this was only one of a series of admonitions from archpriests, stretching back to the turn of the century, which in turn suggests that it was not unusual for Catholic clerics to attend playhouses. Colleton's theoretical justification of antitheatricalism is at many points very similar to the Protestant texts discussed above, resorting like them to St John Chrysostom and St Augustine, and taking a highly negative view of professional actors and the playhouse environment. Leke, on the other hand, bases his defence of the theatre on St Thomas Aquinas's argument that play is necessary within human life, and that actors and their entertainments can be justified if they present nothing contrary to religion and good conduct. Colleton counters this by saying that most playhouse dramas contain irreligious or bawdy passages, though he furnishes an implicit answer to this point when he distinguishes between Catholic playgoers who enquire in advance about a production, and those who do not.

So just as there was a wide spread of attitudes towards drama among Protestants, Catholics did not invariably affirm it – despite the presence of residual Catholic matter in mainstream theatre, and the pronounced association between Catholicism and religious drama both before and after the English Reformation.[38] Some Counter-Reformation writers, such as Carlo Borromeo, Archbishop of Milan, wrote specifically against the theatre; many others disliked specific features of drama such as profanity, bawdry, transvestism, the abuse of sacred material and the appropriation of pagan world-views.[39] Perhaps most typical of the post-Reformation Catholic position, though, is the view that there could be a legitimate role for drama in an ecclesiastical context, a position which ultimately stemmed from the Catholic valorization of images as aids to religious devotion. This, of course, ran counter to one of Protestant antitheatricalism's most important theoretical stances. As several commentators have shown, Protestant iconoclasm – the act of destroying images of God or the saints lest they should provoke idolatry – led to a broader suspicion of imaging which profoundly affected drama.[40] As Michael O'Connell has put it: 'The consciousness of . . . sixteenth-century antitheatrical writers had been formed . . . by revulsion against the possibility of seeing a god within the physical presence of a statue or painting; such a mode of seeing for them was the very essence of idolatry.'[41] In this respect, there is a good deal of common ground between the reformers' position and that developed in an earlier era by the icono-clasts of the Byzantine empire: a circumstance which post-Reformation English Catholic drama exploited within such plays as Joseph Simons's *Leo Armenus*, a tragedy recounting the downfall of an iconoclastic Byzantine emperor, in such a way as to make the analogy with more recent Protestant powers.[42] While iconoclastic views were potentially extendable to all acts of representation, there was a particular concern surrounding religious drama, and especially the legitimacy, or other-wise, of representing God and the saints on stage.

Concerns about this motivated the Protestant suppression of England's popular religious drama, though this was a lengthy and piecemeal process, which in its inception under Henry VIII was only a matter of removing overt references to Catholicism. As commented above, many early reformers made extensive use of the dramatic medium for anti-Catholic polemic, and had no problem about religious drama *per se*. Yet once the concern had been raised, the uneasiness about religious representation was to spread. Murray Roston's influ-ential phrase 'the rungs of sanctity' describes how a prejudice against representing Christ and other figures and episodes from the New Testament spread further, to affect Old Testament and Apocryphal figures, and thence all dramatizations of obviously religious themes.[43] By Shakespeare's time, professional drama reflected this bias. Popular religious drama took a long time to go away, yet it did eventually go; and given how often it has been seen by recent commentators as a joyous instrument of social cohesion and festivity, it is remarkable that the Catholics and social conservatives among Shakespeare's con-temporaries lament its demise so little – which in turn prompts the speculation that it might have seemed rather embarrassing to humanist-educated authors.

Post-Reformation English Catholic drama can, in some ways, be seen as taking over where medieval religious drama left off. Written for semi-private performance in households sympathetic to the old religion, or in the schools and colleges on the Continent set up during Elizabeth's reign to provide a Catholic education for English youths, it is still relatively neglected by scholars.[44] Yet the fact that it was composed by Englishmen at odds with the religious and literary standards prevailing in the country of their birth makes it an essential corrective to standard accounts of post-Reformation English drama. Startlingly accentuating silences and absences within the mainstream, it counters any notion that late-sixteenth and seventeenth-century Englishmen were uninterested in religious theatre. With plots taken from hagiographies, church history and the more recent events of the Reformation, these plays have an unabashed willingness to stage Christ and the saints, to comment on the rise of heresy in England and to celebrate the deaths of recent Catholic martyrs.[45] Passing from them to Shakespeare's theatre reveals the sheer oddness of the English mainstream dramatic experience: plays making little or no attempt to stage the sacred, and with little overt religious reference, produced within an age passionately engaged with religion and a literary culture otherwise saturated by religion.

Yet these were still plays which exploited religious allusion, in a way which would have incurred condemnation from antitheatricalists of all religious persuasions who disliked the admixture of religious and profane material in drama. This is a concern illustrated by the exchange in John Northbrooke's dialogue *A Treatise Against Dicing, Dancing, Plays, and Interludes* (1577), where Youth exclaims, 'I marvel why you speak against such interludes and places for plays, seeing that many times they play histories out of the Scriptures', and Age replies, 'Assuredly that is very evil to do, to mingle scurrility with divinity, that is, to eat meat with unwashed hands'.[46] Looking at a morality play like *Mankind*, which intermingles scatological humour with moral exhortation, or a mystery play like the Wakefield Last Judgement, where the demons act scurrilously in character, his nervousness is understandable. Northbrooke's treatise is one of the earliest interventions in the antitheatricalism debate, reminding us that when he was writing, legislation against religious matter had not taken full effect. But complaints of intermixing continued well after it had done so, and came to be applied more widely. In *Vertues Common-Wealth* (1st edn, 1602), for instance, Henry Crosse described how plays 'intermixe the sacred words of God, that never ought to be handled without feare and trembling, with their filthy and scurrillous Paganisme' (f. P3a).[47] Cited by many antitheatricalists, including Crosse, was the anecdote from the historian Josephus of how Theodectes the tragic poet was struck blind because he had intended to make use of scripture in his writings, then had his sight restored after he had acknowledged his presumption.[48]

DRAMATIZING PAGANISM

The pagan antecedents of drama were another kind of intermixing. While the roots of classical drama in pagan festivity were well known at this date, commentators varied widely on the question of how this was to be judged. Thomas Lodge, responding to Stephen Gosson in a defence of the theatre, calls pagan motives for mixing tragedy with religion 'not discommendable', since 'the first matter . . . was to give thanks and praises to God, and a grateful prayer of the countrymen for a happy harvest'.[49] Countering this specific passage, Gosson remarked that it 'serveth . . . better to overthrow [plays] than establish them: for whatsoever was consecrated to the honor of heathen gods was consecrated to idolatry . . . Being consecrated to idolatry, they are not of God; if they proceed not from God, they are the doctrine and inventions of the devil.'[50] His invective, artificially dualistic as it is, nevertheless reminds us how drama was a locus for concern about pagan idolatry as well as Christian, and how the pagan roots of drama could be seen as fatally compromising the medium for Christians.

If one believed this, the problem could only have been exacerbated by the insistent classical allusions in Elizabethan drama, especially if they took the form of prayer or invocation. The ancient Roman playwright Seneca, perhaps the single greatest influence on English Renaissance tragedy, inspired many dramatic appeals to the gods at times of extreme emotional agony. To take one instance from Shakespeare's work, when Titus Andronicus discovers the names of those who have raped and mutilated his daughter Lavinia, he cries '*Magni dominator poli, / Tam lentus audis scelera, tam lentus vides?*' (4.1.81–82). These words are largely – though as will become clear, not entirely – copied from lines in Seneca's *Phaedra*.[51] The passage can be paraphrased as 'Ruler of the great heavens, are you so slow to hear crimes, so slow to see?' Shakespeare adapts Seneca's periphrasis for Jove, *Magne regnator deum* (Great monarch of the gods), making the divine addressee potentially a monotheistic god; in a play shot through with deliberate anachronism which is often religious in tenor, this has the effect of making any accusation of divine tardiness applicable to the Judaeo-Christian God as well.[52] Ejaculations such as 'How long wilt y[o]u forget me, ô Lord? for ever? how long wilt thou hyde thy face from me?' are, after all, common enough in the Psalms – which is exactly why the passage could have exacerbated uneasiness if an auditor was pre-disposed to find blasphemy in drama.[53] Sometimes the theatregoers of Shakespeare's England were asked to imagine there was no heaven; the antitheatricalists seem to have been afraid it was easy if one tried.

Perhaps, though, this would have been less offensive to the anti-theatricalists than the mimicry of pagan worship. Gosson inveighs against this, in a passage worth quoting in full:

> Though the names of heathen gods or goddesses be of themselves no more hurtful than the names of other men that are dead, yet triumphing under those titles with the Gentiles, and attributing a kind of divinity unto them, as the Gentiles did, is to be defiled with their idolatry. What is idolatry, but to give that which is proper to God unto them that are no gods? . . . Setting out the stage plays of the Gentiles, so we worship that we stoop to the names of heathen idols; so we trust that we give ourselves to the patronage of Mars, of Venus, of Jupiter, of Juno, and such like; so we pray that we call for their succour upon the stage; so we give thanks for the benefits we receive, that we make them the fountains of all our blessings, wherein if we think as we speak, we commit idolatry, because we bestow that upon the idols of the Gentiles which is proper to God. If we make a divorce between the

tongue and the heart, honouring the gods of the heathens in lips, and in gesture, not in thought, yet it is idolatry, because we do that which is quite contrary to the outward profession of our faith.[54]

This kind of play-acting, making as it does a 'divorce between the tongue and the heart', brings to a head the antitheatricalists' concerns about hypocrisy and idolatry. But Gosson also mentions another possibility, that of the actor coming to think as he speaks, and thus bringing questions of belief into the equation. Could he and other antitheatricalists really have been worried about the consequences of invoking pagan gods? On one level, the futility of worshipping them was self-evident, epitomized in the Old Testament story of Elijah and the high priests of Baal: when their god fails to ignite the altar on which a sacrifice is placed, Elijah tells them sarcastically, 'Crye loud: for he is a god: ether he talketh, or pursueth *his enemies*, or is in his journey, or it may be that he slepeth, and must be awaked.'[55] Nor must one ignore the element of sheer point-scoring in Gosson's rhetoric. All the same, his concern over staging pagan religion is not just a rhetorical gambit, but a polemical overstatement of a real, widely shared anxiety. Obviously there were no serious votaries of Jove, Venus, Diana and the rest in Renaissance England, if by that one means believers in their existence who expected favours from them in return for worship. Quite the contrary, allusions to the pagan gods in Renaissance poetic discourse are predicated on not being taken literally. But because they were the quintessence of irony, they were – as ever with irony – vulnerable to misinterpretation by the literal-minded. Emptied gods retained moral value as a way of conceptualizing human qualities, and were also, for the most part, thought of as legitimate playthings; but they could incur accusations of idolatry from those who doubted the value of play, and feared the consequences of distracting humans from the real God. Precisely because they were devoid of devotional significance, they could be seen as vessels for the devil to inhabit, or corpses for him to galvanize. At this period, the devil was often seen as a real entity by learned and unlearned alike, and those who believed with St Augustine that evil was an absence of good would have had cause to be wary of inanity.[56]

In some respects, the above interpretation goes against conventional wisdom. Discussing the function of pagan gods within medieval and Renaissance allegory, C.S. Lewis wrote seventy years ago in a book which deservedly remains on reading-lists: 'The gods must be, as it were, disinfected of belief; the last taint of the sacrifice, and of the urgent practical interest, the selfish prayer, must be washed away from them, before that other divinity can come to light in the imagination. For poetry to spread its wings fully, there must be, besides the believed religion, a marvellous that knows itself as myth.'[57] Thus far, one can agree with Lewis, but there are problems with his formulation too. The imaginative afterlife of the pagan gods depended on author and audience sustaining a complicated equilibrium, given that any claim to worship them needed to be understood allegorically; difficulties would have arisen whenever a respondent insisted – however pig-headedly – on taking such claims at face value. Even the gods' allegorical significance could become problematic when it invited the audience to ask what was actually meant when they were invoked, and the problem could only have been compounded by the fact that the names of classical gods often did stand in for objects of living belief in Elizabethan and Jacobean England.

This reveals a deeper faultline in the intellectual climate of the time. The idea of the Renaissance is synonymous with the scholarly desire across Europe to return to the best classical sources; grammar-school and university curricula were based upon ancient Roman and, to a lesser extent, Greek authors, to the extent that an acquaintance with classical learning became synonymous with education in general. Latin was the normal medium of international scholarly communication, and classical Latin models were used to dictate prose-style. The notion that the intellectual achievement of the ancients could never be surpassed gave them overriding scholarly authority, with moves towards more empirical methods of enquiry only just beginning in Shakespeare's time. Examples of classical wisdom and classical virtue would have been encountered by those at most levels of literacy.[58] Nevertheless, those writing in the present day did have one area of superiority to ancient Greeks and Romans: they were Christians. Writers in early-modern England, as elsewhere in Europe,

exhibit a spectrum of attitudes towards this, not always straightforwardly reinforcing Christian tenets.

Pagan virtue could be used as a reproach to Christians, while the
question of whether virtuous pagans could be saved, one which had
always perplexed the church, was particularly topical in a period when
encounters with the New World exposed Europeans to contemporary
non-Christian belief-systems.[59] To become an ordained member of the
Church of England or the Catholic church, one would have needed an
intimate familiarity with pagan writing. It was commonly acknowledged that examples of pagan virtue could inform Christian morality,
and even be subsumed into it; notably, Christianity inherited from
Stoicism an emphasis on virtuous endurance. The common image of
a bee gathering honey from pagan flowers emblematizes the idea that,
with judicious selection, Christians could learn moral and spiritual
lessons from pagan authors, as well as merely intellectual ones: an
argument central to the didactic aesthetic of mainstream humanism,
and much used by defenders of the theatre. However, there also existed
a position which it may be fair to call anti-humanist, of repudiating
the ancients on the grounds that lessons learned from pagans could
only taint one's religion.[60] At its most extreme, this could foster a
belief that, as William Prynne wrote: 'The very worst of Christians
who shall ever enter Heaven Gates, must transcend the virtues of the
best of Pagans: . . . For Christians then, who should soare above all
others, to stoope to Pagan virtues, . . . is to degenerate into Pagans; to
prove worse, yea, lesse than Christians.'[61] In short, Renaissance
England was a place when humanist extollings of the Graeco-Roman
inheritance could exist side-by-side with anti-humanist denigrations of
it, undertaken in the name of religion. This was not new – one need
have looked no further than the Acts of the Apostles to justify a dim
view of classical paganism – but because classical culture had come to
be so educationally valued in the interim, behaving like an early
Christian could easily develop anti-humanist overtones.

Since the antitheatricalism debate was conducted for the most part
by the highly educated, it is hard not to see them – here, at least – as
reneging on their own learning. But this condemnation of classical
scholarship might also have appealed to a less privileged element in

English society. One can speculate that a degree of class envy operated in some cases, especially since – as already discussed – the rigour of the antitheatricalist position appealed to Puritans, and Puritanism was popular among those who were literate without being highly educated.[62] While it would have been possible for any literate Englishman or woman to pick up a fragmentary knowledge of the classical world from popular literature, gaining a systematic understanding of classical allusion without at least a grammar-school education would have been extremely difficult. But when considering the question of how paganism was regarded and written about in the English Renaissance, one needs to remember that education imparts a state of mind as well as a body of facts – and never more than when considering Shakespeare's schooling. Controversies over whether Shakespeare wrote the plays normally ascribed to him, which persist at the fringe of Shakespeare studies, have at least drawn attention to what a grammar-school curriculum would have contained: insofar as they base their argument on Shakespeare's being too unlearned to have written erudite and allusive plays, they have drawn responses from more orthodox critics which suggest the opposite.[63]

If, in Ben Jonson's famous phrase, Shakespeare had 'small Latin and less Greek' – at least compared to Jonson – he picked up at Stratford-upon-Avon Grammar School a skill which was, perhaps, even more central to a classical education: that of talking about false gods in earnest.[64] In the typical grammar-school curriculum, pagan moralists such as Cicero were presented for admiration and emulation, as were such heroes as Aeneas, praised by Vergil and a host of schoolboy imitators as 'pius' for his devotion to the pagan gods. When it came to original composition in prose and verse, one would have had to mimick the thought-processes of pagan writers as well as their diction. But it is an edginess about this aspect of the classical inheritance which helps to explain one of the key provisos of antitheatricalism. Even antitheatricalists sometimes conceded that drama could be appropriate within an educational context, which carries the assumption that it would be performed by actors and to an audience skilled in how to interpret alternative world-views, especially where to stop believing in them.[65] Even so, the inherent danger in idolatrous invocation might remain. When Prynne summarizes his predecessors' defence of educational drama, it contains the proviso that 'there be no mention or invocation of heathen gods or goddesses in them'.[66] This would have been extremely difficult, given the subject-matter of much university drama; but for that reason, it demonstrates how the very medium of teaching could be seen as compromised by paganism, problematizing what was meant by education in the first place.

Other specific dangers of drama lay in its immediate sensual appeal, and its ability to involve both actors and audience in a fiction. The imaginative contract entered into by audience members willingly watching a drama had, according to some antitheatricalists, the effect of tarring them with the same brush as actors. As Anthony Munday put it, 'all other evils pollute the doers only, not the beholders or the hearers. For a man may hear a blasphemer and not be partaker of his sacrilege, inasmuch as in mind he dissenteth. . . . Only the filthiness of plays and spectacles is such as maketh both the actors and beholders guilty alike. For while they say nought, but gladly look on, they all by sight and assent are actors . . .'[67] It can be hard to see why a theatrical spectator should have been thought any more sinful than, for instance, someone who bought and read a volume of erotic verse, but Munday's singling out of theatre for condemnation testifies to the fact that it was regarded as a uniquely powerful experience, and therefore, perhaps, uniquely pernicious. Munday is perhaps also missing a trick in arguing for a degree of informed complicity in what takes place on stage, which would not necessarily have been true for every audience member. Judging by the plays they were offered, the general level of audience sophistication rose rapidly during the first decades of London's professional theatre, and one can assume at any historical period that most adults appreciate the difference between real life and make-believe. However, the success of drama depends on the temporary consensual blurring of categories between the two, and any imaginative identification with pagan characters, whether among actors or audience, would surely have created another moral difficulty. We have already seen the invocation of pagan gods identified as a potential problem even for educational drama, and much of the antitheatricalist rhetoric quoted above seems to be anticipating what an unlettered apprentice would make of a prayer to Diana or Jove.

Even at their most paranoid, antitheatricalists do not seem to be implying that such an auditor would actually go away from the theatre believing in pagan gods. What they fear is, rather, the temporary imaginative collusion of auditor with actor: a problem for everyone when questions of idolatry are in play, but most acute for those who are not assumed to have the intellectual equipment to register dissent. In essence, this is a suspicion of – to use an anachronistic term – performativity.[68] One could define this term as the process of doing something by saying it – making a promise, for instance. It encompasses both the possibility of saying something without explicit previous internal assent, and the idea that what is said might take effect later. Precisely because saying something without first meaning it would have been anathema to Puritans, they were very well aware of how performativity worked; their suspicion of ritual and devotional repetition was prompted by the fact that these let in efficaciousness by the back door. Of the several critics who have read Elizabethan antitheatricalism in relation to contemporary religious controversy, one of the subtlest is Michael O'Connell; in *The Idolatrous Eye* (2000), he asks why the charge of idolatry should have been levelled at the repertoire of the Elizabethan public theatres as well as biblical drama, and comments: 'it arbitrarily assigns a religious dimension to drama that makes no claims in this direction'.[69] As he says, this is strange. His answer to the conundrum emphasizes the strong association of popery with idolatry among Protestant commentators at this date; my intention has been to supplement this by pointing out that the notion of idolatry has more far-reaching implications still, ones which struck at the basis of the educational system and notions of intellectual authority with their suspicion of classical paganism.

SYNCRETISM AND CENSORSHIP

Here as often elsewhere, it would be a mistake to write the antitheatricalists off as reactionary in comparison to the dramatists they were criticizing. Commentators on both sides of the debate about staging paganism can be seen as uncommonly prescient, anticipating some of the challenges posed to orthodox Christianity by Enlightenment thinkers, as well as the Christian responses to these. This illustrates how drama's pull away from the normative operations of authorial comment and towards imaginative autonomy could have some remarkable consequences; officially debarred from straightforward dramatization of religious topics or direct commentary on the debates between Catholic and Protestant, dramatists were almost invited to leap out of the frying-pan into the fire. Evocations of a godlessness which matched contemporary definitions of atheism, and experiments with scepticism, comparative religion and impious railing at the gods, are not at all hard to find within Shakespeare's own work, or that of his immediate precursors and successors.[70] Certainly, no-one would argue that Shakespeare's work is as obviously audacious as parts of *Dr Faustus* or *Tamburlaine* – Marlowe's canonical centrality can prevent one noticing how much further he goes than most of his contemporaries. In the way that Shakespeare practises religious syncretism while not presenting it as a challenge to received ideas, his dramatic practice is closer to the norm, yet it still contains matter that a religiously motivated antitheatricalist would have found doubtful.

It is time to look at the staging of pagan worship in Shakespeare's drama, and the following example is taken from Act 5.3 of *Much Ado About Nothing*. At this point in the plot, Hero is assumed to have died of shock after having been falsely accused of sexual infidelity by her erstwhile fiancé, Claudio. He and his friends, together with Hero's father Leonato, visit her tomb at Leonato's request to do penance. It may be helpful to quote at length.

> *Enter* CLAUDIO, DON PEDRO, *and three or four* [*Attendants,*
> *including a* Lord *and* Musicians,] *with tapers.*
> CLAUDIO: Is this the monument[71] of Leonato?
> LORD: It is, my lord. [*Reads the*] *epitaph.*
> *Done to death by slanderous tongues*
> *Was the Hero that here lies;*
> *Death, in guerdon of her wrongs,*
> *Gives her fame that never dies;*

> *So the life that died with shame,*
> *Lives in death with glorious fame.*
>
> [*Hangs scroll*]
>
> Hang thou there upon the tomb,
> Praising her when I am dumb.
>
> CLAUDIO Now music sound, and sing your solemn hymn.
>
> [*Music*]
>
> ONE OR MORE SINGERS [*Sing*]:
>
> Pardon, goddess of the night,
> Those that slew thy virgin knight,
> For the which with songs of woe
> Round about her tomb they go.
> Midnight, assist our moan,
> Help us to sigh and groan,
> Heavily, heavily.
> Graves yawn and yield your dead,
> Till death be uttered,
> Heavily, heavily.
>
> LORD: Now unto thy bones good night;
> Yearly will I do this rite.

(5.3.1–23)

While we are probably meant to imagine this taking place in a churchyard, the ceremonies are more syncretic than this might suggest. The participants in this scene sing a 'solemn hymn' not to God but to Diana, the 'goddess of the night': a patron of virgins, a virgin herself, and thus an appropriate recipient of prayers from those admitting, with sorrow, that Hero was a virgin after all. The pagan frame of reference also reminds one of Hero's namesake, the priestess who died for love of Leander. But if the addressee of the prayer points us in one direction, the repentant and confessional quality of the scene steers us in another, towards the Prayer Book that would have been statutory listening for Shakespeare's audience. In Shakespeare's England, the most familiar place for penance would have been the church, where offenders would stand in front of the congregation, sometimes draped in a white sheet.[72] Sometimes they would have confessed their fault, more often they would have had it confessed for them. The General Confession that members of the Church of England would have experienced at Morning Prayer and Holy Communion is also evoked; in the quarto text the confession is assigned to an anonymous lord rather than spoken by Claudio, and it is that lord, rather than Claudio himself, who says: 'Yearly will *I* do this rite.'[73] Since this lord is not himself responsible for Hero's supposed death, the transference may show us Claudio evading a personal admission of penitence; but it has also the effect of applying censure to the entire community, with a hint that the ceremony will become part of the liturgical year.[74] Lastly, the way in which the hymn looks forward to the general resurrection – 'Graves yawn and yield your dead' – would have been reminiscent of the burial service, especially if the monument was physically evoked on stage, and given that Don Pedro's comment at the end of the scene, 'Come, let us hence and put on other weeds' (30), implies that the participants are clothed in mourning.

A mixture of Christian and classical references is unremarkable at this date, both in drama and in poetry. Nevertheless, the kind of syncretism which Shakespeare employs in this scene could be used as a way of not taking God's name in vain on stage, something which was a sensitive area even before the specific prohibitions in the 1606 Act to Restrain Abuses of Players.[75] Audience-members would have been free to substitute Christian equivalents for pagan terms, in a way that would have varied according to denomination – a Catholic in the audience, for instance, might well have picked up on possible comparisons between Diana and the Virgin Mary. There is also another, less learned and more homely kind of paganism operating here, since the liturgy has apotropaic elements designed to ward off evil or unquiet spirits: though comminations and exorcisms involve prayer, they tip easily over into spells.[76] The circular movement evoked by the penitents' chant – 'For the which with songs of woe / Round about her tomb they go' – is less reminiscent of religious ritual than of the witches in *Macbeth*. Spells were common enough in Renaissance England, especially among the uneducated, but regularly evoked disapproval from churchmen of all denominations.[77] A possible Protestant reaction to this scene would have been to notice the conflation of pagan religiosity and church ritual, and see it as something only to be expected in a Catholic country. In the context of the play, disapproval would surely have been mitigated by the fact that Claudio is repenting for the wrong he has done Hero, but even so, auditors would have varied as to how they put it in context. Prayers to pagan gods, which could have been received as offensive in any literary genre, are embodied by the very nature of staging, and as stressed above, one should not underestimate the capacity of an antitheatrical commentator to give a scene a literal-minded reading.

While the type of syncretism we see in this scene has real imaginative benefits, it arises out of a situation of constraint where certain pronouncements were forbidden. Antitheatricalists posed the playwrights of Shakespeare's time with a catch-22 situation: references to Christianity were unacceptable because they ran the risk of treating sacred things profanely or scoffingly, but references to paganism were no better because there was a danger in showing reverence to false gods on stage. There was no right answer, and playwrights attentive to the debate would have had to write off a portion of their potential audience. But there is a difference between the unofficial censure of the antitheatricalists and the official censorship of English drama which took place throughout Shakespeare's lifetime, which had nothing to say about the use of the pagan pantheon in drama but a good deal about reference to the true God. Proclamations censoring religious reference within plays were issued under Henry VIII, Mary I, Elizabeth I and James VI/I. Elizabeth I's proclamation of 1559, arranging for all performances to be licensed beforehand, instructed the officers in question that 'they permit none to be played wherein matters of religion or of the governance of the estate of the commonwealth shall be handled or treated, being no meet matters to be written or treated upon but by men of authority, learning, and wisdom, nor to be handled before any audience but of grave and discreet persons'.[78] Later in Shakespeare's career, the Act to Restrain Abuses of Players imposed a fine on 'any person or persons . . . in any stage play, interlude, show, May game, or pageant' who might 'jestingly or profanely speak or use of the holy name of God, or of Christ Jesus, or of the Holy

Ghost, or of the Holy Trinity, which are not to be spoken but with fear and reverence'.[79]

How would English drama of Shakespeare's time stand up to the proverbial injunction that one should not bring up sex, religion or politics in public? Answering this question tells one a lot about how censorship operates in different ages. Sexual topics, given their strong moral charge and defamatory implications, can have a close relationship to religious and political ones, and the three areas are hard to consider separately at this date. As Richard Dutton has commented, 'it is far from clear that matters of sexual taste and decency had any bearing on the *formal* censorship of drama in this period', yet 'it is all but impossible to distinguish sexual discourse from that of religion and politics'.[80] As this implies, while sexually explicit language and the representation of low life on stage were often complained about by antitheatricalists and other moralists, they never became a matter for government legislation in themselves. References to politics and religion, though, were a different matter, and monitored by the state throughout Shakespeare's working life. By the time Shakespeare started writing, the expansion of the professional theatre had impacted on government bureaucracy, and the Master of the Revels and ecclesiastical licensers censored plays before performance and printing respectively. The Master of the Revels was to take over the job of licensing plays for publication towards the end of Shakespeare's career, in 1606 – also the year of the Act to Restrain Abuses of Players. Janet Clare has traced the ways in which playwrights, playhouse book-keepers and the official censor altered texts to come within the terms of this Act, from which it seems that its most far-reaching effect was to curtail the use of oaths.[81] Profanity is one obvious way in which an antitheatrical consumer could be offended at the use made of religious reference; jokiness is another, as discussed below. But perhaps we need to go further, and recover a mode of thought where even a more neutral reference to the Bible could potentially displease someone when it was put on stage; in a context of pretence, matter edifying in itself could come across as totally inappropriate.

Yet it happened all the time. If direct and extensive reference to religion was difficult, there were many indirect ways that Shakespeare and his contemporaries could exploit a subject of such profound emotional resonance. Shakespeare's plays and poems, like those of most imaginative writers among his contemporaries, are saturated with religious allusion.[82] The Bible – Bible-stories most of all – and the Bible's liturgical offshoots were texts one could count on everyone knowing: which has nothing to do with their religious significance, except insofar as this ensured their wide dissemination. Degrees of familiarity would have varied enormously, but the pleasures of biblical allusion could work on several levels. Even a remote familiarity with Genesis would enable one to spot the allusion to the Flood within Jaques's comment in *As You Like It*, as the characters pair off at the end: 'There is sure another flood toward, and these couples are coming to the ark' (5.4.35–36). But it would take a more erudite and careful listener to pick up the biblical allusion in Bottom's speech at the end of *A Midsummer Night's Dream*. Here, Bottom is waking up from a magically induced sleep after his dalliance with Titania:

> I have had a most rare vision. I have had a dream past the wit of man to say what dream it was. Man is but an ass if he go about to expound this dream. Methought I was – there is no man can tell what. Methought I was, and methought I had – but man is but a patched fool if he will offer to say what methought I had. The eye of man hath not heard, the ear of man hath not seen, man's hand is not able to taste, his tongue to conceive, nor his heart to report what my dream was.
> (4.1.201–210)

As has long been recognized, the last sentence parodies a verse from the first epistle of St Paul to the Corinthians: 'But as it is written, The things which eye hathe not seene, nether eare hathe heard, nether came into mans heart, *are*, which God hathe prepared for them that love him' (2.9).[83] This extraordinary speech presupposes a critical mass of listeners who would have enough verbatim recall of the Bible to pick up on the parody, and who, having done so, would find it amusing rather than shocking. To have God's word scrambled in the mouth of a fool, with a gratuitous dirty joke thrown in – 'his tongue to conceive' – would surely have confirmed the worst suspicions of any antitheatricalist. Yet the resemblance of Bottom's speech to St Paul is never brought above the threshold of innuendo; the distortion might be suggestive, but it also makes the similarity to Scripture just about deniable. Censorship creates an ideal climate for innuendo, since it heightens people's sensitivity to dangerous topics – sometimes to counter-productive effect. On the one hand, reference to religion in the Elizabethan and Jacobean theatre was restricted because it was a matter of such political importance and passionate concern. On the other hand, this made for exciting drama, and with religious innuendo as with sexual, there are climates in which one does not need to say much to get people's minds working.

IDOLATRY AND RELIGIOUS LANGUAGE

Sex and religion could also be linked in a more dangerous way, since idolatry and adultery are frequent bedfellows in early-modern writing. As the notoriously iconophobic theologian William Perkins maintained, 'Adulterie is the punishment of Idolatrie; and Idolatrie the punishment of Adulterie', and again, 'note the order of these sinnes: First, [sinners] are drawn to sit at idols feasts, and then to commit adulterie: where we see that these two sinnes goe together, Spirituall adulterie, that is, idolatry; and bodily adultery, one is the plague & punishment of the other'.[84] As Perkins's wordplay suggests, the frequency of their association must have had something to do with their being near-homonyms, but there are other reasons why they were so frequently juxtaposed. Medieval conventions of courtly love were associated with homage to a woman not one's wife, and so were vulnerable to censure, aiding the already standard connection of love with feminine vanity and masculine weakness. Earthly love of any kind was, in any case, inferior to love of God and posed a potential idolatrous hazard to it, while misogynistic discourse made the connection of woman with idolatry and sexual looseness easier still. A topic vulnerable to moralistic condemnation in medieval England proved equally and differently so after the Reformation.[85] Insofar as late-medieval veneration of the Virgin Mary owed something to courtly love conventions, this would have aided her downgrading by the reformers. Conversely, the common association of the Whore of Babylon and the Catholic church within Protestant apocalyptic literature led to frequent comparisons of woman, idolatry and spiritual adultery – it is not surprising that Perkins's reflections come from a sermon on the Book of Revelation. The fact that woman is so often allegorized as an object of spiritual desire in both medieval and Renaissance poetry is an implicit answer to this jibe, at its most cerebral in such neoplatonic texts as Edmund Spenser's *Four Hymns*, but seldom without defensive overtones.[86]

The connection between idolatry and adultery – and by extension, illicit partiality of any kind – is a commonplace one in the poetry and drama of Shakespeare's time, and could even be extended to hymns which were perceived to have idolatrous subject-matter, as when Walter Haddon inveighed against popish holy days, with their 'songes and sonnettes for the most part idolatrous'.[87] A love poem by Fulke Greville, Lord Brooke, makes unusually explicit a theme which pervades the amorous language of Renaissance literature, the comparison between saints and mistresses, and gives it a post-Reformation twist.

> More than most fair, full of that heavenly fire,
> Kindled above to show the maker's glory,
> Beauty's first-born, in whom all powers conspire,
> To write the Graces' life, and Muses' story,
> If in my heart all saints else be defaced,
> Honour the shrine, where you alone are placed.
>
> Thou window of the sky, and pride of spirits,
> True character of honour in perfection,
> Thou heavenly creature, judge of earthly merits,
> And glorious prison of man's pure affection,
> If in my heart all nymphs else be defaced,
> Honour the shrine, where you alone are placed.[88]

When Greville says 'If in my heart all saints else be defaced', he is, of course, evoking the iconoclasm practised by Protestant reformers from Henry VIII's reign onwards. Iconoclasts went round churches and cathedrals, defacing any statues of God or saints that seemed to them idolatrous. In this context the notion of idolatry has a slightly different inflection from that already encountered in this chapter, since iconoclasts were concerned to destroy anything which appeared to flout the injunction in the Ten Commandments against worshipping images, or led to worship of saints or specific artistic creations rather than God. One can see the results of their labours, which a later age finds it easy to call vandalism, in places like the Chapter House in Ely Cathedral, where there still remain statues without heads, hands and other features.[89] In evoking the notion of defacing saints, Greville's speaker is saying to his real or imagined mistress that he is a good Protestant, disapproving of idolatrous graven images, but that she is different, so good and so beautiful that she shows God's glory and is deserving of religious veneration. Having displaced saints, Greville is putting his mistress in a saint's niche – at least, that is half the story. But what would have complicated an audience's reaction is the fact that this remains dangerous language: still courting idolatry, still dubiously motivated. After all, if it was wrong to displace God by means of saints, it was surely much worse to talk about an earthly woman in quasi-divine terms, especially if it was a way of flattering her in order to obtain sexual favours. The poem walks a very tricky tightrope indeed.

This audacious conflation of love and religion can be found at many points in Shakespeare's work too. Unsurprisingly the Sonnets are among these, since – as contemporary commentators suggest – the conflation of idolatry and adultery especially tainted this genre:[90] Thomas Adams, for instance, described how 'The Adulterer admires the beauty of his harlot, kneeles to a pledge of her memory, by wanton sonnets Idolizes her, turnes his soule to an elephant, and worships this Sun'.[91] Shakespeare's Sonnet 105 seems to be responding to just such a charge: 'Let not my love be called idolatry / Nor my belovèd as an idol show, / Since all alike my songs and praises be / To one, of one, still such, and ever so' (1–4). But it also shapes *Romeo and Juliet*, the play in which Shakespeare most sustainedly interrogates contemporary conventions of romantic love. In Act 1 Scene 5 of the play, during Romeo's first encounter with Juliet, the lovers speak to each other in very formalized language, which includes a sonnet. This is one of the moments in the play where Shakespeare is most obviously conflating religious language with the language of sexual desire, as Fulke Greville is doing above, in company with poets as different as Petrarch – another Italian writer found inspirational by the Elizabethans – and England's John Donne. Yet none of these were writing for an audience in a theatre, and the diverse auditory of drama would have maximized alertness to any potential causes of offence. The sonnet's language of veneration is open to criticism on two fronts: evoking idolatry towards saints, and comparing one's mistress to a saint.[92]

> ROMEO: If I profane with my unworthiest hand
>   This holy shrine, the gentle sin is this,
>   My lips, two blushing pilgrims, ready stand
>   To smooth that rough touch with a tender kiss.
> JULIET: Good pilgrim, you do wrong your hand too much,
>   Which mannerly devotion shows in this,
>   For saints have hands that pilgrims' hands do touch,
>   And palm to palm is holy palmers' kiss.
> ROMEO: Have not saints lips, and holy palmers too?
> JULIET: Ay, pilgrim, lips that they must use in prayer.
> ROMEO: O then, dear saint, let lips do what hands do;
>   They pray, grant thou, lest faith turn to despair.
> JULIET: Saints do not move, though grant for prayer's sake.
> ROMEO: Then move not while my prayer's effect I take.
>
> *He kisses her*
> (1.4.206–219)

There are moments in this passage where, despite the play's Italian setting, we find ourselves transported to post-Reformation England. A line like Juliet's 'Saints do not move' is a slightly odd one if we read it literal-mindedly as coming from a native of Italy, a country where, then and now, supposedly miraculous statues are commonplace. Shakespeare's Protestant contemporaries heartily disapproved of these claims, believing that they encouraged idolatry and lined the Church's pocket by means of the cults they stimulated. So 'Saints do not move' is a line which gives a nod towards polemical exchanges between Catholic and Protestant, and seems to be tending towards the

Protestant view; yet the very next phrase, 'though grant for prayer's sake', shifts one right back into a Catholic world-view where saints, as well as God, respond to intercessions. Perhaps most fascinatingly of all, the lines show Juliet imagining herself into the position of a saint, something which most Renaissance women who were the object of such addresses got no opportunity to do. Saying that she, a saint, responds to prayer is her way of encouraging Romeo without being forward or unmaidenly.

In a play full of religious language transferred onto occasions of secular love, the theme of this exchange is picked up several times. In Act 2 Scene 1, the famous balcony scene, when a suitable object is being sought to validate the vows of love which Romeo wishes to make, Romeo asks 'What shall I swear by?' and Juliet answers:

> Do not swear at all;
> Or if thou wilt, swear by thy gracious self,
> Which is the god of my idolatry,
> And I'll believe thee.

> (115–118)

Here, Juliet's 'Do not swear at all' alludes to Christ's Sermon on the Mount in St Matthew's Gospel: 'But I say unto you, Sweare not at all; . . . But let your communication be, Yea, yea: Nay, nay. For whatsoever *is* more then these, commeth of evil' (5.34.37). Romeo's position, on the other hand, is closer to that described in the previous verse: 'it was said to them of olde time, Thou shalt not forsweare thy self, but shalt performe thine othes to the Lord' (5.33). Those with a good knowledge of the Gospels might well have recalled how the stricture voiced by Juliet follows immediately upon the Sermon's condemnation of sexual misbehaviour, which includes the notorious verse, 'whosoever loketh on a woman to lust after her, hathe committed adulterie w[i]t[h] her already in his heart' (5.28), and a reminder that some marriages end in divorce (31–32). In this context, Juliet's caution seems even more understandable.

Yet it is a caution which passion causes her to override. No sooner has she asked Romeo not to swear than she contradicts herself: 'Or if thou wilt, swear by thy gracious self, / Which is the god of my idolatry'. As remarked above, 'idolatry' is a word charged in all contexts, with particular negative connotations when love and the theatre are in question. Hence, it is no surprise that when Romeo responds 'If my heart's dear love –', Juliet cuts him off: 'Well, do not swear. Although I joy in thee, / I have no joy of this contract tonight: / It is too rash, too unadvised, too sudden' (159–161). Her own word 'idolatry', it seems, has made her conscious that she has gone too far. Deeply in love, but still not absolutely sure of Romeo's intentions, her situation does indeed bear comparison with religious affection illicitly deployed, and it is hardly surprising that she goes on to ask Romeo to expedite their marriage if his 'bent of love be honourable' (186). This might, on the face of it, seem to replace irregular adoration tending towards idolatry with a love legitimized by the church. Nevertheless, even when married, the couple would not have been quite out of danger in some eyes. The perils of matrimonial idolatry were cautioned against by contemporary Puritan commentators: for instance, objecting to the words 'With my body I thee worship' contained in the marriage service of the Church of England, the Puritan John Reynolds suggested that 'They make the new married man . . . to an idol of his wife'.[93]

If Romeo and Juliet's love might be thought of as only just this side of idolatry, the same could be said of the lovers in Donne's poem 'The Canonisation'. As the title suggests, Donne's speaker imagines a future where the lovers die and are venerated:

> And by these hymns, all shall approve
> Us canonized for love:
>
> And thus invoke us: 'You whom reverend love
> Made one another's hermitage;
> You, to whom love was peace, that now is rage;
> Who did the whole world's soul contract, and drove
> Into the glasses of your eyes
> (So made such mirrors, and such spies,
> That they did all to you epitomize,)
> Countries, towns, courts: beg from above
> A pattern of your love!'[94]

The last two lines exactly describe what is happening at the end of
Romeo and Juliet, when the grieving Montagues and Capulets make
peace over the bodies of the lovers, and vow to raise the statues of the
lovers in pure gold as a civic example: 'whiles Verona by that name is
known, / There shall no figure at such rate be set / As that of true and
faithful Juliet' (5.3.300–302). The statues are interpretable as emblems
of public aspiration, while also evoking the idea of commemorative
monuments – the same English Protestants who deplored religious
images in churches had no problem about erecting lifelike and elabo-
rately gilded funeral monuments there.[95] But the language that the
lovers have previously used of themselves also invites a more divisive
interpretation, reminding the audience that towns could be under the
patronage of saints, that these are saints who have died for love rather
than religion, and that the veneration of saints is a controversial
matter. Where, we are led to ask, does exemplarity end and idolatry
begin? With its self-aware evocation of contemporary poetic discourse,
Romeo and Juliet comments upon the interface between love-language
and idolatry as explicitly as some love-poets do. Like them, it shows
attentiveness to the points where imaginative writing on love could be
seen as most morally vulnerable. An antitheatricalist could not have
complained that his points had not been taken on board; but insofar
as they are exploited for titillating effect, this could be seen as part of
the problem.

SECULAR DRAMA, FERIAL DRAMA

Three examples of Shakespeare's use of religious language have now
been discussed in detail, but, to return to the question with which this
chapter began, how would these have affected his audience? It is hard
to see how the invented liturgy in *Much Ado*, or the lovers' hyperbole
in *Romeo and Juliet*, could have done other than confirm the prejudices
of an antitheatrical observer. One of these is syncretically pagan and
Christian, one is interdenominationally Catholic and Protestant, and
both, for interdependent reasons, would have invited accusations of
idolatry. Bottom's speech in *A Midsummer Night's Dream*, on the other

hand, would have been adversely noticed by those who believed that plays mocked the holy Scriptures. Shakespeare's language in these scenes, and elsewhere in his work, is constantly oscillating between sacred, secular and profane, pagan, Catholic and Protestant. It tells us little about Shakespeare's own beliefs, other than that he had no ideological objection to this kind of intermixing. But it reveals a very great deal about the various reactions he expected his audience members to have, and would also have prevented some of his contemporaries from taking any pleasure in his drama at all.

As Paul Whitfield White has said: 'The bias persists that religion had little or no significant representation on the "Renaissance English stage", partly . . . because those who really took their religion seriously – the Puritans – would have no part of it, except to voice their opposition and disgust.'[96] As he goes on to point out, this is a caricature of how things actually were. We have already seen how, despite the strong association between Puritanism and antitheatricalism, not all Puritans were antitheatricalists and not all antitheatricalists were Puritans. As has also been suggested, and as Chapter 3 of this study will argue in more detail, it was possible for individuals of strong personal religious conviction to affirm the theatre's potential for moral instruction, to see it as a legitimate recreation or feel that it was something indifferent in itself. While this study has no space to give the reception history of early-modern drama its due, it is Shakespeare who, more than any of his contemporaries, has been read as morally instructive and beneficent on a par with the Scriptures. But as with the Scriptures, some passages of his work lend themselves more easily to moral transcendence than others. A defender of the theatre in Shakespeare's time could have pointed to, say, the character of Cordelia as a dramatized exemplar of goodness; an antitheatricalist could have countered with any of the above extracts. Yet even at their most outrageous, these testify as eloquently as Cordelia's speeches and silences to a keen engagement with religious language and concerns.

Shakespeare's England was a world where Christianity was dominant, where Christianity's doctrinal variations were a matter of fervent intellectual concern and fierce public debate, where nearly everyone thought within religious paradigms, and where religious allegiance could be a matter of life and death. It was also a world where allusions to Christian belief and practice constituted a common currency, bonding viewers of different social degrees, regions and genders more than anything else could. Given the responsiveness of Shakespeare and his fellow playwrights to this state of affairs, it is remarkable in some ways that the term 'secular' should be so commonly accepted to denote the drama of the period. 'Secular' is an oppositional or negative term, relating to the world as opposed to the church, or indicating an unconcern with religion. While it was familiar to the Renaissance era – Sir Thomas More, for instance, distinguishes between 'holy Scripture' and 'secular literature' in his *Dialogue Concerning Heresies* – it now primarily implies a culture where religion is a private matter, deemed unimportant by the majority, and not figuring significantly in the public sphere.[97] This could hardly be less like Renaissance England. The silences, evasions and indirections that characterize the treatment of religion in the mainstream drama of Shakespeare's time arose because the topic was far too interesting not to be policed. Yet, fortuitously, they mirror our own secular embarrassments; as already suggested, religious language and concerns are most evident in drama at the level of allusion, and because allusions can be taken or left, this has helped to make drama more appealing than many Renaissance genres to those whose outlook is secular. For this and other reasons, the effect that English Renaissance drama has had on the development of present-day secularism is an interesting area of study, to which – as commented in the introduction to this book – Shakespeare's self-presentation and thought is central. Still, there are several steps between acknowledging this and trying to recover the world in which Shakespeare and his contemporaries actually operated.

The assumption that English Renaissance drama is secular has had several effects, both positive and negative, on literary criticism relating to the period. The term has been useful in pointing up the contrast between Renaissance professional drama and medieval religious plays, but by the same token, it has led critics to underestimate how long the latter took to die, and how tenaciously they sometimes survived.[98] The notion also continues to screen out the drama written and performed by English Catholics at home and abroad, which – as commented above – operated in a defiantly religious idiom. It has meant a routine underestimation of religious matter as it pervaded drama within the mainstream: through scriptural and liturgical allusion, through polemic – most often anti-Catholic or anti-Puritan – through moralism and allegory, through a providential mode of thought, sometimes even through reference to contemporary high-profile religious controversies. Lastly – and ironically, given that the term 'secularism' identifies a negative condition – it even prevents a full understanding of how religious concerns negatively affected the content of drama. Thanks to the trend for interdisciplinarity within literary studies, to literary critics' eagerness to learn from historians, and most of all to the present-day suspicion of claims that literature should purvey eternal truths rather than engage with its time, there is now a greater willingness to recognize the religious element in Renaissance drama – which is why the term 'secular drama' can sometimes feel like a hangover from an earlier age.

So an unfamiliar supplementary term will be used in this study: ferial drama. *Feriae* is the Latin for 'holiday' and 'festival', but in church calendars, *feria* is used to indicate a day on which no saint or Gospel event is commemorated. Thus, in a liturgical context, the term 'ferial' has a paradoxical function, pertaining to holidays but not to festivals. The notion of being detached from church festivals, but still operating within an overarching ecclesiastical framework, is a useful one when considering drama in Shakespeare's period, with its complex inheritances, cross-currents and transitions. Two areas of tremendous recent interest in Renaissance studies – the literary response to the changes which Protestantism brought about in the English calendar, and the relationship between early-modern drama and festivity – have helped a fuller recognition of Christianity's shaping power on the literature of Shakespeare's era.[99] As scholars writing on both topics have established, this was a time when a strong association of drama with liturgical festivity continued; looking at the dates when theatrical performances were mounted at court, R. Chris Hassel has traced their correlation with festive seasons and specific feast-days.[100] Given that court patronage was a key reason why professional dramatic companies were tolerated, and that performances at Court were – officially, at least – often

seen as these companies' most important activity, it is hard to over-
estimate the importance of the liturgical calendar to their operations.
More generally, England's festive traditions were plundered for dramatic
effect, across the dramatic genres but particularly within comedy.[101]

But the rise of professional dramatic companies meant that plays
were no longer tied to religious festivals in the medieval manner, and
drastically weakened the link between drama and community-led
festivity.[102] The drama they offered, though often linked to festivals
and offering many of the same pleasures as festivals, was pulling away
from them; after all, to be commercially viable, a play increasingly
needed to have a life beyond a specific festive occasion. Drama tied to
the festive calendar did not need to represent a Christian world, but
often had a specific relevance to the day: sometimes integral to the
plot, sometimes a detachable element such as a customized prologue
or epilogue.[103] At the very least, playwrights, performers and audience
would all have wanted it to be a felicitous contribution to the occasion.
But the day-to-day availability of professional theatre would have
weakened this experience; one would still have watched as a Christian,
but one particular kind of piety, the obligation to receive a play in the
light of its liturgical occasion, would often not have been appropriate.
In a fascinating article, Alison Chapman has identified the unique role
played by shoemakers in the imaginative economy of early-modern
drama. Having the traditional right to choose their own holidays, they
were therefore perceived as having 'authority to shape calendrical and
ecclesiastical observance'; and in the opening scene of Shakespeare's
Julius Caesar, they are seen as doing just that, decreeing a holiday at
grass-roots level to celebrate Caesar's triumph.[104] To apply Chapman's
principle more widely, the rise of the professional theatre extended the
shoemakers' privilege to all playgoers who, on whatever day and for
whatever reason, took time off to enjoy themselves.

Since the term 'ferial' also retains its holiday meaning, it reminds us
that going to the theatre is a recreational activity in itself.[105] Immersion
in the narratives of imaginary or fictionalized characters would, then
as now, have provided a break from day-to-day concerns. This holiday
from real life would have taken effect whether or not the characters of
a play inhabited a world comparable to one's own, and even where real

and fictional experiences were obviously different, religion would not have been the only source of unfamiliarity. A London apprentice watching a tragedy about court life in continental Europe would surely have experienced a disjunction almost as great as a Christian viewing a play about non-Christians. Still, where the characters of a play inhabited a non-Christian world, most audience members' sense of visiting another country could only have been accentuated: not only because the references would be exotic, but because it would have placed the characters at one or more moral removes from the viewer, mitigating the insistent – and to some, perhaps, the relentless – demand in Renaissance literature that one should learn from exemplars.

The extent of this mitigation would obviously have varied with the nature of the dramatized world; for instance, dramatic treatments of ancient Rome could hardly exist in isolation from the fact that classical exemplars were constantly urged on the Renaissance reader, and the ancients venerated in what can often seem an uncritical manner. But there was a great gulf fixed between paganism and Christianity. At all times, it would surely have been relaxing to know that Christians had a built-in superiority not only to the depravity of Sejanus, but to the nobility of Cato; and the mimetic sophistication of English Renaissance professional drama, combined with its flattery of the audience, played up this superiority. Shakespeare, and many other professional dramatists of his time, gave one permission to attend to stories other than one's own salvation, by presenting those stories in a way that played down the author's role as explicit moral arbiter, while placing each audience-member in the position of judge. Thus, some plays would have provided a holiday from the Christian world-view, and most would have enabled one, if so minded, to take a break from the Christian obligation to examine oneself. The notion of ferial drama is perhaps most useful as a way to recapture the experience of an Elizabethan or Jacobean playgoer, but it tells one something about the playwrights and their ethical priorities that they were willing to give playgoers this experience.

So is ferial drama nothing more than escapism? The definition of escapism adopted above is based on the assumption that, while reading is always a process of ethical engagement, and that it is impossible to read in a moral vacuum, some kinds of reading are more personally interrogative than others, and therefore less escapist. An ethical engagement which permits the viewing and judging of fictional or historical characters, but does not oblige the interrogation of one's own mindset and behaviour, was not officially an option for the Renaissance reader; yet it must often have happened in practice, and drama is of all literary genres the most conducive to it.[106] In our own age, when the morally interrogative capacities of imaginative literature are routinely downplayed, it is hard to imagine the sheer relief with which some must have taken up the option of these holidays, but we may be able to gauge its intensity from seeing the antitheatricalists' reaction. Over and above what antitheatricalists alleged to be the intrinsic immorality of drama, there arose questions of legitimate and illegitimate recreation. Puritan elevation of Bible-reading and sermon attendance had the effect of denigrating all leisure-time activity which did not conduce, in some way, to a better understanding of the Scriptures. Given this, drama would have stood condemned on two fronts: when devoid of scriptural or religious reference it was unedifying; when it employed scriptural or religious allusion in a manner intermingled with profane discourse, it was worse still. Thus, it emphasized the polarity between God's word and the human imagination, to the inevitable discredit of the latter; and it is in this light that we must see Shakespeare's more positive claims for imagination.

CONCLUSION: THE TWO IMAGINATIONS

A Midsummer Night's Dream, with its eclectic plot and its marriage of a classical Greek setting with native English fairy lore, is perhaps an obvious place to find one of Shakespeare's highest claims for creativity:

> The poet's eye, in a fine frenzy rolling,
> Doth glance from heaven to earth, from earth to heaven,
> And as imagination bodies forth
> The form of things unknown, the poet's pen

Turns them to shapes, and gives to airy nothing
A local habitation and a name.

(5.1.12–17)

Spoken by Theseus, these are famous lines, important to Romantic conceptions of poetic genius, which have often been used to evoke a pure aesthetic realm where nothing matters except the imaginative artefact.[107] Given this, it is easy to forget that their immediate context is one of suspicion. Theseus introduces his reflection by remarking sceptically about the lovers' strange tale, 'I never may believe / These antique fables, nor these fairy toys . . . / The lunatic, the lover, and the poet / Are of imagination all compact' (2–3, 7–8), while Hippolyta comments how 'all their minds transfigured so together, / More witnesseth than fancy's images' (24–25). The reception history of the passage would be very different if it did not present an attractive view of poetic creativity, but its positioning in the scene shows how hard it was, even in a play with so much to say about the faery world, to get away from the notion that imagination was reprehensible – a suspicion which, as this chapter has demonstrated, is partly a religious one. Not for the first time, Shakespeare is having it both ways.

But Hippolyta's speech continues, admitting that the tale 'grows to something of great constancy; / But howsoever, strange and admirable' (5.1.26–27). In other words, the marvellous need not necessarily be untrue; and, as J.A. Bryant has argued, the passage can also be read as arguing that the imagination has its own integrity.[108] Certainly, religious commentators' condemnatory links between imagination and falsity would have been disingenuous, wherever they failed to admit that imagination was also part of Christian practice. To imagine something is to form a mental concept of what is not actually present to the senses, which need not imply that the imagined object itself goes beyond reality. Thus, as well as bodying forth the form of things unknown, imagination can be used to evoke real objects and set possible events in motion. Then and now, Christians and non-Christians differ as to what it means to say that Christianity is real; but either way, antitheatricalist Christians of early-modern England could have invoked one kind of imagination against another, rather than forswearing imagination altogether.

One sees this happening in Christopher Sutton's devotional tract *Disce Vivere* [Learn to live] (1st edn 1602). Arguing against dissimulation, Sutton asks: 'is it credible that the Christian profession should in anie age put on masking attire, and play her part upon the stage? . . . In the Comedie of Menander there is a Hercules, but not true Hercules: in the course of the world there is a Herod, that pretends worship, but intends the life of an innocent babe . . . One man discerneth another by his habit, God by his hart.' This is a standard link between theatricality and hypocrisy, of the kind that we have already seen. But it is soon dismissed, with Sutton showing more enthusiasm for the imaginative imitation of Christ; as he exclaims at another point, 'who is not animated in minde, when he heares of Christes conflict, and conquest, with, and against the professed enemie of us all?'[109] Antitheatricalism, in other words, was not necessarily a killjoy attitude. So many writers of antitheatrical tracts come across as professional thunderers, committed at some level to what they are saying, but journalistic in their priorities and most interested in presenting the negative side of a case; if they sometimes seem to be saying that theatre should be banned simply for being entertaining, it comes as no surprise, but does give a distorted view of the debate. Christian piety, which the theatres are presented as undermining, could be imaginatively stimulating too; the positive side of antitheatricalism is best discerned by looking at writing like Sutton's, only incidentally antitheatrical, where the author's main aim is to foster spiritual development.

Sutton's attractively written, best-selling book is only one sign that as presented in the vernacular religious literature of Shakespeare's day, the Christian story made compulsive demands on early-modern imaginations. Thousands more could be given, relating to both the providers and the consumers of spiritual discourse: to quote from the life of Margaret Duck again, her biographer explains that she saw no need for the theatre because 'In Gods house . . . she saw enough of the Scene . . . to refresh and delight her soul. Would she see a Tragedy? there she could behold before her eyes Jesus Christ evidently set forth crucified among them.'[110] This evokes the discipline of meditation, a term which overlaps sufficiently with the idea of imagination to make it helpful to distinguish the two; after all, if to imagine something was to form a mental image of something not present to the senses, then this would have occurred not only at the theatre but every time someone prayed or listened to a sermon attentively. Any distinction between the two has partly to do with the process of imaging – 'meditation' has connotations of structured and disciplined thought – and partly with its subject: if the topic being imagined was devotional or edifying, to call it a meditation would have seemed natural to an early-modern commentator.

For literary critics, the term has been associated with the type of spiritualized thought, commonly practised in sixteenth- and seventeenth-century Europe, which Louis L. Martz has described as 'deliberately directed towards the development of certain specific emotions'.[111] Though the practice is particularly associated with the Spiritual Exercises devised by Ignatius Loyola, it had medieval antecedents and achieved considerable interdenominational traffic – as is demonstrated by another religious best-seller of Shakespeare's time, Edmund Bunny's Protestant adaptation of the English Jesuit Robert Persons's *A Booke of Christian Exercise*.[112] Encouraging its readers towards a deeper imaginative understanding of Christianity, this devotional manual demonstrates how the practice of meditation was seen as a way of distinguishing the fervent from the lukewarm believer: 'We believe in grosse the mysteries of our Christian faith, as that there is an hel; an heaven; a reward for vertu; a punishment for vice; a judgement to come; an accompt to be made; and the like: but for that we chew them not wel by deepe consideration, and do not digest them wel in our harts, by the heat of meditation'.[113] As this suggests, the literature of meditation makes rigorous demands on the imagination, inviting the reader to develop emotions conducive to spiritual self-improvement. It was a harder imaginative option than drama, but this is not to say that it was less compelling.

Elizabethan and Jacobean plays are written about by lovers of the drama, who have sometimes found it impossible to imagine why anyone except philistines and misanthropes would have voluntarily eschewed the theatre at a time when Shakespeare was writing.[114] Hence, it may be helpful to turn the question round. Given the overwhelming pressure in post-Reformation England to reap spiritual nourishment from one's reading, and the demonstrably huge appetite among the reading public for the Bible and works of Christian spirituality, why did consumers bother with anything else in their spare time? As ever, there would have been a plurality of tastes, and the period boasted an unprecedented array of leisure-time diversions. The theatres were popular, and so too were devotional manuals. Sometimes their readers would have also been part of the theatregoing public, at other times not. Some Englishmen and women would have loved drama, and some, then as now, would not have seen the point. Some people were more pious than others; if one had nothing against the theatre but preferred one's leisure-time activity to be religious in nature, there would have been very little in the dramatic repertoire which dealt directly with religious matter, and the more obvious thing to do would have been to go to a sermon.

For some, Christianity powerfully engaged the imagination in a way that had the incidental effect of making plays seem trivial or decadent, and repudiation of drama could therefore become part of a conversion experience. The Puritan Richard Norwood confessed in his autobiography that acting a woman's part in a play had made him theatre-mad as a young man – 'I was so much affected with this practice that had not the Lord prevented it I should have chosen it before any other course of life'. Together with such narratives as the *Aeneid* and the *Seven Champions of Christendom*, playbooks distracted him from religion: 'the vain conceits which they begat in me was the principal thing that alienated my heart from the word of God . . . '. He was so engaged with drama that he became a regular at the Fortune Theatre, and even began a play of his own. But the kind of spiritual satisfactions that some enjoyed, and that could alter one's preferences so radically, can be glimpsed in Norwood's account of his conversion: 'Whence is this heavenly fire in my heart that hath heat and light and motion exciting and carrying me to those things whereunto I was formerly altogether averse? . . . I was as one that had found some inestimable treasure which none knew but myself.'[115]

As this suggests, Puritanism did not always equate to joylessness. It would be perverse to deny the intense anxiety about being saved, or the distrust of humour, relaxation and ornament which could go with the territory. Yet the Puritan approach to Christianity also engendered an intense appreciation of beauty and fitness. To speak of a Puritan aesthetic is not a contradiction in terms – quite the contrary, Puritanism was one of the most highly aestheticized religious movements there has ever been. But by the same token, it had a high intolerance of clutter; as lifestyle magazines show, one has to make a case for every single object in an all-white interior.[116] Analogies between Puritanism and architectural modernism do not end there, since modernism was a movement which restricted choice in the name of utopianism, and what made Puritans so controversial and so addicted to controversy was a similar intolerance of whatever did not match their own way of life. Wherever these kinds of beliefs are held by policy-makers and used to engineer other people's lives, the results, whether tower blocks or antitheatricalism, can often seem unpleasantly doctrinaire to a later generation.[117] But just as tower blocks can be highly desirable places to live for those prepared to tailor their lives to the modernist ideal, Puritans would have derived intense pleasure from aesthetically motivated constraint, and eschewing the theatre would often have been part of that. Nor did one have to be a Puritan to derive pleasure from religiously motivated self-denial. Being a serious practising member of any religion can be seen, at this or any date, to be all about pleasure: in the case of Christianity, the pleasure of contemplating God, and of living – or attempting to live – a life completely justifiable in God's eyes. The mellifluous titles of many religious texts in this period – Thomas Playfere's 1593 sermon *Heart's Delight* and Abraham Fleming's religious manual *The Diamond of Devotion* (1st edn. 1581) are typical – address a clientele who found real pleasure in God's word, or saw such pleasure as a desideratum. In this respect, Puritans and other religious antitheatricalists would have been like any other Christians whose religious beliefs and practices were not simply a matter of custom or a source of unease; their differences from them would have arisen first in identifying the theatre as a personal obstacle to religion, and second in applying this across the board.

What is plain from such testimonies as Norwood's, but surprisingly rare in the mainstream theatre of Shakespeare's day, is a sense that religion is sometimes a joyful activity. Certainly, drama as shaped by Shakespeare appears better suited to Claudius's frustrated attempts at prayer in *Hamlet*, or to Henry V's pragmatic petition, 'O God of battles, steel my soldiers' hearts' (4.1.276), than to rapturous internalized communings with God. Even expressions of collective worship are not easy to find in Shakespeare's drama. Occasionally they are referred to: the exultant Henry V, having won the day at Agincourt, declares: 'Do we all holy rites: / Let there be sung *Non nobis* and *Te Deum* . . . ' (4.8.120–121).[118] Perhaps we are to understand these lines as a stage direction, yet they appear to herald a collective exit. In *Much Ado*, as we have seen, pagan invented ceremonies can be staged, yet Christian marriage can only be achieved after the ending of the play. Similarly, in *As You Like It*, though the comic cleric Sir Oliver Mar-Text and the pagan god Hymen foreshadow the promises exchanged in matrimony, Duke Senior's declaration 'We'll begin these rites' (5.4.195) acts as a signal for the play to conclude.[119] In both cases this retreat behind the scenes probably arises from a sensitivity about religious matter being staged: arising in a time and place where religion was of too much public importance for players to tamper with, it foreshadows the privatization of religious observance within secular society.

Can we, as some commentators have argued, see the joys of religion and the joys of theatre as competing with each other? Despite what has been said above, there is considerable overlap between the two.[120] The recent interest in festivity within English Renaissance drama, referred to above, has made it clear how extensively playwrights borrowed from the lighter side of religious observance, showing a continuity with their medieval forebears. Churchgoing and playgoing have often been compared; one recent critic has described the latter as a communal affective response to an aesthetically staged event, akin to religious participation.[121] While this goes beyond what contemporary critics would have articulated, moments such as Prospero's epilogue to *The Tempest*, where he appeals to the audience in specifically religious terms, make it believable: 'And my ending is despair / Unless I be relieved by prayer' (5.1.333–334). The kinship between the two media often increased hostility; complaints that the public are eschewing sermons and flocking to the theatre are common enough among preachers. Later generations have tended to interpret these as an admission of defeat, but they do not necessarily denote embattled individuals presiding over shrinking congregations. Preachers, like other religious writers, were both allowed and expected to inhabit the moral high ground, and had more freedom than professional play-wrights to tell their audience how they ought to act. What Jeffrey Knapp has described as the 'broad cultural authority' of antitheatric-alism was also on their side, to the extent that theatre-loving clerics would have found it difficult to affirm the moral utility of drama in a sermon.[122]

Given this, it is not surprising that the contest between preachers and players, looked at purely as a debate, can seem one-sided. While antitheatricalists constantly complained how people 'shame not to . . . affirm openly, . . . that they learn as much or more at a play than they do at God's word preached', it is hard to find first-hand apologias along these lines, and when the theatrical entrepreneur Philip Rosseter was reported as saying that plays were as good as sermons, he was obliged to recant his statement before the Bishop of London.[123] But play-wrights did, more modestly, assert the moral efficacy of drama, as in Ben Jonson's famous boast that he and his kind were able to 'steer the souls of men'.[124] It would be too cynical to divorce such statements from a genuine moralistic agenda, yet the soothing of tender con-sciences would also have had positive effects from a worldly point of view, increasing the reputation of playwrights and maximizing the playhouses' clientele. Just as preachers had an interest in warning their congregations against the theatre, playwrights had every motive to collapse the division between play and sermon, even while making the most of their imaginative liberties and giving the audience an easier ride than they would have had from a preacher.

Were plays actually more entertaining than sermons? At first this may seem a silly question, yet it is one that that throws up deep issues of cultural relativism. The contemporary reputation of a preacher such as Thomas Adams or John Donne can be compared to that of an actor like Richard Burbage; sermons must often have been as thrilling as the best drama in delivery, and in many cases remain sophisticated and enjoyable reading-matter – but only if one can bear being preached at.[125] In the twenty-first century, what we have been trained to enjoy has less to do with literary merit as such, more to do with whether we, as readers or audience, are attacked or affirmed; even practising Christians, less used than their forebears to being berated from the pulpit, are likely to find much Renaissance religious discourse off-putting for this reason. Given this, it is no wonder that drama, the least cavilling of Renaissance genres, has such canonical pre-eminence. As this chapter has established, antitheatricalists constantly complained that the theatre distracted audiences from the business of salvation, and they would have seen their worst fears confirmed in the literary canon as it stands. There is much we do not know, and will never know, about Shakespeare's personal religious beliefs. But we do know that he saw no contradiction between these and writing for the theatre – and this alone tells us a good deal.

Chapter Two

SHAKESPEARE'S LIFE AND WORKS: CATHOLIC CRITIQUES

INTRODUCTION

In Tudor and Stuart England, reading love-poetry and the erotic exploits of the pagan gods could be seen as immorality on a par with visiting the theatre. The writers and preachers who spoke against the stage, discussed in the last chapter, have something in common with the followers of the Catholic priest, poet and martyr Robert Southwell, who inveighed against profane and sensual verse, and whose theory of literature pervades the discussion below. Like them, Southwell is repudiating certain aspects of the literary education which he would have undergone.[1] Models such as Seneca on the one hand, and Ovid on the other, were central to learning but often seen as vulnerable from the Christian standpoint. Those who received a grammar-school or university education, or – like the period's learned women – were exposed to the classical curriculum in other ways, would have equated the classical canon with most though not all significant scholarship; all the major reformers broadly endorsed classical learning, as did the Catholic church in its various Counter-Reformation educational pro-grammes. The attractiveness of the classical inheritance, and more broadly of imaginative discourse in general, was routinely exploited to sweeten didacticism and doctrine. But depending on one's religious position, the place in one's life for classical writing, or any kind of secular literary pleasure, could fluctuate drastically. Antonius Posse-vinus, a contemporary Jesuit writer whose literary theory has much in common with Southwell's, wrote, 'The first purpose of the poet must be, to make his reader better; his second only, to delight him': profit and pleasure were typically seen as complementary aims, but this comment suggests how the two might clash.[2]

If one was a Catholic, a Puritan or anyone else whose back was to the wall for religious reasons, humanistic literary ideals were likely to come under threat. As already discussed, antitheatrical sentiments could be uttered by Catholics and conformists as well as Puritans. Similarly, the Christian case against profane verse, while strongly associated with Southwell in Elizabethan England, was neither original to him nor restricted to Catholics – especially after his work became popular in the second half of the 1590s – and some Catholics would not have found that it spoke to their condition. Yet the strong association of antitheatricalism with Puritanism, and objections to profane verse with recusant Catholicism, is no coincidence. In a literary context as in the broader sphere of action, the notion of *adiaphora* – things indifferent to salvation – was easier to adopt if your religious position was not oppositional.[3] This chapter will continue the work of the last in looking at Shakespeare's life and work through the eyes of commentators opposed to certain kinds of literary endeavour, and will also be asking what Shakespeare's literary emphases and silences can tell us about his religious position. After several decades when questions of religion have been downplayed within Shakespeare studies, no topic has attracted more recent speculation, both inside and outside the academy, than Shakespeare's religious views and the effect they might have had on his writing.[4] There has been a particularly intense interest in the attitudes towards Catholicism within his work and his biographical connections with Catholics, with some scholars going so far as to see him addressing the beleaguered Catholic community by means of codes and allegories.[5] Hence, this chapter responds to market forces in taking an approach to Shakespeare's life and work which, to my knowledge, has not been sustainedly tried before: looking at how he appeared in a group of writings emanating from the English Catholic community, and how he measured up to these commentators' standards – or failed to do so.

In the first instance, the combination of Shakespeare's works and Shakespeare's life poses a very simple question to do with genre: would someone who was primarily interested in writing about religious topics have written in the fictional mode at all? In many eras he or she might have done, since although fictional writing is not the best vehicle for theological argument, it has immense possibilities for the devotional writer and yields promising didactic opportunities. But though England in Shakespeare's era was an unusually exciting environment for both religious and fictional writing, it was also an unusually discouraging one for those who wished to combine the two. The Protestant distrust of human additions to scripture ensured that the boundaries between sacred and secular writing were policed in many ways – most effectively, perhaps, within the mind of the writer. Among poets this often had a counter-productive effect, trammelling religious inspiration and encouraging secular verse instead.[6] Playwrights who might have been inspired by religious matter in other circumstances would have had their enthusiasm curbed in Elizabethan England, a time and place where the fullfrontal treatment of many religious topics on the mainstream stage was impossible. Despite what has been said about the amount of religious allusiveness in Shakespeare and other playwrights, the narrative emphasis of their drama was necessarily elsewhere. Yet religious material of other kinds featured prominently in the output of English printing presses, and while many of the most prolific writers on religious topics were clerics, some were laymen; it would surely have been possible for a layman as energetic as Shakespeare to make a living this way.

But as has so often been remarked, Shakespeare does not appear to have been particularly interested in writing about religious topics for their own sake. In his surviving writing, engagement with religious issues, while acute and various, is invariably subsumed to dramatic context. Though plays are a more multivocal genre than most, this must have been a conscious decision at a time when even plays are routinely explicit about the sympathies of their authors, whether in their narrative bias, their incidental comment or their paratextual material. It is not surprising that Gary Taylor, among others, has accused Shakespeare's work of being religiously evasive.[7] But if this was a stance designed to deflect questioning at the time, it has certainly not done so since; Shakespeare's beliefs have engendered far more comment than if he had written more about them. Unfortunately – or fortuitously –

for the speculators, hardly any archival evidence survives on the topic either.[8] Thus, biographers and literary critics have more often than not been driven back to the plays, whether to read the gaps, or to attempt an interpretation of the religious signifiers which do exist.

Scanning the plays for Shakespeare's attitudes to Catholicism, as has so often been done, affords a good illustration of the technique. Shakespeare's work yields nothing to compare with the anti-Catholic farce in Marlowe's *Dr Faustus* or the lurid picture of the Catholic hierarchy in Webster's *The Duchess of Malfi*; a striking omission, given that anti-popery went down well with audiences. In *King John*, a play which directly addresses the King's conflicts with the Roman church, he even modifies the anti-Catholicism of such dramatic precursors as the anonymous *Troublesome Reign of King John*.[9] Individual representatives of the Catholic church are a mixed bunch: as religiously fervent as Isabella in *Measure for Measure*, as brave as the Bishop of Carlisle in *Richard II*, as hard to read as Friar Lawrence in *Romeo and Juliet*, as Olympian as the friar in *Much Ado about Nothing*, as Machiavellian as Pandulph in *King John*, or as worldly as the war-mongering bishops at the beginning of *Henry V*. Though all these characterizations betray an intense awareness of the very differing ways that Catholic matter could be read, they are also generic to the kinds of story being dramatized; it would be hard to carry any of them beyond their dramatic occasion, or to see them in aggregate as presenting a coherent view of the Catholic church.[10]

Much attention has also been paid to an alleged strain of Catholic nostalgia in Shakespeare's work, epitomized in the first part of Sonnet 73:

> That time of year thou mayst in me behold,
> When yellow leaves, or none, or few do hang
> Upon those boughs which shake against the cold,
> Bare ruined choirs where late the sweet birds sang;
> In me thou seest the twilight of such day
> As after sunset fadeth in the west,
> Which by and by black night doth take away,
> Death's second self that seals up all in rest . . .

$$(1-8)^{11}$$

As Eamon Duffy has written of line 4, 'Shakespeare's one-line evocation of the ruins of England's monastic past, the ruins of England's Catholicism, can hardly have been casual or unselfconscious, for in Elizabethan England these walls had, if not ears, then mouths, and, in the mode in which Shakespeare chose to evoke them, cried out against the cultural revolution which had shaped the Elizabethan religious settlement.'[12] The line can also be said to anticipate the Gothic strain in later English literature, which evokes Catholic ruins primarily for visual reasons, as part of a picturesque past. The speaker, comparing his time of life to late autumn, uses a metaphor which forces the reader to identify a parallel between the branches of deciduous trees at a time when leaves are falling, and the choirs in abbeys and other religious buildings destroyed under Henry VIII. Yet an awareness of what England lost with the Reformation was not unique to Catholics at this date, and the parallel, when pursued, gives a picture of Catholicism in terminal decline. The 'sweet birds' have gone, and only leaves remain in their place. While the phrase 'Yellow leaves, or none, or few' could certainly be read as playing on uncertainties about how many Catholics remained in England, the metaphor is relentlessly personalized, to an extent which closes off what would otherwise be cyclical overtones in the alternation of night and day, or autumn and spring. If English Catholicism is – however temporarily – to be associated with the speaker, then it appears to be as moribund as him. A wistful, elegiac note is certainly there, and would be an unlikely attitude to find in a Puritan – but then, arguments for Shakespeare's Puritanism have never had much going for them.[13]

How much, though, can one deduce from the way in which Shakespeare distanced himself from Puritan ways of thinking? Following on from what was said in the last chapter about Shakespeare's deployment of anti-Puritan stereotypes, one of the rare contemporary comments on his religious reputation appears to be casting him as a Catholic sympathizer hostile to Puritan heroes.[14] Complaining about Shakespeare's dramatic treatment of the Lollard martyr Sir John Oldcastle, John Speed remarks that the English Jesuit Robert Persons 'made Ouldcastle a Ruffian, a Robber, and a Rebell', and that 'his authority taken from the stage-plaiers, is more befitting the pen of his slanderous report, than the Credit of the judicious, being only grounded from this Papist and his Poet, of like conscience for lies, the one ever faining, and the other ever falsifying the truth'.[15] As this chapter will go on to argue, gossip and detraction can tell one a good deal about the contemporary reputation of a writer. But given that the imputation of popish sympathies was such a common and indiscriminate insult at the time, Speed need have meant no more than that Shakespeare's play and others gave ammunition to Catholics; should more be read into his comment?

As remarked above, Shakespeare's works have sometimes been read as encoding support for a persecuted Catholic minority. Elements of this position have been heavily criticized, as the debate currently stands.[16] But one should be grateful to those scholars who have adopted it, since they have done the wider academic community a valuable service in foregrounding the question: how would one write as a Catholic? As this chapter will demonstrate, this is a question with several possible answers – which is hardly surprising, given the range of ways Catholics behaved in this period.[17] Historians routinely distinguish between Catholic recusants, those who refused to attend Church of England services and suffered a range of penalties as a result, and church-papists, those who conformed to the requirements of the Church of England while also subscribing to elements of Catholic belief and practice. Puritans too could be penalized as recusants if they had conscientious objections to attending their parish church.[18] Hence, though some individuals found themselves on the recusant rolls when they failed to attend church because of illness, a quarrel or fear of being prosecuted against for debt, the term 'recusant' has come above all to connote principled religious refusal.[19] If one maps similar notions onto the period's literary culture, recusancy can be seen as an unwillingness to participate in intellectual and imaginative exchanges which compromised one's integrity or distracted from one's religious practices – though one should not make the mistake of supposing that individuals did not change, or that literary tastes necessarily went hand in hand with policies about church attendance. It is in this sense, and with all these factors in mind, that the term will be used below, and its potential to inspire a rigorist aesthetic will be given particular attention.

From a rigorously recusant standpoint such as Southwell's, there were only a limited number of ways in which a Catholic could conscientiously write. But within a more broadly defined Catholicism, there were several, some of which might have been even more provoking to hardliners than the most pertinacious Puritanism. Thomas Lodge, discussed below, gives us a convenient example of someone who moved from an inclusive to an exclusive literary stance, while always writing as a Catholic; beginning as a writer of romance, an Ovidian satirist and a defender of the theatre, he moved in his later years to a passionate, religiously engaged repudiation of his former work.[20] Then, too, there were individuals whose literary work appears to espouse some elements of Catholicism and repudiate others. Describing the career of Anthony Munday, Shakespeare's probable collaborator on the play *Sir Thomas More*, Donna Hamilton has given us a model of what one might call Catholic minimalism; the Munday she describes is a Catholic so committed to loyalism, and wishing so much to distance himself from any less loyal co-religionists, that he often ends up persecuting them.[21] Shakespeare was, at least, more tolerant than that, though probably less Catholic.

SHAKESPEARE'S RELIGION: FRIENDS AND RELATIONS

Catholicism in Stratford-upon-Avon remained strong in the early years of Elizabeth's reign, and Shakespeare would have known many Catholics during his formative years.[22] More than one of the schoolmasters who probably taught Shakespeare at Stratford-upon-Avon Grammar School were Catholics, or had Catholic connections – though as Park Honan points out, they would have had to accept Church of England practices as part of their job.[23] Simon Hunt may be identifiable with the individual of the same name who matriculated at the Catholic English College at Douai in 1575, and who, interestingly, was a close associate of Southwell's.[24] Thomas Jenkins was an alumnus of St John's College in Oxford, a well-known stronghold of conforming Catholics. John Cottom or Cottam, who succeeded him, had suggestive links with the strongly Catholic Lancashire district in which it has been argued Shakespeare spent his 'lost years' – an issue which will be addressed later on – and had a younger brother, Thomas Cottam, who became a Jesuit and was martyred; in later years, he went back to Lancashire and appears there on returns for recusants.[25] John Frith, the priest who probably married Shakespeare and Anne Hathaway, was described in a Puritan survey of Warwickshire ministers in terms which suggest his religious conservatism: 'an old priest & Unsound in religion'.[26] Thus, like most people in early Elizabethan England, Shakespeare would have run up against many individuals of pronouncedly conservative tastes in religion, and known others whose affiliations to Catholicism were more forward-looking.

Given that Catholicism tended to run in families, it is significant too that members of Shakespeare's own family have been linked with the outlawed faith. Shakespeare's daughter Susanna was cited for not receiving communion in Easter 1606.[27] Of the generation before Shakespeare's own, Shakespeare's mother Mary Arden came of a strongly Catholic family and his father John absented himself from church – though his ostensible reason was fear of being proceeded against for debt. While this was certainly an excuse often used by recusants, Robert Bearman has recently made a very strong case for John Shakespeare's suffering real financial difficulties during the period in question.[28] John Shakespeare's name was also appended to a manuscript document which came to light in the eighteenth century, the so-called 'Spiritual Testament': a Catholic profession of faith in fourteen articles.[29] The Testament's general formula, as distinct from its embodiment in this specific manuscript, is undoubtedly authentic, a version of a devotion traditionally attributed to the Cardinal Archbishop of Milan, Carlo Borromeo.[30] If the manuscript itself were genuine, it would give as much proof as one could reasonably hope that Shakespeare had been brought up in a household not only Catholic, but with some links to Counter-Reformation spiritual trends. Yet there are major objections to seeing it as such. The document itself is missing; Edmond Malone, who had the advantage of seeing the original, eventually decided that he could not link it to any of Shakespeare's family; and Robert Bearman, again, has recently argued that the balance of evidence is in favour of a fake.[31] This uncertainty has had knock-on effects on the hypothesis, favoured by some recent scholars, that the Shakespeare family had links with the Jesuit priest Edmund Campion, who is identified in a contemporary letter as having copies of a 'Testament' for distribution in England; a recent article demonstrates, in any case, that this refers not to Borromeo's Testament but the English-language New Testament about to be published at Douai.[32] Thus on several related fronts, the *prima facie* case for suspecting John Shakespeare's Catholicism was never an unproblematic one and, though perhaps not completely eroded, has been drastically weakened by recent research.

This is only one reason why the following account of Shakespeare's life will spend less time on Shakespeare's father than usual, and more time on Shakespeare's cousin. Robert Southwell, related to Shakespeare through the Arden side of the family as well as more distantly on his father's side, was a Jesuit, a martyr and one of Elizabethan England's most influential poets.[33] His poetic collections, as circulated in manuscript and especially as printed after his execution in 1595, gave the next generation of writers a model for non-biblical religious verse and metrical self-exhortation. It may not be too far off the mark to compare his influence to that of his fellow Elizabethans Sidney or Spenser – though he is seldom explicitly mentioned as an inspiration by non-Catholic writers, given the difficulty of acknowledging a papist among one's literary forefathers.[34] In his poetry Southwell was concerned with setting out a religious alternative to the profane imaginative writing of his day. His longest and most ambitious poem, 'St Peter's Complaint', chronicles Peter's denial of Christ and subsequent repentance with a relentless internality which embroils the reader in Peter's thought-processes, making it a disconcerting read even now. While the story of Peter's repentance was a versatile means of urging contrition, it was thought by the Catholic recusant community to have an especial message for weaker Catholics; a pamphlet written in the person of Christ asks church-papists: 'Doe ye not as Peter deny your selves, to be of my company? . . . what is this but to disclaime from my Religion, to depart from the corps of my universal Church . . . ?'[35] Southwell's poetic example became a way of exhorting the less religiously committed writer, as this section will go on to describe, and this may be an added reason why.

'St Peter's Complaint' would have been written only a few years earlier than Shakespeare's 'Venus and Adonis', and they share the same stanza-form. Otherwise, they could hardly be more different. Shakespeare's poem, telling the story of Venus's love for the beautiful youth Adonis and his subsequent death while hunting, was one of the most popular of his productions, but some contemporaries of Shakespeare's would have found plenty to dislike about it.[36] The erotic subject-matter and the characterization of Venus as dominatrix still have some power to shock. But any offence caused to a contemporary religious commentator could as easily have been on generic grounds. Since its earliest days, Christian poets have had an unstable relationship with the commonplaces of the pagan imagination, sometimes appropriating them and at other times repudiating them; Venus, both as an object of pagan worship and as the personification of eroticism, was especially vulnerable to attack. Thus, 'Venus and Adonis' would have been typical of the kind of poetry Southwell criticized. Writing to an unnamed cousin to present him with a collection of religious verse, he begins, 'Poetes by abusing their talent, and making the follies and feyninges of love the customary subject of theire base endeavors, have so discredited this facultye that a Poett a Lover and a lyer, are by many reckened but three wordes of one significacon': and the prefatory verse to 'St Peter's Complaint' reads: 'Still finest wits are stilling Venus Rose. / In paynim toyes the sweetest vaines are spent: / To Christian workes, few have their tallents lent.'[37]

To condemn Venus is a commonplace, and Southwell may or may not have had Shakespeare's poem in mind, but it has been claimed that he did. The most substantial argument in favour derives from the fact that an edition of his verse, published at St Omer in 1616, expands the dedication to Southwell's cousin, in which the criticisms of contemporary verse occur, by adding the initials 'W.S.': an addition which seems most easily explicable as the incorporation of a manuscript annotation to the printed edition which the typesetter was using as copytext.[38] As is well known, Shakespeare appears to have written 'Venus and Adonis' at a time when the theatres were closed because of the plague, beginning in the summer of 1592. Southwell was arrested in June of that year, and kept under tight security in the Tower of London; unless he had prior knowledge of Shakespeare's project, and wrote his epistle before his arrest, he would have had to find some way of getting it – with or without the accompanying verse – out of the Tower of London and to the editor who was eventually to see to the printing of the verse after Southwell's execution.[39] Prisons were not completely impenetrable, and this is not an impossible scenario; but it is an unlikely one, and an unnecessary one too, since if Southwell had really been moved to reprove Shakespeare, he would have found plenty to disapprove of in Shakespeare's writing prior to 'Venus and Adonis'.[40] In any case, one cannot hang too much on a set of initials. One would leave it there, were it not that one contemporary commentator suggests very strongly that Shakespeare was thought at the time to be the addressee of Southwell's reproof. This does not prove that he was, since mistakes in attribution can happen at any time; yet as far as Shakespeare biography goes, even a mistake would be striking and suggestive, betraying how Shakespeare was perceived by a contemporary. As the next section will discuss, this commentator singles Shakespeare out as an unregenerate profane author, in a way that may suggest a back-story.

CATHOLIC REPROOFS TO SHAKESPEARE

The reference in question occurs in *Saint Marie Magdalens Conversion*, a long religious poem published by a Catholic secret press in England, with a preface dated 1603. In it, the saint repents her former life as a prostitute and rejoices at Christ's resurrection in a manner which derives from Southwell's 'St Peter's Complaint', of which there are also strong stylistic echoes. The author, identified only as 'I.C.', begins with an agonistic gambit that was common enough at the time: the claim that the present poem is superior to previous efforts in a similar vein.

But, just like Southwell's poetic collection, it also makes clear the writer's repudiation of non-religious verse:

> Of Helens rape, and Troyes beseiged Towne,
> Of Troylus faith, and Cressids falsitie,
> Of Rychards stratagems for the english crowne,
> Of Tarquins lust, and lucrece chastitie,
> Of these, of none of these my muse nowe treates,
> Of greater conquests, warres, and loves she speakes,
>
> A womans conquest of her one affects,
> A womans warre with her selfe-appetite,
> A womans love, breeding such effects,
> As th'age before nor since nere brought to light,
> Of these; and such as these, my muse is prest,
> To spend the idle houres of her rest.
>
> Thou blessed Saint, whose life doth teach to live,
> Intreate that loving and best loved Lord of thine,
> That he vouchsafe such lively grace to give
> Unto these dull, and liveles rimes of mine,
> That such as read this good, (though ill told) story,
> May be (like thee) for their offences sorry.
>
> (f. A3a)[41]

The stories alluded to – the tale of Troy, Troilus and Cressida, Richard III, Tarquin and Lucrece – are well known, and the passage may encompass reference to the work of more than one writer: John Trussell, who wrote a long poem about the rape of Helen, and Giles Fletcher, who versified the life of Richard III, would be two possible candidates.[42] But the characters make an eclectic group, and given that all their stories were written up by Shakespeare, an overarching reference to Shakespeare's work is surely intended.[43] Observing that Shakespeare's subject-matter is relatively trivial, the writer is presenting a more serious-minded alternative. Moreover, though the hope 'that such as read this . . . story, / May be . . . for their offences sorry' is put in the plural and directed at all readers, Shakespeare has been invoked as the primary addressee of the poem and can hardly be exempted from this call to contrition. Thus, even if Southwell himself did not call on Shakespeare to repent, this Southwellian writer certainly does.

I.C. describes *Saint Marie Magdalens Conversion* as having been written for the pleasure of some private friends, and a dedicatory verse to Mistress F.B. presents it to her as a New Year's gift. Though printed – an unusual distinction for Catholic verse at this date – it invokes the half-hidden world of Catholic manuscript circulation where Southwell's works appear to have begun. Like these, it portrays imaginative writing as legitimate, but only if it is religious in character and serves spiritually strenuous ends. Even festive New Year exchanges partake of this quality, since in the Christian world-view, festivity is inseparable from suffering; as I.C. reminds us, again in the dedicatory material, New Year's Day is the day when the church commemorates Christ's circumcision: 'This day, the Sonne of blessed MARY shed / His first deare bloud, to make us live b'inge dead' (f. A2a). When I.C. writes that his 'muse is prest, / To spend the idle houres of her rest' in writing the poem, the verb 'prest' has the effect of counteracting the slightly disingenuous word 'idle'. The writer's implication is that he has felt constrained to write, a factor that condemns Shakespeare all the more.

In all, it seems likely that Shakespeare is being attacked on an *ad hominem* basis: which, as will be discussed below, has considerable significance for any attempt to recover his biography. But he is also standing in the dock as the representative of undesirable corporate literary tendencies. In the epistle to the reader, I.C. comments that he chose his subject 'as most fitting this time of death', probably referring to the recent outbreak of plague.[44] As remarked in the first chapter of this study, moralists insistently held the theatre to blame for these outbreaks, and I.C. might have felt an attack on a leading playwright appropriate for that reason. But Shakespeare is also, and not for the first time, being presented as the type of a profane poet. Francis Meres's observation a few years previously that 'the sweete wittie soule of Ovid lives in mellifluous & hony-tongued Shakespeare' is famous, but I.C.'s comments show what a double-edged compliment it could have seemed, to those predisposed to find fault with Ovid and his kindred.[45] If the association of Shakespeare with an Ovidian style of composition was common currency at this date, this would be an added reason to hold him up as an exemplar of irresponsible authorship. There was a long tradition, starting with Ovid's contemporaries, of accusing him and his work of impudence and licentiousness (*lascivia*, *licentia*).[46] As a Christian literary tradition evolved, he was one of the pagan writers whose work was either consciously repudiated, or seen as needing Christianized exposition. Throughout the medieval era, despite his centrality within the classical inheritance, he tended to awake moralizing tendencies in commentators, and this continued into the Renaissance. Despite the fact that only his non-dramatic works survive, his reception at this period is more comparable to the reception of popular drama than in the case of almost any other classical writer. But as compared to the antitheatrical debate, full-blown attacks are rare while defences are common – George Sandys, for instance, included a section on defences of Ovid in the 1626 edition of his translation of the *Metamorphoses*.[47]

This may be a sign of how ingrained the Christianized, allegorized mode of reading Ovid had become. While allegorization is associated above all with medieval hermeneutics, it continued in Shakespeare's time, and presented one way round the peculiar difficulties posed by Ovid. So, more generally, did the tradition of reading him within a Christianized framework. But as Raphael Lyne has commented, one can identify a 'doublethink', whereby writers professed a religious style of interpretation while, in practice, translating with what seem to be different priorities. Arthur Golding, the translator of the *Metamorphoses*, has been seen as a transitional figure for the way that he commends moralizing readings in the dedicatory epistle, while largely letting the stories speak for themselves.[48] In contrast, Shakespeare himself eschews both allegorization and Christianization. The moralizing voice is certainly present in 'Venus and Adonis', whether the speaker muses in a worldly vein, reproving older women who pursue uninterested younger men, or comments more seriously on a man's right to say no. But it is still very different in spirit to the point-by-point expositions relating particular stories to general moral truths, so typical of medieval allegorizations.[49] Nothing is said of morality or Christianity in the dedicatory epistle to the Earl of Southampton, and nothing either at the beginning of the poem, which plummets the reader *in medias res*: 'Even as the sun with purple-coloured face / Had ta'en his last leave of the weeping morn, / Rose-cheeked Adonis hied him to the chase' (1–3). The ending, too, would have seemed very abrupt to those reared in a school of moralized Ovid. Finishing her prophecy about the destructive effects of love, Venus flies away in a chariot drawn by silver doves 'Holding their course to Paphos, where their queen / Means to immure herself and not be seen' (1193–1194). With no allegorical asides and no paratextual justification, the poem's narrative is as classically nude as Venus herself.

One cannot push the comparison between Shakespeare and Ovid further than it will go; after all, 'Venus and Adonis' – arguably Shakespeare's most frivolous composition, as well as one which owes a good deal to Ovid's best-known work, the *Metamorphoses* – is not included in I.C.'s list.[50] Yet to a religiously fervent commentator, still more to a religiously embattled one, Shakespeare and Ovid must both have seemed lightweight writers with suspiciously evasive authorial personas. As Jonathan Bate has commented, 'recent criticism has been much concerned with the "flexibility of the self" in Renaissance literature . . . [but] has not always recognized that the flexible self has a prime classical exemplar in Ovid'.[51] Shakespeare, the *ne plus ultra* of the flexible self, might well have been adversely criticized because he replicated the Ovidian model of an author.[52] Certainly, at many different points in history, commentators have felt the need to allegorise both authors. This has often foregrounded a religious mode of reading; one can think of G. Wilson Knight's Shakespeare criticism, so very productive of Christ-figures, as an *Ovide moralisé* for its time.[53] But allegorical interpretations arising from readerly desire rather than authorial intention are easier at some historical distance, and in the case of post-Reformation English Catholics, the situation is complicated still further by the fierce anti-humanism they so often exhibit. The corpus of their literature does include allegorizations of classical myth, as one would expect with any group of educated writers in the period.[54] But the inadequacy and danger of classical narrative is also a constant motif to their writing. Sometimes they saw no alternative but to repudiate writers on grounds of erotic, unimproving or profane subject matter, even if those writers were central to the classical inheritance:

one Catholic poem on the legend of St Winifred begins 'Ceace Oued [i.e. 'Ovid'] Cease to fayne / would god I had thy skill / then would I scorne to make thy toyes / the objects of my will' (f. 46a).[55]

The post-Reformation British Catholic literature that reached print has been extensively catalogued, but is still under-studied; the manuscript literature, despite the enormous past and present efforts of denominational scholars and growing recent interest within the secular academic community, has yet even to be mapped.[56] In the present state of knowledge, therefore, conclusions about typical modes of address can only be provisional. But in my own experience, within both printed and manuscript sources, attacks on theologians are as ubiquitous as one would expect, but those on imaginative writers are extremely rare. Thus, one has to entertain the possibility that I.C. was attacking Shakespeare for personal reasons to do with religion; a hypothesis which receives further support from another Catholic book, *The Life and Death of Mr. Edmund Geninges Priest* (1614), published at St Omer in the Spanish Netherlands, a centre for English Catholic exiles. This is a martyr-narrative commemorating Gennings's death in 1591. While based on an earlier biography by Edmund's brother John, it appears to have been rewritten, extended and embellished; John Wilson, manager of the college press at St Omer, may have had a hand in this.[57] Among the prefatory material is a verse, entitled 'The booke to his reader':

> Affected wordes, or Courtly complement,[58]
> Do not expect, who ever reades this story;
> Vertu's my ground, it needs no ornament,
> And to deceyve you so, I should be sory.
> If any such there be, post to King Liere,
> He hath applause, seeke not contentment heere.
>
> Poets may paynt, and diversely adorne
> Theyr feygned passions, and Chymera's strange;
> Teaching theyr pennes to weepe as one forlorne,
> And up and downe in barren deserts range.
> But if true griefe do once possesse theyr mind,
> They feele theyr combats in another kind.

> My authour's playne, nor is his griefe a fiction,
> The world can witnesse what himselfe doth prove;
> Read that ensues, t'is writ for thy direction,
> And ease thy passion, as desert shall moove.
> It it [*sic*] be pen'd according to thy fancy,
> Then learne to suffer by his constancy.
>
> (f. A2b)

Whoever authored this poem – John Gennings, John Wilson or a third party – it is a prosopopoeia, a speech for an entity other than the writer. The book is talking, we are invited to believe, and taking another text to task: *King Lear*, which is glossed 'a Book so called'. On its own, this could be taken as referring to the quarto version of Shakespeare's play published in 1608, or *The True Chronicle History of King Leir, and his Three Daughters*, published three years earlier in 1605, and entered in the Stationers' Company Register as early as 1594.[59] But as will be explained below, the poem takes issue with tragedy in a way which fits Shakespeare's play better than the tragi-comic *True Chronicle History*, and the unmistakable reference to Shakespeare's poetry and drama in I.C.'s prefatory verse would support the idea that, here as well, Shakespeare's works are being used to epitomize a kind of literary endeavour opposite to the writer's own.

There are several grounds on which the book of King Lear is attacked. First, it is identified as a source of 'Affected wordes' and 'Courtly complement', an example of the rhetorical artifice that the author is eschewing on the grounds that virtue needs no ornament; an opposition which deliberately evokes the opening of *King Lear* itself, where Goneril and Regan attempt to outdo each other in insincere flattery to their father, while the virtuous Cordelia continues to speak plainly even when threatened with banishment. The author – or rather the book, to play along with the fiction – is taking on Cordelia's role in order to admonish Cordelia's creator, who is identified with Lear himself, and characterized as only interested in 'applause'.[60] Anticipating the harrowing matter to be found in the body of the text, the poem then warns 'seeke not contentment heere', an injunction that concerns both the primary addressee and the readership as a whole.

The third stanza sums up the messages of the first two, 'My authour's playne, nor is his griefe a fiction', and orders 'Read that ensues, t'is writ for thy direction'. For a Catholic verse to announce its intention of directing the reader away from fiction and towards spiritual improvement is a clear Southwellian fingerprint. The next line, 'And ease thy passion, as desert shall moove', may be carrying forward the allusions to tragedy by invoking – if not in so many words – the Aristotelean notion of catharsis, and implying that this is a response more appropriate to a martyr's death than to anything fictional. But the succeeding idea that relief only happens 'as desert shall moove' is an ambiguous one. Applied to Edmund Gennings, his desert is to evoke veneration, which can work towards the easing of a reader's passionate indignation at his fate; applied to the reader, it implies that only the most deserving of them will find their passions eased. The last lines pursue the idea that one's taste in literary style cannot be other than a moral choice, with implications for how one lives one's life: 'It it [*sic*] be pen'd according to thy fancy, / Then learne to suffer by his constancy.' In other words, if the subject and style of the *Life* appeals to a reader, that reader has no option but to follow in the subject's footsteps. Literary appreciation goes hand-in-hand with conversion.

By this token, it is not surprising that the kind of literature being advanced for appreciation is one which makes a virtue of its utilitarian qualities; just as surely as the plain style of a Puritan preacher, it is intended to give the impression of effacing the author and putting centre-stage the object of religious contemplation. Told like a romance and enhanced by some very artful and expensive engravings, the *Life* is not without disingenuousness on this front. But even if the book shows its author's and publisher's recognition that attractive presentation is important, both life and poem set up an opposition between fine writing, of a kind which shows off the author's skill and wins acclaim, and plain writing, where unnecessary ornamentation would detract from the subject's virtue. This, in turn, redounds on Shakespeare as an author more interested in style than substance, seeking applause and personal contentment rather than virtue and religious inspiration.

While *King Lear* would not have been particularly novel in 1614, either as performed play or printed artifact, it is one of the last of

Shakespeare's tragedies, and its genre is crucial to the contrast being drawn in the next stanza between feigned and real grief. The specific references to *Lear* may continue in the description of how poets teach their pens to range 'up and downe in barren deserts' – it would not be the only time that critics have used desert metaphors for the king's mad scene – but more important is the avowal that 'if true griefe do once possesse' the minds of poets, '[t]hey feele theyr combats in another kind'.[61] Fictional grief, by this token, is the preserve of those who have never really had to grieve. At this point, it is worth taking a step back – or forward – and thinking about the critical afterlife of *King Lear*, since there is no play of Shakespeare for which higher spiritual claims have been advanced; Maynard Mack, for instance, claimed that 'it abandons verisimilitude to find out truth'. As R.A. Foakes says in the preface to his edition of *Lear*, many have seen the play 'in terms of universal values, as a kind of objective correlative for the spiritual journey through life of suffering Man'.[62] The poem's author gives us an alternative viewpoint; he might have asked how universal a play can be if it causes offence by advancing fictional equivalents to real suffering, and what truth there can be without verisimilitude. For him, it seems, the evocation of grief for fictional characters cannot be other than a decadent activity. He is, after all, writing about a much-admired individual, who died horribly even by the barbaric standards of Elizabethan executions: 'And being dismembred, through very payne, in the hearing of many, with a lowd voyce he uttered these wordes, *Oh it smartes* . . . ' (p. 86).

This may be a reported anecdote, since John Gennings, it appears from the narrative, was not present at the execution himself. A Protestant at the time, he experienced a conversion to Catholicism some ten days later:

> . . . having spent all that day in sport and joylity, being weary with play, he resorted home, where to repose himselfe he went into a secret chamber. He was no sooner there set downe, but forthwith his hart began to be heavy, and his head melancholy, and he began to waygh how idlely he had spent that day. When he was entred into such conceits, there presently was represented unto his

mind a strange imagination, and apprehension of the death of his Brother, and amongst other thinges, how he did forsake not long before all worldly pleasure, & for his Religion only indured intollerable torments. Thus within himselfe he made long discourses concerning his Religion and his Brothers, comparing the Catholike manner of living with his, and finding the one to desire payne, the other pleasure, the one to live strictly, the other licentiously, the one to fear sinne, the other to runne into all kind of syn, being stroken with exceeding terrour and remorse, he wept bitterly . . .

(pp. 98–99)

Gennings's conversion proved permanent. He became a Franciscan, and was eventually to be appointed the English Provincial of the order: a model conclusion, from the recusant point of view.[63] Exemplary too is his account of how imagination should be used, opposing idleness to religious meditation in a way that – as we have seen in Chapter 1 – Puritans too would have endorsed. Yet Gennings, or his biographer, is describing a time when he had not yet converted. The author clearly wishes to imply, by the phrase 'there presently was represented unto his mind', that this was not a willed meditation, but an image vouchsafed Gennings by the grace of God and the intercession of his martyred brother. The entire biography can be seen as replaying this moment of truth, which in itself counterbalances a remarkable earlier episode: the description of how Edmund Gennings came to London to search out John, his only living relation, and urge him to become a Catholic. Disappointed not to find him, but resigned to God's will, he prepares for his departure. But on passing someone in the street, 'heat strived to expell cold, and cold heate, all his joynts trembled, as dreading some great trouble, or misfortune to ensue: . . . his innocency fearing the worst, looked backe to see who followed him. And behold no man of marke, but a youth in a browne coloured cloake: . . . stedfastly viewing the yonge man, presently he was stroken with this cogitation, *This* (quoth he) *may be my brother*' (pp. 56–57).

They converse; Edmund finds John 'wilfully given to persist in his Protestancy' but promises to return to London for further conference; and on keeping this promise, he is arrested without seeing his brother

again (p. 60). As described in retrospect, John 'rather rejoyced' on hearing of his brother's death 'then any way bewayled the untimely & bloudy
end of his nearest allyed, hoping therby to be rid of all perswasions,
which he mistrusted he should receyue from him touching Catholique
religion' (p. 98). This suggests another reason why Gennings after his
conversion, or someone who knew Gennings well, might have found
the story of King Lear both a poignant analogue to his, and a deeply
unsatisfactory one. *King Lear*, too, is a story of truth acknowledged too
late to avoid tragedy, and of family members reunited only to be
separated again by death. Even the coincidence of two Edmunds – dis-
similar in character as they are – may have struck home. Perhaps too,
the author of the 'Lear' poem – like so many critics since – read *King
Lear* as expressing pagan hopelessness, and disliked it for that reason.
After all, as Gennings felt obliged to prove in his own actions, his brother's death was a tragedy, but one which could have positive effects
on the living. For anyone who believed in the Catholic doctrine of the
communion of saints – still more for anyone who aspired towards believing in it – lines like Lear's lament for Cordelia would have had an especial
discordancy: 'O, thou wilt come no more. Never, never, never.'[64]

Whoever it is that speaks to us as Cordelia in the 'Lear' poem, John
Gennings takes on aspects of Lear in the body of the book. But he is
a Lear who profitably outlives his revelation. If the *Life* is a tragedy at
all – and this word is used – it is surely a *tragoedia sacra*, in which a
martyr's death has an affirmative effect which outweighs the bloody
circumstances of their execution. Yet if so, it gives more space than
usual to sorrow.[65] Many authors of Reformation martyr-narratives
knew their subjects personally, and of those, most managed to hold in
equilibrium their personal grief at the loss of a friend and their joy
that he or she had won a martyr's crown.[66] But in this book, despite
the fact that it is written from well inside the Catholic fold, one sees
this balance put under unusual strain. At times the work reads like a
spiritual autobiography, and a peculiarly unresolved one at that,
vividly expressing the guilt felt by John at his obduracy towards
Edmund when living. Evoking the emotions of those who have
experienced real grief, the prefatory poem points to tensions of which
its attack on *King Lear* is a wider sign; both throw up an irresolvable

difficulty which goes beyond particular cases. For some, tragic and other fictional scenarios can be truer than what happens to any individual, as applying generally to the human condition, and can improve a reader's compassion for this reason. For others – and the author or authors of this book seems to have been among them – there are real-life tragedies which make all fictional ones seem pointless, even when they are written by Shakespeare.

But was Shakespeare really among the implied readers of this *Life*, or I.C.'s poem? One writer can attack another without expecting to be read or responded to, and while I.C. published his poem right in the middle of Shakespeare's career, the later reproach from St Omer would have been badly timed in one sense, since Shakespeare had stopped writing for the stage by 1614. Yet the possibility could not have been have ruled out, and everything about the texts implies that their authors would have liked Shakespeare to have read what they had to say. They have transformative aims on their audience in general; Shakespeare is singled out as needing reformation; thus, they do urge a transformation of life on Shakespeare that, though inspired by literary matters, goes far beyond them. In his line, 'Of these, of none of these my muse nowe treates', I.C. points out how Mary Magdalen's conversion, taken as a poetic subject, cannot avoid reflecting badly on the profane author Shakespeare. The implication is that Shakespeare would do well to think about conversion: of a theological kind as well as a literary, since edifying literature is likelier to spring from an orthodox and zealous writer. It is followed up by the hope, addressed both to the saint and to an earthly audience, that 'such as read this good, (though ill told) story, / May be (like thee) for their offences sorry'. The author of the 'Lear' poem goes further still along the didactic path: 'Read that ensues, t'is writ for thy direction, / And ease thy passion, as desert shall moove. / It it [*sic*] be pen'd according to thy fancy, / Then learne to suffer by his constancy.' The injunction is to be contrite and to suffer; the context is one of confessional Catholic literary culture. Hence, these writers' definition of contrition would necessarily have involved a turn to oppositional Catholicism, a move which could never come too late while someone was alive. Richard Davies, vicar of Sapperton in Gloucestershire in the late seventeenth century, recorded a piece of gossip that Shakespeare 'dyed a papist'.[67] If Shakespeare did not die a papist, it would not have been these writers' fault.

It is Southwell's work, above all, which provides the literary model for their exhortations; and whether or not there was a direct link between Southwell and Shakespeare, it is Southwell's voice which speaks to Shakespeare through these intermediary Catholic authors. There is no evidence that Shakespeare ever read them – it would be optimistic to expect any. It is likely that he encountered Southwell's verse: perhaps before its printing, very probably when 'St Peter's Complaint' became a best-selling book in the later 1590s, as part of his general acquaintanceship with the London literary scene. There is no evidence that he took Southwell to heart.[68] Yet Southwell's call to repentance was certainly heard and attended to by Thomas Lodge, whose early literary career bears some comparison with Shakespeare's. Tempting as it is to think of authors as religious or secular according to the genres with which they are most associated, there was heavy traffic between piety and profanity; all the same, Lodge's career shows that authors sometimes found themselves in a one-way street. While nothing like as prolific a playwright as Shakespeare, Lodge was a defender of the theatre – as we have seen in Chapter 1 – and a productive professional writer in other genres: especially the prose romance, a type of imaginative writing which, like the drama, could be criticized as frivolous. The most recent account of his life follows early biographers in picturing Lodge as someone who might have had Catholic affiliations throughout his adulthood, and tracing how these might have affected his career. As its author remarks, 'Lodge's Catholicism later in life is undisputed', and perhaps the most significant turning-point in both Lodge's life and his writing was the publication in 1596 of *Prosopopeia. Containing the Teares of the Holy, Blessed, and Sanctified Marie, the Mother of God*. As much as he could in a work published in the mainstream, he comes out as a Catholic here; as part of this, he repudiates his former writing and turns to religious subject-matter. Thus, he mirrors what I.C. and the author of the 'Lear' poem would have liked Shakespeare to do.[69]

Prosopopeia emblematizes the author's repentance for a life of profane writing, and has a more outwardly directed polemical agenda as well. As its title suggests, it is a long speech written in the persona of the Virgin Mary contemplating the crucified Christ. Alluding to the tradition of Catholic devotions such as the *Stabat Mater*, and explicitly pointing to the testimony of church fathers who have endorsed Marian devotion, Lodge mounts an attack on the 'superstitiously ignorant' who will 'accuse me for writing these teares, desiring rather . . . to impaire the honor of the mother of God, than . . . to inhance it' (f. A5b). Referring to the contemporary notion that bats had weak sight because the eye's crystalline humour had been translated to their wings, Lodge writes: 'These bats betoken these proud neglecters, who by how much the more they strive to flie, by so much more are they deprived of the grace of the divine light, because all their intention, which ought to bee in consideration of heavenly things, is translated into the feathers of ambition, so that all their thought is howe they may ascend by degrees the steps of dignitie, not descende in imitation of thee, to the bosome of humilitie' (f. E2a). This is one of many places in *Prosopopeia* where Mary is given lines less relevant to her own situation than to that of a country where openly practising the Catholic faith was inimical to worldly advancement. General in its implications, the text nevertheless resonates with the more specific accusations that the author of the 'Lear' poem levels at Shakespeare.

Anne Barton has described the spectators of medieval drama as being 'exhorted, threatened and harangued'.[70] The same could be said of the readers of *Prosopopeia*, as well as of Southwell's verse, I.C.'s poem and Gennings's *Life*. Every text written from a confessional standpoint has explicit designs on the reader, and it is hardly surprising that these authors, like so many writing from within post-Reformation British Catholicism, should place exhortation, threat and harangue in the foreground. Not only are they didactic, they assert that any other, less didactic form of writing cannot possibly be justified. At a time when the idea of didacticism is unfashionable, and the very word is usually employed with pejorative intent, the position of these writers is difficult to appreciate without a full-scale reversal of one's usual literary standards, and a venturing with them into the kind of moralistic biographical speculation which is usually off limits. But if one does this, aiming only to entertain can also be seen as looking no further than the author's own honour and glory, and arising from impulses of selfishness rather than charity. Here, the emphasis is not on the pleasure given to the reader, but on the writer's motives for writing. Moving one stage further, the two become inseparable. For these writers, the quality of the aesthetic experience gained from a book is entirely governed by its writer's perceived motives, and so they can gain no pleasure from a work if the writer's reasons for writing it are felt to be inadequate. As a member of a hard-pressed religious community, used to scrutinizing one's neighbour for soundness or the opposite, it must have been natural to apply the same hermeneutics to one's reading – and the result is a desire, even a hunger, to ascertain an author's motives for writing and judge him accordingly.

It is hard to imagine how reasons for authorship could be compared more starkly than they are by these Catholic writers – or more provocatively for literary critics of the twenty-first century, so much more likely to sympathize with Shakespeare's implied position than with that of his attackers. Lines like the comparison of Catholicism and Protestantism in the Gennings *Life*, 'finding the one to desire payne, the other pleasure', are likely to evoke the misplaced zeal of suicide bombers rather than elicit nods of approval – for that matter, this holy masochism could well have gone too far for the contemporary English Catholic hierarchy, always sensitive to the charge that they were unnecessarily making martyrs.[71] But in fairness to the past, one must at least give space to these religiously charged spokesmen for a persecuted minority, as they reflect on Shakespeare's work. Devoting oneself to the production of pure literature, standing at a distance from theological controversy and commitment, may be the best way to ensure the transferability between cultures and near-universal acceptability with which literary greatness is so strongly associated; but as I.C. and the author of the 'Lear' poem might have retorted, in the very exceptional conditions of Shakespeare's England it also had the effect of saving Shakespeare's skin.

As commented above, these kinds of attack are rare in the literary culture from which these works come. But Shakespeare was not the only author to whom Catholic poets issued literary reproaches. In 'Hyemall Pastimes', Thomas Willford's manuscript collection of his own occasional verse, there survives an 'Epitaph upon the most learned Comedian and Moderne Poet, Benjamin Johnson who left the Church and died . . . [1630]'. In it, Jonson's life and apostasy from Catholicism is recounted as a tragic narrative:[72]

> Here Johnson lies, who spent his days,
> In making sport, and Comicke plays:
> His life a Play, perform'd the worst,
> The last Act did disgrace the first,
> His part he plaid, exceeding well,
> A Catholike; untill he fell
> To Sects and Schismes, which he did chuse,
> Like to a fiction of his Muse. . . .
> When Death his bodie did surprise,
> The Fatall Sisters clos'd his eyes,
> And tooke him to his tyring roome,
> Where I will leave him to his doome;
> But wish that I could justly raise,
> Memorialls of eternall praise.
> But Ben, from whence thy mischiefe grew,
> I mourne, but must not say, A due.

The last two lines, with their pun on 'Adieu' and 'a due', can be read as a mitigation of the harsh things said in the body of the poem, and an expression of hope that Jonson may not be entirely damned. Yet Willford's volume contains several other poetic epitaphs, mostly illustrated by coffins adorned with crosses; chillingly, the picture that illustrates Jonson's epitaph shows a coffin completely unmarked.

How does this poem compare with those on Shakespeare that we have already read? The two cases are, of course, not directly comparable: Jonson's conversions to and from Catholicism are far better documented than any evidence we have about Shakespeare's religious convictions, and Willford is criticizing Jonson's apostasy, not his dramatic subject-matter. Nevertheless, all three Catholic poets convey an overwhelming sense of having been let down by the writers they reproach. And so it is at this point that one question, not confronted so far, obtrudes itself: do the contemporary responses to Shakespeare's writing rehearsed in this section have anything to tell us about Shakespeare's religion? At the very least, they show Shakespeare being singled out and personally responded to by Catholics, and thus need to be looked at in conjunction with other biographical pointers towards possible Catholic sympathies and associates. In itself, they neither prove nor disprove them; as ever, each piece of evidence must be taken on its own terms. But the material discussed above is consistent with Shakespeare being identified by some contemporary Catholics, rightly or wrongly, as a fellow-traveller – well-affected enough to rouse hopes, uncommitted enough to disappoint. Thus it also supports the hypothesis that Shakespeare was a member of the established church, a conclusion almost forced upon one by the lack of positive evidence to the contrary. One cannot prove that Shakespeare was not a church-papist, or did not have Catholic sympathies; certain features of both his life and his work, as rehearsed above, can be interpreted as tending in that direction. But his authorial ethics deeply offended those Catholics who approached the literature of their time in a spirit of recusancy.

The fact that Shakespeare's literary stance downplays personal religious engagement may lie behind some Tudor and Stuart rewritings of his work. In an adaptation of Sonnet 116 set to music by Henry Lawes, the famous lines 'Let me not to the marriage of true minds / Admit impediments; love is not love / Which alters when it alteration finds, / Or bends with the remover to remove' (1–4) are altered and augmented to read 'Selfe blinding error seazeth all those mindes; / who with falce Appellations call that love / w[hi]ch alters when it alteration findes / or with the mover hath a power to move / not much unlike [th]e heretickes p[re]tence / that scites trew scriptures but p[re]ventes ther sence' (1–6).[73] Later on, the speaker avers that love is '[n]oe mowntebanke with eie-deludeing flashes / But flameing Martyr in his holly ashes' (11–12). In contrast, William Barksted's narrative poem *Hiren* (1611) tells the story of its heroine's apostasy from Christianity in a way that deliberately recalls Shakespeare's 'The Rape of Lucrece'. Both texts are inspired by Shakespeare's work; both construct a riposte to it in a way that draws attention to the lack of Christian matter in the original. In this context, John Weever's assertion that the 'sugred tongues, and power attractive beuty' of Shakespeare's characters 'Say they are Saints althogh as Sts they shew not / For thousands vowes to them subjective dutie' can be read as fending off similar criticism.[74] If religion was sometimes felt to be a significant absence in Shakespeare's work, as these three authors suggest, then the Catholic writers discussed above give us this criticism at its sharpest and most personally aggrieved.

'THE HISTORY OF PURGATORY' AND 'HAMLET'

But what sort of play might have been written by a Shakespeare whom I.C. and the author of the 'Lear' poem would have approved of, someone passionately concerned to promote the Catholic faith through drama? The school plays written at the British Catholic schools and colleges overseas were touched on in the last chapter, and Martin Wiggins has recently identified how one such play, *Innocentia Purpurata*, contains several passages from Shakespeare's *Henry VI: 3*, as well as alluding to other Shakespeare plays. The effect is to redeploy Shakespeare's work towards dramatic veneration of Henry VI, regarded as a saint by many, whose life and martyr's death would have struck a chord with other Englishmen who felt themselves persecuted.[75] Valuably augmenting other evidence that Shakespeare was read – if sometimes in censored form – in the English Catholic colleges overseas, the play shows how wrong it would be to deduce from commentators such as I.C. and the author of the 'Lear' poem that Shakespeare was disliked by all British Catholics throughout the early-modern period.[76] Back in England, opportunities to write and put on plays would probably have been fewer and certainly more circumscribed, because of the necessity to be discreet. Yet it could have happened, especially if one joined the entourage of a nobleman who supported both plays and the old religion.

It has been speculated that Shakespeare is the 'William Shakshafte' who is mentioned in the will of Alexander Hoghton, a Lancashire Catholic nobleman, in August 1581. Arrangements are made for Shakshafte to pass into the service of Hoghton's brother-in-law, Thomas Hesketh, while the previous clause bequeaths musical instruments and playclothes to Hesketh in the event that Hoghton's heir, his brother Thomas, should not wish to maintain players: a juxtaposition which has been interpreted as suggesting that Shakshafte himself was a player or musician. As E.K. Chambers was the first to point out, Hesketh often visited Henry Stanley, the fourth Earl of Derby, whose son Lord Strange was an early patron of Shakespeare's, and may even have brought a troupe of players on one visit.[77] The Shakespeare/ Shakshafte hypothesis has moved in and out of fashion, but has recently received a good deal of attention. The implications are fascinating for all sorts of reasons, not least because if Shakespeare and Shakshafte are to be identified with each other, it would mean that Shakespeare cut his dramatic teeth in a recusant household. Suggestive arguments have been advanced on both sides; the case stands at stalemate, particularly since 'Shakshafte' was a common name in the area, though the strong association of Shakespeare's schoolmaster John Cottom with this part of Lancashire is a reason to keep the file open.[78] Commentators have, perhaps, been most helpful when they have used the speculation to draw attention to the rich tradition of dramatic productions outside London and the universities.

There would also have been some opportunity to write drama for companies of travelling players who catered for clients with Catholic tastes. While there is little evidence for the period that 'William Shakshafte' would have been operating, the late 1570s and early 1580s, an interesting case study survives from the early seventeenth century. In 1611 Sir John Yorke of Gowlthwaite Hall, Yorkshire, was charged in Star Chamber for having hosted a subversive dramatic presentation two years previously, by the Simpson players, a touring company of Catholic actors. The resulting documents are well known to historians of early-modern English drama, and reveal that the Simpsons' repertoire included, cheek by jowl with Shakespeare's *King Lear* and *Pericles*, a miracle play on the life of St Christopher and an anti-Protestant interlude. Unfortunately, neither of the non-Shakespearean texts survives; yet this remains a tantalizing episode, which illustrates that not all Catholics disliked plays about King Lear as much as the author of the 'Lear' poem did, and turns the spotlight on what seems to have been a rich and well-organized dramatic tradition – albeit a badly documented one.[79] However, in addition, a play has recently emerged which seems to have been written for performance by early-seventeenth-century Catholics, and therefore contributes to the picture: *The History of Purgatory*. This section will give it critical consideration for the first time, and since, fortuitously, it shares the subject of purgatory with *Hamlet*, the two plays will be compared.

Robert Owen, its possible author, was a resident of Shrewsbury, and *The History of Purgatory* seems to have been part of a polemical programme. As far as is known, it survives in one copy only: in the British Library, bound with several controversial pamphlets copied for manuscript circulation, some definitely put together by Owen.[80] The text as a whole is devised to defend the notion of purgatory, and its form is basically that of a morality play: a courtroom drama in which a devil and a guardian angel battle for a pilgrim's soul with St Michael as judge, and Ladies Mercy and Grace speaking for the defence. Plot-wise, there are heavy borrowings from Guillaume de Guileville's *Le Pèlerinage de l'Âme* (Pilgrimage of the Soul), a fourteenth-century text.[81] Yet it would be misleading to call the play a throwback, since it reads more as a conscious attempt to re-create medieval tradition than as evidence of that tradition's unconscious survival. There were a number of ways in which a Catholic dramatist could have respected the integrity of his medieval inheritance, while bringing it up to date and setting it in an oppositional context; *The History of Purgatory* can be seen as a hybrid production, a play conceptualized in a basically medieval manner but with a post-Reformation paratextual commentary.

This consists in part of an alternative liturgy for the dead. The first scene after the prologue shows the soul declaring his readiness to die; the third scene gives us a combat between the soul's guardian angel and Satan, which leads on to the courtroom drama described earlier. But the second scene, in which this liturgy is included, takes us away from this specific soul's spiritual combat for a while. Instead, it forces the audience to reflect on the general state of souls in purgatory. The play seems to have been written with an eye to performance in a great hall containing a screen, and this scene is presented in a curtained space set some way back from the main action, which would be compatible with this type of setting. As far as the play's conceptual schema goes, this has the effect of setting the scene on a different plane, literal rather than allegorical. Since the speakers are a priest and his clerk, it also evokes a chancel or the choir of a cathedral, with the audience standing in as congregation.

The text does not sustainedly borrow from any particular liturgical source; among Catholics just as much as Protestants, there might well have existed sensitivities in both author and audience which worked against the reconstruction of 'real' services on stage. But it reads as a pastiche Divine Office: an assemblage of several texts traditionally read by Catholics as giving biblical warranty for purgatory, set out in such a way as to invite an antiphonal delivery by priest and clerk, the latter of whom speaks for the congregation as a whole. Two of the versicles and responses read as follows:

> *Priest*
>
> Open the eies, of the blynded parson
> and bringe forth the prisoners out of prison
>
> Esay [i.e. Isaiah]. 42. [7]
>
> *Answere*
>
> We most of force confesse, some other hell . . .
> *Priest*
>
> Thou hast, in the bloode of thy Testament
> let forth thy prisoners, out of prisment
> But of late, wherin ys no water   Zach: 9.11
> the true knowledge, as they did requier
> *Answere*
>
> We most of force confesse, some other hell[82]

This phrase, 'some other hell', refers, of course, to purgatory. In particular, it sets itself up against the reformers' insistence that every soul went either to heaven or to hell after death, referring as well to the traditional notion that the pains of purgatory were like those of hell, though of limited duration and ultimately conducive to good. When comparing the two biblical texts against their originals, the polemical glosses are clear.[83] Isaiah says only that God will open blind eyes, not the eyes of blinded parsons, and Zachariah refers only to prisoners in 'the pit wherein is no water', but this play reads the water as a metaphor

for knowledge.[84] The idea that the water of knowledge has dried up –
with the Reformation, we infer – cuts two ways: those who were born,
brought up and died as heretics will linger in purgatory longer than
they might otherwise; and because the culture of praying for the dead
has now officially been abolished, purgatorial agonies will not be cut
short by the prayers of the faithful to anything like the degree that happened in the past. This scene is a stirring call to action, but also very
oppressive. A well-affected Catholic would surely have felt the recent
unprayed-for dead pressing in upon them, soliciting more prayers than
anyone could possibly utter. More than that, the scene would have
reminded all Catholics of what they were to expect after death, dissolv-
ing the boundaries between actor and audience in a way that harks
directly back to pre-Reformation drama.[85] A later speech picks up the
notion of a commonly shared plight, with the third-person plural
sliding naturally into first-person: 'So many Actors, in our Tragicke
sceane / as in this Tragedye, were never seene / In Purgatorie paynes,
we tossed are / Bowels rent, and our harts, enflamed their . . . ' (p. 70).

Yet as it continues, this speech also contains heartening reminders
of continuity:

> Church Sacrifice, Almes, Praier, sent to us
> on the Arke of memorie, done for us
> Are a most riche, an hidden treasuarie
> Phisitions, Balme, in Purgatorie
> Of that to God, to make an Imolation
> which AEgipt holdeth, for a bomynation
> And armed thus; how we in good arraye
> may stande against our foes, both night and daye . . .
>
> (p. 71)[86]

Like the spokesmen for many religious minorities before and since, the
author compares his community to the Israelites in Egypt. Showing its
writer's usual alertness to polemic, the speech deplores the downgrading of church tradition typical of 'AEgipt', or Protestantism. Then,
alluding to the Ark of the Covenant, here re-christened the 'Arke of
memorie', he invites the audience to see this as a repository for Catholic
tradition: something which, among much else, maintains connections

with the wider church by means of alms and prayer for the dead. Elsewhere too this play, itself a vehicle for religious memories, deploys the notion of memory in a highly self-aware fashion.

The notion of church tradition, which for Catholics is an authority on equal footing with Scripture, bears a striking resemblance to the more secular idea of a collective or cultural memory.[87] Within both literature and history departments in recent years, there has been a lot of interest in the interface of cultural memory and historical trauma: something which has become especially high profile through being deployed in holocaust studies, but which can also usefully be read back onto earlier traumatic events such as the Reformation. For Shakespeare, the work has already been done in specific cases: for instance, as editors of *Hamlet* have often noticed, the madness of the traumatized Ophelia embodies itself in snatches of Catholic material.[88] Some of this, like the song about St Valentine's Day, is bawdy and profane: 'By Gis and by Saint Charity, / Alack and fie for shame, / Young men will do't if they come to't: / By Cock they are to blame' (4.5.58–61). More decorously, the medieval custom of pilgrimage is also evoked in relation to love, as in so many lyrics of the time: 'How should I your true love know / From another one? / By his cockle hat and staff, /And his sandal shoon' (23–26). Daringly for post-Reformation England, with its prohibition on praying for the dead, Ophelia's lament for an unnamed dead man ends 'His beard was as white as snow, / Flaxen was his poll. / He is gone, he is gone, /And we cast away moan. / God'a'mercy on his soul', which is followed by the ejaculation 'And of all Christians' souls. God buy you' (187–192). While the scene sets up cues for Catholic nostalgia, it can also be read as supporting the inference that Catholics and madwomen inhabited the same twilight world. In one of Shakespeare's most explicit acknowledgements of interpretive diversity, a bystander's speech passes the buck to the reader:

> Her speech is nothing,
> Yet the unshaped use of it doth move
> The hearers to collection. They yawn[89] at it
> And botch the words up fit to their own thoughts
> Which, as her winks and nods and gestures yield them,

> Indeed would make one think there might be thought,
> Though nothing sure, yet much unhappily.
>
> $(4.5.7-13)^{90}$

Here, the word 'botch' needs to be paused upon. Though it is possible to use the word at this date simply to denote the repairing of holes or gaps, the examples given for this and related words in the Oxford English Dictionary show pejorative meanings paramount, relating to disfiguring patches and clumsy workmanship. In the context of the play, the speaker is reflecting sadly on how, despite one's best efforts, the intentions of the insane are unreadable. But read as a paratextual commentary on the business of interpretation, the passage seems to be pointing in two opposite directions: first suggesting the possibility that Ophelia's speeches may be intended for audience-members to supplement, then being dismissive of any attempts on their part to do so. On one level, it admits that Ophelia's words are pathetically suggestive. On another, it acts as a pre-emptive strike against both sympathetic and hostile hearers inclined to read too much into the words of madwomen – which should give a warning to literary critics, too.

Yet against this one needs to set the play's reverberant injunctions to remember: in this scene, Ophelia's 'There's rosemary: that's for remembrance. Pray you, love, remember. And there is pansies; that's for thoughts' (170–172), and in an earlier episode, the Ghost's injunction to Hamlet, 'remember me' (1.5.91). As has often been pointed out, the latter speech powerfully evokes the practice of praying for the dead, and seems designed to evoke complex feelings of guilt in audience members forbidden to do so by their church. The situation is made particularly harrowing by the fact that Old Hamlet dies such a sudden and unprepared death:

> Thus was I sleeping by a brother's hand
> Of life, of crown, of queen at once dispatched,
> Cut off even in the blossoms of my sin,
> Unhouseled, disappointed, unaneled,
> No reckoning made but sent to my account
> With all my imperfections on my head.
>
> (1.5.74–79)

The audience infers that the Ghost is in purgatory because of his earlier comment that he is '[d]oomed for a certain term to walk the night' till his crimes are 'burnt and purged away' (1.5.10, 13). Having died 'unhouseled, disappointed, unaneled' – without having received the host in the Eucharist, and unprepared, without the benefit of Extreme Unction – his term in purgatory is longer than it would have been otherwise. Thus, while it is highly unlikely that Shakespeare knew *The History of Purgatory*, an early-seventeenth-century Catholic drama bearing that name is a useful text to read side by side with *Hamlet* and *Hamlet*'s critics.[91]

The play reminds us that one cannot make the blanket assumption, occasionally slipped into by Stephen Greenblatt in his recent, movingly elegiac and personal account of *Hamlet*, that purgatory belonged to the past at the time Shakespeare was writing.[92] For Catholics in the audience, it remained part of the future, and since *The History of Purgatory* was probably composed within a very few years of *Hamlet*, one cannot even assume that the dramatization of purgatory was a thing of the past when Shakespeare's tragedy was written.[93] No-one would deny that the Ghost in *Hamlet* is conceived with intense and well-informed attention to the divergent emotional currents which the topic of purgatory would have stimulated at the time.[94] But this attention tells us less about Shakespeare's own beliefs than about his concern to move a diverse audience by imaginatively improvising on this most sensitive of issues. There can be few places in the history of literature where dramatic sophistication works against ideological clarity so much as it does in the characterization of the Ghost; all we can deduce is that the Ghost was conceived by someone who felt able to indulge in the luxury of theological ambivalence.

While the Ghost describes himself as emanating from purgatory, it is famously left unclear whether he does. The theology of ghosts, always a fringe area, did not receive the attention from contemporary theologians that it does nowadays from critics of *Hamlet*, but much could be inferred at a popular level from its dependency on the more mainstream topic of purgatory. Just as the Catholic advocacy of purgatory could be used to support the idea that a middle state did exist for souls, the Protestant debunking of purgatory most commonly implied that ghosts were not souls, but demons – though, as Peter Marshall has commented, 'in the process of telling the people what to think about ghostly apparitions, reformers were working it out for themselves, and the answers were not always clear and consistent'.[95] Hamlet himself reacts to the ghost in lines which positively invite the audience to supply the missing term of purgatory: 'O all you host of heaven, O earth – what else? – / And shall I couple hell?' (1.5.92–93). Similarly, in the previous scene, he describes the spirit as coming in a 'questionable shape' (1.4.43) on his first encounter:

> Let me not burst in ignorance but tell
> Why thy canonized bones hearsed in death
> Have burst their cerements, why the sepulchre
> Wherein we saw thee quietly interred[96]
> Hath oped his ponderous and marble jaws
> To cast thee up again.

$$(1.4.46–51)$$

The word 'sepulchre' has, here as elsewhere in Shakespeare, strong associations with the place of Christ's interment as described in the Gospels. Shakespeare's language draws explicit attention to this, and in some members of his audience might well have stimulated memories of the quasi-dramatic presentations in which the Marys and the disciples discover the empty tomb; as Beatrice Groves has described, these were a feature of the Easter liturgy up until early Elizabethan times.[97] But the return of Hamlet's father's ghost, or of any ghost, parodies Christ's harrowing of hell, and the emphasis is on parody here. The sepulchre is personified as a monster with 'ponderous and marble jaws' reminiscent of the hell-mouth of medieval mystery plays, whose vomiting of dead bodies further reminds one how the harrowing of hell prefigures the Apocalypse.[98]

This serves only to complicate the question of the Ghost's *bona fides*, particularly since – as an audience member alert to the conventions of Senecan tragedy might also have reflected – 'hell' was a term used at the time to denote the infernal regions within both Christian and classical cosmologies.[99] Here as elsewhere, the Ghost and reactions to him combine Catholic, Protestant and pagan fields of reference: hence the level of ambiguity that critics have detected, and the impossibility of giving him any clear religious cast. A ghost who describes himself as being from purgatory and then unchristianly calls his auditor to revenge is true to his mixed antecedents, but would never have passed the internal censor of someone who had a serious interest in promoting Catholicism through drama. Nothing better sums up the differences between *Hamlet* and *The History of Purgatory* than the differing stimuli given in each play by acts of remembrance. For the author of the latter play, as for his dramatic speakers, remembrance of the souls in purgatory stood for the wider need to keep faith with the true religion through cultivating Catholic traditions and memories of the past; but for Hamlet, admittedly distraught, a similar remembrance translates merely into revenge. In response to the Ghost's parting injunction, 'Adieu, adieu, adieu, remember me', Hamlet replies:

> . . . Remember thee?
> Ay, thou poor ghost, whiles memory holds a seat
> In this distracted globe. Remember thee?
> Yea, from the table of my memory
> I'll wipe away all trivial fond records,
> All saws of books, all forms, all pressures past
> That youth and observation copied there
> And thy commandment all alone shall live
> Within the book and volume of my brain
> Unmixed with baser matter.
>
> (1.5.91, 95–104)

As part of this remembrance, Shakespeare does elegise and exploit the supposed pastness of England's old religion, in *Hamlet* and elsewhere. Such phrases as 'Catholic residue' and Stephen Greenblatt's phrase 'evacuated rituals' are now standard currency within early-modern studies, usefully drawing attention to the intensive use that post-Reformation writers made of the Catholic past; but it is no coincidence that the latter phrase was first devised to describe how Shakespeare functions.[100] The play being commented on was not *Hamlet* but *Lear*, and the essay in question, which has deservedly achieved classic status, reads the move from Catholic to Protestant as directly prefiguring not only secularization, but a move away from religious belief. Even in the 1980s this had an old-fashioned feel, at odds with what historians and sociologists of religion were saying. In the 2000s, when even literature departments are having their tranquil agnosticism disturbed by diversities of belief and unbelief, it is the one element of the essay to look seriously dated; and at no time did it give adequate tribute to the overarching importance of faith in Shakespeare's age. Yet as far as *Lear* itself goes, Greenblatt's comments remain trenchant. Describing the end of the play, for instance, he writes: 'Lear's sorrows are not redeemed; nothing can turn them into joy, but the forlorn hope of an impossible redemption persists, drained of its institutional and doctrinal significance, empty and vain, cut off even from a theatrical realization, but . . . ineradicable.'[101] As this demonstrates, and as the author of the 'Lear' poem may have intuited long ago, *King Lear* does indeed lend itself exceptionally well to a post-Christian reading; and for some readers, this has been a reason to call it Shakespeare's most profound play. But one must be wary of seeing this interpretation, only one of many possible readings, as revelatory of Shakespeare's worldview outside this specific dramatic occasion – and still warier of letting Shakespeare's work, especially such an unusual work as *Lear*, dictate the paradigms for an entire era.

What *Lear* does for Christianity, *Hamlet* does for Catholicism, artificially consigning it to another time, then bringing it back as a way of making his audience beautifully sad. But juxtaposing *The History of Purgatory* with *Hamlet* demonstrates that Catholic ritual remained alive for other playwrights of Shakespeare's era. The notion of a Catholic 'past' is loaded, and sometimes even impertinent, if one does not qualify it with the consciousness of a Catholic present. Catholic England ceased at the accession of Elizabeth I, but many English people continued Catholic – for that matter, some do to this day. Read onto the affairs of its time, the Catholic references in *Hamlet* have the effect of first stifling, then artificially reanimating, the lively presence of Catholicism in England of which Shakespeare must have been aware throughout his working life. Yet it is not very different from how Shakespeare treats other versions of Christianity, showing as he does a ruthless subordination of religious matter to dramatic effect, and a preference for eclectic imaginative synthesis over theological consistency.[102] Many eras, including our own, witness a stand-off between Shakespeares and Southwells: those who subsume religious or other ideological considerations to aesthetic ones, and those whose convictions make them impatient with all cultural activity not obviously directed towards important ends. The conscientious difficulties that prevented some Catholics from going to church in Elizabethan and Jacobean England could become an aesthetic recusancy. Unlike them, Shakespeare was a subsumer, someone who could be interpreted as sacrificing theological coherence on the altar of imaginative amplitude; and the result in *Hamlet* is universally agreed to be great writing. One kind of piety would end here, but this chapter has aimed to juxtapose two kinds.

Illustrating her belief that art should not shun political implications but be above and beyond politics, the historical novelist Mary Renault wrote: 'if a writer thinks he can do more good by suppressing his work than propagating it, no matter to whom, he has signed off as an artist and had better make an honest living selling nylons or something. Shakespeare was put on by people who were burning Catholics alive for nothing but being Catholics, and if he'd said no, there'd be no Shakespeare today.'[103] Throwaway and historically questionable as they are, her comments encapsulate two assumptions common among twentieth-century *bien pensants*: that the best art transcends historical circumstance, and that Shakespeare was right not to jeopardise his literary career by speaking out on controversial issues. Even if this generation is more suspicious of the literary canon and the notion that high art is necessarily apolitical, both contentions would still find support today. But the Catholic authors discussed above, knowing the costs of plain speaking, would have unhesitatingly connected Shakespearian literary sophistication with personal cowardice and unregeneracy. Rather than dismissing the position out of hand, it may be a useful piece of role-play to think oneself into it, and to remember that for some of Shakespeare's contemporaries, an exemplary writer would, as John Donne said of himself in another context, '[seek] not your acclamation to himselfe, but your humiliation to his and your God'.[104] Even among readers without a god, few can regard with indifference the spectacle of rhetorical skill divorced from moral accountability, and the fact that Shakespeare, of all writers, was accused of this ought to startle us.

Why, though, were Shakespeare's secular literary aesthetics judged especially shameful by some Catholic commentators? This essay will perhaps reorientate the debate about the place of Catholicism in Shakespeare's biography. We do not know for sure why I.C. and the author of the 'Lear' poem singled out Shakespeare for reproof; while their strictures are one reason among many to rule out recent claims that Shakespeare acted as a spokesman for English Catholics, they complicate rather than resolve the wider question of his relationship with England's Catholic community.[105] This chapter can only hope to draw attention to the topic, and other commentators are sure to improve upon the tentative conclusions I have reached. But the issues that these Catholic writers pose, and which other writers discussed in this chapter reflect upon in practice, transcend local circumstance. There remains an irreconcilable difference, which they identify and which makes them sorrowful, between a literary aesthetic which values the explicit declaration of beliefs and a clear-cut spiritual utility, and one which privileges ambiguity, multivalency and a deferral of personal commitment on the part of the writer. Theirs was a partial point of view and will always be a minority position, but still, they too must have their say; it is not taking sides to point out that there are other sides than Shakespeare's to take.

Perhaps the last word should go to Graham Greene, the most distinguished writer to have commented on the theme which has dominated this chapter, the irreconcilable difference between Shakespeare and Southwell. Accepting the University of Hamburg's Shakespeare prize in a characteristically subversive spirit, Greene remarked: '[Southwell] is a greater hero for the writer than Shakespeare. Perhaps the deepest tragedy Shakespeare lived was his own: the blind eye exchanged for the coat of arms, the prudent tongue for the friendships at Court and the great house at Stratford.'[106] Where I.C. and the author of the 'Lear' poem condemned profanity and authorial vaingloriousness in writers like Shakespeare, Greene censures establishment smugness. This advocacy of Southwell, matched elsewhere in Greene's writing, comes with especial force from a writer who is as fascinated as Southwell by the attributes of sainthood, but whose characterizations, like Shakespeare's, fight shy of conventional sanctity.[107] It is perhaps not surprising that a writer so consciously Catholic as Greene should look to England's recusant heritage as an inspiration, though a *bon mot* from the same speech, 'The writer is driven by his own vocation to be a protestant in a Catholic society, a catholic in a Protestant one', betrays his very twentieth-century view of the Reformation: less a period when truth was pitted against falsehood than one where the virtues of disloyalty could be strikingly fulfilled. Looking at Shakespeare and Southwell together, Greene identifies an extreme ethical divergence and throws in his lot, in his own words, with 'poets who dared to reveal themselves whatever the danger'. In his comments, one can hear a distant echo of the outrage at Shakespearean models of authorship that impelled I.C. and the author of the 'Lear' poem to write. He is the latest writer, though perhaps not the last, to place Southwell above Shakespeare as they did.

Chapter Three

GOOD WORKS: SHAKESPEARE'S USE OF RELIGIOUS MORALISM

> This moral men may have in mind.
> Ye hearers, take it of worth, old and young.
> And forsake Pride, for he deceiveth you in the end.
> And remember Beauty, Five Wits, Strength, and Discretion –
> They all at the last do every man forsake,
> Save his Good Deeds there doth he take.
> But beware! And they be small,
> Before God he hath no help at all.[1]

> One asked another what Shakespeares works were worth all being bound together? he answered not a farthing; not worth a farthing said he why so? he answered that his plays were worth a great deale of mony but he never heard that his works were worth any thing at all.[2]

The first of these quotations comes from the epilogue of the early-sixteenth-century morality play *Everyman*, a drama centred round the topic of conversion that shows the protagonist's preparation for death. The second is an anecdote recorded in a joke-book two decades after Shakespeare's death, which affirms the economic value of Shakespeare's writing but dismisses him as a moral agent. Its humour comes from the conflation, then the separation, of literary works and good works; looking back to the last chapter, it is tempting to identify a

Catholic undertow to it, given that a stress on good works as a means of salvation was usually typified as Catholic. But the sentiments could have issued from anyone who believed that an author's life should be more religiously exemplary than Shakespeare's: a judgement which bypasses any beauty, wit, strength and discretion in his plays, and focuses on their author's perceived lack of good deeds.

Had Shakespeare written plays like *Everyman*, which combined affecting drama with an explicit moral agenda, they would have been harder for the speaker to dismiss; in such a case, a play would have itself been a good deed. But the way that a Shakespeare play addresses an audience is very different from the dramatic call to conversion epitomized in *Everyman*. Given that Shakespeare does dramatize changes of character as well as of external circumstance, sometimes following or mimicking the Christian model, he cannot be seen as eschewing the possibilities of conversion. But it is striking how often such conversions happen offstage, as if Shakespeare were making a conscious decision not to harangue his audience in the way that medieval theatre had done, and sermons still did. Similarly, the way in which he deploys the moralistic discourse of Elizabethan and Jacobean England maximizes an audience's judicial pleasures, while playing down adverse personal criticism. This chapter will describe the relationship between moralism and the professional theatre in Shakespeare's time, bringing scenes from his plays into dialogue with a variety of contemporary moralistic texts; the aim is to demonstrate Shakespeare's oblique approach to the topic of religious conversion, and the way that he avoids arraigning his audience.

MORALISTIC LITERATURE AND THEATRE IN SHAKESPEARE'S TIME

'Consider therfore thy misery. 1. In thy life. 2. In thy death. 3. After death', Lewis Bayly cautioned the unregenerate in a best-selling tract, first published in 1612. 'Who can describe or paynt in his colours the severitie of his judgement', Luis de Granada concurred in a devotional manual popular both in England and on the Continent, adding: 'This exhortation then beeing so good and so fruitfull, I beseeche thee deare brother, sucke out the sappe and sweete thereof for thy commoditie.'[3] These two examples, the first from an indigenous Puritan writer and the second from a continental Catholic writer whose translated work achieved wide mainstream distribution in England, are picked almost at random from the religio-moralistic fulminations which comprised a huge part of what Shakespeare's contemporaries were given to read and hear. A literary culture so directed towards constructive spiritual humiliation is not one that most twenty-first-century readers can easily relate to. But if we ignore it, we miss something very important about Shakespeare's England, as market forces alone would suggest. In a monumental study of early-modern religious literature, Ian Green has identified a series of 'best sellers and steady sellers', most of which inhabit the large area of overlap between Christianity and secular moralism.[4] Injunctions to remember your latter end, such as those which have already been quoted, are only one example of how popular wisdom and Christian obligation interpenetrated, making it impossible to separate the two.

Tracts like these seem to contradict the picture given by the antitheatricalists and the opponents of profane verse in the first two chapters of this book. If we were to believe those commentators, we would have to see most English people of Shakespeare's time as interested only in superficial entertainment, with a stalwart few colonizing the moral high ground. But publishing history shows that readers of the period had a real, widely shared, economically powerful appetite for moral and spiritual betterment that, in an age when the generic range of literature was wide, cannot be explained by a lack of alternatives. Some consumers would have confined their purchases to moral and spiritual reading, others to imaginative literature, while many would have built up a library containing both.[5] It is always difficult to distinguish between what is read for duty and what for pleasure, and the two are not necessarily antithetical. But while admitting the power of the ferial experience, one cannot assume that the consumption of moralistic tracts, entirely supererogatory to the Christian practice demanded by the law of the land, was always regarded as a wearisome obligation.

It is standard in Renaissance rhetoric both to characterize moralism as bitter on first encounter, and to compare it to honey-drops. Despite the doom-laden quotations above, moralistic works were not in the business of providing unalloyed pain, since a Christianized optimism was central to the message they gave the well-affected reader. As Luis de Granada puts it: 'And though at the beginning thou be appalled and affrighted vehemently, yet have patience a whyle, for thy colde feare shal be qualified and tempered with the heate of love, as the black night is turned by little and little into the brighte shyning day.'[6] Lewis Bayly turns to the Song of Songs to express the joy of the saved: 'The Winter of our affliction is now past: the storme of our misery is blowne over, and gone. The Bodies of our Elect Brethren appeare more glorious, then the Lilly flowrs of the earth; the time of singing Hallelu ah [sic] is come; and the voyce of the Trumpet is heard in the Land.'[7] Looking past the drama of one's own salvation to what these and similar tracts had to say about social behaviour, it is even easier for us to see what would have kept people reading, and to identify the overlap between this world and the world of the stage. Our moralisms are not always those of Shakespeare's time, but at every period one must be sensitive to the complex interplay between aesthetic pleasure and judgementalism, as invited by an author or engaged in by a reader: a contention which Renaissance literary theorists would have supported by quoting the Horatian tag *Dulce et utile*.[8]

At grammar school, Shakespeare himself would have engaged in debates on provocative topics, where the felicitous deployment of moralistic commonplaces would have been crucial to rhetorical success.[9] This early training comes over in the way that dramatic situations are set up to invite strongly divided responses from the audience, and sometimes too in fully staged debates such as that in Act 4:3 of *Othello*. Emilia is helping Desdemona to undress and prepare for Othello's return, and the two converse about whether it is ever right for a wife to commit adultery. Desdemona's question to Emilia, 'Wouldst thou do such a deed for all the world?' contains a conventional hyperbole which Emilia takes up, logic-chopping and imagining a world where she could make and unmake moral conventions at will. 'Why, the wrong is but a wrong i'th'world; and having the world for your labour, 'tis a wrong in your own world, and you might quickly make it right' (63, 79–81). Making due allowances for atypicality, one can identify morally normative reactions that the scene would arouse now, and would have aroused then. One should not assume that speakers in a more religious age than ours would have been more cautious about using religious terms flippantly – if anything, the contrary is true – but in some cases, their potential for offensiveness would have been more carefully monitored. Thus, Emilia's jocular comment that she would 'venture purgatory' for an adulterous deed (76) does not seem obtrusive now, but would have been likely to attract adverse notice when *Othello* was first performed, raising the hackles not only of the anti-Catholic contingent within the audience, but of Catholics annoyed that their church's doctrine of repentance was being distorted. Adultery, being a mortal sin, would have put one in danger not of purgatory but of hell if one did not repent, and the underlying assumption that one could buy one's way out of hell and into purgatory would have played directly to anti-Catholic stereotypes.[10] Either way, it would have confirmed a sense of Emilia being morally flawed. Conversely, Emilia's feisty assertion of women's essential similarity to men, 'they see, and smell, / And have their palates both for sweet and sour / As husbands have' (93–95), is not without parallel in proto-feminist voices of the Renaissance, but it is likely to generate a more standard agreement now; thus, it has taken on a new degree of moralistic authority since Shakespeare's time.

Given continued mainstream prejudice against adultery, or at least against infidelity within stable relationships, there would be less divergence between eras regarding the scene's central question. Even if lip-service is paid to the good one might do with money or power – Emilia says 'who would not make her husband a cuckold to make him a monarch?' (74–75) – a respondent is bound in the end to affirm that sexual loyalty is preferable to riches, unless they want to be thought of as a gold-digger, or a cynic whose own experience of such relationships has been unhappy. Here, though Emilia's morally unorthodox generalizations are undertaken in a humorous spirit, they remind the audience of her marital difficulties: a reaction echoed by Desdemona, when she says 'God me such usage send / Not to pick bad from bad, but by bad mend!' (103–104).[11] While this could be addressed to Emilia in performance, Desdemona is primarily addressing God, secondly exhorting herself not to think as Emilia does; even while remembering Emilia's misfortunes, she is attempting to use Emilia's misguided thoughts and her own miserable situation as a means towards religious self-improvement. The rhyming couplet, which ends the scene, has its part to play in giving her response the stamp of finality.

Thus, in signalling her disagreement with Emilia, Desdemona is given a reaction that blocks any over-enthusiastic audience reactions to what Emilia has had to say. It is a moment of moralistic meta-theatre, showing Shakespeare's awareness of the notion that *exempla vitii* could work to suggest vice rather than discourage it. Early-modern commentators who disliked the theatre were concerned that its examples of bad behaviour might encourage emulation: John Greene, for instance, declared with heavy irony, 'if you will learn to condemn God and all his laws, . . . and to commit all kind of sin and mischief with secrecy and art, you need not go to any other school, for all these good examples may you see painted before your eyes in interludes and plays'.[12] The antitheatricalists' case was at its strongest when they drew attention to the potential vulnerability of the moralistic stance on sin; after all, it provides ample material for misreading. So it is not surprising to find playwrights inserting pointers in exchanges such as the above; they leave visible the detailed consideration of immorality and vice within the text, acting as an exit sign where an antitheatrical commentator might have preferred a brick wall, but they still have considerable symbolic importance. Paratextual commentary, especially in prologues and epilogues, was another means of damage-limitation, though one less used by Shakespeare. Famously – though how disingenuously, it is still debated – the epilogue to Marlowe's *Dr Faustus* turns what the audience have witnessed into a moral exemplum: 'Faustus is gone. Regard his hellish fall, / Whose fiendful fortune may exhort the wise / Only to wonder at unlawful things, / Whose deepness doth entice such forward wits / To practice more than heavenly power permits.'[13]

This scene from *Othello* is not, of course, the only moment in Shakespeare's drama where a guiding authorial moralism can be detected behind the process of dramatic interchange. However, one of the reasons that Shakespeare ranks so high in the canon is his interpretive openness and, to quote a recent commentator, an avoidance of 'simplistic or even moralistic conclusions', which begs the question of why dramatic moralism is so often linked with over-hasty closure.[14] The association of the two is often well deserved, a problem of which Shakespeare himself was aware: Cleopatra's objection that she does not wish to see 'some squeaking Cleopatra boy my greatness / I' th' posture of a whore' (5.2.220–221) betrays both the character's obsession with shaping her historical persona and her creator's wry acknowledgement of this pull towards reductiveness. Yet morally normative reactions can also involve the audience, maximizing rather than short-circuiting the pleasures of moral judgement. Cleopatra cannot be simply pigeonholed as a whore, but the question of whether there is a whorish element in her behaviour reasserts itself within every performance, production and reading. If moralistic closure is often hard to come by in Shakespeare's drama, few texts have ever been so moralistically suggestive.[15] Though the term 'problem play' now looks so dated, one can add that there is undoubtedly a special relationship between tragicomedy and moralistic debate in Shakespeare's writing; and if debate operates best in environments where it is made difficult for the audience to take sides, then a play like *Measure for Measure*, with the evasive Duke, the hypocritical Angelo and the rigorist Isabella, calls every audience member to argue flexibly.

Shakespeare's audience were not only invited to evaluate and judge dramatic characters, but given plenty of material to continue moralistic interchange outside the theatre. Any assessment of Shakespeare's moralism must point to his constant, creative deployment of proverbs and commonplaces, and even more, his phenomenal ability to coin utterances that have subsequently become proverbial: he is one of the most quoted writers in the English language.[16] Impersonally commenting on what are held to be universal truths, such aphorisms evoke common wisdom even when – as so often in Shakespeare – they are spoken for the first time; looked at as a rhetorical gambit, they do more to empower quoters than embarrass listeners. In Renaissance rhetoric, after all, the artful deployment of aphoristic wisdom is often more to do with demonstrating one's intellectual agility than any desire to change the outside world. In Act 2.1 of *As You Like It*, the First Lord's account of Jaques commenting on the fate of a stricken deer demonstrates this well, as he describes how 'big round tears / Coursed one another down [the] innocent nose' of the 'poor sequestered stag' (38–39, 33) and how Jaques observed the scene. Duke Senior asks eagerly 'Did he not moralize this spectacle?', and being told how Jaques has compared the deer's tears into the stream to 'worldlings' bequeathing riches to those who are rich already, and the rest of the herd to 'fat and greasy citizens' ignoring someone in misfortune, leaps up and declares 'I love to cope him in these sullen fits / For then he's full of matter' (44, 48, 55, 67–68). There is a striking disjunction between the animal's tears and Duke Senior's glee. We are probably meant to notice how all the characters in the scene think of the deer less as a suffering creature than as an excuse for rhetorical plenitude; if so, this would be a way for an audience to critique, even to moralize, the spectacle of moralism divorced from active compassion.[17]

But despite the reminder of suffering, this is a scene where the element of playfulness in moralism comes across clearly. As many critics have observed, Shakespeare is drawing on an emblematic tradition in this passage, and with their interplay of moralism, ingenuity, visual stimulus and verbal point, emblems epitomize the Renaissance desire that moral instruction should be entertaining.[18] But even if moralizing itself could be fun, being on the receiving end of adverse judgements is painful in any era. Like gossip, moralism is central to how a community functions, but has endless potential to create bad feeling: one reason why both words have such strong pejorative overtones.[19] Imaginative literature, though, brings with it the possibility of unilateral, risk-free moralizing.[20] The professional theatre must have been a relaxing environment in the post-Reformation England of Shakespeare's time, where religious diversity, and especially the upsurge of Puritanism, ensured that one's *modus vivendi* was constantly being challenged. The godly, almost by definition, felt morally impelled to intervene in other people's lives: sometimes over matters which lay outside the law, sometimes by invoking or changing the law. Much recent work on Puritanism has emphasized how 'godly regimes deployed . . . communitarian and social disciplining alongside an emphasis on interior, private contrition, so that spiritual correction was also influenced by social ordering'.[21] Insofar as it was a safe forum for moralistic debate, the theatre can be seen as providing an alternative to this kind of utopia. Here, it is worth considering Shakespeare's reputation for tolerance. The ability to evoke sympathy and understanding for a diverse range of characters has been seen as one of Shakespeare's main strengths – arguably his greatest. But however high tolerance now ranks as a virtue – and for most readers of this book, that will be very high indeed – one should not make the mistake of thinking of it as above justification or historical circumstance. In Shakespeare's age as in our own, the limits of tolerance, and the notion of tolerance in itself, had political implications for decision-makers, and pragmatic ones for every member of a community; it is hardly surprising that they should have had literary ones too.[22]

For this period, Annabel Patterson has influentially characterized the relationship between writers and players on the one hand, and censors on the other, as a contract where each side knew the limits of what could be said.[23] One can see the relationship between Shakespeare and his audience as a contract similar to this; since Shakespeare was not in the business of exhorting his hearers, he depicts instances of virtue and vice while deliberately, even ostentatiously, leaving the rest to inference. This can be best seen at those dramatic moments when a character is called to account within a play, whether by death or accusation, and this chapter will now move on to discuss a selection of these: Richard II's last dying speech; the accounts of Falstaff's death; and personal application within drama and satire, as seen in Claudius's reaction to the play-within-a-play in *Hamlet*, Jaques's defence of the satirical medium and the admissions of human weakness in *Measure for Measure*. Though diverse in nature, these are all moments where the literary genres and motifs being employed would have reminded contemporary audiences of calls to repentance within moralistic discourse, and where Shakespeare is correspondingly at pains to limit the applicability of what is said.

DYING SPEECHES: ARNOLD COSBIE
AND RICHARD II

The theatre of the scaffold, and the genre of dying speech, have been much attended to by scholars in recent years. Surprisingly downplayed within these accounts, though not in the texts themselves, is a sense that God is being addressed by those about to die – is, indeed, the most prominent addressee of all. With their public exposure of an individual's worst crimes and their exaction of punishment, execution-scenes anticipated the day of judgement, but could be seen as staving off final damnation if proper use was made of them. If the final speeches of condemned individuals can sometimes appear moralistic and uniform, this is exactly the point, since they were an opportunity for exemplary public atonement. Sometimes delivered from the scaffold itself, sometimes dispatched from prison, they redefined the malefactor as a repentant Christian. Expressing contrition, resignation to an untimely end and the hope of mercy, they would have elicited prayer-ful support from the crowd in a way that no condemned individual would have regarded indifferently. J.A. Sharpe has remarked on the 'active co-operation of the condemned' in these staged spectacles, and this may be one reason why.[24]

Prayers do not often come in blank verse; nor, outside drama, do condemned men's final utterances. But shortly after the execution of Arnold Cosbie in January 1591/2 for murdering John, Lord Burgh, a pamphlet on the affair appeared, advertising 'certaine verses written by the said Cosby in the time of his imprisonment'.[25] There is every reason to believe the attribution. Like the scaffold, prison was com-monly seen as necessitating exemplary behaviour, and prison-verses written by those under sentence of death are not uncommon.[26] But Cosbie's is a highly unusual poem: written in blank verse, reading like a dramatic soliloquy, and figuring emotional fluctuation in a way which risks undermining the piece's final exemplary message, only to rein-force it triumphantly at the end.

As this suggests, Cosbie's real-life dying speech is closely attentive to fictional analogues, borrowing the idea of biographically structured personal lamentation from the contemporary genre of complaint, best exemplified in the *Mirror for Magistrates*.[27] Crucial to this is an acknowledgement of how the speaker's present woes contrast with his past honour, and Cosbie's use of this is all the more touching for not being strictly exemplary. Reminiscing about his glory-days on the battlefield, he asks his 'Frends, countrie men, and kinsfolkes' either to forget him entirely or to imagine that he died in combat.

> My name, my face, my fact, ô blot me out,
> Out of the world, put me out of your thoughts,
> Or if you thinke, o thinke I never was,
> Or if you thinke I was, thinke that I fell,
> Before some sorte, some holde in Belgia,
> With this suppose beguile your sorrowes friends . . .
>
> (f. A4a)

But because this shows the speaker thinking boastful thoughts and ignoring the obligation to instruct his audience, it is only a provisional exhortation. Cosbie pulls himself back to the path of contrition – 'A wretched man to talke of honors heigth, / Fallen so basely into the pit of shame, / The pit of death: my God, my God forgive me. / Next to my God, my countrie pardon me' (f. A4a) – and the temporary lapse, if anything, helps to authenticate Cosbie's concluding requests for pardon from God and England. The quasi-dramatic verses achieve real dramatic tension by showing exemplarity forcibly arrived at, and the struggle authenticates a final couplet which might otherwise come across as too pat: 'Flie thou my soule to heaven the haven of blisse, / O bodie beare the scourge of thine amisse' (f. A4a). This is both a penultimate utterance and one from beyond the grave, having been printed after Cosbie's execution; but the reader's privileged access to Cosbie's contrition, unqualified by any negative editorial comment about his demeanour on the scaffold, seems designed to elicit real hope that he achieved a good death.

Given that Cosbie's imprisonment and execution came just after the concentrated period of English dramatic excellence which saw Kyd's *Spanish Tragedy* (*c.* 1585–1589), Marlowe's *Tamburlaine I & II* (*c.* 1587–1588) and Shakespeare's first two *Henry VI* plays, it may not at first seem surprising that he should have bidden farewell to the world in this way. But given that prison-verse and dying speeches compelled authors to present contrition in the most rhetorically efficacious manner possible, it is still remarkable that Cosbie should have chosen to write in a style – blank verse – and a genre – the soliloquy – so strongly associated with the theatre, and therefore with feigning. His verse reads so like a passage from a late Elizabethan tragedy or history play that, even now, it gives one a start to remember that his death was real. What would read like conventional hyperboles in a play, such as Cosbie's opening gambit, 'Breake heart, be mute my sorrowes past compare, / *Cosbie* complaine no more, but sit and die', and his further injunction to himself, 'Bleed heart to thinke what these accursed hands / Have perpetrated' (ff. A3a, A3b), are given emotional authority by the reader's knowledge that poet and speaker are, for once, to be identified with each other. Contrition, after all, can be performative as well as internal. In an epideictic paradox that no fictional speaker could ever have achieved, Cosbie commends himself to his audience all the more by accusing himself so publicly and so dramatically; his testimony validates a quasi-dramatic medium by injecting real experience and real suffering into it.

Most of Cosbie's readers and those who witnessed his execution would not, obviously, have been murderers themselves. Yet the theatre of death could never be just a spectator sport. For some its effect would have been cautionary, but others would have used it as a means of preparing for their own end. As suggested by the quotations from Bayly and de Granada, all Christians were obliged to consider themselves sinners and criminals before the judgement-seat of God; they would not all have practised vicarious mortification themselves, but they would certainly have known how it was done, and have noticed when others failed to do it. In the penultimate scene of *Richard II*, where the imprisoned king is anticipating death, this common knowledge is sometimes referred to, and implicitly counterpoints Richard's lack of conventional moral courage throughout the scene. Both dramatic speeches, Cosbie's and Shakespeare's, can lay claim to considerable psychological subtlety in the way they chart the mental switchbacks of a condemned man. But if one took them out of context, in the New Critical manner, Cosbie's verses on an empirically experienced situation would look more artificial than Shakespeare's on an imagined one, simply because university-educated readers of this and similar literature have been trained to see exemplarity as psychologically unconvincing. If one discards this presupposition, comparing the two has the effect of undermining facile distinctions between art and life; most actual condemned men at this period would not have wanted, and could not have afforded, to look as heterodox and fallible as the imagined Richard. Conversely, there are reasons why Shakespeare might have wished to deny Richard an exemplary death. If Richard's speech is all too human, this is precisely what would have incited contemporary audiences to will him on towards conformity with the exemplary ideals he has invoked earlier – as many critics have observed, Richard often compares himself to Christ.[28] Yet the spectacle of Richard's imperfection, and the experience of knowing better than him, would have given auditors the option, at least, of resting in that knowledge, rather than using his mistakes as a spur towards self-betterment.

The beginning of Richard's soliloquy reads as follows:

> I have been studying how I may compare
> This prison where I live unto the world,
> And for because the world is populous
> And here is not a creature but myself,
> I cannot do it. Yet I'll hammer't out.

> (5.5.1–5)

Fully to understand the force of this, one needs to be aware of what Richard is doing with a cliché. The literary comparison between the prison and the world was a standard one, not least in writings by prisoners themselves, and could be used to introduce a number of improving reflections: most frequently, perhaps, how the world itself was a prison for a soul which aspired heavenwards. But Richard is closer to despair than exemplary resignation; he begins by interpreting this commonplace metaphor in a perversely literal manner, and this has the effect of defamiliarizing it. The 'world is populous', but he is alone, and to make the comparison fit, he must – as he goes on to reflect – breed thoughts to inhabit the microcosm of prison. By expressing the intention to 'hammer' the comparison out, or make it a display of conscious ingenuity, he signals both his awareness that prisoners are expected to think in this way, and the fact that, in his case, it comes only by expending unnatural effort. But the phrase also carries connotations of religious meditation. It is no coincidence that if one subtracts the plot-related material from Richard's soliloquy, one ends up with something similar to the meditative religious verse that was starting to be written in England around the time *Richard II* was composed. At its most psychologically sophisticated, this type of verse often began by presenting a speaker who, like Richard, is aware of his own inadequacy as a respondent to edifying propositions; at its most audacious, it addressed contemporary religious controversies in a sceptical spirit.

The next few lines of Richard's speech could have been written by Donne. Thinking about how he stands with God, Richard opens up the question – one could almost say, shifts the blame – by setting one Scriptural text affirming God's generosity in salvation against another that implies salvation is very hard to achieve.

> For no thought is contented. The better sort,
> As thoughts of things divine, are intermixed
> With scruples, and do set the word itself
> Against the word –
> As thus: 'Come, little ones', and then again
> 'It is as hard to come as for a camel
> To thread the postern of a small needle's eye.'

$$(5.5.11-17)$$

Here, as so often in Shakespeare's work, something may make sense within the world of the play while also conveying a specific topical message by means of studied anachronism. On the face of it, Richard's complaint is a fairly standard one. The speech deplores how 'thoughts of things divine' are inseparable from controversial and polemical interchange, something that could be said at any stage in the history of Christianity. But audience members and readers of the mid-1590s, better accustomed than Richard's contemporaries to seeing 'the word itself' set 'against the word', would have started up at the particular examples Richard chooses to prove his point; indeed, where the Folio reads 'word', the Quarto reads 'faith', gesturing even more strongly towards scepticism. Richard is alluding to portions of two texts from the Gospels: 'Suffer the litle children, and forbid them not to come to me' and 'It is easier for a camel to go through the eye of a needle, then for a riche man to enter into the kingdome of God'.[29] As selectively quoted by him, they are made more inclusive than they are in their fuller form, and much more contradictory of each other. The first text, instead of referring specifically to the episode in Matthew's Gospel where children are allowed to come to Jesus instead of being driven away, spreads its net more widely to take in all God's children. The second text goes further, exhibiting not merely an allusive approach to the scriptures, but – as several previous critics have pointed out – a misreading of them. The original, after all, specifies that it is a *rich* man who is likely to have difficulty entering the kingdom of heaven. As far as Richard's characterization goes, the misremembering seems almost perverse. Richard is dispossessed and no longer rich, so the text in its original form might seem to give him hope; as it is, it seems unnecessarily to exacerbate his despair.

But Richard's misquotation of his second text has an effect similar to his very partial quotation of the first: both are detached from their original contexts just sufficiently to enlarge their reference to human-kind in general. This means that, when they are juxtaposed, the first text shows God inviting humankind to Himself, only to turn them away in the second text by making the conditions of salvation impossibly difficult. This has the effect of pointing to the painful con-trast between the Protestant ideal of evangelism and the Protestant doctrine of predestination, in a manner which, again, post-dates Richard's own era but was acutely topical at the time the play was first performed.[30] Juxtaposing the two texts also has the effect, superficially at least, of presenting the Bible as internally inconsistent. One should not underestimate the theatrical shock-value of this; while it was common enough to quote seemingly contradictory biblical texts, most speakers had an interest in resolving them rather than leaving contra-diction hanging in the air as Richard does. It is a sceptic's meditation; yet the more biblically literate members of the audience, seeing the partial and inaccurate operations of Richard's memory, would have identified it as a self-induced and unnecessary scepticism, particularly deplorable in one who is near his end and knows it.

Richard moves on from religion to analyse 'thoughts tending to ambition' (18), which induce him to plot futile escapes from prison; then he entertains the comforts of stoicism, only to reject them:

> Thoughts tending to content flatter themselves
> That they are not the first of Fortune's slaves,
> Nor shall be not the last, like silly beggars
> Who, sitting in the stocks, refuge their shame
> That many have and others must set there,
> And in this thought they find a kind of ease,
> Bearing their own misfortunes on the back
> Of such as have before endured the like.
>
> (23–30)

Thanks to Boethius' *Consolations of Philosophy* and its imitators, Christianized stoicism was very common among prison writers. But this passage, so contemptuous in tone, shows Richard pulling away not only from a stoical stance but from exemplarity in general. Unifying his disparate self-begotten thoughts by amalgamating them into his self-portrayal as actor, he arrives not at a stance appropriate for a condemned man, but at an acknowledgement of his confusedly multiple subjectivities: 'Thus play I in one person many people, / And none contented. Sometimes am I king, / Then treasons make me wish myself a beggar, / And so I am' (31–34). At this point in the scene, Richard even seems to be entertaining the un-Christian notion of death as annihilation – 'But whate'er I be / Nor I nor any man that but man is / With nothing shall be pleased till he be eased / With being nothing' (38–41) – which could only have increased an auditor's dismay at his lack of integrity.

To those anxiously waiting to see whether Richard will achieve a good death, the succeeding excursus on time seems to promise a moral and spiritual unification of his scattered thoughts; but again he fails to deliver. As he says:

> I wasted time and now doth time waste me,
> For now hath time made me his numbering clock.
> My thoughts are minutes, and with sighs they jar
> Their watches on unto mine eyes, the outward watch,
> Whereto my finger like a dial's point
> Is pointing still, in cleansing them from tears.
> Now sir, the sound that tells what hour it is
> Are clamorous groans that strike upon my heart,
> Which is the bell. So sighs and tears and groans
> Show minutes, times and hours. But my time
> Runs posting on in Bullingbrook's proud joy
> While I stand fooling here, his Jack of the clock.
>
> (49–60)

Richard's failure here is all the more striking because his theme is another meditational commonplace. The medieval church's monitoring of time, through the monastic offices or their various equivalents for lay people – Books of Hours for the literate, or the regular chiming of the Angelus bell as a call to prayer – had some analogues in Protestant England. For this and other reasons, a consciously prayerful awareness of time's passing was one of the many methods of holy living that Catholics and Protestants had in common. A best-selling devotional manual on the subject by a German Jesuit, Jeremias Drexelius, translated into English around 1630 under the title *The Angel-Guardian's Clock*, gives a good idea of how the theme was often developed. The movements of a clock and the bells striking the hour are metaphors for how humans will be called to account at the end of their lives, and parallels are routinely drawn with alarm bells and passing bells. *The Angel-Guardian's Clock* is typical in using this as a means of imaging self-examination:

> Thy Conscience is to thee a bell, which is often and daily strictly to be examined. Descend into thyself, and looke into thy Life; & do not only heede what thou intendest to do, but consider often, what thou hast done; use in this manner to sound that bell, and daily search into thy conscience; and finde out, what have bene thy thoughts, thy words and thy deedes during that whole day;

> Thus make use of the respit of time, which at the instant of
> death, thou wouldst perhaps in vaine seeke for, and now is
> granted thee. LEARNE TO DIE; . . . [31]

As with Bayly and de Granada, one needs to remind oneself that texts
of this kind are making use of scare tactics to convey a fundamentally
optimistic message. Drexelius's remark that at one's death one might
search for a respite 'perhaps in vaine' is both chilling and reassuring,
reminding the sinner that something practical can be done in the
meantime, and also warning against last-minute desperation
stemming from a lack of trust in God's grace. The signs of contrition
are easy to confuse with those of despair, and Richard's 'sighs and
tears and groans' which 'show minutes, times and hours' could
connote repentance when taken out of context. But his despondent
self-characterization, 'I wasted time and now doth time waste me, /
For now hath time made me his numbering clock' recalls – perhaps
deliberately – the last speech of a notorious damned sinner, Dr
Faustus.[32] Marlowe's play also features clock-watching as a prelude to
eternity, and both of these final speeches exploit the theatrical tensions
resulting from deferred repentance. The question of Faustus's
destination after death is more obtrusive, and he is more concerned
than Richard to escape his fate, but both protagonists share an
inability to profit from the time that remains to them. Though Richard
has every reason to believe these are his final hours, he exhibits no
sense of anxiety to make up for lost time; more than anything else,
this frustrates the expectations set up by his speech's edifying
beginning, as well as the moment where, in his earlier scene with the
looking-glass, he describes his body as 'the very book indeed / Where
all my sins are writ' (4.1.273–274). A further frustration occurs in
the exchange with the groom which divides Richard's soliloquy from
the entry of his murderer Exton, where Richard bitterly reflects on the
news that his favourite horse bore Bolingbroke in the coronation
procession, and exclaims 'Forgiveness! Horse, why do I rail on thee'
(90).[33] To an audience holding its breath for Richard to ask forgiveness
of God, this would have had a grossly parodic feel. His speech never
has a hope of reclaiming itself until his very last lines, 'Mount, mount

my soul. Thy seat is up on high / Whilst my gross flesh sinks downward, here to die' (111–112) – and even then, any reclamation this constitutes is very imperfect. Given Richard's eleventh-hour and fifty-ninth-minute haste, not to mention the fact that he has just killed two men, the audience is left wondering whether his assurance of salvation may not be misplaced.

A normatively minded contemporary reader of Cosbie's soliloquy, seeing its writer winning through to an exemplary position, could only have cheered him on, and filed the example away for future reference. But a similar auditor of Shakespeare's play, giving breathless attention to Richard flunking his last test, would have found so little to emulate, and so much to pity and criticize, that outwardly directed adverse judgement might well have substituted for self-interrogation. Shakespeare has often been characterized as a writer with a compassionate attitude towards human imperfection, and the death of Richard, a bravura display of psychological particularity, shows this compassion at work. But looked at against Cosbie's verse, the limitations of this approach appear alongside its strengths. Learning to read imaginative literature entails gaining pleasure from the depiction of psychological sophistication, and Shakespeare's writing has done much to inculcate awareness that human beings cannot be categorized in black-and-white terms. But, perversely, his authority has sometimes encouraged readers not to believe accounts of exemplary behaviour, or to equate them with literary crudity, which is an unhelpful way of approaching both fiction and fact at this date. For the martyrs of whom Shakespeare's age was so full, and for repentant criminals too, heroic exemplarity had a reassuring and empowering function; as this discussion began by observing, exemplary behaviour on the scaffold was common enough at this period, as it was for other publicly attended deathbeds.[34] The real-life Cosbie, contemplating his imminent death, must have found comfort in modelling himself along exemplary lines. But Shakespeare's fictional characters are seldom allowed this liberty, and for readers and audiences at any time, this has the effect of closing off imaginative options.[35]

CALLED TO ACCOUNT:
BELLMEN AND THE DEATH OF FALSTAFF

Another exercise in popular chrono-moralism, Thomas Tymme's pamphlet *A Silver Watch-Bell* (1st edn 1605), describes how desperation might affect the unrepentant sinner: 'In the one eare, Security sounding, It is not yet time: In the other eare, presumption singing, It will be time still. And thus . . . they swim in delights, when destruction is nearest: Till at last, Desperation, the handmaide of Securitie, plaieth her part, sheweth them the houre-glasse, and wofully telleth them the time is past.'[36] The 'watch-bell' of Tymme's title evokes the figure of the bellman, or night-watchman, whose job was to ring a bell and call out the hours at night in towns, and who came to symbolize the inexorability of time and death. Because he walked at night, as rogues and vagabonds were supposed to do, he also became proverbial as a witness for dark deeds, which is why, when Lady Macbeth waits nervously for her husband to come back from murdering Duncan, she is reminded of a bellman on hearing an owl hooting: 'It was the owl that shrieked, the fatal bellman / Which gives the stern'st good-night' (2.2, 3–4). The frontispiece of an early-seventeenth-century moralistic tract shows the bellman on his nightly perambulation, superimposed on scenes of murder, brawling and tavern revelry; the inset image of him acts as a shaft giving onto heaven above and hell beneath, with the legend 'Heavens Glory, Seeke It[.] Eart[h]s Vanitie, Flye It. Hells Horror, Fere It' (Fig. 4, p. 141).[37] Similarly, the speaker of Thomas Dekker's *The Bel-man of London* (1608) relates how the book's protagonist 'discovered unto me the properties of his walkes, as how farre his boundes reached, what mad hobgoblings he oftentimes encountred with, what mischiefs he now and then prevented, [and] what knaveries he was now and then an eye witness to' (f. C3a).[38]

For these reasons, bells and bellmen regularly acted as a point of imaginative intersection between Christian moralism and sin. In *Henry IV: 2*, Shakespeare plays an ironic variation on this set-piece in Act 3.2, the scene where Justice Silence prompts Justice Shallow to reminisce about his wild youth.[39] This in turn proves a reminder of mortality:

SHALLOW: Jesu, Jesu, the mad days that I have spent! And to see
how many of my old acquaintance are dead.

SILENCE: We shall all follow, cousin.

SHALLOW: Certain, 'tis certain; very sure, very sure. Death, as the
Psalmist saith,[40] is certain to all; all shall die. How[41] a good
yoke of bullocks at Stamford Fair?

(30–36)

Like the justice characterized by Jaques in *As You Like It*, Shallow is full
of 'wise saws and modern instances' (2.7.157). But though intoning
that 'all shall die', his mind immediately turns to the price of livestock,
suggesting that, despite being so near his own grave, he remains
fleshly and venal: a mental oscillation which makes him comic, but
also cautionary. Throughout the scene, though his mind never quite
moves from death, he seems oblivious to any personal application this
might have; thoughts about material goods succeed those of mortality,
and he brags wistfully about his wild youth rather than repudiating it.
The casually blasphemous 'Jesu, Jesu', altered to 'Oh' in the Folio
edition in response to the 1606 Act to Restrain Abuses of Players,
points up his unconverted state.[42]

The entry of Shallow's old acquaintance Falstaff spurs Shallow and
Silence to further reminiscence, again checked by a consciousness of
time's passing:

SILENCE: That's fifty-five year ago.

SHALLOW: Ha, cousin Silence, that thou hadst seen that that
this knight and I have seen! Ha, Sir John, said I well?

SIR JOHN: We have heard the chimes at midnight, Master
Shallow.

SHALLOW: That we have, that we have, that we have; in faith,
Sir John, we have. . . . Jesus, the days that we have seen!

(203–209, 211)[43]

The phrase 'chimes at midnight', implying both night-time revelry and
the admonitions of the clock, sums up the intimations of mortality
already so prominent in this scene: it is not surprising that Orson
Welles chose it as the title for his 1965 cinematic reworking of the

HEAVENS GLORY
SEEKE IT
EARTS VANITIE,
FLYE IT.
HELLS HORROR,
FERE IT.

FIGURE 4   Samuel Rowlands, *A most excellent treatise containing the way to seek heaven's glory* © The British Library Board, C.21.49.

Henry IV plays. But Shallow fails to pick up on the double meaning which the ironist Falstaff intends. His cheerful concurrence, 'in faith, Sir John, we have', points up the distinction between hearing the chimes at midnight and listening to them, while reminding us of the gaps elsewhere between word and intention in his use of religious language. As the above quotations demonstrate, Shallow's character as originally conceived blasphemes a good deal. The scene presents him as someone obsessed by the loss of time and aware of his own mortality, but imperfectly prepared for death: an indictment all the more serious because he is a justice, supposedly wiser than average. Most pitiable of all, as Falstaff points out after Shallow has gone, is the element of self-delusion in Shallow's memories: 'This same starved justice hath done nothing but prate to me of the wildness of his youth, and the feats he hath done . . . and every third word a lie' (290–293). The audience are invited to reflect on the folly of an old man who wishes to exaggerate the sins of his young manhood. Here as elsewhere, Shallow functions as a foil to Falstaff, throwing into relief the latter's greater self-awareness, though his plea earlier in the play, 'Peace, good Doll, do not speak like a death's head, do not bid me remember mine end' (2.4.232–233) has reminded the audience that he himself is little better than Shallow.

Bellmen and chimes are only signifiers of death's inevitability, not death itself, and where the latter impinges on scenes of low life, it is bound to have an even greater admonitory effect. The juxtaposition is familiar within morality plays: for instance, Fellowship in *Everyman* promises 'if thou wilt eat, and drink, and make good cheer, / Or haunt to women the lusty company, / I would not forsake you while the day is clear', and, true to his proviso, departs from Everyman when the imminent death of the latter becomes obvious.[44] But within *Henry V*, in keeping with Shakespeare's usual reluctance to stage Christian rites of passage, the opposite happens: Falstaff does not appear to the audience in his last hours, and his off-stage death throes interrupt bawdiness and brawling in Act 2.1, when Hostess Quickly summons his friends to his deathbed. His last words are recalled in two scenes' time:

BARDOLPH: Would I were with him, wheresome'er he is, either
    in heaven or in hell.

HOSTESS: Nay, sure he's not in hell. He's in Arthur's bosom, if
    ever man went to Arthur's bosom. A made a finer end, and
    went away an it had been any christom child. A parted
    ev'n just between twelve and one, ev'n at the turning o'th'
    tide – for after I saw him fumble with the sheets, and play
    with flowers, and smile upon his finger's end, I knew there
    was but one way. For his nose was as sharp as a pen, and a
    babbled of green fields. 'How now, Sir John?' quoth I. 'What,
    man! Be o' good cheer.' So a cried out, 'God, God, God',
    three or four times. Now I, to comfort him, bid him a
    should not think of God; I hoped there was no need to
    trouble himself with any such thoughts yet. So a bade me
    lay more clothes on his feet . . .

$$(2.3.7–21)^{45}$$

The scene is well known as one that blends comedy and poignancy,
partly because of the sport it makes with conventional deathbed ideals
through Hostess Quickly's reportage. From the moralistic point of view
she is plainly far from ideal as a deathbed attendant: like the figure of
Security in the quotation from *A Silver Watch-Bell* given above, she
assures Falstaff when he talks about God that 'there was no need to
trouble himself with any such thoughts yet' – though as the word 'yet'
shows, even she recognizes that a time may come for him to do so.
Meanwhile, she exhorts him to 'be o' good cheer' rather than compos-
ing himself to repentance, the irony being that, from her account, his
demeanour has already shown visionary contentment. An uncertainty
about how far to believe her relation and interpretation of Falstaff's
death partly explains the conflicting readings which this scene has
inspired, which pivot on the question of whether he dies well or badly.
His cry 'God, God, God' has lent support to both camps, and Paul
Cubeta, for instance, has contended that 'consolation is not to be found
in any recognition that Falstaff tried to die well'.[46] This perhaps
underestimates the scene's designed ambiguity. Hostess Quickly may
be morally questionable and a poor interpreter of what she sees, but

in this context she is an unlikely dissembler, and the particularities of
the scene she describes give real support to her sentimental conviction
that Falstaff must be in 'Arthur's bosom': signalled as comic and scripturally uninformed by her confusion of King Arthur with Abraham,
but for all that, a sign of hope for Falstaff's well-wishers. Her observation, 'A made a finer end, and went away an it had been any christom
child' – a child anointed at baptism with a mixture of oil and balm,
the oil of chrism – might have recalled another Scriptural text: 'except
ye be converted, and become as litle children, ye shal not enter into
the kingdome of heaven' (Matthew 18:3). But in the context of
Hostess Quickly's describing how Falstaff babbled of green fields, it
probably also alludes to Psalm 23: 'He maketh me to rest in grene
pasture . . . thou doest anoint mine head with oyle' (verses 2, 5).[47] If
so, in death as in life, we are to think of Falstaff's cup as running over.

But if Falstaff is saved, when does he repent? As has long been
recognized, Hal's rejection of him in Act 5 Scene 5 of *Henry IV: 2*
plays out one of St Paul's injunctions on repentance: 'cast of,
concerning the conversation in time past, the olde man, which is corrupt through the deceiveable lusts; . . . And put on the new man,
which after God is created in righteousnes, and true holines.'[48] Acting
up to Christian stereotypes of repentance is, after all, part of the long
game that Hal is playing. Anyone who had read or seen *Henry IV: 1*
would have recalled his prediction, 'My reformation, glitt'ring o'er my
fault, / Shall show more goodly and attract more eyes / Than that
which hath no foil to set it off' (1.2.201–203), when the Archbishop
of Canterbury ingenuously declares in *Henry V*: 'Consideration like an
angel came / And whipped th'offending Adam out of him/ . . . Never
came reformation in a flood / With such a heady currence scouring
faults' (1.1.29–30, 34–35). But when one gives allegorical figures an
individuated existence, they too can repent rather than being merely
the leavings of other people's repentance. For all its cruelty, Hal's dismissal 'I know thee not, old man. Fall to thy prayers' (5.5.46) reminds
us that there is ample room for reform in Falstaff's life.[49] Even corrupt
old men are capable of reforming, though admittedly, we see no sign
of this first-hand; in the last conversation Falstaff ever has on stage,
we hear him brazening his rejection out to his friends: 'This that you

heard was but a colour' (83–84). But if any character of Shakespeare's ever had a robust offstage existence, Falstaff is surely the one. Not much time has elapsed between the end of *Henry IV: 2* and the beginning of *Henry V,* but it is more than enough for an offstage repentance. If we are to make the deductions from a serene and prayerful deathbed that Shakespeare's contemporaries would have made, it may be one of the greater ironies of the play that, at the last, Falstaff did what Hal told him.

All the same, for such a legendary low-liver to die at peace with God is counter-intuitive, and the second-hand and divergent reports of conversations leading up to his death do nothing to clarify matters:

> NIM: They say he cried out of sack.
>
> HOSTESS: Ay, that a did.
>
> BARDOLPH: And of women.
>
> HOSTESS: Nay, that a did not.
>
> NIM: Yes, that a did, and said they were devils incarnate.
>
> HOSTESS: A could never abide carnation, 'twas a colour he
> never liked.
>
> BOY: A said once the devil would have him about women.
>
> HOSTESS: A did in some sort, indeed, handle women – but then
> he was rheumatic, and talked of the Whore of Babylon.
>
> (2.3.25–35)

All this suggests that Falstaff refers to his past sins in his deathbed utterances, but leaves unclear exactly what he says, and whether it comprises repentance or not. Given the close association of apocalypticism and Protestant theology in Shakespeare's time, Falstaff's unspecified comments on the Whore of Babylon from the Book of Revelation may be teasing the audience with a throwback to the connections between Falstaff and the Lollard hero Sir John Oldcastle, played upon in *Henry IV: 1* and, after protests from Oldcastle's descendants, somewhat disingenuously denied in *Henry IV: 2.*[50] But in any case, the past theatrical connection of the two knights is relevant to Falstaff's good death. Shortly after the real Henry V became king, Sir John Oldcastle was hanged in chains as a traitor and burned as a heretic because of his links with the Lollards, early religious radicals who in Shakespeare's time were seen as prefiguring Protestantism through their advocacy of the vernacular Bible and resistance to the church establishment. The epilogue to *Henry IV: 2* hinted that, though Falstaff might die in the next instalment, his death would not be one to foster further comparisons with Oldcastle: 'for anything I know, Falstaff shall die of a sweat . . . For Oldcastle died a martyr, and this is not the man.'[51] This was, of course, precisely the way to make the first audience of *Henry V* watch out for buried connections between the two. What they witnessed would have both frustrated and fulfilled expectations. Falstaff's death, if not that of a martyr, is at least that of a victim – Hostess Quickly diagnoses that 'The King hath killed his heart' (2.1.84) – and, as outlined above, it has exemplary elements, even though it concludes the least exemplary of lives.

On one level, this could be read simply as the witty exaggeration of a standard Protestant premise: that salvation and reprobation are entirely in God's gift, and not affected by man's endeavours. If a Falstaff can be saved, then God's decrees are indeed unsearchable, but it is not for man to question them. There may, though, be more going on. As Kristen Poole has shown, Falstaff's characterization owes much to contemporary satirical depictions of Puritans as gluttonous and sybaritic tavern-haunters.[52] These satires in turn point to the link perceived by non-Puritans between Puritanism and antinomianism: the notion that God's elect are above the law, which was believed to promote lawless behaviour. In satire as in real life, it was just as common for Puritans to come under attack for the opposite fault, an ostentatious preoccupation with godly behaviour and the visible signs of a Christian life. But this seeming contradictoriness results from an underlying similarity; both forms of anti-social behaviour could be seen by a hostile commentator as deriving from an over-emphasis on election, thought to be characteristic both of Puritanism and radical Christianity. Despite the hint of a more standard psychomachia in the Boy's recollection, 'A said once the devil would have him about women', Falstaff's death can be counted among the many ways that his character refracts ideas associated with radical religion. His faith in God appears to be testified to by Hostess Quickly; his repentance is not clearly shown; but if a belief in God's saving grace is sufficient for salvation, one's past life is irrelevant, and even repentance can be seen as unnecessary. So Falstaff's radical faith may bypass conventional repentance; alternatively, he may repent in a manner we do not see. Either way, this last phase of his life can be read as posing a suggestive, rather attractive contrast to the carefully planned, ultra-visible conversion of Hal, which can hardly be called repentance at all.

If so, though, it remains a highly discreet repentance by any standards, especially early-modern ones. As remarked above, it takes place just offstage; a turn to God is strongly hinted at, but is also deniable, especially as it is not witnessed first-hand by the audience. Thus, they are not confronted with the painful spectacle of Falstaff repenting everything that made him such a well-loved dramatic character in his prime. The religiously conscientious are allowed to imagine whatever they find comforting; others could have taken away from this scene the equally soothing feeling that if Falstaff can achieve a good death, anyone can.[53] The Hostess's comment 'I hoped there was no need to trouble himself with any such thoughts *yet*' reminds us how much could hang on the perceived efficaciousness of last-minute repentance;[54] after all, even those contemporaries of Shakespeare's who sat most lightly to conventional morality and religion would, in all but a tiny number of instances, have believed that the Christian heaven and hell existed. It fits with Shakespeare's abhorrence of the stereotypical that tropes associated with edifying deathbed scenes should be employed to send Falstaff, of all characters, to his heavenly home.

'MARRY, HOW TROPICALLY!': 'HAMLET' AND REAL-LIFE REPENTANCE

As this illustrates, Shakespeare often uses religious and moralistic matter to enhance the dramatic experience, and does not prevent a religiously scrupulous member of the audience from applying this personally; but his plays are also full of escape-clauses. While this undoubtedly widened their appeal in some directions, as well as helping them cross over to a secularized culture such as our own, it would have troubled anyone who felt that Christians could not take up the option of ignoring their own salvation. As most early-modern religious commentators would have seen it, one distinction between the unconverted and the regenerate was that the former would shy away from being reminded that their behaviour fell short of the Christian ideal, while the latter would welcome this.[55] Several commentators have recently, and rightly, compared the experience of listening to a sermon to that of watching a drama, but in this context the difference between the two genres stand out plainly. It would, of course, have been possible to sit through a sermon while ignoring any personal application it might have had. But the implicit contract between an early-modern preacher and his audience, hardly diminished by the element of compulsion in church-attendance, was that he spoke, and the congregation came, in the general expectation that his words were intended to effect moral and spiritual improvement. Moralism had a less integral function within professional drama; self-accusatory moralism would have been more of a minority taste than an outward-looking moralism which cast explicit blame on others; and so it is hardly surprising that Shakespeare wrote, wherever possible, to affirm a variety of behavioural choices.

But there were times when dramatic strictures hit home, especially when audience members witnessed a scene in a play analogous to their own sin. We shall never know how often this happened in private; in public the phenomenon was probably not common, judging by how often the same anecdotes recur. But the notion that it could happen was immensely important to the arguments of apologists for the theatre, who could also draw on such classical examples as Alexander of Pherae, whose unwillingness to be seen weeping at plays was legendary. Asserting that 'the high and excellent Tragedy, that openeth the greatest wounds, and showeth forth the ulcers that are covered with tissue . . . maketh kings fear to be tyrants', Sir Philip Sidney commented:

> how much it can move, Plutarch yieldeth a notable testimony of
> the abominable tyrant Alexander Pheraeus, from whose eyes a
> tragedy, well made and represented, drew abundance of tears,
> who without all pity had murdered infinite numbers, and some

of his own blood: so as he, that was not ashamed to make matters for tragedies, yet could not resist the sweet violence of a tragedy. And if it wrought no further good in him, it was that he, in despite of himself, withdrew himself from hearkening to that which might mollify his hardened heart.[56]

As Sidney clearly recognizes, this story describes a case where theatre ultimately failed to act as a moral scourge. Yet it did lend itself well to one conventional means of praising an affecting performance, the assertion that it would make evildoers repent. Describing a performance of *Richard III* acted at St John's College in Cambridge, Sir John Harington alludes to it, and his comment is paraphrased by Thomas Heywood in his *Apology for Actors*: 'had the tyrant Phaleris beheld [Richard's] bloody proceedings, it had mollified his heart, and made him relent at the sight of his inhumane massacres'.[57] It supports Heywood's argument that the drama can provide its audience with an array of edifying personal exemplars:

Art thou addicted to prodigality? envy? cruelty? perjury? flattery? or rage? Our scenes afford thee store of men to shape your lives by, who would be frugal, loving, gentle, trusty, without soothing, and in all things temperate. Wouldst thou be honorable? Just, friendly, moderate, devout, merciful, and loving concord? Thou mayest see many of their fates and ruins who have been dishonorable, unjust, false, gluttonous, sacrilegious, bloody-minded, and broachers of dissention. . . . What can sooner print the modesty in the souls of the wanton than by discovering unto them the monstrousness of their sin?

(p. 244)

Heywood clinches the case by citing two anecdotes of murderesses whose consciences were troubled by the plot of a play, to the point of making a public confession. One of these episodes was brought on by the play *The Four Sons of Aymon*, in which a virtuous labourer is killed by his less industrious fellows driving a nail into his skull; during a performance of this by a company of English players at Amsterdam, a woman suffered a breakdown, and was later found to have murdered her husband by similar means. The other occurred at King's Lynn in Nor-folk during a performance of the play *Friar Francis*, which concerned

> a woman who, insatiately doting on a young gentleman, had . . .
> murdered her husband, whose ghost haunted her, and at diverse
> times in her most solitary and private contemplations, in most
> horrid and fearful shapes, appeared and stood before her. As this
> was acted, a townswoman (till then of good estimation and
> report) finding her conscience (at this presentment) extremely
> troubled, suddenly screeched and cried out Oh my husband, my
> husband! I see the ghost of my husband fiercely threatening and
> menacing me. At which shrill and unexpected outcry, the people
> about her . . . inquired the reason of her clamour, when pres-ently, unurged, she told them that seven years ago she, to be
> possessed of such a gentleman . . . had poisoned her husband,
> whose fearful image presented it self in the shape of that ghost:
> whereupon the murderess was apprehended, before the Justices
> further examined, and by her voluntary confession after con-demned.

Heywood is evidently anxious to authenticate the story: 'That this is true, as well by the report of the actors as the records of the town, there are many eye-witnesses of this accident yet living, vocally to confirm it' (p. 245).[58] The anonymous play, *A Warning for Fair Women*, performed by Shakespeare's company in 1599, makes use of the incident, describing the murderess as 'ever haunted with her husbands ghost': she 'was so mooved with the sight thereof, / As she cryed out, the Play was made by her, / And openly confesst her husbands murder'.[59] The phrase 'the Play was made by her' vividly suggests shock at finding the workings of one's conscience externalized.

As a number of commentators have pointed out, the episode is echoed in the plot of *Hamlet*. When the travelling players visit Elsinore, Hamlet asks them to perform 'The Murder of Gonzago' – a play in their repertoire that bears an obvious resemblance to Claudius's murder of Old Hamlet – with an insertion by him; and he reflects at the conclusion of the scene:[60]

> Hum, I have heard
> That guilty creatures sitting at a play
> Have by the very cunning of the scene
> Been struck so to the soul that presently
> They have proclaimed their malefactions.
> For murder, though it have no tongue, will speak
> With most miraculous organ. . . .
> The play's the thing
> Wherein I'll catch the conscience of the King.
>
> (2.2.523–529, 539–540)[61]

During the play's performance, the following exchange takes place:

KING: What do you call the play?
HAMLET: *The Mousetrap.* Marry, how tropically! This play is the image of a murder done in Vienna. Gonzago is the duke's name, his wife Baptista. You shall see anon 'tis a knavish piece of work, but what of that? Your majesty and we that have free souls – it touches us not. Let the galled jade wince, our withers are unwrung.

> (3.2.230–236)

When Hamlet says 'Marry, how tropically!', he is explicitly asking the audience, on and off stage, to interpret the image as a moral commonplace – or, as he says, a trope.[62] The notion of mousetraps catching sinners would have been a natural metaphor for everyday life to yield, but it also carried reminiscences of St Augustine's aphorism *Muscipula diaboli, crux Domini* (The devil's mousetrap, the cross of the Lord); this poses the paradox that the cross, epitomizing human sin, is a mousetrap set for Christ by the devil, but that Christ's sacrifice has the effect of trapping the devil.[63] The trope, together with Hamlet's heavy irony in this scene, 'Let the galled jade wince, our withers are unwrung', draws attention to the exemplary function of drama in a way which seems gratuitous to those not in on the secret – but which, we infer, is shortly to aid Claudius's recognition that his crime has been discovered. When an actor pours poison in the duke's ear, mimicking the way in which Old Hamlet was done to death, Claudius may not leap up and confess his guilt, but he is obviously affected by the scene. Several aspects of his subsequent behaviour – his departure in confusion, and his subsequent plans to have Hamlet disposed of on a trip to England – could be explained as no more than his reaction at being discovered. But when, in Act 3.3, he confesses his fratricide to God in an abortive attempt at repentance, the audience are made aware that the king's conscience has been caught – however imperfectly and temporarily.

As William A. Ringler has commented, the fact that the mousetrap succeeds can be read as an intervention in contemporary debates about the legitimacy of theatre, but with significant qualifications: 'Shakespeare followed his contemporaries in asserting that a play was an image of truth, but he was also aware that knowledge of the right does not necessarily lead a person to righteousness.'[64] Like Alexander of Pherae, Claudius knows himself to be condemned by analogy, but the knowledge effects no long-term alteration of either man's behaviour. Conversely, Hamlet, who believes in the power of the theatre to bring about repentance, can be seen as falling victim to presupposition: he desists from taking his revenge on Claudius because he has no desire to kill him in the act of prayer, when he is 'fit and seasoned for his passage' (3.3.86). In making two fundamental mistakes – assuming Claudius is repentant, and leaping to conclusions about how someone troubled in conscience might behave – he himself has been caught in the mousetrap of the trope. As the audience later find out, Claudius's attempt to repent was unsuccessful: 'My words fly up, my thoughts remain below. / Words without thoughts never to heaven go' (97–98). The question of his eternal destination, if he had been killed by Hamlet at that juncture, is more complicated than Hamlet believes at the time, and is left hanging.

Just as Claudius's conscientious distress is imperfect, *The Mousetrap* is not a straightforwardly edifying example of a guilty conscience entrapped by a play – despite Hamlet's words, and despite the long history of commentators who have made the connection with occasions such as those described by Heywood. As a play deliberately staged to prick a particular conscience, *The Mousetrap* has less in common with these than it does with the staged re-enactments of murders enacted before suspects in the last chapter of an Agatha Christie novel – it is no coincidence that Christie used that title for what has become the longest-running play in London's West End.[65] In *Hamlet*, the villain is known and the mousetrap is set for him – with a few teeth left over for Gertrude – and this can only limit the moralistic relevance of both plays.[66] The off-stage audience, meanwhile, has it both ways. The fact that the play makes Claudius declare his guilt would have provided a powerful, if fictional, buttressing for theatre's apologists, but the device of a play-within-a-play dilutes this. The audience members, so far from being embroiled in the painful business of personal application, are in the supremely flattering, quasi-divine position of being able to predict the action and pass judgement on the wrongdoer, which would have played to antitheatricalists' suspicions that exemplary messages within plays were easy to shrug off.

William Prynne may even be referring specifically to the play-within-a-play in *Hamlet* when he writes: 'Yet beloved, you must know, that the Devill takes more by pleasures, then by feare. For why doth he daily set the Mouse-trap of Stage-playes, the madnesse of filthy studies and pleasures, but that he might take those whom he hath lost with those delights, and reioyce that he hath found that againe which he had lost?'[67] In picturing the mousetrap as set not for sin but by sin, Prynne shows how, like so many tropes, it could sustain two completely opposite meanings.[68] More broadly, the play in *Hamlet* would have fallen victim to the counter-arguments that antitheatricalists advanced against assertions that the theatre was edifying. These sometimes questioned its supposed ability to elicit repentance: in *M. Some Laid Open in his Coulers* (1589), a satirical Puritan tract attributed to Job Throckmorton, the speaker makes the following observation:

> I know right wel, that a godly man may even then be edified by
> the worde, when it is most blasphemed by a hellish mouth, and
> I knowe that a man may be edified some times & stroken with
> remorse upon the sight of some horrible murther, as he may
> also at on of these plaies, or Theater Spectacles, as some have
> not let to give out, *That they for their parts have bin more edified*

> *by a play then by all this preaching*: neverthelesse I hope no man
> of sence will say that either murther or blaspheming the worde
> of God, or the same word wretchedly prophaned in a play, is
> therefore an ordinarie meanes to edifie: And what warrant hath
> any man to seeke for Edification there where there is noe pro-
> mise he shall be edefied? Though the worde it selfe be an
> edefieng word, yet may not the Lord chuse whether it shall be
> an edifying word to us or no, especially when we make noe
> conscience of repairing thither, where we knowe before hand
> his holy ordinance is prophaned?

(p. 118)

This is part of the tract's broader argument about intentionality; later
on the author maintains that 'Noe popish Priest as a Priest, Noe Papist
as a Papist, Noe Witch as a Witch, did ever say the Lords prayer rightly
in his life . . . ' (p. 119). While God may choose to turn good out of
evil, this does not excuse those who speak holy or edifying matter in
the wrong spirit, or within a profane context. Thus, by asserting that
the theatrical medium was irredeemably corrupt, antitheatricalists
could trump the best card played by theatre's apologists.

   As already remarked, the incidents related by Heywood are unpre-
dicted and fortuitous reactions to episodes in secular drama, which
would have made them easier to explain away as an instance of God's
grace acting through a corrupt medium. But it might have been
harder for antitheatricalists to dismiss theatrical mousetraps with
deliberate designs on the conscience of the audience, especially when
these could and did have a more general application than the one in
Hamlet does. On the Continent, a play exactly contemporary to *Hamlet*
gained a reputation for bringing about conversions among audience
members: Jakob Bidermann's *Cenodoxus*, first staged at the Jesuit
College in Augsburg in 1602. The plot concerns a scholar who falls
prey to the sin of pride, and poses an interesting contrast to Marlowe's
Doctor Faustus.[69] Unlike Faustus, Cenodoxus lives a life that is outwardly virtuous, though dominated by hypocrisy and self-love. When
he dies, his corpse rises up three times, first announcing that he is
accused, then that he is sentenced and finally that he is damned; Bruno,

a witness of the miracle, is awed by what he sees, experiences a conversion and founds the Carthusian Order. Thanks to the polarizing of Cenodoxus and Bruno, the ending is a tragicomic one, combining horror and edification. In conjunction with the graphic scenes involving demons, and the suspenseful cross-cutting between Cenodoxus's funeral and his appearance at the heavenly tribunal, this seems to have had spectacular effects on contemporary audiences. The preface to the 1666 edition of the play describes the effect of one particular performance, staged in Munich in 1609: the jokes and laughter accomplished more good in a few hours than a hundred sermons – a point familiar to apologists for the theatre – while the spectators were numbed and silent during the final trial, as if they themselves were threatened with damnation. After the performance, fourteen men asked to make a retreat for the purpose of practising Ignatius Loyola's Spiritual Exercises, while the actor who played Cenodoxus was subsequently to join the Jesuits and lead an exemplary life in the order.[70]

Jesuit drama, with its often spectacular staging and unambiguous Counter-Reformation message, operated with an affective sophistication very different from Shakespeare's own – which is only one reason why a similar scene could never have taken place in Shakespeare's England. A play like The History of Purgatory, written in the same decade and discussed in the last chapter, does share the theme of judgement after death and the determination to involve the audience in the protagonist's trial, drawing on medieval traditions of stimulating the collective consciousness through drama. Yet since it was written for a besieged minority, performance conditions would have been much more constrained than for Bidermann's play – even assuming it was performed at all. The Munich and King's Lynn anecdotes, for all their differences, both relate to drama which is mainstream within their country, and both demonstrate an exceptional, newsworthy audience reaction to the power of dramatic narrative. But setting them side by side throws into relief the relative modesty of the claims made by the English writers who allude to the King's Lynn anecdote. Citing the confessions of murderesses demonstrated that theatre was edifying, but posed no real threat to the ferial experience; less spectacular sinners could sit back and enjoy themselves in the knowledge that their recreation was valid, a validity which was partly demonstrable through the fact that plays pricked other people's consciences. While *The Mousetrap* and its surrounding play can certainly be seen as an intervention in the debate between antitheatricalists and apologists for the theatre, it makes only limited use of the theatre's supposed moral efficacy. In Munich in 1609, Christ could appear on stage, condemning Cenodoxus, converting Bruno and sweeping up the audience in a dynamic process of contrition. In the London where *Hamlet* was first performed, a playwright would not have been free to use that subject-matter. Yet *Hamlet*'s play-within-a-play typifies the kind of liberation that resulted from English playwrights' lack of freedom to address religious topics. Scapegoating murderers had the effect of emancipating the rest of the audience, and their elevation from prisoner in the dock to jury member is never more evident than here.

SATIRE AND REPENTANCE: JAQUES AND THE CONVERTITES

The limited moral efficacy of fictional mousetraps with an outwardly directed, specific target is nowhere better demonstrated than in Henry Parrot's *The Mous-Trap* (1606). This is a collection of satirical epigrams referring to *Hamlet* in its title, like another from Parrot's pen, *Laquei Ridiculosi, or, Springes for Woodcocks* (1613).[71] As Parrot says in his dedicatory epistle, he is only concerned with small-time sinners: 'Alasse you see tis but the silly Mouse, I onely aime at, for any greater or more venomous vermine, I leave them altogether to the cunning Rat-catcher' (f. A3a). This throwaway attitude towards his subject-matter, publishing it on the one hand and trivializing it on the other, is by no means uncommon in Renaissance dedicatory material, but here forms part of a more complicated paratextual game which Parrot plays with his audience. In a rhyme to a hypothetical curious reader, imagining him asking 'And why the Mouse-trap . . . ?', Parrot replies that he only wishes to 'unfold by way of borrowed rime, / some few fantasticke humors of our time: / Wherein (if ought thats pleasing) may content thee / take it: If not, suppose no harme was meant thee . . . '

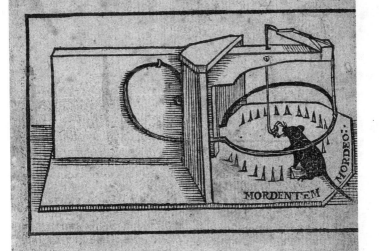

FIGURE 5   Henry Parrot, *The Mous-Trap* © The British Library Board,
4412.e.34.

(f. A4b). Conflating aesthetic pleasure with the condition of remaining unscathed by the satire, Parrot flatters his reader and promotes his own work by the assumption that only the vicious will be displeased by what he has to say. The possibility of readerly reform is only admitted obliquely at the end of the volume:

> Thus have I waded through a worthlesse taske,
> Whereto (I trust) ther's no exceptions tane:
> For (meant to none) I answer such as aske,
> 'tis like apparell made in *Birchin lane*.
> If any please to sute themselve and weare it,
> The blame's not mine, but theirs that needs will beare it . . .
>
> (f. F3a)[72]

This sartorial image extends the proverb 'If the cap fits, wear it', signalling general judgementalism but protecting the person passing judgement, if a specific individual takes exception to their satire. Birchin Lane, in the City of London, was a street where ready-made clothes were sold; the metaphor does not mean that the clothes are necessarily ill-fitting, merely that their fitting well can only be fortuitous.[73] Thus, Parrot acts as vendor to his verses, not ruling out the possibility that they might prove personally and morally efficacious, but presenting himself as dissociated from attempts to render them so. For a satirist, dependent on the condemnation of evil and folly, it is an uncomfortable posture to assume; given that Parrot does in fact attack specific individuals in his verse, it is a little disingenuous too.[74] But it epitomizes the satirist's difficulties, obliged as he is to scourge on the one hand and to please on the other.

All communicators, whether in speech or in writing, neglect at their peril the rhetorical obligation to please their audience. For some, satirists included, this brings about a tension with their generic obligations; among playwrights in this period, it is to Jonson rather than Shakespeare that one must look to see these tensions writ large.[75] In particular, any satirical writer who gained financial benefit, however slight, from having his work publicly disseminated would have been pulled in two directions.[76] Yet while stroking one's audience the right way was only prudent for authors wanting that audience's cash or approval, one cannot take a crudely market-driven approach to the trade-off between punishment and pleasure. Many best-selling moralistic tracts chastised the reader, and for well-affected listeners, the judgementalism of sermons was an essential part of their appeal – though the fact that sermons were either free or financed by those with a taste for inwardly directed moral rigour would have given preachers a freer hand than most.[77] For every literary genre, tracts and sermons included, laws relating to libel and slander would have limited one's ability to bring specific offenders to book, and led authors to rely on indirect statement and readerly inference if they wished to make *ad hominem* comments. This could, and sometimes did, encourage a move from particular to general condemnation, in which the reader was potentially implicated. But for genres such as satire, the scourging of other individuals – sometimes real, sometimes blatantly imaginary – was all part of pleasing and flattering one's respondent, often encouraging the assumption that those under attack formed no part of the interpretive community. Thus, the opposition is less between flattering and scourging, more between genres which draw attention to the reader's own imperfections and those which are more outwardly directed. Satire and drama, closely related in so many ways, are both guaranteed to please those with a keener eye for other people's flaws than their own.

Thus, despite the fact that satire's declared aim is to change people's behaviour, its relationship with the idea of conversion is a difficult one, simply because the two are so akin. No one confronts this more directly than John Donne in his Satire III, a poem whose familiarity may lead to an underestimation of its unusualness in the context of its time. If the satiric stance depends on being outwardly directed, Satire III breaks the mould. Its speaker gives us Theophrastean portraits of those whose religion is deficient, and withholds a ruling on what religion is the right one, yet enlists his audience in the struggle to find out: 'On a huge hill, / Cragged, and steep, Truth stands, and he that will / Reach her, about must, and about must go.'[78] Though scepticism is often a bystander's position, it here becomes a reason to join in the climb, since the speaker's survey of alternatives is strictly provisional: of religion, he says: 'unmoved thou / Of force must one, and forced but one allow, / And the right' (69–71). While specific directions on conversion are lacking, the idea of conversion is central to the endeavour, making it easy to see why Satire III has been so much discussed by those who see Donne's own move from Catholicism to the Church of England as central to his writing.[79]

Shakespeare's most sophisticated satirist, Jaques, adopts a similar position at the end of *As You Like It*.[80] On hearing from his namesake Jaques de Boys that Duke Frederick has been converted by an 'old religious man', Jaques asks him, 'If I heard you rightly / The Duke hath put on a religious life / And thrown into neglect the pompous Court'. Receiving a reply in the affirmative, he declares: 'To him will I; out of these convertites / There is much matter to be heard and learned' (5.4.158, 178–180, 182–183). The word 'convertite' has a number of distinctive overtones at this date, denoting conversion to religion in general as well as the religious life in particular. In a sermon printed around three decades after *As You Like It* was first performed, Lancelot Andrewes wrote: 'We condemne not *Conversus sum in aerumnâ:*[81] Many are so turned; and GOD is gracious and rejects them not. But, we commend . . . that man, . . . who being under no arrest, no bridle in his jawes, shall in the dayes of his peace, resolve of a time to turne in, and take it; . . . And thus much for *Convertite.*'[82] Andrewes is punning, here and throughout his sermon, on the noun 'convertite' and *convertite*, the plural imperative form of the Latin verb, reminding his audience how the spectacle of someone publicly turning towards God could act as an exhortation. Looking at Andrewes's emphases makes it easier to identify Shakespeare's gaps: we never get the chance to see Duke Frederick in his regenerate condition, and no audience-directed imperatives arise from Jaques's proposed sojourn with religious men. Jaques remains outwardly directed to the last in his mock-bequests to members of the assembly, some of which have a satirical edge: for instance, he bequeaths the recently partnered Touchstone to 'wrangling, for thy loving voyage / Is but for two months victualled' (5.4.189–190).[83] Since these bequests come immediately after Jaques has announced his future plans, they have, among much else, the effect of fending off queries.

Another facet of the convertite's persona could be the public repudiation of a licentious former life.[84] In this connection, one remembers

the earlier scene in which Duke Senior, a figure of considerable moral
authority throughout the play, accuses Jaques of being 'a libertine /
As sensual as the brutish sting itself' (2.7.65–66). While Jaques immediately – and characteristically – goes on the attack, he does not deny
the charge, and perhaps we are expected to assume that he has
something to repent.[85] What he does say deserves to be looked at in
more detail. Continuing to explain to Jaques why he is unworthy to be
a satirist, Duke Senior declares that 'all th'embossed sores and headed
evils / That thou with licence of free foot hast caught / Wouldst thou
disgorge into the general world' (2.7.67–69). This damagingly identifies the satirist's perennial problem, how he can present himself as
knowledgeable about sin but untainted by it, and pins Jaques into a
corner. Jaques does not – and, if Duke Senior's accusations are true,
cannot – reply along Martial's lines, 'What I write is impudent but my
life is upright'.[86] Instead, he chooses to redirect the debate:

> Why, who cries out on pride
> That can therein tax any private party?
> Doth it not flow as hugely as the sea
> Till that the weary very means do ebb?
> What woman in the city do I name,
> When that I say the city-woman bears
> The cost of princes on unworthy shoulders?
> Who can come in and say that I mean her,
> When such a one as she, such is her neighbour?
> Or what is he of basest function,
> That says his bravery is not on my cost –
> Thinking that I mean him – but therein suits
> His folly to the mettle of my speech?
> There then – how then, what then? Let me see wherein
> My tongue hath wronged him. If it do him right,
> Then he hath wronged himself. If he be free,
> Why then my taxing like a wild goose flies
> Unclaimed of any man.

(2.7.70–87)

Though this speech is a bravura response to Duke Senior's accusation, it is no sort of an answer – as the audience is surely expected to notice. Orlando's unexpected arrival is fortuitous from Jaques's point of view, preventing any challenge from his on-stage companions. His attempt to move the debate away from the potentially embarrassing topic of the satirist's fitness to criticize others, and towards the satirist's standard assertion that he is identifying general trends rather than criticizing specific individuals, can be read as a little disingenuous off-stage as well; Richard McCabe has suggested that the ease of identifying individuals in satire prompted the Bishops' Ban of June 1599, around the time the play was written.[87] Still, it hints suggestively at the moral limits of satire.

If satire is effective in identifying faults and presenting them as loathsome, Jaques's speech shows how its aims then diverge from religious discourse. Anyone who thinks he is being personally criticized not only identifies himself as contemptible, but as 'of basest function', with attendant implications of unsophisticated literal-mindedness. Since seeing oneself in a satirical representation is tantamount to identifying inadmissible comment, the satirist has every interest in saying that only knaves and fools would do so. In any case this is dangerously incomplete as an exemplary stance, since the assumption is that one will be angry, rather than contrite, at having one's faults pointed out. Thus, in a nod to its pre-Christian origins, satire inverts conversion: the more you can avoid self-accusation, the more virtuous you are. General accusation, which acts as a public call to repentance in medieval drama, here has the effect – latent even in the earlier period – of giving each individual member of the audience an excuse not to repent personally. This also has the effect of strengthening the satirist's case, by making it appear that vice is so widely diffused that it would be pointless to accuse any one individual; as Jaques says, no city woman can say she is being specifically criticized when they are all as bad as each other.

Jaques's speech is ironic, and nowhere more so than where he identifies the faultlines of satire. When he says, 'who cries out on pride / That *can* therein tax any private party?', there is considerable virtue in the verb: not only because of censorship difficulties, but because certain courtesies are due to a paying audience.[88] Elsewhere, he describes himself as 'ambitious for a motley coat' (2.7.43); the assumption that fools had more liberty than wise men to utter sharp criticism derives from the jester's role in early modern courts, and again is a way of flattering the audience members, making them comparable to royalty.[89] But as an earlier speech by Jaques makes clear, while a motley coat invites derision, it is also a way of making the satirist unassailable:

> I must have liberty
> Withal, as large a charter as the wind
> To blow on whom I please, for so fools have,
> And they that are most galled with my folly,
> They most must laugh. And why, sir, must they so?
> The why is plain as way to parish church.
> He that a fool doth very wisely hit
> Doth very foolishly, although he smart,
> Not to seem senseless of the bob. If not,
> The wise man's folly is anatomized
> Even by the squandering glances of the fool.
>
> (2.7.47–57)

Appropriating for himself the liberties of the Holy Spirit – 'The winde bloweth where it listeth, & thou hearest the sounde thereof' (John 3:8) – Jaques is claiming a God-given right to speak as he wishes. His simile, 'The why is plain as way to parish church', draws mischievous attention to the similarities between the roles of satirist and preacher. Certainly, the vigorous and imaginative abuse of many preachers exploits the common ground between a satire and a sermon. Yet the differences between the genres are even more palpable, and have to do, more than anything, with the role taken on by the speaker. A preacher's job was to speak as the Spirit moved him and turn his congregation from sin, but edification appears to figure less highly on Jaques's agenda than the exercise of literary power for its own sake. Correction administered by inference and privately received was nevertheless still an option. As the verb 'seem' makes clear, while a wise man does not evince any sign that a fool's satirical barb has hit home, it is still open to him to take the fool's lesson on board without appearing to; the passage's criticisms all relate to people who make the mistake of confessing their own similarity to satirical characters. In other words, one can respond to satire in an exemplary manner, but only if one does not let one's response show, and if the satirist is not identified as intending personal criticism. Again, this can be interpreted as an advance in courtesy. But like the fool's coat, it is also a practical way of muting the satirist's theoretical claim to act as moral arbiter, protecting him from such criticisms as Duke Senior's – which is perhaps why, after all, Jaques does not need to respond to the Duke.

At the end of the play, we cannot assume that Jaques has been converted as Andrewes, or another religious writer, would have defined conversion. He only presents himself as wishing to hear and learn from the convertites – a modern analogy would be going on a retreat – and while there is a possibility that he has turned his criticisms inward and is seeking to amend his own life, we never know for sure. Like the speaker of Satire III, he defers commitment; unlike that speaker, he does not explain his reasons, and remains private to the last. As with Falstaff, we are given the option of assuming that repentance might have happened off-stage, but the dramatist's gaze is turned away. As on so many other occasions when religious conversion is hinted at, Shakespeare swivels the character in question towards a secular exit. The secularist assumption that religion is a private matter is most often invoked in early-modern studies as a means of charting the move towards freedom of worship, but perhaps it should be extended to identify moments like this: the shielding of a character's soul from public inspection, which in turn lifts the auditor's obligation to embrace repentance or be reminded of his unregeneracy.[90]

MOTES, BEAMS AND APPLICATION: 'MEASURE FOR MEASURE'

What has been said about satire above is also more broadly true of how human imperfection was depicted in the drama of Shakespeare's time. This era saw a number of spectacular developments in the theatre: a move away from religious allegory, the liberty to dramatize a range of stories which had minimal or no relevance to Christianity, and rapid technical advance in the psychological depiction of individual characters. All these maximized points of divergence from an auditor, weakening if not destroying their edifying function. While this drama played to an audience well versed in Christianized moral discriminations, it made outwardly directed judgementalism compulsory and self-examination optional. Its allurement, and for some its danger, was that it maximized the pleasures of moralism while minimizing its impertinences, bringing with it the freedom not to be exhorted, challenged and changed. One can speculate – if nothing more – that this change of direction was due to the conditions of the professional theatre, which had every interest in treating its audience members like the patrons they were.

As this chapter has already suggested, moralistic tracts urging the need for repentance would have figured prominently in any best-seller lists of the time. But in the disengagements, tactfulnesses and voids by which Shakespeare defers to the sagacity of a paying audience, one can see a distinctive appetite being born, and a new product created: popular then, dominant now. While it is not impossible to identify elements of crossover between drama and sermon, it is not surprising either that, in this period, literature generated by the professional theatre should differ so much from religious literature. The printing press, and the rise of the professional playhouses, helped to give Englishmen a more differentiated choice of textual experiences than they had ever had, which in turn would have freed the hands of playwrights whose primary imaginative interests lay elsewhere. One reason why explicit religious self-interrogation was kept to a minimum in the professional drama of the English Renaissance may have been because those who liked it were well catered for by other literary genres, and those whose spirituality did not take that form would not be repelled. On the other hand, maximizing the pleasures of outwardly directed judgementalism while forgoing the pains of self-interrogation would surely have increased the attractiveness of drama for those unwilling to undergo self-accusation, and have provided a ferial experience for many of the pious; if so, the antitheatricalists would have had a point on both counts.

Yet even if this would have limited the drama's value for some of Shakespeare's contemporaries, it is possible to identify other, more religiously positive functions of moralism which would have been as powerful in drama as elsewhere. Since after the Reformation there was much broader agreement on how a Christian should live than on what a Christian should believe, moralism could act as a means of ecumenical bonding, and was also a way to get the best out of non-Christian cultures. Shakespeare's era was particularly well aware of the common ground between classical stoicism and Christianity.[91] But an emphasis on virtuous action rather than orthodox belief would have troubled those alert to Pelagianism, the heretical notion that one could be saved through one's own attempts rather than through Christ's sacrifice. A kind of practical Pelagianism was, it is true, intrinsic to Renaissance scholarship and imaginative writing: as Debora Shuger has pointed out, the notion of 'religious literature' was not a familiar one to practitioners of humanist poetics, who 'valued "poesie" for its ethical rather than redemptive force'.[92] If drama was criticized for valorizing virtue in isolation from Christian repentance, the same would have been true of the educational curriculum in general; even in an age when *sola scriptura* was so often invoked, the notion that education ought to comprise nothing but the Bible and other Christian texts was one which would have been thought suitable only for the lower orders. It may, indeed, be possible to see the criticisms levelled against drama as a kind of scapegoating which identified, but occluded, a wider problem: the tainted nature of scholarship for the Christian. At a popular rather than an academic level, Ian Green has identified semi-Pelagian tendencies at this period within the 'great majority' of ballads and 'penny godlies', religious chapbooks intended for the semi-literate.[93] As Green remarks, such texts were very much at odds with attempts, made by Puritans and non-Puritans alike, to improve lay ignorance through cheap print. But, like drama, they were a readily available, popular source of moralistic example; and though Green does not discuss drama, the notion of semi-Pelagianism can be carried over to that genre wherever it emphasizes good and bad deeds and public accountability.[94]

One consequence of this accountability, as suggested above, is to allow the audience of a play to attack, defend and judge the on-stage

sinners. Eavesdropping on a whole dramatic world, Shakespeare's audience is quasi-divine; but in fostering judgementalism within its audience while postponing a last judgement, Shakespeare's drama
illustrates a deference and a paradox which are both scriptural in
origin. At any period, trying to live by Christian principles necessitates
moral discrimination and provisional condemnation, as one measures
everyday human conduct against the standard set by Christ and the
saints; but the obligation to practise charity is often interpreted as
enjoining tolerance, and in reminding the reader to 'judge not, that ye
be not judged', the Bible refers all final judgements to God. Even so,
provided that one acknowledged God's goodness in forgiving sin,
adverse self-judgement was encouraged within all the Christian traditions that Shakespeare would have known. The passage of the New
Testament from which the above text is taken, Christ's Sermon on the
Mount, makes explicit the link between charity towards others and
rigorousness towards oneself: 'For with what judgement ye judge, ye
shal be judged, and with what measure ye mette, it shall be measured
to you againe. And why seest thou the mote, that is in thy brothers
eye, and perceivest not the beame that is in thine owne eye?'[95]

Shakespeare knew this passage well enough to source the title of a
play from it: a play that this chapter will conclude by briefly discussing. Perhaps Shakespeare's richest venture into moralistic discourse,
Measure for Measure brings together many themes that have figured
above. Like bellmen, the Duke and his deputies bring dark deeds to
light, and the condemned characters show an unpreparedness for
death which recalls Richard II's. Like Hamlet, the Duke makes the
guilty parties aware that their crimes are known. In the same scene,
the play's denouement, he undermines the would-be satirist Lucio by
asserting that his slurs are unfounded (5.1.326–354, 503–510). As this
indicates, the Duke is the play's primary means of conveying judgement and admonition. Acting the part of a friar for most of the play,
he unmasks villains *in propria persona* and rises to the challenge of
tempering justice with mercy. As Debora Shuger has pointed out, his
character embodies some early modern notions of sacral kingship.[96]
But merely as an individual, he is not above criticism: either in his
implementation of the bed-trick or in permitting Vienna to develop a

sordid moral climate in the first place. Throughout the play, his world-
view is governed less by consistent ideals than by pragmatic responses
to a given situation: sometimes pious, sometimes looking no further
than casuistical advantage or pagan moralism. His exhortation to
Claudio in Act 3.1, 'Be absolute for death . . . What's in this / That
bears the name of life? Yet in this life / Lie hid mo thousand deaths;
yet death we fear, / That makes these odds all even' (5, 38–41) embodies
a stoicism untempered by Christian hope. Ironically, it is Claudio, not
the Duke, who introduces the notion of immortality in his response: 'I
humbly thank you. / To sue to live, I find I seek to die, / And seeking
death, find life. Let it come on' (41–43).[97]

But while the Duke's counsel comes strangely from someone posing
as a priest, there was nothing to stop laymen giving spiritual advice.
Sacraments, on the other hand, were reserved for priests to administer,
and the Duke's comment on Mariana, 'I have confessed her, and I
know her virtue' (5.1.519) tells us that – off-stage at least – he has
illicitly deployed at least one. The third scene of the play, in which he
converses with a friar, shows him exploiting the sacrament of
confession in a different way. Admitting that the friar will want to
know why he has been asked to give the duke 'secret harbour', he
says, 'Now, pious sir, / You will demand of me why I do this', and the
friar answers, 'Gladly, my lord' (1.3.4, 16–18). This exchange is one
worth pausing upon. In isolation the Duke's remark could be read
merely as acknowledging the friar's natural curiosity; but the friar's
response, 'Gladly, my lord', combined with the confessional tone of the
Duke's next speech, points up its other implication: the Duke is
invoking the friar's priestly role, and all but commanding him to act
as confessor. As he goes on to say:

> We have strict statutes and most biting laws,
> The needful bits and curbs to headstrong weeds,
> Which for this fourteen years we have let slip, . . .
>   Now, as fond fathers,
> Having bound up the threatening twigs of birch,
> Only to stick it in their children's sight
> For terror, not to use, in time the rod

> Becomes more mocked than feared; so our decrees,
> Dead to infliction, to themselves are dead,
> And liberty plucks justice by the nose,
> The baby beats the nurse, and quite athwart
> Goes all decorum.
>
>   (19–21, 23–31)

Even in the context of this quasi-confession, the Duke's language initially shirks full acknowledgement of personal responsibility and repentance. The ducal 'we' has the effect of spreading blame for this undesirable state of affairs; the flesh given to the abstract personifications Liberty and Justice has the effect of granting them autonomy too, suggesting that they are somehow beyond human control.[98] The friar intervenes, with an unmistakable though appropriately decorous reproof: 'It rested in your grace / To unloose this tied-up justice when you pleased' (31–32). The Duke's response is simultaneously frank and shifty, combining a sense of personal unfitness with a Machiavellian wish to divert resentment onto another.

> Sith 'twas my fault to give the people scope,
> 'Twould be my tyranny to strike and gall them
> For what I bid them do; for we bid this be done,
> When evil deeds have their permissive pass
> And not the punishment. Therefore, indeed, my father,
> I have on Angelo imposed the office,
> Who may in the ambush of my name strike home,
> And yet my nature never in the fight
> To do in slander.
>
>   (35–43)

Our unease at the Duke's employment of a hatchet-man should not mean that we ignore the element of real self-accusation here. The friar's reminder that he has misused authority has the effect of making him fully acknowledge his sin, even to the point of over-scrupulousness. In a distinction which would have been familiar within the Catholic environment of the play as well as in the early Stuart

Church of England, his has been a sin of omission rather than commission, but his gloss of the word 'bid' denies any difference between the two: 'we bid this be done / When evil deeds have their permissive pass / And not the punishment.'[99] But the Duke's penitential discourse has clearly defined limits. As a pious ruler, he wishes to confide his former wrongdoing to a representative of the church; as an absolute one, he states his future intentions to that representative rather than asking for guidance. Since the scene ends here, we never get to hear the friar's response; we may be intended to interpret the line 'Mo reasons for this action / At our more leisure shall I render you' (48–49) as the Duke's response to his enquiring demeanour, forestalling further queries for the time being. But a half-confession, after all, need receive no kind of absolution, and in temporal terms no friar is in a position to question a duke's proposed actions. While the Duke exploits the Church's spiritual facilities, he is not ultimately answerable to it; the play is set in Catholic Vienna, but his Erastian practices may constitute an oblique satire on the monarch's headship of the Church of England. On a more personal level, the scene encourages us to think both better and worse of the Duke; his admission of past weaknesses and miscalculations gives him greater spiritual authority, yet exposes him to adverse criticism almost as much as his doubtful means of amendment.

Here as throughout the play, the audience's voyeuristic role removes any element of reciprocity from the penitential process. Its members are, of course, not guilty of the specific sins committed by the characters, but they are not prompted either to use them for self-examination. It is no coincidence that the play's most blatant acknowledgement of general sinfulness comes in the context of a plea for tolerance, Isabella's fiery defence of her brother to Angelo: 'Who is it that hath died for this offence? / There's many have committed it' (2.2.89–90). It is the kind of moment where auditors are jolted into speculating about the sex-lives of the people next to them, and forced to remember any past lapses of their own. But even so, the context is anything but condemnatory. Isabella's remark can be approved both from the moral high ground and outside it, a circumstance foreseen and undercut by the staging of the scene. Lucio, a concealed onstage auditor of

Isabella's tirade, interjects an enthusiastic aside, 'Ay, well said' (90), which, coming from a notorious fornicator, suggests a response along the lines of, 'He would say that, wouldn't he?' Meanwhile, auditors whose consciences might be pricked are immediately presented with a series of excuses: that fornication is common, that Claudio is plainly undeserving of extreme punishment and that even the spotless Isabella is pleading for mercy towards him.

Measure for Measure is surely one of the era's most sophisticated meditations on penance, but at no point does it turn to the audience and ask them to participate in the penitential process. A play like *Everyman* takes a position standard within Christian moralism – that human weakness is universal – and uses it for admonitory effect. But Shakespeare, like most of his contemporaries in the Elizabethan and early Stuart professional theatre, has more to say about human weakness within the play than outside – an emphasis which may be inseparable from inviting audience members to evaluate and judge what they see in front of them. Relating developments in Elizabethan theatre to the practice of trial by jury, Lorna Hutson has made a distinction between medieval 'sacramental theater . . . concerned with the audience's experiencing feelings of complicity in human guilt, which lead to feelings of contrition and renewed community', and 'mimetic Renaissance drama' which 'invites the audience to speculate on and evaluate the motives and intentions embodied by actors as *dramatis personae*'.[100] Analogously, Ruth Lunney has suggested that throughout the period Shakespeare was writing, audiences were increasingly being invited to assess not whether characters should act in a certain way, but instead why they acted as they did.[101] While both these approaches do much to illustrate the changing priorities of English Renaissance drama, it may be more helpful still to develop a model that reminds us how 'complicity in human guilt' continued to be embodied in other, popular literary genres, and how drama's comparative lack of reproachfulness could taint the entire medium. As we have already seen, some contemporary commentators disliked the drama of Shakespeare's time, and Shakespeare's drama in particular, for not explicitly reminding respondents of their own weakness and need for God's grace. Opprobrious and exhortatory moral messages do feature in Shakespeare's plays; those watching or reading are seldom actively prevented from applying those messages to themselves, but they are not explicitly encouraged to do so, and are certainly not ordered to. If the cap fits, one is at liberty to wear it, but there is no overt suggestion that one should try it on.

Cornelius Burges is only one moralist who compared playwrights to preachers who failed to apply their doctrine, for fear of offending their hearers: 'It is rather for a Parasite upon the Stage than a Divine in the Pulpit to flatter thus. *I need not to apply. I know your wisdome and discretion. I leave it to your godly care to make the application. I need not to exhort* &c. when many times he knowes too well his hearers are too farre from such a care.'[102] Burges is referring to a common distinction between general and personal application, general application being a speaker's request that all his hearers should examine their consciences concerning a particular vice, while personal application involved strong personalized hints or naming and shaming. The notion that characters within a drama could be deployed to invite personal application was a familiar and sensitive one in early-modern England. Of recent years it has most often been considered in relation to censorship, and the interface between drama and politics: both areas where *ad hominem* criticism would typically have dealt with the highest in the land.[103] But it may be helpful to turn the spotlight away from them and onto more ordinary theatregoers: those too unimportant to elicit personal criticism, who were now not even being addressed as sinners *en masse*. Burges's antitheatrical complaint points to a quintessentially post-Reformation situation, and if anything, he underestimates the move away from moral application that professional drama helped to bring about.

While one must never underestimate Shakespeare's debt to medieval theatre, the sophisticated character differentiation that he brought to the drama of his time can be seen as tending away from it. On the one hand, it drew on the excitements of personal application while minimizing its dangers; on the other, it downplayed general admonition, accentuating the distance between the judging audience and the fallible people on stage. It is precisely the vacuousness of Everyman that makes him hard for the audience to escape.[104] But one can embody a vice in a dramatic character while not asking for either general or personal application from the audience, and this is Shakespeare's most common technique by far. Though dramatic representations of sin and weakness abound, they are realized in a highly specific manner: Iago, so reminiscent of the medieval Vice, is also embodied as a resident of Venice, and this has the effect of containing the allegorical character's search for a host. Shakespeare was not, of course, the only writer whose work reflects this trend. But his work epitomizes how between the medieval and early-modern eras, mainstream drama was transformed from a lively and attractive realization of the call to repentance, into an opportunity for audience members to judge others, while bypassing if they chose the personal summons to conversion still ubiquitous in many other genres. In his play *The Conflict of Conscience* [1570–1581], Nathaniel Woodes shows a prophetic awareness of this difficulty. This drama, which can be seen as a half-way house between earlier morality plays and Shakespearian theatre, was explicitly inspired by the religious fluctuations of a real-life individual, Francisco Spira, but Woodes decided nevertheless to widen its moral relevance by giving his protagonist the allegorical name 'Philologus': 'Againe, nowe shall it styrre him more, who shall it heare or see, / For if that SPERA had ben one, we would strayght deeme in mynde, / That all by SPERA spoken were, our selves we would not finde.'[105]

Still, choice can work both ways, as Debora Shuger's *Political Theologies in Shakespeare's England* (2001) has demonstrated in recent years. This book-length discussion of *Measure for Measure*, which asks what lessons politicians can learn from the play's staging of reconciliation, advocates a way of reading which is thoroughly Renaissance in inspiration: the study of fictional exemplars for what they might tell us about virtuous living.[106] Though Martha Nussbaum, among others, has recently posed similar questions in discussing the relationship between literature and ethics, Shuger's stance is unusual within current mainstream literary-critical discourse.[107] But at this or any period, Shakespeare's drama can stimulate readers interested, like her, in exploring the workings of Christianized self-examination and contrition, or concerned with more secular forms of public reconciliation and personal self-knowledge. All the same, the initiative has to come from them; Shakespeare's distance from his medieval predecessors is nowhere more pronounced than in his lack of moral directiveness. So this chapter will end by posing a series of questions. The common assumption that didacticism and literary sophistication are incompatible deserves a critique more prolonged than it can receive here. But, if nothing else, should we pause and think before automatically preferring Shakespeare's dramatic tactics to, say, the author of *Everyman*'s? How far is it greater literary expertise that prompts our preference, how far a dislike of being exhorted? Professional critics, in particular, need to be careful that they do not praise Shakespeare's skill and judgement simply because he shows such respect for theirs. Is there, indeed, something troubling about a writer who motions his audience to a seat outside the forum of moralistic interchange, and about a critical body that has taken up this invitation to voyeurism so readily? 'Hypocrite, first cast out the beame out of thine owne eye, and then shalt thou se clearely to cast out the mote out of thy brothers eye.'[108] Often enough, Shakespeare's deployment of moralism has been morally inspirational; yet it also allows his audiences, if they choose, to practise a kind of hypocrisy.

Chapter Four

PROVIDENCE, FATE
AND PREDESTINATION:
FROM TRAGEDY TO TRAGICOMEDY

A Gentleman falling off his horse brake his necke, which sod-
daine hap gave occasion of much speech of his former life, and
some in this judging world, judged the worst. In which respect a
good friend made this good Epitaph, remembring of S. Augustin.
Miserecordia Domini inter pontem et fontem.[1]

> My friend judge not me,
> Thou seest I judge not thee:
> Between the stirrop and the ground,
> Mercy I askt, mercy I found.[2]

This quatrain, recorded in the collections of the antiquarian
William Camden, does something similar to *Measure for Measure* in
reiterating the Sermon on the Mount's warning 'Judge not, that ye be
not judged', and affirming the notion that sudden and invisible repentance could be acceptable to God. In the process, it condemns the kind
of providentialist gossip that interpreted accidental death as God's
judgement on an evil life.[3] But though it is orthodox to assert God's
boundless mercy, the epitaph would never have been written if the
death it commemorated had not thrown up hard questions about the
destination of the victim's soul. In the aftermath of the English

Reformation, authors working in genres that depicted or threatened violent and sudden death were similarly alive to the religious implications of their plots. In exploring Shakespeare's use of the classical notion of fate, and the Christian ideas of providence and predestination, this chapter will read a selection of his later plays in the light of early-seventeenth-century theological anxieties.

DETERMINISM AND FREE WILL
IN THE RENAISSANCE

'Is the individual a rigidly defined link in a universal chain of being in which birth, life and death have been entirely pre-ordained by physical cosmic forces? Or can the individual control his life and, by means of more or less independent decisions, direct it to some consciously chosen goal?'[4] One of Renaissance philosophy's most central questions, handed down from the ancient world, was complicated at the time of the Reformation by sharp denominational differences among Christians on the topics of predestination and free will.[5] Posed in more secular terms, the problem continues to resonate in our own age. While neo-Darwinian writers like Richard Dawkins pursue a hard-line genetic determinism and sociologists continue to foreground the importance of environment, intellectual positions which acknowledge the influence of both internal and external factors on the individual are likely to command the widest assent. Recent advances in the study of genetics have seen to it that the third millennium has begun in a deterministic mood. Still, within a society more meritocratic than any in the early-modern world, the idea that success or failure is largely down to individual motivation is one which has far more impact on day-to-day behaviour than a consciousness of genes or environment.

When Cassius declares in *Julius Caesar*, 'Men at some time are masters of their fates. / The fault, dear Brutus, is not in our stars / But in ourselves, that we are underlings' (1.2.138–140) his statement has a similar self-help quality. He is alluding to, and dismissing, the belief in astrology that some of Shakespeare's original audience would have shared, and all would have recognized as a powerful metaphor for factors outside an individual's control. Over the course of the play, though, he comes to believe that prognostications may be valid: in Act 5 Scene 1, just before the battle at Philippi in which he is killed, he describes how the eagles which have accompanied his regiment so far have been replaced by birds of worse omen, 'ravens, crows, and kites', and despondently admits, 'You know that I held Epicurus strong / And his opinion: now I change my mind / And partly credit things that do presage' (84, 76–78).[6] As with the move from scepticism to belief experienced by Horatio in *Hamlet* after he has seen the ghost of Hamlet's father, this is a metatheatrical nod to the idea that anything can happen within drama: it is no coincidence that Horatio's words remind us of the earlier play when he describes the supernatural portents before Caesar's assassination.[7] But Cassius's change of heart also has implications crucial for the plot, heralding the blend of self-will and fatalism that characterizes him for the rest of his life. Seeing things go badly for his side in the battle, he determines that his birthday shall also be his death-day – 'Time is come round; / And where I did begin, there shall I end' (5.3.23–24) – and commits suicide by getting Pindarus, his slave, to stab him. Thus, he contrives both to die both at the hands of another and in a self-determined way. Pindarus has been promised his freedom if he carries out Cassius's demand, and after the deed has been done, reflects: 'So, I am free; yet would not so have been / Durst I have done my will' (5.3.47–48).

His comment, while highlighting the way in which the episode polarizes freedom and constraint, also poses questions about the limits of human agency. Cassius has certainly taken matters into his own hands: but is he simply pre-empting inevitable death at the hands of the opposing forces? – might things have been different if he had not given way to despair? – or is his death simply, at this point, written in the stars? He is not the only major character of Shakespeare's to provoke such speculations. We are used to thinking of tragedy as being precipitated by a combination of dire external circumstances and aspects of a hero's own personality – not necessarily negative ones – and much Shakespeare criticism has been an attempt to determine the exact interplay of the two. A differentiation between outward and inward factors, and a feeling that the latter are more within an individual's control, are easy default positions to adopt in literary criticism. But believing that autonomy is within one's power is not, of course, the same thing as being autonomous. Richard III's self-characterization, 'I am determinèd to prove a villain' (1.1.30), illustrates how the idea of personal autonomy was a double-edged one in Shakespeare's age; it can be read as expressing a conscious and willing embrace of villainy, but also as meaning that Richard's behaviour has been predetermined by the powers that gave him a misshapen body and a malevolent mind. Both meanings would be in character; both have a striking implicit relevance to one of the most divisive issues of the Reformation, the exact relationship of providence, predestination, fortune and fate.

Providence is the way in which Christians interpret natural phenomena and the vicissitudes of individual human lives and collective entities – countries, churches or families – as part of God's divine plan for the world. In Shakespeare's time, there was a consensus among orthodox Christians that they lived in a providential universe, even though considerable debate occurred over whether providence operated on humankind mainly through its primary cause, God, or secondary agents such as nature.[8] Since Puritans were likely to de-emphasize natural causes for events while stressing divine immanence and God's direct intervention in human life, one's stance on these questions would partly have depended on churchmanship. But across the board, it was – and indeed had to be – a versatile instrument for justifying divine activity. Ill-fortune to one's enemies could be seen as providential, while one was obliged to read the same ill-fortune as purging sin and testing the sinner when it happened to oneself. As this indicates, providence was a more uniformly optimistic idea than either predestination or fate, because of the notion that divine justice existed and would be implemented in the fullness of time. This has literary analogies, since like the phenomenon of narrative itself, providence has been seen as meeting a need for imaginative compensation. R.A.D. Grant has argued for the affinities of the two: 'The case for a moral universe can only be saved by the premature introduction of an additional, invisible world in which outstanding accounts are finally squared.'[9] But though drama certainly had a compensatory function, it could also be used to give human shape to cases which threw up difficulties with the Christian world-view. The very existence of ideas about providence was a response to the observed fact that in the world around, there was no easy equation between virtue and good fortune, and much that seemed obviously wrong. One should not underestimate its satisfactions – most Christians in the Reformation era used the idea of providence as a last and highest appeal when confronted with inexplicable sadness or evil – but it was not without its difficulties either.[10]

Certainly, on the question of why evil should exist at all, it had less to say. Going the extra mile, and asking how the existence of evil was reconcilable with a supremely good and all-powerful God, led to the branch of philosophy known as theodicy: the attempt to demonstrate, without sacrificing any of the Christian God's conventional attributes, how God and evil could both exist. Though the term 'theodicy' was first used by the philosopher Gottfried Leibniz in a book of essays published in 1710, it describes a question which had existed for longer than Christianity.[11] As set out in the Book of Job, it is central to the Old Testament canon. As a result of a wager with Satan, God inflicts suffering on Job to test his faith; the victimised and abject Job calls on God to justify his actions, but when God speaks out of the whirlwind to Job, he magnificently asserts his power but gives no answer to the questions Job has posed him. St Augustine, however, did attempt a cluster of answers to the problem of evil, collectively the most authoritative to be undertaken before the Reformation; he took the position that evil was an absence of good, and hence could not be traced to God's positive will.[12] To the question of why God should permit evil, Augustine replied that good drawn out of evil was better than what is merely good to begin with, and that God's redemptive power was revealed in how He turned to benign ends the disordered choices of free rational agents.

Augustine's formulation was sophisticated, but not immune to challenge. From the late seventeenth century – at first at the level of discreet philosophical enquiry, then as a more generally diffused opinion – the difficulty of reconciling a good God with the existence of evil opened the way for radical questions to be asked about whether Christianity was workable at all. Given how a play like *King Lear* exploits the spectacle of unrelievable suffering, and contains speakers who express some very cynical views of deity, Shakespeare himself has been seen as anticipating this trend – which, among recent generations of intellectuals, has accrued almost entirely to his credit.[13] While present-day scholars are often wary of asserting Shakespeare's progressiveness, they can agree that he would have encountered both atheism and a sceptical suspension of judgement about the Judaeo-Christian God as intellectual possibilities, and that certain aspects of his drama lend themselves to being read in light of these.[14] Within drama, some would have found it exciting to see how far a Christian could go without intellectual dissociation or emotional repugnance; the current chapter is written in the belief that drama, with all its built-in ability to repudiate what it was saying, could indeed exploit the shock-value of heterodox world-views. For Shakespeare or any other writer of this era, it would be anachronistic to go into the whole history of Enlightenment thought as a way of explaining early-seventeenth-century dilemmas about the problem of evil; even the phrase may be inappropriate for an age where all but a few were thinking within Catholic or Protestant versions of the Christian paradigm, and evil was largely treated as a datum. Plays, though, could present the possibility of a failing god, a god tolerant of evil or a godless world as a nightmare: sharply realized and transient, soliciting emotional awe rather than intellectual assent, and not attempting a relevance beyond the drama itself.

Scholarly attention in the Reformation, as distinct from imaginative attention, focused less on the motivation of God in allowing evil, more on the attributes of God and the nature of the relationship between Him and the agents of evil, both diabolic and human. The Protestant belief in the absolute sovereignty of God and the absolutely evil nature of unregenerate man, first articulated by Luther and most uncompromisingly set out in the thought of Calvin, had the advantage of explaining why evil operated in the world, and why some humans were good nevertheless: God's grace, quite simply, had been granted to some individuals and not to others. Defenders of the position known as 'supralapsarianism' or 'high Calvinism', which would have included most Elizabethan bishops at the time Shakespeare began writing plays, held that God's decree of predestination must have antedated his decision to allow the fall of Adam, and must therefore have been irrespective of human sinfulness. High Calvinists cited St Paul's Epistle to the Romans to prove the absolute power that God had over man, as over the rest of His creation: 'shal the thing formed say to him that formed it, Why hast thou made me thus? Hathe not the potter power of the claie to make of the same lompe one vessel to honour, and another unto dishonour?' (9.20–21)[15]

The logic of this was to attribute everything to God's grace and nothing at all to individual merit. This could be perceived as a comforting doctrine, which is certainly how it is presented in sermons preached by its advocates.[16] But it was also bound to throw up the problem of why a good God should choose to create some human beings, only to withhold His grace from them and damn them; the Calvinist view of predestination would not have become one of the Reformation's most divisive issues if the Calvinist God had not been a God who invited despair and accusations of unfairness. One should not exaggerate the novelty of the concept: like so much else in Reformation thought, predestination had been prefigured in medieval Catholicism, which accepted God's foreknowledge from eternity of what human beings experience as past, present and future, and suggested that God had incorporated all human choices into the plan for creation devised at the beginning of time. But the difference, and the divisiveness, stemmed largely from the Calvinist practice of foregrounding the question of whether one was saved, building one's spiritual life around it, and asking the same question of others. It never commanded uniform assent even within the Protestant camp, and it goaded Catholics into an even greater emphasis on man's free will. Thus, the Reformation was a period constantly asking whether humankind was really free, and often coming up with a negative answer, which helps to explain why attitudes towards predestination have been seen as the most important factor dividing Catholics from Protestants, and Protestants from each other, throughout the Reformation period.

Every well-informed Christian of the Reformation era would also have encountered another manifestation of determinism: the concepts of fate and fortune that figure so prominently within the classical pagan world-view. Stemming from a belief-system long superseded, these were superficially incompatible with Christianity; after all, Christianity in its earliest days had repudiated pagan ideas of fate.[17] Yet the goddess Fortuna came to have a considerable iconographical importance within medieval Christianity, and ideas of fate and fortune were central to writers whose work figured prominently within Renaissance education.[18] The strongly fatalistic quality of much Greek, Hellenistic and Roman thought would have been experienced by readers in the English Renaissance via such works as Cicero's *De Natura Deorum*, which figured in the grammar-school and university curriculum.[19] Both as abstract nouns and personifications, the concepts of Fate and Fortune also entered popular discourse, and would have become familiar to many who had no Latin or Greek: for instance, a well-known ballad-tune was called 'Fortune my foe'.[20] Classical notions of fate encompassed both individual destinies and the overwhelming power that was believed to predetermine those destinies, even directing the gods themselves. This power, sometimes an abstract entity, was also personified as the three Furies Alecto, Megaera and Tisiphone where situations appeared to invite supernatural vengeance.

Fortune too was personified as a goddess, sometimes holding a rudder to indicate her role in steering human affairs, at other times a cornucopia signifying the gifts of fortune. She tended to be a more attractive conception than fate, though not necessarily more benign. A third common attribute of hers was a ball signifying instability; images of Fortune's wheel, which raised men to great heights before flinging them down, were part of the English Renaissance's moralistic inheritance from the medieval world, pervading tragic drama and the tragic mode throughout imaginative literature.[21] Though inexorable fate and capricious fortune seem opposite at first, this is deceptive.[22] Different personality-traits are certainly attributed to the personifications, but both are ways of imaging situations apparently outside human control, and both throw up questions about supernatural agency and how humans should respond to undesirable events. The ancient Roman philosophical system of Stoicism, which later interbred with Christianity, provided one answer to the latter question – to the extent that many Renaissance readers identified the Stoic philosopher

Seneca as a good Christian.[23] Stoic moral philosophy addressed the problem of how to adjust to sudden downturns from happiness and prosperity, and praised the maintenance of self-control and personal dignity under unfavourable circumstances. Boethius's sixth-century text *Consolations of Philosophy*, written while its author was in prison, was well known to both medieval and Renaissance readers as a pattern of this internal resourcefulness; Shakespeare and Fletcher's *The Two Noble Kinsmen*, discussed below, is only one play that it influenced.[24]

Renaissance drama, like so much imaginative literature of the period, often speaks as if the gods, fate and fortune were all still valid: a rhetorical posture, but one which can betray real slippage between pagan and Christian habits of thought.[25] A similar hybridity can be seen outside imaginative literature too. The phenomenon of Christian stoicism is only one example of how classical ideas of fate continued in dialogue with Christianity, and hence with Christian determinisms; in this as in other respects, theological discussion was profoundly indebted to classical paradigms. Such terms as 'fate' and 'fortune' were widely used in Reformation England to denote God's subsidiary workings, and an exchange from a catechism compiled by Thomas Becon in the 1570s illustrates how they could be seamlessly incorporated into Protestant discourse: 'What is fortune? It is fate, or destiny chaunsing to any man by the will of God, without mans providence.'[26] But not everyone was able to speak with this catechetical certainty, especially as anti-Calvinism gathered momentum in the early seventeenth century. Writing fifty years later in 1626, the Calvinist Daniel Featley admits the similarity between pagan notions of fate and what he regards as orthodox notions of God, but expresses uneasiness about the terminology: 'Wee maintaine not *Fate*, or fatall necessity under the name of grace; but if it please some men to call the omnipotent will of God under the name of *Fate*, we seeke indeed to avoid prophane novelty of word, but wee will not contend about words.'[27] The remark illustrates, above all, how vocabulary of this kind could be defamiliarized or disowned by calling attention to its pagan origins. Whatever he might say, Featley is choosing his words carefully here, probably out of awareness that Calvinists could be criticized by their opponents for courting neo-paganism. Certainly the clerical writer Thomas Gataker, a friend and intellectual ally of Featley's, explicitly dissociates himself from the opinion that 'Fortune is no other than but God nicnamed'.[28]

To summarize: in the first instance, one can see notions of fate and fortune at this date as providing a powerful metaphor for notions of free will and predestination, transposed from a different discursive world; the former are more typical of imaginative literature and the latter of theological. This picture is complicated, though, by the fact that there was some overlap between these worlds: the classical terms were often used within theological discourse, either as a way of conceptualizing the separate operations of divine providence in a recognizable manner, or as a means of imputing profanity to one's opponents or oneself. Sometimes both these operations take place at once. Featley's recognition that there is a suspicion of profanity in equating fate and God is paralleled in the history play *Sir Thomas More*, in a passage frequently attributed to Shakespeare: 'It is in heaven that I am thus and thus, / And that which we profanely term our fortunes / Is the provision of the power above / Fitted and shaped just to that strength of nature / Which we were born [withal].'[29] As observed above, the drama of Shakespeare's time shows many instances of slippage between pagan and Christian determinisms: partly because dramatists so often found themselves pastiching the classical world-view while writing for a contemporary audience, but also because the rise and fall of a protagonist like More provided ample opportunity to reflect, speculate or fantasise upon the unseen forces that governed the trajectories of individual lives.[30]

In English terms, the linkage of drama and determinism can be thought of as a characteristically Renaissance phenomenon. The humanist renewal of interest in classical texts affected drama as it did every other branch of literary endeavour, bringing classical philosophies more into play on the stage. Besides, in medieval religious drama, as in medieval Christianity as a whole, there existed a very strong link between personal culpability and human free will: a link which would have been challenged by Reformation ideas, and sometimes broken. One must not exaggerate the difference, since medieval imaginative writing frequently addresses the vicissitudes of fortune through the *de casibus* tradition and the mystery of reprobation through the figure of

Judas.[31] Nevertheless, the notion of fate derived from classical tragedy undoubtedly provided a powerful metaphor for Protestant anxieties.[32] Critics of English Renaissance drama have long recognized how the high Calvinist obligation to see human beings as saved or damned from the beginning of time, irrespective of their own efforts, resonates unnervingly with the idea, central to both the metaphysics and the structure of classical tragedy, that one cannot escape one's fate.[33] Though this seems obvious to the twenty-first-century reader, it was little commented upon by Shakespeare's contemporaries – not surprisingly, as there would have been strong taboos against comparing Graeco-Roman deities with the Christian God.

But polemic was an exception to this. Debates between Calvinists and their opponents on the topic of predestination show a tendency for writers of anti-Calvinist sympathies to accuse their opponents of quasi-pagan fatalism, a gambit that became more overt as the seventeenth century progressed: writing in 1658, for instance, Thomas Pierce inveighed against those who saw God as a puppet-master, and humans 'like Wooden Engines . . . moved only by wires at the meer pleasure and discretion of the Engineer, . . . [which] were by inevitable consequence to uncreate his creature'.[34] Closer to Shakespeare's own time and genre, there was another way in which religious controversy could have helped to override the age's usual inhibitions. The polemical dramatization of obviously unbalanced Christianities is common in Renaissance drama, and in anti-Catholic tragedies such as John Webster's *The White Devil*, the popish participants in the drama are seen spiralling inexorably towards damnation. On one level, this would have been a straightforward way of urging orthodoxy by counter-example. On another, insofar as the drama elicited sympathy for the characters, it could well have provoked questions pertaining to predestination: why did God choose to let so many so-called Christians live and die without the light of a scripturally based religion, and could any Catholic in this position be saved? While the controversial literature of early-modern England often poses similar questions in the abstract, characterization would have brought about a huge difference, and the requirements of empathy sometimes impel drama to develop in unorthodox directions.

'KING LEAR' AND SUBMISSION TO PROVIDENCE

Most unorthodox would have been the suggestion that there was no God at all. Of all Shakespeare's plays *King Lear* has most often lent itself to an atheistical reading, whether one interprets that in twenty-first-century terms, as setting forth a world in which no god exists, or in terms more typical of early-modern Europe, as illustrating raillery against God or the gods. Certain of its characters' atheistical statements are very familiar, such as Gloucester's lament: 'As flies to wanton boys are we to th' gods; / They kill us for their sport' (4.1.36–37).[35] But part of the play's fascination is that, while inviting both atheistical and Christianized readings, it resists a totalizing explanation, and the context of these famous lines show that they are no exception. They are not only spoken after Gloucester's blinding, surely an excuse for strong language, but in the context of his imminent rescue by Edgar, which can be read in providential terms: after all, Gloucester has just said of Edgar, 'Might I but live to see thee in my touch, / I'd say I had eyes again' (23–24). This is not the only scene in *Lear* to have attracted metaphysically divergent readings, and two others – the storm scene, and the death of Cordelia – will be discussed below. Both have been read as displaying the senseless agonies of a world where God is dead or absent, but both also deserve particular scrutiny in the context of early-modern providentialist and predestinatory discourse: both for how the characters themselves react to the terrifying natural events around them, and for how a contemporary audience might have interpreted those events and reactions. It should become clear that every heterodox reading invited by the sorrows of the main characters can be countered by another showing orthodox early-modern providentialism at its most severe.

It has been very common to see the pathos of the storm scene as residing in the combination of Lear's appeal to the heavens and the heavens' failure to be affected; Susan Snyder's comment about the 'uncaring heavens' is representative.[36] For a society where believers and non-believers are similarly unlikely to see a storm as manifesting divine wrath, it is an understandable reaction. But if we are to recover a more early-modern way of thinking, perhaps we should attend to

Lear himself, who does not appear to think that the forces governing the weather are indifferent to his plight. Quite the reverse, he sees them as signalling a displeasure which it is the spectators' job to interpret.

> Let the great gods,
> That keep this dreadful pudder o'er our heads,
> Find out their enemies now. Tremble, thou wretch,
> That hast within thee undivulgèd crimes
> Unwhipped of justice. Hide thee, thou bloody hand,
> Thou perjured and thou simular of virtue
> That art incestuous. Caitiff, to pieces shake,
> That under covert and convenient seeming
> Has practised on man's life. Close pent-up guilts,
> Rive your concealing continents and cry
> These dreadful summoners grace. I am a man
> More sinned against than sinning.
>
> $(3.2.47–58)^{37}$

This is the language of popular providentialism, and as such would have been familiar to Shakespeare's original audience.[38] Discussing the final causes of storms in a tract of the 1570s, Thomas Hill listed among these how 'the almightie God thundereth in the clowdes, to the ende that men may be procured unto a due reverence and feare towards him: and they abashed, and warned of the devine yre, may heartily repent', and how 'the wicked, obstinate, and impenitent, which even like Gyaunts wage battle against heaven, maye be destroyed . . . '.[39] While to see weather as a manifestation of divine wrath is not inappropriate to the play's pagan setting, Lear is interpreting the storm in a way which would have been familiar to all early-modern Christians, constantly urged as they were to scrutinize unusual and extreme natural phenomena for what these might reveal about God's will.

Familiar too would have been the idea that they had personal relevance. Lear has begun the scene by calling down providential justice on himself in the form of lightning – 'You sulph'rous and thought-executing fires, . . . Singe my white head' (3.2.4, 6); and this speech broadens the remit, with its warning that all sinners should beware. Yet this is also where the scene takes a non-exemplary turn, as Lear uses his consciousness of general wickedness not to perfect his personal repentance, but to articulate his sense that, compared to those who have wronged him, he is 'a man more sinned against than sinning'. In suggesting that divine anger should have limits when applied to himself, this goes well beyond standard providentialist exhortations, while identifying a tension which characterizes many of them; storms, like other meteorological marvels, could be interpreted simply as an awful warning to one's political enemies, glossing over any pejorative relevance to oneself. Thus, the passage appears to be soliciting a complex response from the audience. On the one hand, they have seen the maltreatment of Lear and have every reason to sympathise with his self-characterization. On the other, exemplary self-abasement had no limits and admitted no qualifications, so anyone who called himself a man more sinned against than sinning would have invited an audience to retort that this was not for him to say.[40] As the action continues, Lear rails against his daughters in a way that removes him still further from the repentant self-knowledge he temporarily achieved. While his wandering wits – another affliction traditionally supposed to be brought about by storms – would have mitigated charges of self-pity brought against him, and while the audience is led to appreciate the reasons for his overriding bitterness, the impression of imperfect self-interrogation remains.[41]

Yet, in the end, the storm can be seen as bringing Lear to a greater knowledge of his own weakness, and as aiding what repentance he does achieve: functions which would be in keeping with a notion that bad weather called men to contrition. 'Thunder and lightning' is a familiar stage direction within the early-modern theatre, and it has recently been argued that these special effects were a conventional means of establishing or confirming a supernatural context in the minds of the audience.[42] Thus, plays could have been as ordinary a means of purveying popular providentialism as a sermon. To quote Thomas Hill again: 'God thretneth: the devine to such as will heare, cryeth repentaunce: to such as can not away wyth that kinde of speach, but desireth sweeter and more delectable geare, the Player

with his stage matters, by an other kind of more pleasant mean
admonisheth, and by a plaine demonstration putteth every man ›
minde of his vocation . . .'[43] Perhaps, therefore, the world of *King Lea,*
is not quite a godless one, given its shocking weather, but even so, the
question of interpretation is foregrounded. The providentialist way of
reading a storm, or any other singular occurrence, would have
encouraged the notion that the divine will was discernible, but this
was not the same thing as deriving the right message from it.

In other plays too, Shakespeare makes a link between bad weather,
the supernatural world and characters' behaviour, and whereas the
lessons to be learnt are straightforward in some cases, others foreground similar hermeneutical questions. In *A Midsummer Night's Dream,*
Titania admits that her quarrel with Oberon has displeased the moon,
bringing about a 'distemperature' which leads to human beings stop-
ping their worship of the moon, and thus to even more inclement and
unseasonable weather: 'The human mortals want their winter cheer. /
No night is now with hymn or carol blessed. / Therefore the moon, the
governess of floods, / Pale in her anger, washes all the air . . . ' (2.1.106,
101–104). The cause for this bad weather is more obvious than in
Julius Caesar: in the latter play the elements act in conjunction with
other natural and supernatural portents of change, not obviously
supporting either party except insofar as they reveal the will of fate.
The audience is invited to share Cicero's scepticism, not so much about
the portents themselves as about the possibility of interpreting them
correctly: 'Indeed it is a strange-disposed time. / But men may
construe things after their fashion, / Clean from the purpose of the
things themselves' (1.3.33–35). Certainly it is the responses to portents, rather than the portents themselves, that bring about the play's
catastrophe: Caesar, for instance, manifests a fatal hubris in the way
he reacts to the soothsayer's warning, 'Beware the Ides of March'
(1.2.18), and other portents.

Both *Julius Caesar* and *King Lear* articulate sceptical as well as
believing positions towards portents: a scepticism that relates less to
their existence than to the ever-present possibility of interpreting them
wrongly. On the related topic of augury, Caesar orders a sacrifice, but
goes on to misinterpret the augurers' findings in a way which, in

...oman world-view dramatized in the play, seems
...ble; in response to the Servant's information that
...find a heart within the beast' (2.2.40), Caesar replies,
...this in shame of cowardice. / Caesar should be a beast
...heart / If he should stay at home today for fear' (41–43).
...urers' message is the same as that conveyed by the descrip-
...of freakishly bad weather, and reminds us that even though
...gury as such was not practised in early-modern England, prodigious
...mperfections in animals could be and were read side by side with
meteorological portents. Astronomical marvels, again described in both
plays, would have been a third invitation to providentialist speculations; on this latter topic, the pagan settings should not prevent us
realizing that both plays are imaginatively exploiting, at one remove,
contemporary disagreements on the question of how far astrology
could be Christian.[44] Astrology could be seen as a way of reading the
world for providential signs, but also as superstitious, and in *Lear*,
Edmund begins by expressing disbelief in it.[45] Reacting to his father
Gloucester's bodeful comment that 'these late eclipses in the sun and
moon portend no good to us', he says contemptuously:

> This is the excellent foppery of the world, that when we are sick
> in fortune, often the surfeits of our own behaviour, we make
> guilty of our disasters the sun, the moon, and stars; as if we
> were villains on necessity, fools by heavenly compulsion, knaves,
> thieves, and treachers by spherical[46] predominance, drunkards,
> liars, and adulterers by an enforced obedience of planetary
> influence; and all that we are evil in, by a divine thrusting on.
> An admirable evasion of whoremaster man, to lay his goatish
> disposition on the charge of a star!

(1.2.104–112)

His dismissal of astrological determinism is reinforced by the fact that
he sees in it only a political tool, immediately and cynically appropriating Gloucester's point of view in order to unsettle Edgar. This is
played up more in the Quarto text, as follows:

I am thinking, brother, of a prediction I read this other day,
what should follow these eclipses . . . I promise you, the effects
he writes of succeed unhappily, [as of unnaturalness between
the child and the parent, death, dearth, dissolutions of ancient
amities, divisions in state, menaces and maledictions against
king and nobles, needless diffidences, banishment of friends, dissipation of cohorts, nuptial breaches, and I know not what].[47]

Edgar asks, again in the Quarto text, 'How long have you been a
sectary astronomical?' 'Sectary' here can bear two meanings. Edgar is
certainly expressing a well-founded surprise that Edmund is speaking
like someone who studies astrology, but at this date the term was
already being used within anti-Puritan discourse to condemn religious
dissent and division, and hence could apply to Puritans in general.[48]
If an anti-Puritan point is being made, it would only be by analogy;
as Keith Thomas has commented, this most theologically deterministic
of groups was unusually concerned to refute the idea that the stars
could influence man's life, at a time when astrology was believed in by
many Protestant Christians.[49] Still, such an interpretation would fit
with Shakespeare's other anti-Puritan asides, and even be a reason
why the reading in the Folio text is altered to 'Do you busy yourself
with that?'[50] Read providentially, the play has the effect of refuting
disbelievers in astrology, Puritan or not; just as in *Julius Caesar*, ignoring the weather's message turns out to be a mistake. In the passage
just quoted, Edmund thinks he can master the stars not as a magician
but as a Machiavellian, rationally exploiting others' superstitious fears
about them to gain political advancement; but an audience is bound
to notice that the plot bears out Gloucester's interpretation of the
eclipses in ways that precede Edmund's confession and extend outside
his subsequent brief, bearing him down in the process. Not attending
to the stars' exemplary message is part of Edmund's arrogance, and
hence his downfall. So whether we are to see the storms and stars in
Lear as divinely governed or not – and the play allows either interpretation – we are definitely invited to ask whether the characters use
them as an opportunity for self-examination. To interpret an eclipse

merely as something exploitable for political ends is to refuse the providentialist invitation to repent.

To view a storm as primarily an occasion for self-pity rather than contrition is to do something similar; here and elsewhere, the way in which Shakespeare plays up the pathos of Lear's situation can be seen as yet another way to avoid the staging of exemplary repentance. If imperfection is an inability to follow a train of thought through to an exemplary conclusion, then a sympathetic and pitiable imperfection marks Lear's reaction to the death of Cordelia. Critics have often asked, with Dr Johnson, why Cordelia had to die: a question which has been given added force by the fact that both in *The True Chronicle History*, one of Shakespeare's sources, and in Nahum Tate's popular Restoration rewriting, she does not.[51] Yet this seems to miss the point of much early-modern providential discourse, which was not concerned with an obvious happy ending so much as wresting consolation from miserable circumstances. Instead, therefore, one should ask: given that Cordelia dies so harrowingly, what are we to make of Lear's response to this? When children died, whether they were of childish years or not, the exemplary response was to resign yourself to providence; a whole genre of didactic literature, while admitting that some grief was unavoidable and even desirable, exhorted against excessive grief.[52] Inevitably this threw up the question of what was legitimate grief and what was not, but protracted and over-intense grief were both potentially condemnable.

The leading Huguenot writer Philippe de Mornay displays a typical trajectory of reactions in a tract on the death of his son, like Cordelia a young adult at the time of his decease.[53] First de Mornay laments, 'Alas, thou Lord of mine, are thine eares become deafe? is thine heart growne obdurate also: is that that [*sic*] eternall, never-dried fountaine of thy free mercy, frozen with colde, or dryed with heate, when I come to drinke, and unto none but mee?' Immediately, though, he answers himself by paraphrasing the Book of Job, 'It is true, Lord that *If I should dispute with thee, I should not answere thee to one thing in a thousand*': a quotation which would have reminded a biblically literate reader that Job too was a bereaved father. After this, he addresses God with a fitting resignation: 'Therefore are thy judgements deep, & thy

mercies a boundles, a soundlesse depth: thou givest these, as Cauter-
ismes in Phisick, not as hurtes in hostilitie.'[54]

As this indicates, railing against God in the event of a child's death
was something which one could display oneself as doing, but only
provided that this questioning was succeeded by a prayerful resignation to Providence. Thus, when Lear cries, 'O, you are men of
stones. / Had I your tongues and eyes, I'd use them so, / That heaven's
vault should crack' (5.3.231–233), the potentially blasphemous implications of this in a Christian context could have been neutralized, even
turned to exemplary ends, by a subsequent display of resignation.

But though Lear gives us the spectacle of despair and hope treading
on each other's heels in the scene following, we never detect the
exemplary submission to events that, in Christian terms, would have
been the right reaction. Nor is he given any time to arrive at a
resignation of this kind. He dies of grief before the scene is over,
posing two chilling unanswered questions: why he should have died
just then, and what happens to those who die in such an unresigned
spirit. In Q, his despairing reaction is left hanging in the air, condemnable as it stands, yet also serving to qualify condemnation because it
so obviously arises out of misery: 'Break, heart, I prithee break.'[55] In
F, his famously enigmatic last words 'Do you see this? Look on her!
Look, her lips. / Look there, look there' (284–285) can be read as
suggesting a final hope that she is reviving: a possibility which he has
described earlier as a 'chance which does redeem all sorrows / That
ever I have felt' (240–241). Thanks to the word 'redeem', with its
Christological overtones, this points to the idea that contingency can
have a place in an overarching providential scheme. Yet the fact that
Lear remains fixated on his own desires and sorrows suggests that he
perceives redemption in a dangerously limited manner, as only operating through an ending that he himself would find happy; whether
one goes along with redemptive readings of *Lear* or not, one should
beware of making the same mistake.

Even the saddest ending can be mitigated by notions of the Christian afterlife, but the relationship of *Lear* to the Christian revelation is
at best an indirect one. The status of those who lived and died without
hearing the gospel was a topic of some debate, both in Shakespeare's

time and earlier; as Erasmus's ironic petition 'St Socrates, pray for us' (*Sancte Socrates, ora pro nobis*) suggests, the question was hardest in the case of virtuous pagans who might seem to deserve not only salvation but canonization.[56] As one of them, Cordelia might well have been identified as someone who could be saved, or would be able to enjoy heavenly bliss in a limited degree; it is probably fair to see the play as setting up the question of whether this is going to happen. If no such special pleading can be advanced for ordinarily imperfect pagans, like Lear, this does not mean that his life and death cannot be read in Christian terms; imposing anachronistic Christian standards on pagans was a very common Renaissance mental habit, the other side of the coin to routinely acknowledging the superior authority of the ancients in so many fields of enquiry. As many critics have commented, Shakespeare often uses anachronism as a deliberate device to set up imaginative reverberations between past and present. In *Lear*, we do not know whether the characters go on to an afterlife, but some conception of an afterlife is certainly articulated within the play: one which is described in terms that could be either pagan or Christian. Lear describes Cordelia as a 'soul in bliss' and himself as 'bound / Upon a wheel of fire' (4.6.43–44), evoking the sinner Ixion's fate in the classical underworld simultaneously with images from medieval popular theology.[57] All this is described in the present tense rather than the future, thanks to Lear's mental confusion, and this has the effect of evoking a God like Calvin's, whose decrees on humankind have been set from eternity. Like so much else in the play, this can be read as faithfully transposing uncomfortable doctrines from the orthodox mainstream Christianity of Shakespeare's time onto a pagan setting.

Nothing in *King Lear*, in fact, is incompatible with the Christianity of the time and place it was written. But that being so, why has it so often been read as a play which calls the very existence of God into question? And why, conversely, have the play's redemptive elements been overstressed to an extent which cheapens its irresolvable sadness? As remarked at the beginning of this section, the play has invited both nihilistic and Christian readings. The stand-off between critics of each camp might be said to have reached a stalemate; yet the debate has to be revisited here, if only to point out that both parties have tended to take their bearings from a version of Christianity more accountable to human notions of fairness than was early-seventeenth-century English Protestantism. For most of those in the play's first audience, it would hardly have needed saying that a play illustrating God's providence did not have to end happily for everyone, and did not have to explain individual unhappy endings, other than by saying they were what every sinner deserved. Relevant here is Jesus's comment when told about the Galileans whose blood Pilate had mingled with their sacrifices: 'Suppose ye, yt these Galileans were greater sinners then all the *other* Galileans, because they have suffered suche things? I tell you, nay: but except ye amende your lives, ye shal all likewise perish' (Luke 13:2–3). But the question of why only some got their temporal deserts remained a pressing one. It was partially answered by the notion, potent for dramatists, that some were singled out as an example to warn others: partly too by the belief that the justice of God's decrees would become manifest at the end of time. In other words, though the whole appeal of popular providentialism was the idea that God's judgements could be understood, there were tensions to it, given the wider awareness that God's deeper plans were unsearchable by man.[58] It is a hallmark of Shakespeare's dramatic sophistication that he picks up on this, in an age when so many other dramatists confined themselves to a less nuanced understanding of providence.

Put at its simplest, the debate has been between 'Christian' interpreters, stressing the play's redemptive vision, and proponents of darker readings, who see it as pointing to an absent God, or one who is not interested in relieving extreme misery.[59] The interpretations of *Lear* that have tended to consolidate Shakespeare's reputation most with twentieth- and twenty-first century readers have belonged to the latter group. Even now, though it would be wrong to make blanket assumptions about the metaphysical convictions of Shakespeareans, those writing more or less explicitly from a non-Christian perspective have been in the majority in recent years, and for them the play has looked forward to a time when divine absence is the norm. But the notion that *King Lear* is utterly nihilistic now looks dated, and the fact that a more optimistic reading has also proved sustainable should tell us something.[60] Like many recent commentators on *Lear*, I am not

concerned to adjudicate on which reading is the more correct, merely
to acknowledge the very differing reactions the play has elicited. R.A.
Foakes has suggested that 'for many critics there can be no return to
simply optimistic or pessimistic readings of the play', a phenomenon
which may have its origins in the religious divergences of Shakespeare's own time.[61] Uncertainty, after all, was the besetting malaise
of Protestants: not because God's judgement was anything other than
fixed, but because man's discernment of God's certainties was inevitably imperfect, and so much rested upon it. While this uncertainty
focused on the question of whether one was personally saved or
damned, it also had wider implications when it came to interpreting
the outside world: though one was obliged to judge one's surroundings
with the help of scripture, the acknowledgement that God's decrees
were inscrutable would have infused doubt into the process. Above all,
this mental position would have created an uncertainty about endings.
This could have led to hope as well as to despair: an inscrutable God
is not the same as an uncaring God. But if the appeal to divine inscrutability could be seen as comforting, for the Calvinist it was necessarily
made in the context of a world where only God could ensure that one
attended to God's signs correctly. For many critics of the last few
generations, perhaps the majority of them, *King Lear* sets out a world
where no god alleviates suffering. To an early-modern viewer the play
is more likely to have played to fears about one's own imperfection:
how, even when the hand of God was manifested, one might not react
appropriately to it.

TRAGICOMEDY AND CRITIQUES OF CALVINISM

So far, this chapter has considered the relationship between the Christian notion of providence, the Protestantized notion of predestination
and the pagan notion of fate, with a view to how these are manifested
in the world-views of Shakespeare's comedies and tragedies, and how
these might be read against the high Calvinist version of Christianity
dominant in England when Shakespeare began to write. The following
section will continue the story, outlining the critiques of and departures

from high Calvinism that gained ground in the early years of the seventeenth century, and arguing that these are mirrored and anticipated in two of Shakespeare's later tragicomic plays.[62]

The doctrine of supralapsarianism, the notion that from eternity God had decreed salvation or damnation for every human soul, has been discussed above, as has its rigidly determinist quality.[63] As Calvin's ideas and those of such followers as Theodore Beza became more familiar in England, it emerged as a doctrine that worked better in the abstract than at grass-roots level. Both learned and unlearned started questioning the picture of a God who, seemingly arbitrarily, had damned certain individuals from the beginning of time. Its various pastoral disadvantages, and the despair it stimulated in some unlucky individuals, also explain why it rapidly fell from favour in the early years of the seventeenth century.[64] Though it did not go away entirely, it was modified in various ways. Among Calvinists, for instance, a more moderate theory of predestination gained ground, known as 'infralapsarianism' or 'sublapsarianism', whereby God's decree of predestination came after, not before, his decree to permit the fall of Adam. Human sinfulness had a more obvious part to play in this scheme: the damned were damned because of their sins, as an act of divine justice, while, through divine mercy, the saved were saved in spite of their sins. The idea that God's predestination applied to sinful mankind in general – a 'corrupt lumpe', *massa perditionis* or *massa damnata* – was the distinguishing claim of the infralapsarian position.[65] While still a pessimistic doctrine to the modern way of thinking, it brought relief through making salvation more personal and damnation less so: damnation was the ordinary lot, but if you were plucked from the *massa damnata*, it was a positive favour.

Even while having a developed theology of predestination in place, moderate Calvinists tended for pastoral reasons to discourage speculation about predestinatory matters, claiming that they were beyond man's understanding. In this, if in few other respects, they would have seen eye to eye with the English theologians who, from the early years of the seventeenth century, were influenced by the Continental thinker Jacobus Arminius.[66] In his work, Arminius argued that free will played a part in the process of salvation, thus contradicting Calvinist notions of man as an utterly passive recipient of God's grace, and turning the spotlight back on the active efforts of the individual.[67] Thus, the fact that high Calvinist notions of predestination were pastorally problematic was crucial to directing further theological enquiry, as Arminians challenged the so-called 'Calvinist consensus' which had evolved over the Elizabethan period and ultimately reconfigured what the Church of England regarded as orthodoxy. While conceding that drama is not theology, this chapter has been arguing that Shakespeare's drama does something similar: that it was affected by the fortuitously close resemblance of pagan tragedy to Christian ideas of predestination in their most uncompromising form, and that certain of Shakespeare's tragedies contain an emotional response to the notion of determinism which was relevant in both a pagan and a Christian context. This section extends the suggestion by plotting the rise of tragicomedy against the fall away from high Calvinism, and the search for doctrinal alternatives to it. One can be sceptical about how far theological fashion would have affected the world of drama, but it is remarkable how closely these two cultural trends mirror each other.

It has been said that all Christian drama is tragicomic, which is true if the playwright emphasizes the notion of God's providence, less so if he foregrounds questions of predestination. Medieval religious drama in England and elsewhere did have a tragicomic trajectory, the period's strong theological emphasis on free will lending itself to the idea that characters' deserts should be demonstrably just.[68] This world-view was not entirely without stress-points, particularly when sustained consideration was given to the character of Judas.[69] Nevertheless, because of the emphasis placed on earning salvation by obedience to the Church's teachings, the period gives us a dramatic world that directs attention away from unanswerable questions about the nature of God, while playing up the interrelationship between theatre and ideas of justice. Later, given the neoclassical impulses at work in the Renaissance, the poetic justice of a tragicomic ending could be seen as a serious flaw from the theoretical point of view. Aristotle's disparaging comments on tragedies with double endings set the tone for many commentators at this date: 'Second-best is the structure which some say comes first . . . which ends with the opposite outcome for better and worse people. It is thought to come first because of the weakness of audiences; the poets follow the audiences' lead and compose whatever is to their taste.'[70] Following in this critical tradition, Sir Philip Sidney was dismissive of contemporary tragicomedy in his *Defence of Poesy*, while acknowledging that there was classical precedent for it: 'I know the ancients have one or two examples of tragicomedies, as Plautus hath *Amphitryo*; but, if we mark them well, we shall find that they never, or very daintily, match hornpipes and funerals.'[71]

It is striking that in a work devoted to advancing a moral justification for imaginative literature, Sidney gives no space to the argument that a tragicomic vision could be seen as reflecting God's providence more accurately than either the tragic or the comic: perhaps an indication of how far his literary tastes were governed by academic rather than religious correctitude. But according to Giambattista Guarini, perhaps the most influential tragicomic theorist of Renaissance Europe, the genre reflected Christian belief more accurately than any other.[72] Defending his pioneering tragicomedy *Il Pastor Fido*, he famously asked: 'What need have we today to purge pity and terror with tragic sights, since we have the precepts of our most holy religion, which teaches us with the word of the gospel?'[73] Conscious of Greek tragedy's religious origins, Guarini saw catharsis as unnecessary now that a true, Christian world-view had superseded the false one of the pagans: a pious assertion, and also a highly effective means of countering Aristotle's contempt for tragedies with happy endings.[74] A disclaimer appended to another Italian play, Giambattista della Porta's *Ulisse*, is even more explicit, declaring 'The present tragedy is enacted by Gentiles; and therefore if in it are to be found these terms – fate, destiny, chance, fortune, the power and coercion of the stars, gods and the like – they have been used to conform to their ancient customs and rites. But according to the Catholic religion, these words are but emptiness, for all consequences and all events are to be attributed to Blessed God, the supreme and universal cause.'[75] One should not conclude that dramatic determinism was dispensed with altogether outside Protestant countries: throughout this era, notions of fate and fortune are pervasive in the drama of both Protestant and

Catholic Europe. Nor, as Chapter 1 of this study cautioned, should one necessarily see Counter-Reformation mores as hospitable to theatre. In 1605, Cardinal Bellarmine told Guarini that his drama had caused as much harm to morals as Luther and Calvin had to religion: a reminder that the backlash against Guarini's play was to involve ethical concerns as well as theoretical.[76] This suggests that Guarini's claims for the religious efficacy of tragicomedy may have had an opportunistic and defensive element. But for whatever reasons, the theoretical development of tragicomedy in Italy had to some degree the effect of defending Catholic piety against pagan precedents and contemporary neoclassicists, with an implicit relevance to debates on free will and determinism between Catholic and Protestant.[77]

No mainstream dramatist in Shakespeare's England would have found it easy to confront the relationship between religion and dramatic determinism as explicitly as Guarini or della Porta did, however much their plays were inspired by its practical outworkings. It is probably fairest to see the English and Italian traditions as exhibiting parallel developments with points of convergence, rather than engaging in dialogue – not least because the English response to Guarini had a very different series of agendas in mind.[78] In the English context, Guarini was relevant less because of his own passing comments about drama and religion than because he was a powerful apologist for tragicomedy, and tragicomedy was a remarkably versatile means of reflecting upon the Christian dispensation. One could have recognized the similarity between God's providential plan for mankind and the tragicomic form without having read any theory. But looked at more closely, early-modern European tragicomedy begins to ramify in several directions, each of which has different predestinatory overtones. Corneille's tragicomedy *Le Cid* is a famous affirmation of man's free will, inflected by Jesuit theologians' emphasis on the topic and Corneille's own Jesuit education.[79] Conversely, the idea of a world in which death is threatened but never actually takes place, and a happy ending extends to all the dramatic participants, is central to Guarini's theory but, despite his protestations, at something of a distance from Christian orthodoxy; one could call it a universalist dramatic overstatement, at the opposite extreme from fatalistic Calvinist-inspired nightmares. A more orthodox case can be made for the *tragedia mista* or *tragedia di lieto fin* associated with the Italian theorist Giovanni Battista Giraldi Cinthio, in which the good end happily and the bad unhappily, or the *tragoedia sacra* dramatizing the happy deaths of Christian martyrs.[80] In addition to all these, tragicomedy can act very like tragedy in foregrounding issues of fate and subsuming individual endeavour to events outside human control. Despite the views of Guarini and della Porta quoted above, the genre could also affirm determinism: in Christian terms, a demonstration of how God's dispensations are both marvellous and just.

As has been commented above, the Calvinist belief in predestin-ation could seem both an invitation to personal despair and an optimistic vision, reinforcing the absolute sovereignty of God and the absolute justice of his decrees. This combination of doubleness and optimism would have mapped easily onto plays where the good end happily and the bad unhappily, which is true to different degrees of tragedy, comedy and tragicomedy, but has a particular importance for the latter. The two plays discussed below, *The Winter's Tale* and *The Two Noble Kinsmen*, both set out what can seem a harsh notion of fate and show people punished beyond their moral deserts; while neither obvi-ously critique deterministic forces, both set out their human cost.[81] There is an overriding similarity of endeavour between negative res-ponses to high Calvinism in theology, and the use of drama to explore the human fallout of determinism; in terms of early-seventeenth-century England, this suggests that it may be fruitful to compare Shakespeare's late plays with the views of the moderate Calvinists and Arminians referred to earlier. It is a comparison that should not be pushed too far; here as elsewhere in this study, one must stress the indirect nature of the relationship between theological discourse and the professional theatre, and in any case, the grand showdown between Calvinist and Arminian in the 1620s and 1630s post-dates Shake-speare's death. But dissenting voices were beginning to be raised against high Calvinism at the time Shakespeare was writing his last plays; thus, it seems legitimate to see early-seventeenth-century contro-versies between high and moderate Calvinists, and between Calvinists and Arminians, as addressing the fault lines of Calvinism in ways that were emotionally tracked – even at times anticipated – in the theatre. No argument is being mounted for an Arminian Shakespeare, or even for an anti-Calvinist one – merely for a Shakespeare who apprehended and aestheticized the sorrows of predestination.

It would, of course, be wrong to make the blanket assertion that Calvinists did not visit the theatre. Still, Puritans continued to adhere to a Calvinist world-view at a time when other alternatives had become available to English Protestants, and as discussed in Chapter 1, there was some connection between Puritanism and antitheatricalism. Hence, a typical London theatre audience of the early seventeenth century might have contained, relative to the city's population in general, a disproportionately large number of those who consciously recoiled from Calvinist doctrine – even without allowing for the incalculable number of Englishmen who were frightened by what they believed, and consciously or not, valued theatregoing because it faced up to uncomfortable religious issues more than a sermon could. On another tack, it is tempting – though the subject for another study altogether – to see the partial displacement of tragedy by tragicomedy in the English dramatic mainstream over the 1620s and 1630s as occurring in tandem with the rise of Arminian thought.[82] Tragicomedy, however deterministic and however dark, tends to take a more positive view of man's destiny than tragedy, and the message of Arminianism was certainly easier to receive as optimistic than that of high Calvinism; not because it necessarily postulated more people being saved, but because to see free will as figuring in the process of salvation seemed fairer from the mortal standpoint. In a period where theatrical fashion was highly responsive to court preference, tragicomedy would also have resonated with Arminian and pro-Catholic theological moods within the court, as well as chiming in with the dramatic fashions which Charles I's queen Henrietta Maria imported.[83] But looking ahead in this way should not prevent one identifying the specificities of the Shakespearean tragicomic vision, and recognizing how closely this responds to the notions of fate and destiny that had so disturbing an analogue in high Calvinism. In *The Winter's Tale* and *The Two Noble Kinsmen*, happy endings give us good reasons for optimism, but these are severely qualified by the dramatic use made of fate and death.

A CONVERSION AND A BAD DEATH:
'THE WINTER'S TALE'

'Once a day I'll visit / The chapel where they lie, and tears shed there / Shall be my recreation', Leontes declares of the dead Mamilius and of Hermione, whom he presumes dead, in Act 3 of *The Winter's Tale*. When he next appears in Act 5, it is sixteen years later, and Cleomenes reassures him, 'Sir, you have done enough, and have performed / A saint-like sorrow' (3.2.235–237; 5.1.1–2). Shakespeare's depiction of Leontes's repentance is interesting for what it depicts, what it omits and where it comes in his oeuvre, given how often his last plays recast earlier work. The first three acts of *The Winter's Tale* give us a miniature tragedy. Like *Othello*, they demonstrate the tragic implications of unreasonable and uncontrollable jealousy; like *King Lear*, they chart the dreadful effects of a monarch going mad. Othello dies raving, by his own hand; Lear also dies, perhaps in despair. Leontes, on the other hand, is spared several more years to repent, and lives to witness Hermione's return.

Any dramatic death has soteriological implications, whether or not it takes place within a Christian setting, and conversions such as Leontes's have too. If one focuses on him, the play's didactic message might seem obvious and cheerful: he repents, and is rewarded by the unlooked-for grace of Hermione's return. Given Shakespeare's penchant for brief, discreet and off-stage repentance, *The Winter's Tale* is unusual in the space it affords the topic, and Leontes's admission 'I am ashamed' (5.3.37) is, for once, borne out by what the audience actually sees. All the same, the glancing, almost squeamish quality which Shakespeare more often imparts to penitence remains visible, in Time's speech at the beginning of Act 4. As many previous commentators have recognized, Time's probable costume, combined with the fact that his speech is written in rhyming couplets, make him a visual and aural throwback within early-seventeenth-century drama, seemingly straight out of a morality play or moral interlude. Yet Shakespeare's Time brusquely dismisses what these genres would have dilated upon, Leontes's repentance: 'Leontes leaving – / Th'effects of his fond jealousies so grieving / That he shuts up himself' (4.1.17–19). His hourglass works like a remote-control. To a twenty-first-century audience this might seem a tactful dramaturgical device, fast-forwarding a dull element of the narrative, but an early-modern audience, more prepared to savour the niceties of repentance, might not have agreed. In Leontes's characterization too, we can detect a resistance to exemplarity, as where he snaps at Paulina, 'She I killed! I did so; but thou strik'st me / Sorely to say I did' (5.1.17–18). Here as elsewhere in Shakespeare, individuation works against any general didactic message.

But if Leontes remains a sinner, and if the audience feels at the end of the play that he is still not good enough for Hermione, this illustrates a point familiar to every Christian, with a particular shaping importance for Protestants: that grace is a free gift, which no human being can be said to deserve. The play is shot through with references to grace, both social and sacred, and in the play's last scene, Hermione's role takes on Christian connotations.[84] Like Christ, she is an innocent victim; a scene where she is brought back from the dead is bound to remind audiences of the Resurrection; and her final embrace of Leontes emblematizes reconciliation. The possible miraculous significance of the play's denouement has been much commented on, though never without an acknowledgement of Paulina's directorial role, as Susan Snyder and Deborah T. Curren-Aquino have remarked: 'Shakespeare seems to want it both ways: as marvel and as something that can be explained in human terms.'[85] The idea of providence is, after all, wide enough to encompass both miracle and human action. But as indicated by Paulina's admonition in front of the statue, 'It is required / You do awake your faith' (5.3.94–5), belief by the audience on- and off-stage is essential to the providential drama. The line can be read two ways – is it Paulina who requires the awakening of faith, or some other agent? – and in the polemical context of its time, it comes over as both provocative and reconciliatory. Looked at in one way, it sets out a blatantly popish claim for the spiritual efficacy of images; in another, it makes a reformed point about the all-encompassing necessity of faith. Either way, Leontes's good works, his outward expressions of repentance, may have prepared the ground but are not enough in themselves.

Yet two provisos are appropriate. First, as so often in Shakespeare, quasi-religious language and ritual are being employed to enhance the secular power of theatre. Second, the world being dramatized is not exactly Christian. The term 'gentile', taken over from Jewish discourse and employed by Shakespeare's contemporaries as a catch-all for those who were neither Jewish nor Christian, fits not only *The Winter's Tale* but all the plays discussed in detail in this chapter, with their broadly pagan, coherent but strikingly eclectic world-views. Dramatic gentilism had a free-form, imaginative quality which encompassed Christian elements too, paralleling the syncretism which occurred every time an ostensibly Christian character in drama, poetry or romance gave more credence to the gods or to pagan-inflected notions of fate than an early-modern Christian would have done. Since religious matter with an immediate contemporary application was difficult to stage openly in Elizabethan and Jacobean England, it would have been natural to look to other cultures and other religions to examine questions relating to salvation or damnation, wherever these verged on the controversial; and here too, the notion of gentilism is appropriate as an overarching, negative means of definition.[86] Yet within this, it has the potential for considerable variety. As explored in the introduction to this study, many of the English Renaissance's more sophisticated playwrights used the relative imaginative freedom of drama to create different hetero-cosms, or micro-climates, for different plays: an eclecticism which directs attention towards reader- and viewer-response.[87] When reflective audience members came out of the theatre, or even while they were immersed in the drama, they could hardly have avoided comparing a play's world-view with the Christian orthodoxies of their time.[88] In a culture where tales about non-Christians were so commonly mapped onto a Christian grid within sermons and popular literature, readers at every level would have been well aware that honey could be culled from gentile flowers. Thus, the earliest audience of *The Winter's Tale* would surely have recognized, just as later critics have done, how the story of Leontes evokes Christian repentance within a gentile setting; and in some sense, they would have reacted as if he were saved.

But given this, how would they have interpreted the death that so chillingly terminates the first half of the play, and is deliberately recalled in its denouement? Leontes's sight of Hermione parallels the dream-vision that Antigonus reports just before his death, and in the play's penultimate speech, Antigonus's widow Paulina forcibly reminds her auditors of his loss:[89]

> Go together
> You precious winners all; . . .
>   I, an old turtle,
> Will wing me to some withered bough and there
> My mate, that's never to be found again,
> Lament till I am lost.
>
> (5.3,130–135)

In response, Leontes issues her with Camillo as a new husband. Given Paulina's continued loyalty to Leontes, and the fact that she has already expressed gratitude to him, 'All my services / You have paid home' (5.3.3–4), it is probable that she goes along with this.[90] Yet as a palliative, its inadequacy is manifest. Leontes has publicly repented for his behaviour towards his wife and son, but not for the ghastly fate of his all-too-faithful courtier or the sorrow of Paulina, to whom his debt is so great – which is a conspicuous omission, even for a king. Thus, his silencing of Paulina's complaint, 'O peace, Paulina!' (135), cannot entirely suppress the intruded memory of Antigonus which adds a melancholy note to the ending.[91] The exchange can be seen as the tying-up of a loose end, and on one level it is. But it also continues to disturb the final tableau with its reminder that not every sinner gets a second chance, which is why, when *The Winter's Tale* was first performed, Antigonus's fate would have played on topical theological sensitivities about the exceptional nature of grace.

Famously, *The Winter's Tale* is structured like a diptych, with a tragic first half succeeded by a comedy of regeneration. In contemporary theoretical terms, it could be typified as having features in common with the *tragedia mista*, where – as described above – a double ending ensures that good and bad characters both get the fate they deserve. While tragicomedies of this kind did not, like Guarinian tragicomedy, necessarily exclude death, one way of mitigating its sting was to place it halfway through the action. This is what happens with the character of Mamilius, who pines and dies in Act 3 and is not explicitly referred to in the final scene.[92] So what is Shakespeare doing, and why, when he makes Paulina remind us of Antigonus in the final scene of the play? Most obviously, he is recalling the most conspicuous death in the drama – all the others happen off-stage – and presenting us with that Shakespearean trademark, an emotionally complicated ending. Antigonus, we are invited to remember, is a character whose distress and mental uncertainty have been portrayed in sympathetic detail: a man who falls foul of ill fortune, and who believes with some cause that he has been cursed. Given that Leontes is the greater sinner of the two, while Antigonus merely carried out his orders, their respective fates pose a marked and painful contrast with each other.

One should not overstate the case. We are likely to feel Antigonus's fate unfairer than a contemporary of Shakespeare's would have done; his story would have reminded any early-modern Christian that the agents of a sinful action risked being cut off by the hand of God. Antigonus's wrongdoing is contingent on Leontes's, and something for which Leontes, as king, is ultimately responsible; yet he is not just a whipping-boy. The play gives us a sharp critique of monarchical absolutism, and we are intended to condemn Antigonus's misguided loyalty to the king, in particular his oath to carry out Leontes's instructions concerning the infant before knowing what they are.[93] But though Antigonus is culpable as an instrument of Leontes's injustice, he is an unwilling sinner; as he reports the dream-vision of Hermione saying, fate has singled him out for this action 'against [his] better disposition' (3.3.27). Though the scene in which he recounts this vision throws up some positively Sophoclean questions about free will and determinism, Antigonus is certainly aware that he could act otherwise. Responding to the dream-Hermione's request to deposit the child on the shores of Bohemia, he follows the request through, explicitly stating that he believes he is acting in accordance with Apollo's decrees, but also identifying an element of perversity in his own behaviour.

> Dreams are toys,
> Yet for this once, yea superstitiously,
> I will be squared by this. I do believe

> Hermione hath suffered death, and that
> Apollo would, this being indeed the issue
> Of King Polixenes, it should here be laid . . .
>
> (3.3,38–43)

Thus, in a self-fulfilling prophecy, it is Antigonus's conscious effort to believe in supernatural revelation that brings about his doom. Saying 'yea superstitiously, / I will be squared by this', he follows this position through, demonstrating for the audience the willed nature of his belief in it. But superstition is wrong, and all the more so if it is self-conscious. Perhaps Antigonus has only himself to blame if he acts on the dream, even while remarking that 'dreams are toys' and it is superstitious to pay any attention to them at all – in any case, his interpretation of it is false insofar as he believes the child to be Polixenes's. But in a further twist, the dream can be seen to have a prophetic authority when looked at in the context of the play as a whole. Though the question of whether it is stimulated by divine revelation or human imagination is left open, Antigonus's report of it is one of the moments where the play's providentialism is most overt – or its deployment of fate most terrifying. Just as in his earlier exchange with Leontes, he is framed by his own willingness to act under orders. If he begins by acknowledging that he has a choice about whether to believe the dream or not, the scene ends with his exhibiting the authentic circularity of despair; he not only believes he is cursed but colludes with the curse, with obedience to his king and fulfilment of the curse becoming one and the same. If his sin is one of despair, that despair is not causeless.

In a man who believes himself to be accursed, Antigonus's fluctuations and wrong turns are psychologically plausible. But this begs the further question: does he have an objective reason for thinking this or not? While we are meant to believe in the oracle in *The Winter's Tale*, no actual gods appear in the play; a dream – as Antigonus acknowledges – can simply be a dream; and bad weather and wild beasts do not necessarily equate to divine anger. Yet Antigonus's diagnosis of a curse finds support when other characters testify to the malefic stars. As the Mariner comments, not only Antigonus but he himself, and his whole entourage, seem to have incurred the displeasure of the heavens: '[T]he skies look grimly / And threaten present blusters. In my conscience, / The heavens with that we have in hand are angry / And frown upon 's' (3.3.3–6). Antigonus replies 'Their sacred wills be done!' (7), and on abandoning Perdita, he characterizes himself as 'most accursed . . . To be by oath enjoined to this' (51–52).

If Antigonus is cursed, he is not unique in falling foul of heavenly anger; the Mariner, and all the passengers on the ship, also die as a result of his mission. As the Third Gentleman comments near the end of the play, 'all the instruments which aided to expose the child were even then lost when it was found' (5.2.60–62). And as this suggests, one is not allowed to forget that the actions prompted by Antigonus's dream prove, against the odds, to be the saving of the child: a factor which argues for the dream's supernatural authority, but intensifies the sense that Antigonus has been set up by heaven. After all, even where the dream-Hermione seems to be pronouncing most sternly on Antigonus's future fate, 'For this ungentle business / Put on thee by my lord, thou ne'er shalt see / Thy wife Paulina more' (3.3.33–35), she stresses the secondary, contingent nature of what Antigonus has done, and places the main blame on Leontes. Moreover, what the dream-Hermione actually tells Antigonus to do is no less cruel than what Leontes has agreed to, though it does include a hint that Antigonus needs to repent of the action: 'There weep, and leave it [the child] crying' (31). To this, as we have already seen, Antigonus rejoins 'Weep I cannot, / But my heart bleeds, and most accursed am I / To be by oath enjoined to this' (50–52). If characters other than tragic heroes can be allowed to have fatal flaws, Antigonus's is too great an obedience to his monarch; he could, after all, have imitated Camillo in carrying out a pious fraud on Leontes, or instead of carrying out Leontes's instructions for exposure, he could have found a safe home for the child in a foreign country. As it is, he obeys both king and queen but approaches the task in a fatalistic spirit.

Famously, Antigonus 'exit[s] pursued by a bear' (57) and is mauled to death, once he has completed his mission. This has been seen as echoing the fate of those who foolishly mocked at the prophet Elisha, and were eaten by bears.[94] Given that mariners used the constellations

Ursa Major and Ursa Minor (Great Bear and Little Bear) to steer by, and that steering a ship was a very common metaphor for life, one could also interpret it as an astrological figuration both of Antigonus's doom, and of the Mariner's with his crew. As already commented, the cosmology of *The Winter's Tale* does allow for true oracles, and though the play's only curse against Antigonus is uttered by a human being, Paulina, it too can be interpreted as oracular, in keeping with her later role as *dea ex machina*. Her pronouncement 'For ever / Unvenerable be thy hands, if thou / Tak'st up the Princess by that forced baseness / Which he has put upon't' (2.3.76–79) can also be read as a prophecy, like her comment in Act 3 Scene 2 that her lord 'is lost too' (228), which precedes the scene where he dies. But even when Paulina laments her bereavement, she never regrets the curse, or retracts it as she does her harsh words towards Leontes; thus, it should be read less as a manifestation of anger than as an impersonal, sibylline pronouncement on Antigonus's fate.

Antigonus's is, on the face of it, a bad death. His last words, 'I am gone forever!' (3.3.57) and the gruesome suddenness of his demise both draw on familiar cautionary exemplars concerning bad deaths: one of many ways in which *The Winter's Tale* harks back to the tropes of medieval Catholicism, while recasting them to take Protestant alternatives into account. The notion that a good death was a sign of salvation is commonplace within medieval popular Christianity, and Protestant funeral sermons show that it was also exploited by the reformed faith. Where they had polemical reasons to do so, both Catholics and Protestants would also have pointed to bad deaths as sure signs of God's anger. But both before and after the Reformation, pastoral considerations also demanded that all religious groups had to find ways of holding out hope for the victims of real-life tragedies. All denominations would have pointed out the need to assess the dead person's life as a whole, and to judge charitably. Protestants would have stressed the inscrutability of God's judgements, while also dismissing as popish the notion that a quiet and penitent death was a guarantee of salvation; for Catholics, the mechanism of purgatory was still in place. Finally, as the quotation at the beginning of this chapter indicates, much emphasis was placed on the last moment before death, when the soul could cleave to God in a way not obvious to outside observers.[95]

So even if *The Winter's Tale* had been set in an explicitly Christian environment, there would have been ways to bypass the automatic conclusion that a bad death spelt damnation. And as the play stands, it is surely wrong to imagine people coming out of the Globe and assuming, without qualification, that Antigonus was damned. The text underplays the idea of an afterlife, pagan or Christian, and even relatively unsophisticated viewers would have been aware that salvation and damnation were problematic categories when applied to gentiles, in a play that presents no explicit Christian alternative to the gentile world-view. Yet in this most bifurcated of Shakespeare's plays, whose very structure depends on contrasting Antigonus's cursed death with Leontes's continued existence and eventual happiness, the play's shaping stress on the prime Christian virtue of repentance enables it to be read very easily against a Christian grid – which, as suggested above, would have been a contemporary's likely first approach to this text or any other. Within this alternative cosmology, faith in God, which all Christians would have regarded as essential to salvation, is not demanded as a prerequisite of the happy ending. Leontes's repentance is not arrived at through faith in Christ, but through a combination of factors appropriate to gentilism: a realization of his bad behaviour and a belief in oracles. For eternal damnation, the play substitutes the idea of finite divine punishment in this life, while retaining the sense of judgemental pronouncement.

Leontes's and Antigonus's respective fates are both to be seen as punishment; both are finite, but only Antigonus's is final. Thus, in terms of the play, damnation is replaced by a final summing-up; and as the two sinners' fates are contrasted, one bespeaks penitence and the other acts as a warning. Yet in its stress on the idea of repentance, and its acknowledgement that this is not allowed to everyone, the play does provide a sustained commentary on Christian notions through the idea of fate. Fate, like predestination, is inscrutable, but unlike it, was not explicitly off-limit in drama. Commenting on fate would have been bound to throw up questions about predestination, with the advantage that one would have had a relatively large amount of imaginative freedom in exploring them. It would be a mistake to see this as dictating Shakespeare's imaginative endeavours; the play's exploitation of the topic goes no further than to contrast the fates of individuals. Yet it is precisely at the level of personalities that the topic would have impinged most on the doubts and fears of ordinary audience members; here and elsewhere, Shakespeare is intensely aware of how to stimulate post-Reformation sensitivities.

Though the play can be fruitfully read in the light of contemporary debates about the nature and operation of grace, there is a larger point to be made too: all early-modern Christians, irrespective of denomination, had to accept that it was part of God's plan for some humans to receive no benefit from divine grace. This has an impact on tragicomic drama that lends itself as obviously as *The Winter's Tale* to being read in Christian terms, since Christianity itself is tragicomically structured in two respects. Verna A. Foster has commented of medieval religious drama, looking at it in Guarinian terms, that 'tragic and comic effects moderate one another, but (though there may be local discordances) apparently tragic incidents are ultimately subordinated to the comic order'.[96] Christ's atonement for the fall of man could be read as a tragedy with a happy ending, while the convention of the double ending, where good and bad characters each receive their deserts, could be used to prefigure the separation of saved and damned at the end of time. The Book of Revelation itself pivots from tragedy to comedy just as *The Winter's Tale* does after Antigonus's death; the Old Shepherd's line, 'thou met'st with things dying, I with things newborn' (3.3.101–102), has routinely – and sometimes callously – been quoted in this context. But to set against this, we have the remark of the Third Gentleman in Act 5 Scene 2: 'But O, the noble combat that 'twixt joy and sorrow was fought in Paulina! She had one eye declined for the loss of her husband, another elevated that the oracle was fulfilled' (62–64). Picturing Paulina's face as a tragicomic mask, this comment is just as much a genre signal as the Old Shepherd's, but unlike his, admits the full difficulty of both tragicomedy and religion. Paulina's response suggests to the audience that rather than simply passing from sorrow to joy, they should acknowledge that the fulfilment of divine decrees may engender simultaneous joy and sorrow.

On the face of it, unfortunate characters like Antigonus need not have rendered the conclusion of a tragicomedy any less just and optimistic. Catholics and Protestants would both have agreed that reprobates were justly damned by God, and that the damnation of some individuals was an inalienable part of his divine plan. When mainstream theologians from all denominations argued about the topic of predestination, they were seeking no more than to establish how and why people were damned; questions such as whether damnation actually happened, or whether it was just of God to damn, would have been outside the purview of orthodox Christianity altogether. Yet the employment of discredited pagan belief systems within drama gave playwrights of Shakespeare's age an opportunity to ask questions about fate that, before too many generations had passed, would enter the intellectual mainstream in relation to providence. How far Antigonus's end can be read as positing divine unfairness, how far this is neutralized by the pagan setting, are tactfully left up to the respondent; but it is hard to believe that Shakespeare would not have calculated the heterodox reverberations of this episode, since being left with a sense of unfairness is central to the scene's emotional impact.[97] This, indeed, becomes a matter of formal contrast when looking at the play as a whole. The dramatic wonder in the final scene, as Hermione is restored to Leontes, fits this story of grace – but its sheer unlikelihood would have been a reminder to Protestants that grace could not be looked for as a matter of course. Similarly, what happens to Antigonus earlier could be seen as simulating what a sinner had every reason to expect, in cases where grace was not obviously forthcoming; and a story showing the granting of grace to one sinner, and seemingly withholding it from another, would have been especially moving at a period when the means of grace were so hotly disputed.

At the time when *The Winter's Tale* was first performed (1609–1611) the point at issue between supralapsarian and sublapsarian Calvinists was whether individual souls had been saved or damned from the beginning of time, or whether mankind had incurred wholesale damnation as a consequence of Adam's fall, from which certain individuals were rescued by God's grace. Though reformed ministers seem to have avoided the arcana of predestinarian theology at a pastoral level, the topic excited keen popular curiosity, and clerical avoidance of it might positively have invited playwrights to fill the gap.[98] While it would be reductionist to read *The Winter's Tale* as falling into one or another of the above-mentioned theological camps, it can surely be seen as reacting to, and even commenting on, this excitement at a distance – particularly as no other play of Shakespeare's foregrounds repentance to quite the same degree. Stephen Orgel has commented on the unusualness of this plot-line compared with other Shakespearean dramas featuring monarchs, asking 'Why . . . the intense focus on the preservation and rehabilitation of Leontes?'[99] One answer is surely that an interest in the mechanisms of sin, redemption and grace was one which tragicomedy was uniquely well equipped to explore, and that the early-seventeenth-century English fashion for tragicomedy has a symbiotic relationship with contemporary theological debate on these topics. No sides are being taken, since the play's emphasis on wonder in its near-miraculous last act fits well with either doctrine: Antigonus's fate is what every sinner has the right to expect, Leontes's displays a marvellous and exceptional instance of grace.

But given that Antigonus's fate remains disturbing, how are we to react? On one level, this section has argued for nothing more than treating him seriously. Shakespeare's debts to medieval drama in *The Winter's Tale* are undeniable, but to appreciate the complexity of what Shakespeare is doing with Antigonus, he has to be read as more than an unrepentant sinner or the old Adam.[100] Still more importantly, one needs to recognise that a wild beast's bloody dismemberment of a terrified man trying to do his duty is not particularly amusing. But courtiers usually are subordinate to kings, and so is Antigonus to Leontes. In terms of the play's structure, his death has most importance as a foil to Leontes's story; Leontes's moral improvement is the play's fulcrum, his repentance its overriding exemplary theme.[101] So is this seeming unfairness a result of dramatic and social hierarchy, a sense that the king's story should be the main focus of a narrative, whereas courtiers are dispensable? Certainly the contemporary tendency was to read plays in terms of the moral lessons set out by the central characters, which obviously puts Leontes in the limelight and relegates Antigonus to the wings.[102] Still, right at the end, we are reminded of Antigonus's fate again, and we should not allow the reminder to go unheeded. There is a well-founded tradition of reading *The Winter's Tale* as a parable of divine grace, though with this comes the danger of writing it off as backward-looking or transhistorical; looking at the play in terms of its immediate theological context helps us to avoid this, while also responding to the full tragicomic implications of grace in post-Reformation England.[103] Mapped onto a Christian grid, the play invites us to rejoice at exceptional grace, but in passing – and perhaps with a dangerous compassion – it also deplores the fact that grace is exceptional.

CONCLUSION: 'THE TWO NOBLE KINSMEN' AND DIVINE INSCRUTABILITY

The preoccupations of *King Lear* and *The Winter's Tale* are typical of their age, since no factor was more important in shaping the plot of a Renaissance play than notions of fate and providence.[104] The idea that a deity or deities could intervene in human life was central to both, and even though the Christian God could not appear on stage in mainstream Elizabethan drama, playwrights could invoke a sense of divine immanence within both gentile and Christian settings. Between providence and fate, a whole generic spectrum is encompassed: since providence is a more optimistic notion than fate, it has a comic and tragicomic bias, while tragedy and fate are natural partners. For orthodox Christians of all denominations, a drama demonstrating God's providence would have provided a straightforward continuum with the world outside the theatre, while issues of fate would have been entered into as an imaginative or historicist exercise, with relevance to the contemporary Christian remaining largely implicit. There were some situations, mostly tragic, in which only pagan gods could be used. Where the fate of a particular individual presupposed a malevolent or uncaring universe, it would have seemed quite incompatible with the just, all-powerful and all-loving Christian God. But within the confines of drama, the classical pantheon could again be seriously believed in;

this in turn meant that the fates could be presented as arbitrary and cruel without impugning the Christian God's predestinatory wisdom, while heavenly powers could be railed at without incurring accusations of atheism.[105]

Can one therefore see Senecan-inspired tragedy, of which this is most consistently true, as a safety-valve for the age?[106] Both the tragedy and tragicomedy of the time can be read as demonstrating adverse emotional reactions to Calvinism and its predestinatory edicts, and these often have a fortuitous resemblance to the harder questions which, a few generations later, were beginning to be asked of Christianity. But while there is a case to be made for Enlightenment Shakespeare, his plays are never other than drama. In no case do they go past the emotional apprehension of theological difficulties to the systematic abstract questioning which was to lead to religious heterodoxy and atheism in later generations, and our wish to bring great minds into dialogue should not lead us to suppose that they do. On a similar tack, it may be missing the point to read Shakespeare alongside Luther or Calvin, as some critics have done. Like autobiographical reflection or poetry, the dramas of Shakespeare's time give us not official theologies but unofficial reactions to theological discourse, usually themselves removed from Luther, Calvin and other originatory theologians by a multitude of written and oral means. Hence, debates between professional theologians are perhaps most directly helpful not when they discuss predestination itself, but where they foreground pastoral concerns about how, and whether, the doctrine of predestination should be conveyed to laymen.

Nor is it particularly appropriate to think, in the new historicist manner, of specific religio-political events giving rise to this interest. *King Lear*, for instance, was probably begun soon after the 1604 Hampton Court Conference, which saw prolonged and high-profile debate upon the topic of predestination;[107] yet where it raises questions pertaining to this, *Lear* is to be seen less as responding to a specific moment than as diagnosing a longer-standing mood. Though one can argue that fashions in dramatic genre tracked the ameliorations of high Calvinism that mark early-seventeenth-century English Protestantism, this is a pattern which only emerges over decades.[108]

Imaginative literature could, of course, be used to give intellectual consideration to questions of predestination; the poet and closet-dramatist Fulke Greville is one contemporary of Shakespeare's who did exactly that.[109] But writers tend to take their bearings not merely from contemporary theological debate but from classical myth foregrounding the mystery of perverse behaviour, exemplified in the comment of Ovid's Medea: 'I see the better way, and approve it; but I follow the worse.'[110] Whether because of censorship, audience preference or a pragmatic consciousness of what was likely to dramatize well, there is little sign in the professional theatre of detailed engagement with the intellectual niceties of predestination; what we see instead is the exploitation of fear and bewilderment at the very idea of it.

William B. Hamlin has suggested that the professional drama of Shakespeare's era contains 'the most searching moral philosophy of the age'.[111] Yet the insights are so oblique, so tied to character, that the question of intentionality remains a huge one; sadly, it cannot be explored in any detail here, though a few reflections may be appropriate. Questions about divine justice were not foreign to religio-philosophical inquiry at this date, and fiction allowed such questions to be left hanging in the air in a way that, were the genre non-fictional, would have been unlikely to reach a mainstream audience. But condemning Christianity for its similarities to an exploded pagan belief-system was an idea whose time had not quite come in non-fiction; in fiction it can only be seen as one imaginative entertainment among others; and in the multivocal medium of drama, sceptical or atheistical gambits would have made most readers or viewers cleave to orthodoxy all the more tightly. A situation of seeming injustice could have suggested the malevolence of God or the gods, possibly even their non-existence; but equally, it could have pointed to His or their inscrutability, acting as a reminder that divine decrees were too high for humans to comprehend. Similarly, the way in which drama probes areas of contemporary theological discomfort could be seen not as venturesome heterodoxy, but as a warning to desist one's questioning, or indeed as a reminder of divine favour: the horror of a world without Christianity would, for many of Shakespeare's contemporaries, have been the single most potent argument that Christianity was true. Science fiction invites its readers to feel awe at imagined technological innovations, but is not, on the whole, written with the explicit purpose of encouraging these, and is often deeply wary about them. Where it appears to anticipate the freethinkers and atheists of a later age, the tragedy of Shakespeare's time may be serving a similar cautionary function.

But even within Shakespeare's own oeuvre, divine inscrutability could have different and even contradictory literary effects. With plots based in each case around a king whose growing awareness of culpability is central to the play's dramatic interest, *King Lear* and *The Winter's Tale* both illustrate how the theme of repentance became more central in the later years of Shakespeare's career, and it is no surprise that both, despite their pagan settings, have sometimes been read as purveying the Christian message of redemption. But both plays also generate a cluster of questions which problematise this kind of didactic and optimistic reading. Why do some people repent and others not, and why are some people unable to sustain their repentance?[112] Are some people incapable of repenting? Why do some people die badly, backsliding or before getting the chance to repent? More broadly, both plays invite one to interrogate fate and the gods, often through asking whether natural events have a supernatural origin: are stars to be read as intimations of a superhuman plan, or storms as a sign of divine wrath? Both plays, one a tragedy and one a tragicomedy, ask a question which has been central to tragedy from the beginning, and became almost as important to the tragicomic genre as it metamorphosed in the Renaissance: for good or ill, are human beings the helpless pawns of powers outside their control? Yet a play that followed shortly afterwards, *The Two Noble Kinsmen*, swerves away from this nexus of concerns, illustrating how questions of determinism could be detached from those of repentance altogether.

Thanks to the presence of a co-author, *Two Noble Kinsmen* has tended to be awkwardly marginal in the Shakespeare canon. But John Fletcher, the other playwright involved, was an important figure in the development of Guarinian tragicomedy in England, and if one places the genre of tragicomedy rather than the figure of Shakespeare in the foreground, it throws the play into greater relief.[113] Like *A Midsummer Night's Dream*, Shakespeare's earlier retelling of a story appropriated

from Chaucer's 'Knight's Tale', it is set during the wedding celebrations of Theseus and Hippolyta.[114] The close friendship of the two
main characters, Palamon and Arcite, turns to rivalry when both fall
in love with Emilia; their duel is interrupted by Theseus who, in
accordance with the Athenian laws against duelling, arranges an alternative form of combat, where the winner will receive Emilia's hand in
marriage and the loser will be put to death. The final act of the play
dramatizes a series of petitions to the gods, as Palamon, Arcite and the
rest ask that the outcome of the duel should be in accordance with the
divine will. In the end, Arcite wins the duel and Palamon prepares for
execution, but finally attains Emilia's hand when the news comes
through that Arcite has been thrown from his horse and killed.

As Eugene M. Waith has commented, the impossible situation in
which Palamon and Arcite find themselves 'present[s] a parallel to the
mysterious and seemingly arbitrary decisions of the gods'.[115] Though
the play's quasi-tragic denouement can certainly be put down to
human causes as well as divine ones – Palamon and Arcite's stubborn
rivalry, Theseus's imposition of the death penalty for the loser of the
tournament, Emilia's reluctance to choose between her two suitors –
the notion of divine immanence is pervasive throughout, preparing the
audience for an ending precipitated by external event rather than character. Theseus provides a typically legalistic explanation that raises
more questions than it answers:

> Never Fortune
> Did play a subtler game. The conquered triumphs;
> The victor has the loss; yet in the passage
> The gods have been most equal. – Palamon,
> Your kinsman hath confessed the right o'th'lady
> Did lie in you, for you first saw her and
> Even then proclaimed your fancy. He restored her
> As your stol'n jewel and desired your spirit
> To send him hence forgiven.
>
> (5.4.112–120)

But even if Arcite has been divinely punished for not ceding Emilia to
his friend, this invites more questions than it answers: in particular,

why both men should have desired Emilia so vehemently in the first place. Here, the play provides no counter to Palamon's melancholy wonder 'That we should things desire, which do cost us / The loss of our desire! That nought could buy / Dear love, but loss of dear love!' (110–112). But like its counterpart in Chaucer, Theseus's speech continues in a manner which acknowledges the insufficiency of human rationalization:

> Oh, you heavenly charmers,
> What things you make of us! For what we lack
> We laugh, for what we have are sorry, still
> Are children in some kind. Let us be thankful
> For that which is, and with you leave dispute
> That are above our question.
>
> (131–136)[116]

The play reflects its source in the way that Theseus first tries to justify the turn of events, then gives up and turns to more pragmatic reflections. As A.C. Spearing comments in a classic essay on 'The Knight's Tale', 'From an assertion of order, Theseus has passed to one of inevitability, and now he leaves metaphysics behind entirely, . . . [moving] from unconvincing philosophical speculation to sensible practical advice'.[117] As Spearing goes on to say, Theseus's view is not one that entirely coheres with medieval Christianity. But even though its perception of the gods toying with humans owes so much to paganism, the opinion that Theseus goes on to express, that one should not speculate about matters beyond human knowledge, was perfectly assimilable to Christianity in both the medieval and the Reformation eras, and in fact had some very contemporary resonances at the time Shakespeare and Fletcher were writing.

As described above, modifications of high Calvinism were already gaining currency in the last years of the sixteenth century. The authors of these are not necessarily to be seen as proto-Arminian, since they often take pains to stress their Calvinist credentials. But their attempts to draw attention to the mysteries of predestination and man's unfitness to investigate it was a way for those who disagreed with the hardline Calvinist position to signal their dissent, while also stressing what their opponents made a point of acknowledging: God's sovereignty and the high incomprehensibility of His decrees. While plainly a response to the pastoral problems caused by high Calvinism, this is considerably more than an abdication of intellectual responsibility or a plea for pragmatism.[118] Its stress on divine incomprehensibility, which can seem intellectually obscurantist to a later age, was intended above all as a mitigation of over-zealous attempts to discern the marks of salvation in oneself, attempts which might culminate in despair. Yet high Calvinism had only been taking to its logical conclusion the notion that man was utterly passive before God, which from Luther's writings onwards was central to early Protestant theology, and which, as suggested above, has deep resonances with classical ideas of fate. Set against a classical background and betraying its medieval source in its emphasis upon aristocratic honour, *The Two Noble Kinsmen* is an eclectic text in many ways, yet it is perhaps more thoroughly post-Reformation than any of Shakespeare's tragedies in its portrayal of man's lack of agency before the divine.[119]

Striking in this context is the near-interchangeability of Palamon and Arcite, and the element of arbitrariness in who wins and who loses. This could have evoked texts familiar within predestinatory discourse, such as: 'Then two men shalbe in the fields, the one shalbe received, and the other shalbe refused. Two women shalbe grinding at the mil: the one shalbe received, & the other shalbe refused' (Matthew 24:40–41).[120] Even sublapsarianism would not have soothed anxieties about how to distinguish the elect from the reprobate. The religious eclecticism of Shakespeare's dramas always defies a reductive reading, and Palamon's valediction to the dying Arcite, 'Thy brave soul seek Elysium!' (5.4.95), strikes an optimistic note and reinforces the play's classical paganism. Yet to the play's first auditors, nothing would have been more emotive than a divine dispensation that rose above what seemed fair, and Shakespeare did not need to set stories against a Christian background, or even employ concepts of the afterlife, to turn the screw on it. Wherever natural rather than supernatural factors play a visible part in a protagonist's downfall, this draws back from the full imaginative implications of predestination; but fatal flaws and similar notions make very little sense with regard to a play like *The Two*

Noble Kinsmen, given its near-total separation of character from destiny. Illustrating how human desert and divine justice need bear no obvious relation to each other, the play is a virtuoso exercise in pre-destinarianism – nothing at all to do with repentance, scarcely to do with character, everything to do with divine decretal. As such, it provokes a certain piety in its audience, though, as the conclusion to this study will explore, we are left wondering whether this is towards God or the author.

CONCLUSION

'CEDO NULLI':
ENDINGS AND AUTHORIAL DIVINITY

This study has been looking at how the idea of conversion was both exploited and avoided by Shakespeare at different points in his writing career. But as the last chapter implied, his later plays also ask insistent questions about who is in control of conversion. In these fictional analogues to real-life dramas of salvation, the author's relation to his characters mimicks that of the Calvinist God's to humankind, as he makes them good or bad at his pleasure, or, as in *The Two Noble Kinsmen*, simply lucky or unlucky; after all, as fictional constructs, they can have no agency and no free will. The title of Thomas Beard's famous tract *The Theatre of God's Judgements* shows how a common early-modern metaphor, the world as theatre, could be mapped onto questions of salvation and damnation, and it was a playwright's endings above all which enabled him to play God in this way; as a lord of limit, a dramatist could control providence within his fictional world and mete out final dispensations. It is against this background that this conclusion will discuss allusions to Terminus, the classical god of endings, in Shakespeare's final plays, as well as the wider ways in which Terminus's operations could be compared to an author's.

Terminus was a well-known figure in Renaissance iconography, though one whose identity was fluid and evasive, very much in keeping with the period's fondness for composite classical deities.[1] Most commonly depicted as a classical herm, a limbless statue combining a bust and a quadrangular pillar, he had links to the Greek god Hermes and his Roman counterpart Mercury, to whom statues of this kind were erected, and the words 'herm' and 'term' are often interchange-able.[2] Most often referred to as male, Terminus had some female incar-nations, a circumstance that could only have been helped through association with the sexual ambiguity of Hermes's child Herma-phroditus, and by the fact that herms sometimes combined the faces of different deities.[3] He presided over endings and boundaries, which gave him an obvious function within dramatic narrative. The most explicit allusion to Terminus within the Shakespeare canon comes in *The Two Noble Kinsmen*, where Palamon and Arcite bid farewell to each other before fighting a duel for Emilia's hand in marriage, and Arcite declares: 'So hoist we / The sails that must these vessels port, even where / The heavenly limiter pleases' (5.1.28–30).[4] But *The Winter's Tale* also exploits the figure of Terminus towards its end, via the character and dramatic function of Hermione.

As all recent editors of the play have noted, Hermione's name marks a departure from Shakespeare's source, Robert Greene's *Pandosto*, where the queen is called 'Bellaria'.[5] With its blend of pagan and Christian referents, it is one of the most syncretic names borne by any Shakespearean character, and its latent puns should be attended to.[6] One recalls recent interest in the scene's evocation of Catholic ritual: 'herm' was a familiar abbreviation of 'eremite' at this period, and concealed in Paulina's 'removed house' (5.2.91) for sixteen years, Hermione certainly qualifies as such.[7] Given the connotations of mercury in alchemical studies and within writings attributed to Hermes Trismegistus, another points towards occultism; Shakespeare's last plays have, indeed, sometimes attracted hermetic approaches.[8] But the present reading advances a more limited claim: that a character called Hermione, who appears as a standing statue in the final scene of a play, is intended both to suggest herms and to evoke elements of the Terminus myth.[9]

There are a number of possible reasons why. Within early-modern theological discourse the word 'terminus' had predestinatory connota-tions, being used to denote a 'bande or limit [wherefore] the elect are seperated a sunder from them that are not elect'.[10] Thus, like the fate of Antigonus discussed above, it invokes God's inscrutable purposes, albeit with a more optimistic sense of providence. Most obviously, the scene ends the play, though not without asking us to reflect on the provisionality of dramatic termini. As we are reminded earlier in *The Winter's Tale*, tragedy can mutate into comedy, and winter always turns into spring. Like Janus, as double-faced as any herm, Hermione's statue looks backward and forward simultaneously; given Terminus's strong association with Mercury, god of crossroads and messenger between the living and the dead, it also suggests how the ending of one phase heralds the start of another, and how the pangs of bereavement can be mitigated by remembrance. And as Hermione breaks her pose and takes up her former position at court, her role as Terminus itself comes to an end. Finally, the allusion is interesting in the light of the play's gender politics. As commented above, Terminus was sometimes given female attributes, a factor that poses interesting tensions with the god's power to command.[11] In an emblematic rhyme by Henry Peacham, Terminus even changes gender half-way through:

> A Pillar high, erectèd was of stone,
> In former times, which TERMINUS they nam'd:
> And was esteem'd, a God of every one:
> The upper part, was like a woman fram'd . . .
> Which when JOVE passed by, with sterne aspect,
> He bad this God remoove, and get him gone,
> But TERMINUS as stoutly did neglect
> His heste, and answer'd, I give place to none:
> I am the bound of thinges, which God above
> Hath fixt, and none is able to remoove.[12]

Peacham's poem refers to the story that when Tarquinius Superbus decided to dedicate a temple to Jupiter, the auguries decreed that a stone dedicated to Terminus on the same site could not be removed, and so it was allowed to remain within the sanctuary walls of the new temple.[13] This suggests how the myth could resonate with dramatic representations of capitulation, or celebrations of immovable integrity such as Hermione's. Here and elsewhere, as a play based around the theme of unfounded marital jealousy, *The Winter's Tale* invites comparison with Shakespeare's earlier *Othello*, and especially, perhaps, with Desdemona's dying lie as to who is responsible for her murder:

'Nobody. I myself, Farewell' (5.2.122).[14] Unlike Desdemona, Hermione never swerves in her protestations of innocence, and though a king and a husband, Leontes is eventually brought to admit that he is wrong. Ceding to the statue, 'Does not the stone rebuke me / For being more stone than it?' (5.3.37–38) he reminds us that even if '*The Winter's Tale* ends with patriarchy intact', Hermione's moral authority is supreme.[15]

Another of Shakespeare's last plays, *Cymbeline*, more directly dramatizes the motif of Jupiter yielding.[16] Considered as a whole, *Cymbeline* strives less for psychological realism than for experimentation with form, and uses the issue of destiny more to foreground the creator's role than to examine his creatures' predicaments.[17] This is true not only for the play's villains, the Queen and Cloton, but for the more central, more sympathetic character Posthumus. His speech in jail, where he describes his conscience as being 'fettered / more than [his] shanks and wrists' and asks 'You good gods, give me / The penitent instrument to pick that bolt' (5.3.102–104), sketches his personal repentance in what is, for Shakespeare, some detail.[18] But this functions less as a denouement in itself than as a prelude to showing how human fates are disposed by author-gods. In the succeeding, highly metatheatrical episode, one of the very few in Shakespeare's work where a god appears on stage, Jupiter is called upon to change the ending of the play from a tragic to a tragicomic one. Posthumus asks that his life be taken in exchange for Innogen's, and as he falls asleep, the ghosts of dead family members appear in a dream to remonstrate with Jupiter about this unhappy potential fate. As Martin Butler has commented, one line from their plea predicts that 'the action will eventually reenfold tragedy under the aegis of romance': 'No more, thou Thunder-master, show thy spite on mortal flies' (5.3.124) rewrites Gloucester's lament in *King Lear*, 'As flies to wanton boys are we to th'gods; / They kill us for their sport' (4.1.36–37).[19] As Posthumus's father Sicilius concludes the chorus with an invocation which is almost a threat, 'Peep through thy marble mansion, help, or we poor ghosts will cry / To th'shining synod of the rest against thy deity' (5.3.154–155), Jupiter appears, and declares in fury:

FIGURE 6 *Symbola Cedo Nulli*, from Andrea Alciati, *Emblematum liber*, Lyon, 1550. By permission of Glasgow University Library (Sp Coll S.M. Add 265).

Poor shadows of Elysium, hence, and rest
Upon your never-withering banks of flowers.
Be not with mortal accidents oppressed;
No care of yours it is; you know 'tis ours.
Whom best I love, I cross; to make my gift,
The more delayed, delighted. Be content.
Your low-laid son our godhead will uplift;
His comforts thrive, his trials well are spent.

(161–168)

Does the ghosts' plea have the effect of actually changing Jupiter's decrees, or has their intervention itself been foreseen and incorporated into the divine plan? We are never given a clear answer, but the checks on Jupiter's power have been explicitly invoked by Sicilius, and we are at least invited to consider the possibility that, whether in time or in eternity, Jupiter has noted this and is responding to it. Through his response, the play turns definitively away from tragedy; but if the contest is partly to do with genre, just as much in question is the agency by which the ending should be achieved. The prognostication which Jupiter gives the ghosts for Posthumus, which both foretells and precipitates the climax, can be seen as defiantly reappropriating augury for himself: 'This tablet lay upon his breast, wherein / Our pleasure his full fortune doth confine' (173–174). But the tablet, emblematizing the act of authorship as it does, begs another question: is Jupiter the author, or is he being made to point to the fact that he himself has been authored?

No Renaissance play is more explicitly engaged than *Cymbeline* with the issue of endings, and who is responsible for them. The play's unusually long-drawn-out last act, long seen as one of its defects, has attracted apologists in recent years, and while it certainly taxes the patience of a modern-day audience, it does make better sense to treat it as a deliberate aesthetic decision, rather than evidence of an ageing playwright's sloppiness.[20] As a formal celebration of resolution it can, in one sense, hardly be too long – as Cymbeline comments, 'This fierce abridgment / Hath to it circumstantial branches which / Distinction should be rich in' (5.4.382–384). But a stretched-out ending that

rejoices in the act of termination, paralleling the spatial expansion of
Rome in temporal terms, can be seen as a narrative tribute to the god
of boundaries. It sets the wheels in motion for an ending that, while
it celebrates personal happiness, subordinates this to a political circumstance: the restoration of tribute to Rome and Rome's bounds
being extended.[21] Connecting the checks on Jupiter's power with the
expansion of Rome's boundaries again evokes Terminus, who had
particular charge over Rome's borders as far as they extended; as the
description of the god in Ovid's *Fasti* concludes: 'To other races territory is granted with a fixed border. / The world's the limit for the city
of Rome.'[22] It is no coincidence that the play's closing lines mention
one of Jupiter's temples, reminding the classically educated viewer of
Terminus's stubborn presence in another:

> Laud we the gods,
> And let our crookèd smokes climb to their nostrils
> From our blest altars. Publish we this peace
> To all our subjects. . . .
>> So through Lud's Town march,
> And in the temple of great Jupiter
> Our peace we'll ratify, seal it with feasts.
> Set on there. Never was a war did cease,
> Ere bloody hands were washed, with such a peace.
>> (5.4.474–477, 479–483)

As suggested above, the myths surrounding Terminus were obvious
ones to bring into dialogue with Christian notions of providence and
predestination. But well before the Reformation, they had also become
a way of asking who was ultimately responsible for endings. In *The
City of God*, Augustine argued that because Jove was greatest, the lords
of limit Janus and Terminus had to yield to him – a Christianization
of the myth, satirically elaborated to demonstrate the absurdity of
polytheism.[23] There were other ways too that the story of Jove's
yielding could be Christianized, as demonstrated by Peacham's verse
quoted above. By having Terminus explain that he represents 'the
bound of things', Peacham co-opts the god into a Christian schema;
thus, Terminus's snub to Jove becomes a way of demonstrating how

Christianity is bound to conquer paganism. But as dramatized by Shakespeare in *Cymbeline*, the spectacle of Jove's concession is different again: not a straightforward pastiche of classical piety, not a normative Christian reading of the Terminus myth like Peacham's, it bespeaks his awareness of an author's general power and his own particular talents.

The fluidity of Terminus's identity, and Shakespeare's, invites comparisons with Proteus and with the Ovidian model of authorship, discussed in the Introduction and Chapter 2 of this study. But for a Renaissance author to associate himself with Terminus had also been an emblematic way of declaring authorial pre-eminence, ever since Erasmus had adopted an image of Terminus for his *impresa*, with the motto *Cedo nulli* (I yield to none). As an English translation of Paulus Jovius's treatise on emblems puts it, Erasmus meant by his choice that 'he would not give place to any other Writer'.[24] As a writer's tutelary deity, Terminus could stand for an aim to be first among equals; as the god of ends, he emblematized belief in the surpassing importance of stylistic refinement and textual satisfaction. Here it may be appropriate to consider a quality which has often been thought to lie at the heart of Shakespeare's greatness, the subordination of everything to art, influentially articulated by August Wilhelm von Schlegel in his notion of organic unity:

Form is mechanical when, through external influence, it is communicated to any material merely as an accidental addition without reference to its quality; as, for example, when we give a particular shape to a soft mass that it may retain the same after its induration. Organical form, again, is innate; it unfolds itself from within, and acquires its determination along with the complete developement [*sic*] of the germ. We every where discover such forms in nature throughout the whole range of living powers, from the crystallization of salts and minerals to plants and flowers, and from them to the human figure. In the fine arts, as well as in the province of nature, the highest artist, all genuine forms are organical, that is, determined by the quality of the work. In a word, the form is nothing but a significant

exterior, the speaking physiognomy of each thing, disfigured by
no destructive accidents, which gives a true evidence of its
hidden essence.[25]

This famous passage is preceded by Schlegel's contention that works of
art whose form is dictated by external forces are necessarily inferior to
those that, like Shakespeare's, demonstrate organic unity. In the same
series of lectures – to glance back at the introduction to this study –
Schlegel visualises Shakespeare as protean, in terms which reinforce
these aesthetic criteria: '. . . from the diversity of tone and colour,
which he assumes according to the qualities of objects, [he is] a true
Proteus.'[26] The picture of Shakespeare drawn in the present study,
which comes at him from another direction, is nevertheless remarkably similar to Schlegel's: of someone constantly ready to appropriate
religious matter wherever it enhances his artistic vision, but who
invariably subordinates it to the requirements of the individual artefact.
Because the truth-claims insisted upon by Christianity, and by many
other religions, have an intrinsically overriding quality, they can be
seen as imparters of mechanical form – and hence artistically inferior,
according to those who take their artistic bearings from Shakespeare.
Every time a work of art is condemned for didactic or proselytizing
features, Shakespeare is one of the authorities behind the pointing
finger.

To think of religious doctrine, discipline and practice as entirely
separate from aesthetic considerations would, of course, be wrong – if
only because aesthetic creeds too can be interpreted as imposing rigorous and self-denying demands on their adherents.[27] Besides, returning
to Schlegel's description, it does hint – despite his loud affirmation of
organic unity – at two possible ways of articulating the idea that truth
and beauty are one. Shakespeare's admirers have nearly always
praised his detachment from dogma and been fascinated by his biography; this, in turn, may suggest that his supremely well-achieved
literary artifacts were always intended to subordinate ideologies more
communally authored than his own works of art, leaving the author
himself as the final object of readerly contemplation. Schlegel's metaphor pictures the work of art, with Romantic disingenuousness, as

unfolding almost independently of an author's ministrations; but poems and plays do not in fact write themselves. Just as the notion of mechanical form can describe the subordination of creative effort to externally imposed ideologies, the notion of organic unity privileges the individual creator. With the one, religion can be seen as governing the author. With the other, the author trumps religion: to adopt Terminus as a cultic figure enabled one to claim precedence even of the gods, surely one reason why Erasmus's contemporary Carvayalus was reported as criticizing the device for its arrogance.[28] Foregrounding the question of outcomes, as any consideration of Terminus must, one can see the omnipotent Jove and the immovable herm as representing the two teleologies, religious and artistic, that have run side by side throughout this study.[29]

As the god of ends, Terminus could also represent death. Erasmus, in fact, claimed in response to critics that this was all he meant by his emblem.[30] There are certainly close connections in the Renaissance between the god and emblematic depictions of death, not least because Hermes and Mercury acted as mediators between the dead and the living.[31] But if anything, this plays up the connection between herms, fame and memorializing, especially since cairns – piles of stones which were believed to have originated as grave-markers – were a common way to depict herms in the Renaissance.[32] And to return to where this study began, the church of Holy Trinity, Stratford-upon-Avon, it is at least a historical serendipity that at some point – we do not know when – Shakespeare's own gravestone was allocated to one of the positions closest to the altar there. Like Terminus, it quite literally jostles God, which may suggest that it was moved to its current position at a time when Shakespeare had begun to be regarded with a quasi-religious awe.[33] Still bearing Terminus in mind, can one even speculate that Shakespeare might have pictured his gravestone as somewhere in the sacred space of the chancel?[34] The well-known verse on it objects as steadfastly as Terminus to the idea of being moved, and what has often been interpreted as a warning against transferring bones to a charnel-house may have classical resonances too.[35]

Good frend for Jesus sake forbeare,
To digg the dust encloased heare:
Bleste be ye man yt spares thes stones,
And curst be he yt moves my bones.

As so often with apotropaic texts, this rhyme deploys the idea of benediction and malediction in such a way as to leave it unclear who is cursing and blessing: is it Death, claiming ownership of the bones, or the dead person acting in a prophetic or priestly role, even annexing powers which belong only to God? If late-seventeenth-century commentators were correct in attributing it to Shakespeare himself, this ambiguity will not have been lost on the author.[36]

Diana Price has suggested that this gravestone, and the monument to Shakespeare that also survives in the church chancel, may together have formed part of a larger commemorative ensemble, which either was not erected or does not survive.[37] Early-seventeenth-century funeral monuments of distinguished people – which, like termini, often combined a portrait bust with a lapidary support – were commonly erected within church chancels. For the classically educated, the visual reminder of Terminus could have been irresistible, leading to metaphysically audacious imaginings.[38] Such a classicization, limiting the remit of the Christian God if not putting him in his place,

FIGURE 7   Shakespeare's Grave, Shakespeare Birthplace Trust. © Shakespeare Birthplace Trust Records Office

seems a possible way to look at Shakespeare's monument as well as Shakespeare's gravestone. Not uniquely among those of its era, the monument is more concerned to locate its subject within the classical pantheon than within the Christianity of its surroundings: 'A Pylus in judgement, a Socrates in genius, a Maro in art, / The earth buries him, the people mourn him, Olympus possesses him.'[39] The writer of this inscription finds the most natural analogues for Shakespeare among pagan masters of language; he, and all those responsible for devising the monument, clearly saw Shakespeare's literary fame as the most important aspect of his life to commemorate, and believed that this could most effectively be done by coupling him with non-Christian authors. As mentioned earlier, another of the gods with whom the figure of Terminus has been consistently linked is Mercury, god of eloquence; but one need not argue, in conspiracy mode, for any hermetic meaning to observe how Shakespeare's monument commemorates verbal skill, not personal piety. As a secular monument, one which must have been felt to be appropriate to the man it commemorated, it reiterates Jonson's tribute 'Soul of the age!' in his dedicatory poem in the First Folio.[40] The emphasis is shared by many church monuments at this date; it may be a time-worn historical adage that the Renaissance saw God being jostled by man, but sometimes adages are apt.

When evoked by authors as able as Shakespeare or Erasmus, the god Terminus with all his mythological resonances must surely remind one that supreme literary achievement is the best means of ensuring posthumous fame for that author's works. But some of the critics discussed in this book would have replied: what about the eternal destination of the author himself? This is a terrible question, though perhaps one which belongs to the past; even critics who are practising Christians would be unlikely to put it so bluntly today. But related questions – how can creative artists please if aspects of their life or work are doctrinally or ethically offensive; are moral criteria irrelevant to works of art? – are as piercing as ever. The notion of Jupiter and Terminus jostling for pre-eminence allegorizes the continued stand-off between those whose aesthetic appreciation is governed or consciously influenced by ethical and religious considerations, and those who claim an overriding authority for artistic creation and its creators. It seems fair to place Shakespeare in the latter camp, and, as we have seen, Shakespeare's work was disliked by contemporaries whose notions of pleasure were focused mainly, or exclusively, on religion. Their reactions tell us something about how he could be perceived: as a secular writer, a profane writer, an idolatrous writer even. Shakespeare's confessional invisibility during his life makes it likely that he was a conforming member of the Church of England. His will is a standardized, nominally Protestant document, commending his soul 'into the hands of God my Creator, hoping and assuredly believing through the only merits of Jesus Christe my Saviour, to be made partaker of life everlasting'.[41] Here as earlier in his career, we shall never know for certain how he saw religious faith as relating to his own life and afterlife. But what we do know is the side he came down upon: that his writing treated all religions, including the Christian doctrine of his time, as subservient to artistic unity and closure; that he was a worshipper of the god Terminus, and has caused others to worship him.[42]

NOTES

INTRODUCTION

1. Information from www.stratford-upon-avon.org/shakespeare.html.
2. G.L. Remnant, *A Catalogue of Misericords in Great Britain* (Oxford: Clarendon, 1998). The misericords are illustrated in Mary Frances White, *Fifteenth Century Misericords in the Collegiate Church of Holy Trinity, Stratford-upon-Avon* (Stratford-upon-Avon: M.F. White, 1974). On Holy Trinity Church, see Paul Jeffery, *The Collegiate Churches of England and Wales* (London: Robert Hale, 2004), pp. 383–385.
3. Clare Asquith, *Shadowplay* (New York: Public Affairs, 2005). For a famous critique of 'the 'school of Knight', see Roland Mushat Frye, *Shakespeare and Christian Doctrine* (Princeton: Princeton University Press, 1963), esp. Ch. 1.
4. While concepts of the aesthetic post-date Shakespeare, his work has often been read in terms of its implicit ideas about art and aesthetic practices: see, recently, Hugh Grady's *Shakespeare and Impure Aesthetics* (Cambridge: Cambridge University Press, 2009).
5. Cf. Remnant, *Misericords*, p. 57. At several periods, misericords could have been damaged by iconoclasts and moralists: see p. xviii in the same volume. Little information is available on Reformation alterations to the fabric of Holy Trinity Church, as the vestry minutes only survive from 1617. My thanks to Mairi Macdonald at the Shakespeare Centre Library for this information.
6. For introductory accounts, see J.A. Guy, *Tudor England* (Oxford: Oxford University Press, 1988); Penry Williams, *The Later Tudors: England 1547–1603* (Oxford: Clarendon, 1995); Susan Brigden, *New Worlds, Lost Worlds: The Rule of the Tudors, 1485–1603* (London: Allen Lane, 2000), and for the later period, Barry Coward, *The Stuart Age: England 1603–1714*, 3rd edn (Harlow: Longman, 2003).
7. I must apologize that a lack of space prohibits adequate consideration of Judaism and Islam, but these important topics have been well covered elsewhere. On Judaism, James Shapiro, *Shakespeare and the Jews* (New York: Columbia University Press, 1996) discusses both the Jewish presence in Shakespeare's England (pp. 58, 62–88) and the myths surrounding Jews. On the execution of Roderigo Lopez, the Queen's physician and a conerted Jew, see (most recently) Stephen Greenblatt, *Will in the World: How Shakespeare Became Shakespeare* (New York: W.W. Norton, 2004), Ch. 9. On the Islamic presence in England around the same period, see Nabil Matar,

Islam in Britain, 1558–1685 (Cambridge: Cambridge University Press, 1998). See also Matthew Dimmock, *New Turkes: Dramatising Islam and the Ottomans in Early Modern England* (Aldershot: Ashgate, 2005), Daniel J. Vitkus, *Turning Turk: English Theater and the Multicultural Mediterranean* (New York/Basingtoke: Palgrave, 2003); and Vitkus (ed.), *Three Turk Plays from Early Modern England* (New York: Columbia University Press, 2000), introduction. London's Globe Theatre had a 'Shakespeare and Islam' season in the autumn of 2004. On Othello as converted Muslim, see Dimmock, pp. 204–206, and Matar, pp. 129–130.

8. David Cressy, *Birth, Marriage and Death: Ritual, Religion and the Life-Cycle in Tudor and Stuart England* (Oxford: Oxford University Press, 1997). ✗

9. The oath is perhaps too mild to have fallen foul of the Act to Restrain Abuses of Players (1606), for which see Tanya Pollard (ed.), *Shakespeare's Theater: A Sourcebook* (Malden, MA: Blackwell, 2004), p. 328.

10. W.B. Patterson, *King James VI and I and the Reunification of Christendom* (Cambridge: Cambridge University Press, 1997); Christopher Durston, *James I* (London: Routledge, 1993).

11. Michael A. Mullett, *Catholics in Britain and Ireland, 1558–1829* (Basingstoke: Macmillan, 1998); John Bossy, *The English Catholic Community, 1570–1850* (London: Darton, Longman and Todd, 1975).

12. G.R. Elton, *The Tudor Constitution: Documents and Commentary* (1960: repr. Cambridge: Cambridge University Press, 1968), pp. 363–368.

13. Margaret Aston, *England's Iconoclasts: Vol. I. Laws Against Images* (Oxford: Oxford University Press, 1988). For the later period, see Trevor Cooper (ed.), *The Journal of William Dowsing: Iconoclasm in East Anglia During the English Civil War* (Woodbridge: Ecclesiological Society/Boydell, 2001).

14. On this point, see Alexandra Walsham, '"Domme Preachers": Post-Reformation English Catholicism and the Culture of Print', *Past and Present*, 168(1) (2000), pp. 72–123.

15. See Patrick Collinson, Arnold Hunt and Alexandra Walsham, 'Religious Publishing in England, 1557–1640', Ch. 1 in *The Cambridge History of the Book in Britain, Volume 4, 1557–1695*, ed. John Barnard and D.F. McKenzie with Maureen Bell (Cambridge: Cambridge University Press, 2002), p. 29; and Ian Green and Kate Peters. 'Religious Publishing in England, 1640–1695', Ch. 2 in the same volume, p. 67.

16. See Naseeb Shaheen, *Biblical References in Shakespeare's Plays* (1999: revised edition Newark: Delaware University Press/London: Associated University Presses, 2002); Steven Marx, *Shakespeare and the Bible* (Oxford: Oxford University Press, 2002); Maurice Hunt, *Shakespeare's Religious Allusiveness: Its Play and Tolerance* (Aldershot: Ashgate, 2003); R. Chris Hassel, Jnr, *Shakespeare's Religious Language: A Dictionary* (London/New York: Thoemmes Continuum, 2005); Ramie Targoff, *Common Prayer: The Language of Public Devotion in Early Modern England* (Chicago: Chicago University Press, 2001); John W. Velz, 'Shakespeare and the Geneva Bible: The Circumstances', Ch.7 in Takashi Kozuka and J.R. Mulryne (eds), *Shakespeare, Marlowe, Jonson: New Directions in Biography* (Aldershot: Ashgate, 2006).

17. The Prayer Book Psalter was Miles Coverdale's version of the Psalms, which first appeared in the Great Bible (Shaheen, *Biblical References*, p. 11; Shaheen's work also calculates which books of the Bible Shakespeare uses most often). On psalm-singing, see John Craig, 'Psalms, Groans and Dogwhippers: The Soundscape of Worship in the English Parish Church, 1547–1642', Ch. 6 in Will Coster and Andrew Spicer (eds), *Sacred Space in Early Modern Europe* (Cambridge: Cambridge University Press, 2005), and Hannibal Hamlin, *Psalm Culture in Early Modern England* (Cambridge: Cambridge University Press, 2004).

18. The first book of homilies was issued in 1547, the second in 1563. See *Certain Sermons or Homilies Appointed to be Read in Churches* (Oxford: Oxford University Press, 1844).

19. Shaheen, *Biblical References*, esp. pp. 64–66; Richmond Noble, *Shakespeare's Biblical Knowledge, and Use of the Book of Common Prayer* (London: SPCK, 1935); Targoff, *Common Prayer*; Timothy Rosendale, *Liturgy and Literature in the Making of Protestant England* (Cambridge: Cambridge University Press, 2007).

20. See John Spurr, *English Puritanism, 1603–1689* (Basingstoke: Macmillan, 1998), Ch. 3.

21. The Douai/Rheims Bible was available from 1582 (NT) and 1609 (OT), though since it would have been difficult to get hold of and a compromising possession, even those of Catholic sympathies might have used other translations: see David N. Beauregard, *Catholic Theology in Shakespeare's Plays* (Newark: Delaware University Press, 2008), Appendix 1. However, Beauregard's study also critiques the methodology of Shaheen and earlier commentators, arguing that the extent of Catholic language and liturgical allusion in Shakespeare has been underestimated.

22. Lucy Beckett, *In the Light of Christ: Writings in the Western Tradition* (San Francisco: Ignatius Press, 2006) is a distinguished recent example.

23. Shaheen, *Biblical References*, p. 53.

24. See p. 254, fn. 8. On members of the Church of England at this date, see Judith Maltby, *Prayer Book and People in Elizabethan and Early Stuart England* (Cambridge: Cambridge University Press, 1998).

25. See Alexandra Walsham, *Church Papists: Catholicism, Conformity and Confessional Polemic in Early Modern England* (1993: this edn, Woodbridge: Boydell, 1999). The literature on Puritanism is more extensive, but for a good overview of the topic, see Christopher Durston and Jacqueline Eales (eds), *The Culture of English Puritanism, 1560–1700* (Basingstoke: Macmillan, 1996). On religious terminology at this period, see Peter Lake, 'Religious Identities in Shakespeare's England', Ch. 5 in David Scott Kastan (ed.), *A Companion to Shakespeare* (Oxford: Clarendon, 1999), esp. pp. 58–59. On the notion of 'voluntary religion', see Lake, 'Religious Identities', pp. 75, 78, and Patrick Collinson, *The Religion of Protestants* (Oxford: Clarendon, 1982), Ch. 6.

26. See Peter Lake, *Anglicans and Puritans? Presbyterianism and English Conformist Thought from Whitgift to Hooker* (London: Allen and Unwin, 1988), and *Moderate Puritans and the Elizabethan Church* (Cambridge: Cambridge University Press, 1982).

27. On Arminianism, see Nicholas Tyacke, *Anti-Calvinists: The Rise of English Arminianism, c. 1590–1640* (Oxford: Clarendon, 1987); Anthony Milton, *Catholic and Reformed: The Roman and Protestant Churches in English Protestant Thought, 1600–1640* (Cambridge: Cambridge University Press, 1995); Peter Lake and Michael Questier (eds), *Conformity and Orthodoxy in the English Church, c.1560-1660* (Woodbridge: Boydell, 2000); Charles W.A. Prior, *Defining the Jacobean Church: The Politics of Religious Controversy, 1603-1625* (Cambridge: Cambridge University Press, 2005), esp. Introduction; Kenneth Fincham (ed.), *The Early Stuart Church* (Stanford: Stanford University Press, 1993); Kenneth Fincham and Nicholas Tyacke, *Altars Restored: The Changing Face of English Religious Worship, 1547-c.1700* (Oxford: Oxford University Press, 2007).

28. See Jesse M. Lander, *Inventing Polemic: Religion, Print and Literary Culture in Early Modern England* (Cambridge: Cambridge University Press, 2006).

29. See, most recently, Frank Brownlow, *Shakespeare, Harsnett and the Devils of Denham* (Newark/London: Delaware University Press/Associated University Presses, 1993); John L. Murphy, *Darkness and Devils: Exorcism and King Lear* (Athens, OH: Ohio University Press, 1984); and Stephen Greenblatt, *Shakespearean Negotiations* (Oxford: Clarendon, 1988), Ch.4.

30. Garry Wills, *Witches and Jesuits: Shakespeare's* Macbeth (New York/Oxford: New York Public Library/Oxford University Press, 1995).

31. On deliberate polemical anachronism, see p. 185. Cf. the interpretation in Robert S. Miola, ' "An Alien People Clutching Their Gods": Shakespeare's Ancient Religions', *Shakespeare Survey*, Vol. 54, ed. Peter Holland (2001), pp. 31–45, who sees Aaron more in terms of a Protestant reformer enforcing an oath from the 'popish' Lucius (p. 34).

32. Jean-Christophe Mayer, *Shakespeare's Hybrid Faith: History, Religion and the Stage* (Basingstoke: Macmillan, 2006).

33. Alexandra Walsham, *Charitable Hatred: Tolerance and Intolerance in England, 1500–1700* (Manchester: Manchester University Press, 2006).

34. See Graham Bradshaw, *Shakespeare's Scepticism* (this edn, Ithaca: Cornell University Press, 1990); John D. Cox, *Seeming Knowledge: Shakespeare and Sceptical Faith* (Waco, TX: Baylor University Press, 2007); Benjamin Bertram, *The Time Is Out Of Joint: Skepticism in Shakespeare's England* (Newark: Delaware University Press, 2004); Richard Strier, 'Shakespeare and the Skeptics', *Religion and Literature*, 32:2 (2000), pp. 171–186; William Hamlin, *Tragedy and Scepticism in Shakespeare's England* (Basingstoke: Palgrave, 2005). The classic historical account is Richard Popkin, *The History of Scepticism* (1979: rev. and expanded edn, New York: Oxford University Press, 2003).

35. See Emma Smith's introduction to Kyd's *The Spanish Tragedie* (London: Penguin, 1998), p. xiii.

36. See Ch. 4, pp. 186–196, and on the overtones of 'atheistical', Ch. 1, p. 52. For a reading of Shakespeare's work in the light of more recent atheistical preoccupations, see Eric S. Mallin, *Godless Shakespeare* (London: Continuum, 2007).

37. *Dr Faustus*, epilogue, 6–8. Quoted from *Doctor Faustus and Other Plays*, ed.

David Bevington and Eric Rasmussen (Oxford: Oxford University Press, 1995, this ed. 1998), A-text.

38. The career of John Dee exemplifies the overlap of religion, magic and science at this date: see Nicholas H. Clarke, *John Dee's Natural Philosophy: Between Science and Religion* (London: Routledge, 1988). In *The Occult Philosophy in the Elizabethan Age* (1979: this edn, London: Routledge, 2001), Chs. 14–15, Frances Yates argues for Shakespeare's sympathy with certain elements of occultism. On the question of devil-worship at this date, see Alec Ryrie, *The Sorcerer's Tale: Faith and Fraud in Tudor England* (Oxford: Oxford University Press, 2008), esp. pp. 170–177.

39. There has been a long critical tradition of interpreting the subject-matter of *Macbeth* as a tribute to James VI/I's interest in witchcraft. See *Macbeth*, ed. A.R. Braunmuller (Cambridge: Cambridge University Press, 1997), p. 8.

40. 'Shakespeare's Religious and Moral Thinking: Skepticism or Suspicion?', *Religion and Literature*, 36: 1 (2004), pp. 39–66.

41. However, cf. Martin Butler's comment that the terms relating to fairies and witches were sometimes interchangeable: *Cymbeline*, ed. Butler, p. 119.

42. See *Daemonologie*, ed. James Craigie and Alexander Law, in *Minor Prose Works of King James VI and I* (Edinburgh: Scottish Text Society, 1982). p. 51.

43. Regina Buccola, *Fairies, Fractious Women and the Old Faith* (Selinsgrove: Susquehanna University Press, 2006), Ch. 5, and Jensen, *Religion and Revelry*, pp. 103–114.

44. Buccola, *Fairies*, p. 174.

45. John Boys, *An Exposition of the Festivall Epistles and Gospels Used in our English Liturgie* (1615), f. E6a.

46. See Justin Champion, *Republican Learning: John Toland and the Crisis of Christian Culture, 1696–1722* (Manchester: Manchester University Press, 2003).

47. See Ch. 1, pp. 46–47.

48. Buccola, *Fairies*, discusses the connection of fairies and Catholicism.

49. On Catholic nostalgia, see Eamon Duffy, 'Bare Ruined Choirs: Remembering Catholicism in Shakespeare's England', Ch. 2 in Richard Dutton, Alison Findlay and Richard Wilson (eds), *Theatre and Religion* (Manchester: Manchester University Press, 2003) and Ch 2 below.

50. See Ch. 1, pp. 67–68.

51. See Helen Cooper, 'Shakespeare and the Mystery Plays', Ch. 1 in Stuart Gillespie and Neil Rhodes (eds), *Shakespeare and Elizabethan Popular Culture* (London: Arden, 2006). Anne Barton (Righter), *Shakespeare and the Idea of the Play* (1962: this edn, Harmondsworth: Penguin, 1967) explores his metatheatrical continuities with medieval drama. Beatrice Groves, *Texts and Traditions* (Oxford: Clarendon, 2006) is a recent, richly documented account of the verbal and visual reminiscences of pre-Reformation religious drama in Shakespeare's earlier plays.

52. E.g. Greenblatt, *Will in the World*, pp. 36–38.

53. See *OED* under 'doom'.

54. For background on the different denominational interpretations of ghosts, see Peter Marshall, *Beliefs and the Dead in Reformation England* (Oxford: Oxford University Press, 2002).

55. See Ch. 4, pp. 204–205, and Velma Bourgeois Richmond, *Shakespeare, Catholicism and Romance* (New York: Continuum, 2000).

56. See p. 283, fn. 7.

57. Alexandra Walsham, *Providence in Early Modern England* (Oxford: Oxford University Press, 1999). I discuss Catholics' attitude to the miraculous in 'St Winifred's Well and its Meaning in Post-Reformation British Catholic Literary Culture', pp. 271–280 in Peter Davidson and Jill Bepler (eds), *The Triumphs of the Defeated: Early Modern Festivals and Messages of Legitimacy* (Wolfenbüttel: Harrassowitz Verlag, 2007).

58. One should not, of course, ignore the interplay and exchange that took place between the two media: see Ch. 1, esp. pp. 38, 76–78.

59. e.g. Dorothy L. Sayers, *The Mind of the Maker* (1st edn, London: Methuen, 1941).

60. *Shakespeare: The Invention of the Human* (New York: Riverhead, 1998), p. xvii. On Bloom's unspoken debt to Matthew Arnold, see Christy Desmet, 'The Function of Shakespeare at the Present Time', paper delivered at the Shakespeare Institute, July 2000 (http://virtual.park.uga.edu/cdesmet/stratford.html) accessed March 2007.

61. 'Forms of Opposition: Shakespeare and Middleton', *English Literary Renaissance*, 24:2 (1994), 283–314.

62. Comparisons between Shakespeare and Proteus were commonplace within the work of such Romantic critics as Schlegel (see also the conclusion to this study), Coleridge and Hazlitt. See Younglim Han, *Romantic Shakespeare: From Stage to Page* (Madison: Fairleigh Dickinson University Press/London: Associated University Presses, 2001), pp. 91–92, 154; Jonathan Bate, *Shakespeare and the English Romantic Imagination* (1986: this edn, Oxford: Clarendon, 1989), esp. pp. 14–16, 43; Theresa M. Kelley, 'Proteus and Romantic Allegory', *ELH: A Journal of English Literary History*, 49 (1982), pp. 623–652, and *Reinventing Allegory* (Cambridge: Cambridge University Press, 1997). For two typical comparisons between Proteus and Shakespeare, see Robert H.F. Carver, *The Protean Ass: The Metamorphoses of Apuleius from Antiquity to the Renaissance* (Oxford: Oxford University Press, 2007), p. 364, and Trevor McNeely, *Proteus Unmasked: Sixteenth-Century Rhetoric and the Art of Shakespeare* (Bethlehem/London: Lehigh University Press/Associated University Presses, 2004), Ch. 1. On the figure of Proteus in the Renaissance, see William E. Burns, ' "A Proverb of Versatile Mutability": Proteus and Natural Knowledge in Early Modern Britain', *Sixteenth-Century Journal*, 32: 4 (2001), pp. 969–980; James Nohrnberg, *The Analogy of* The Faerie Queene (Princeton: Princeton University Press, 1976), esp. pp. 111–114, 582–597; Jonas Barish, *The Antitheatrical Prejudice* (Berkeley: California University Press, 1981), pp. 96–117. On Proteus's relevance to humanist ideals, see A. Bartlett Giamatti, *Exile and Change in Renaissance Literature* (New Haven: Yale University Press, 1984), Ch. 7, which reprints pp. 437–475 of Peter Demetz, Thomas Greene and Lowry Nelson Jnr (eds), *Essays in Literary Theory, Interpretation and History* (New Haven: Yale University Press, 1968), and Thomas Greene, 'The Flexibility of the Self in Renaissance Literature', pp. 241–264 in the latter volume.

63. See Giamatti, *Exile*, pp. 122–123, 125.

64. See Terence Cave, *The Cornucopian Text: Patterns of Writing in the French Renaissance* (Oxford: Clarendon, 1979), pp. 23, 62–63, 110, 333.

65. *verum ubi correptum manibus vinclisque tenebis / tum variae eludent species atque ora ferarum* (*Georgics* 4, 405–406; see also 396–400). Quoted from *Virgil. Eclogues. Georgics. Aeneid I–VI*, trans. H. Rushton Fairclough, rev. G.P. Goold, Loeb Classical Library (Cambridge, Mass.: Harvard University Press, 1999). See also Homer, *Odyssey*, Books 1–12, trans. A. T. Murray, rev. George E. Dimock, Loeb Classical Library (Cambridge, Mass.: Harvard University Press, 1995), Book IV, 365–569; and Ovid, *Metamorphoses*, ed. R.J. Tarrant (Oxford: Clarendon, 2004), 8: 730–737.

66. *The Golden Booke of the Leaden Goddes* (1577), f. 20r.

67. On Proteus's negative moralistic connotations, see Barish, *Antitheatrical Prejudice*, and Cave, *Cornucopian Text*, p. 93. On the connections between Proteus and the dramatic Vice, see Jensen, *Religion and Revelry*, p. 61 ff. For a classical depiction of Proteus as a gifted actor, see Lucian, *Saltatio*, 19:2 (from Lucian, *Works*, trans. A.M. Harman and M.D. Macleod, 8 vols (London: Heinemann, 1913–1967), vol.5). See also Bate, *Shakespeare and the English Romantic Imagination*, p. 165.

68. *The Supremacie of Christian Princes* (1573), p. 151. The Latin (from Horace, *Epistles*, 1: 1, 90) can be translated as 'With what knot can I hold this face-changing Proteus?': quoted from *Horace. Satires, Epistles and Ars Poetica*, trans. H. Rushton Fairclough, Loeb Classical Library (London/New York: William Heinemann/G.P. Putnam's Sons, 1926). Bridges is answering a Catholic tract, Thomas Stapleton's *A Counterblast to M. Hornes Vayne Blaste* (1567), p. 39, which levels the same quotation against Protestant disunity. See also Elizabeth Heale, 'Spenser's Malengine, Missionary Priests, and the Means of Justice', *Review of English Studies*, n.s., 41, no. 162 (1990), pp. 171–184, which features the same quotation and discusses criticisms of the Jesuit order for proteanism.

69. See my *Catholicism, Controversy and the English Literary Imagination, 1558–1660* (Cambridge: Cambridge University Press, 1999), p. 191. This probably alludes to Erasmus's *Adages*: see William Barker (ed.), *Compendium of Proverbs* (Toronto: Toronto University Press, 1991), p. 167.

70. The Thirty-Nine Articles (1563, revised 1571), produced primarily by Archbishop Matthew Parker, were a revision of the Forty-Two Articles of 1533, overseen by Thomas Cranmer. After 1571, clergy were required to subscribe to them. See Peter Toon, 'The Articles and Homilies', Ch. 2 in part IV of Stephen Sykes, John Booty and Jonathan Knight (ed.), *The Study of Anglicanism* (London: SPCK/Fortress Press, 1998), esp. pp. 147–150.

71. Peter Heylyn, *A Full Relation of Two Journeys* (1656) compares his career not only to Proteus's but to another convert's, Henry IV of France (Book 2, p. 56). See also Patrick Collinson, 'Perne the Turncoat: An Elizabethan Reputation', Ch. 8 in *Elizabethan Essays* (London: Hambledon, 1994).

72. The comparison of Proteus to Machiavelli was standard: see Barish, *Antitheatrical Prejudice*, pp. 98–99.

73. For an allegorizing neoplatonic reading of *Two Gentlemen of Verona*, taking its bearings from Proteus's name, see Richard Cody, *The Landscape of the Mind: Pastoralism and Platonic Theory in Tasso's* Aminta *and Shakespeare's Early Comedies* (Oxford: Clarendon, 1969), Ch. 4. See also Giamatti, *Exile*, pp. 142–149.

74. This assumes, as most commentators have done, that Proteus authors and sings the song. On this question, see the edition by William C. Carroll, p. 241.

75. On the question of Valentine's apparent offer of Silvia to Proteus, see Carroll (ed.), pp. 276–277. Also see Michael D. Friedman, *'The World Must Be Peopled': Shakespeare's Comedies of Forgiveness* (Madison/London: Fairleigh Dickinson University Press/Associated University Presses, 2002), p. 19. Friedman's study discusses how perfunctory repentance and unmerited forgiveness demand resolution in the context of performance.

76. *Miscellanea*, f. a3a; Montagu is quoting from 1 Corinthians 4:9 and paraphrasing Philippians 3:14. On the resonances of the former text within the English Catholic community, see my essay, ' "We Are Made a Spectacle": Campion's Dramas', in Thomas McCoog and Joseph Munitiz (eds), *The Reckoned Expense: Edmund Campion and the Early English Jesuits* (1996: rev. edn, Rome: Institutum Historicum Societatis Jesu, 2007), pp. 103–118.

77. See *The Shepherd's Paradise*, ed. Sarah Poynting, Malone Society, Vol. 159 (Oxford: Malone Society, 1997), pp. xii–xv.

78. See below, Ch. 4.

79. John Donne, *Fifty Sermons* (1649), pp. 271–272: from Sermon 31, 25 August 1622, on Job 36:25. The passage relates to Elihu, a 'naturall man', testifying to God.

80. The phrase is Northrop Frye's: *The Secular Scripture* (Cambridge, Mass.: Harvard University Press, 1976). Frye's book, dealing with the structure of romance, makes heavy use of Shakespeare.

1: ANTITHEATRICALISM IN SHAKESPEARE'S AGE

1. However, on the uncertainty of dating Shakespeare's early writing, see Wells and Taylor, p. xx. On antitheatricalism, see Jonas Barish, *The Antitheatrical Prejudice* (Berkeley: California University Press, 1981), particularly useful on the movement's neoplatonic antecedents, Thomas Postlewait, 'Theatricality and Antitheatricality in Renaissance London', pp. 90–126 in *Theatricality*, eds. Tracy C. Davis and Thomas Postlewait (Cambridge: Cambridge University Press, 2003) (my thanks to Gillian Woods for this), and Jeffrey Knapp, *Shakespeare's Tribe: Church, Nation and Theater in Early Modern England* (Chicago: Chicago University Press, 2002). Many pamphlet interventions in the debate about theatre's legitimacy have been edited by Tanya Pollard in *Shakespeare's Theater: A Sourcebook* (Malden, MA: Blackwell, 2004).

2. It has sometimes been argued that civic authorities' dislike of the theatre led to a willingness to sponsor attacks on the stage: see Tracey Hill, ' "He Hath Changed His Coppy": Anti-Theatrical Writing and the Turncoat Player', *Critical Survey*, 9: 3 (1997), pp. 59–77.

3. Ordinances against Sunday playing were not always strictly enforced: see William Ingram, *The Business of Playing: The Beginnings of the Adult Professional Theater in Elizabethan London* (Ithaca: Cornell University Press, 1992), pp. 202, 208–209. I am grateful to Eva Griffith for this reference.

4. However, J. Leeds Barroll sees the city fathers' legislation against crowding as demonstrating awareness of an infective element in the spreading of plague: 'without actually saying so, [they] turned their backs on the highly providential orientation to be found in preludes to most treatises on plague' (*Politics, Plague and Shakespeare's Theater* (Ithaca: Cornell University Press, 1991), p. 95).

5. Barish, *Antitheatrical Prejudice*, p. 66.

6. See Ingram, *Business of Playing*, p. 64, and Janet S. Loengard, 'An Elizabethan Lawsuit: John Brayne, his Carpenter, and the Building of the Red Lion Theatre', *Shakespeare Quarterly*, 34: 3 (1983), pp. 298–310.

7. E.g. in Dudley Fenner, *A Short and Profitable Treatise* (1590), p. 20.

8. Anonymous biography appended to William Gouge, *A Funerall Sermon Preached . . . at the Funeralls (sic) of Mrs Margaret Ducke* (1646), pp. 26–27, quoted in Allan Pritchard, 'Puritans and the Blackfriars Theater: The Cases of Mistresses Duck and Drake', *Shakespeare Quarterly*, 45: 1 (1994), pp. 92–95 (quotation p. 93). See also Charles Whitney, *Early Responses to Renaissance Drama* (Cambridge: Cambridge University Press, 2006), Ch. 5. On Gouge's Puritanism, see *ODNB*.

9. Cf. Patrick Collinson's comments: 'Paradigms such as Puritanism, which were deployed to construct and manipulate a semblance of reality, soon became part of the reality on which they imposed themselves . . . by a process of negative stigmatisation, but also by a measure of reciprocal self-recognition in the stigmatised' ('The Theatre Constructs Puritanism', pp. 157–169 in David L. Smith, Richard Strier and David Bevington (eds), *The Theatrical City: Culture, Theatre and Politics in London, 1576–1649* (Cambridge: Cambridge University Press, 1995), quotations pp. 169, 157–158). See also Tom McAlindon, 'Perfect Answers: Religious Inquisition, Falstaffian Wit', *Shakespeare Survey*, 54, ed. Peter Holland (2001), pp. 100–107, and Peter Lake, 'Anti-Puritanism: The Structure of a Prejudice', Ch. 5 in Kenneth Fincham and Peter Lake (eds), *Religious Politics in Post-Reformation England: Essays in Honour of Nicholas Tyacke* (Woodbridge: Boydell, 2006), esp. pp. 95–96.

10. See Kristen Poole, *Radical Religion from Shakespeare to Milton: Figures of Nonconformity in Early Modern England* (Cambridge: Cambridge University Press, 2000), Jensen, *Religion and Revelry*, pp. 154 ff., Whitney, *Early Responses*, Ch. 2, and Peter Corbin and Douglas Sedge (eds), *The Oldcastle Controversy: Sir John Oldcastle, Part I and The Famous Victories of Henry V* (Manchester: Manchester University Press, 1991).

11. *Ten Sermons* (1627), part 1 ('Three Sermons *Ad Clerum*'), sermon 1 (preached 1619), p. 38. On Sanderson's complex anti-Puritanism, see his entry in *ODNB*.

12. Stephen Longstaffe, 'Puritan Tribulation and the Protestant History Play', Ch. 3 in Andrew Hadfield (ed.), *Literature and Censorship in Renaissance England* (Basingstoke: Palgrave, 2001), esp. pp. 38–39. Longstaffe compares

the stage's antipathy to Puritans to the attempts of high-ranking clerics to suppress critics of the established church, especially in the wake of the Marprelate controversy.

13. See Margot Heinemann, *Puritanism and Theatre: Thomas Middleton and Opposition Drama Under the Early Stuarts* (Cambridge: Cambridge University Press, 1980); Pollard (ed.), *Shakespeare's Theater*, pp. xvi–xvii. On the antitheatrical commentator Stephen Gosson's opposition to Puritanism, see Arthur F. Kinney, *Markets of Bawdrie: The Dramatic Criticism of Stephen Gosson* (Salzburg: Salzburg Studies in English Literature, 1974), pp. 27–28.

14. The play was performed at Cambridge, and probably Oxford, in the 1570s: see Thomas S. Freeman's entry on Foxe in *ODNB*.

15. On Calvinist drama on the Continent, see Catharine Randall, 'Calvinism and Post-Tridentine Developments', Ch. 49 in *The Cambridge History of Literary Criticism. Volume III. The Renaissance*, ed. Glyn P. Norton (Cambridge: Cambridge University Press, 1999).

16. Janet Clare, '*Art Made Tongue-Tied By Authority': Elizabethan and Jacobean Dramatic Censorship* (1990: 2nd edn, Manchester: Manchester University Press, 1999), p. 23.

17. Peter Happé, *John Bale* (New York: Twayne, 1996); Thomas Dorman, *A Proufe of Certeyne Articles in Religion* (1564), f. 123b.

18. Patrick Collinson, *From Iconoclasm to Iconophobia: The Cultural Impact of the Second English Reformation* (Reading: Reading University Press, 1988); see also *The Birthpangs of Protestant England: Religious and Cultural Change in the Sixteenth and Seventeenth Centuries* (Basingstoke: Macmillan, 1988), Ch. 5, on the move away from exploiting popular culture.

19. See below, pp. 74–78.

20. *The School of Abuse*, quoted from the extract in Pollard (ed.), *Shakespeare's Theater*, p. 25. Junkets = delicacies; abroach = public, open.

21. *A Very Fruitfull Exposition of the Commaundements* (1583), pp. 317–318.

22. Hill, '"He Hath Changed His Coppy"', argues for a stock antitheatricalist persona assumed by Anthony Munday and others.

23. *The Parable of the Sower and the Seed* (1621), p. 99. For the dates of pamphlet exchanges, see the table of contents in Pollard (ed.), *Shakespeare's Theater*. On Taylor's moderate Puritanism, see his entry in *ODNB*.

24. See note 3 above, Bryan Crockett, *The Play of Paradox: Stage and Sermon in Renaissance England* (Philadelphia: Pennsylvania University Press, 1995), and Knapp, *Shakespeare's Tribe*.

25. *A Second and Third Blast of Retreat from Plays and Theaters* (1580), in Pollard (ed.), *Shakespeare's Theater*, p. 71.

26. Kinney, *Markets*, pp. 13–14; Rankins's entry in *ODNB*.

27. Hill, '"He Hath Changed His Coppy"'. Sheldon P. Zitner suggests that *The School of Abuse* was written at the request of an agent of the city authorities, though as he points out, this need not necessarily impugn Gosson's sincerity: 'Gosson, Ovid and the Elizabethan Audience', *Shakespeare Quarterly*, 9: 2 (1958), pp. 206–208. Hill's view of Munday's antitheatricalist period as opportunist, expressed in the above article and in *Anthony Munday and Civic*

Culture: Theatre, History and Power in Early Modern England (Manchester: Manchester University Press, 2004), Ch. 4, contrasts with Donna Hamilton's in *Anthony Munday and the Catholics, 1560–1633* (Aldershot: Ashgate, 2005); Hamilton sees Munday as aligning himself both with Gosson's position and with post-Tridentine standards, '[conforming] outwardly to antitheatrical Protestant fervour, while ventriloquising Catholic values' (p. 18).

28. On palinodes, see Patricia Phillippy, *Love's Remedies: Recantation and Renaissance Lyric Poetry* (Lewisburg, PA/London: Bucknell University Press/Associated University Presses, 1995).

29. See Frederick O. Waage, *The White Devil Discover'd: Backgrounds and Foregrounds to Webster's Tragedy* (New York: Peter Lang, 1984), Ch. IX; and Guillaume Coatalen, 'Shakespeare and Other "Tragicall Discourses" in an Early Seventeenth-Century Commonplace-Book from Oriel College, Oxford', *English Manuscript Studies 1100–1700*, 13 (2007), pp. 120–164. I am grateful to Arnold Hunt for the latter reference. For two later clerics who copied and quoted from Shakespeare, see Arthur S. Kirsch, 'A Caroline Commentary on the Drama', *Modern Philology*, 66: 3 (1969), pp. 256–261, discussing Abraham Wright's commonplace book, and Mary Hobbs (ed.), *The Sermons of Henry King (1592–1669), Bishop of Chichester* (Aldershot: Scolar, 1992), p. 53. Further research on the softening of clerical antitheatricalism later in the century would be desirable.

30. The cipher is a very simple one which, as Coatalen remarks, 'was probably meant to ward off someone peeping over [the compiler's] shoulder for the briefest instant': 'Shakespeare and Other "Tragicall Discourses"', p. 154.

31. Zitner, 'Gosson, Ovid and the Elizabethan Audience'; Barish, *Antitheatrical Prejudice*, Ch. 2. On the use of *De Spectaculis* in *Gosson's Playes Confuted*, see Kinney, *Markets*, pp. 269–291.

32. See Michael Camille, *The Gothic Idol: Ideology and Image-Making in Medieval Art* (Cambridge: Cambridge University Press, 1989), pp. 44, 61–62, 267–268.

33. *Ten Sermons Upon the First, Second, Third and Fourth Verses of the Sixt of Matthew* (1602), pp. 36–37.

34. Barish, *Antitheatrical Prejudice*, Ch. 6; Michael O'Connell, *The Idolatrous Eye: Iconoclasm and Theater in Early-Modern England* (New York: Oxford University Press, 2000), pp. 14–15, 33, 71; Regina Schwartz, *Sacramental Poetics at the Dawn of Secularism* (Stanford: Stanford University Press, 2008), p. 42; and Adrian Streete, *Protestantism and Drama in Early Modern England* (Cambridge: Cambridge University Press, 2009), Ch.5. The imaginative implications of transubstantiation in this period have been discussed by, among others, Catherine Gallagher and Stephen Greenblatt, *Practising New Historicism* (Chicago: Chicago UP, 2000), Ch.5, and Douglas Burnham and Enrico Giaccherini (eds), *The Poetics of Transubstantiation: From Theology to Metaphor*, Studies in European Cultural Transition, Vol. 27 (Aldershot: Ashgate, 2005).

35. See Ch. 2 below.

36. 'Trent Revisited: A Reappraisal of Early Modern Catholicism's Relationship with the *Commedia Italiana*', *Journal of Religion and Theatre*, 1: 1 (2002) (online).

37. Folger, MS 4787, f. 13: discussed in I.J. Semper, 'The Jacobean Theater Through the Eyes of Catholic Clerics', *Shakespeare Quarterly*, 3: 1 (1952), pp. 45–51.

38. On the question of Catholic 'residue', see Ch. 2, pp. 111–116.

39. See Barish, *Antitheatrical Prejudice*, p. 122; O'Connell, *Idolatrous Eye*, p. 32; and Ch. 4 below, p. 200.

40. The literature on iconoclasm is extensive. For a recent assessment of work on England, see Alexandra Walsham, 'Angels and Idols in Britain's Long Reformation', Ch. 6 in Peter Marshall and Alexandra Walsham (eds), *Angels in the Early Modern World* (Cambridge: Cambridge University Press, 2006). However, the Reformed tradition did make some use of imagery: see William A. Dyrness, *Reformed Theology and Visual Culture: The Protestant Imagination from Calvin to Edwards* (Cambridge: Cambridge University Press, 2004).

41. *The Idolatrous Eye: Iconoclasm and Theater in Early-Modern England* (New York/Oxford: Oxford University Press, 2000), p. 20.

42. See the translation of the play in Richard E. Arnold *et al.* (trans. and eds), *Jesuit Theater Englished* (St Louis: Institute of Jesuit Sources, 1983).

43. Murray Roston, *Biblical Drama in England from the Middle Ages to the Present Day* (London: Faber and Faber, 1968), esp. pp. 115–120.

44. See Ch. 2, pp. 107–111.

45. See William H. McCabe, *An Introduction to the Jesuit Theater*, ed. Louis J. Oldani (St Louis: Institute of Jesuit Sources, 1983), and my *Catholicism, Controversy and the English Literary Imagination, 1558–1660* (Cambridge: Cambridge University Press, 1999), Chs 5–6.

46. Edited in Pollard (ed.), *Shakespeare's Theater*, p. 7; cf. Munday, *A Second and Third Blast of Retreat*, in Pollard (ed.), *Shakespeare's Theater*, p. 78.

47. Quotation taken from the 1603 reissue, STC 6070.5.

48. From the translation of *Jewish Antiquities* in Thomas Lodge (trans.), *The Famous and Memorable Workes of Josephus* (1602), p. 295. See also (e.g.) Northbrook, *Treatise*, in Pollard (ed.), *Shakespeare's Theater*, p. 7, and Prynne, *Histrio-Mastix*, f. 553.

49. *A Reply to Stephen Gosson's School of Abuse* (1579), in Pollard (ed.), *Shakespeare's Theater*, p. 52.

50. *Plays Confuted in Five Actions* (1582), in Pollard (ed.), *Shakespeare's Theater*, p. 89.

51. *Phaedra*, 671–672: *Hippolytus* is *Titus*'s alternative title. These comments draw upon the translation of *Titus* in the Loeb Classical Library series: Seneca, Vol. VIII, *Tragedies*, ed. and trans. John J. Fitch (Cambridge, Mass.: Harvard University Press, 2002). Cf. Jonathan Bate's comments in his edition of the play (p. 30).

52. See Nicholas Moschovakis, ' "Irreligious Piety" and Christian History: Persecution as Pagan Anachronism in *Titus Andronicus*', *Shakespeare Quarterly*, 53: 4 (2002), pp. 460–486.

53. Psalm 13, verse 1.

54. *Plays Confuted*: Pollard (ed.), *Shakespeare's Theater*, pp. 98–99.

55. I Kings 18:27.

56. A famous formulation of Augustine's belief comes in his *Enchiridion*, Ch. 4:

    Augustine: Confessions and Enchiridion, ed. Albert C. Outler (London: SCM, 1955).

57. *The Allegory of Love: A Study in Medieval Tradition* (1936: this edn, New York: Galaxy, 1958), p. 83.

58. Natascha Würzbach, *The Rise of the English Street Ballad, 1550–1650* (1981: trans. Gayna Walls, Cambridge: Cambridge University Press, 1990), discusses uses of well-known literary material in popular ballads (p. 210).

59. See Ch. 4, pp. 181–185.

60. The range of contemporary examples given for the word 'pagan' in the *OED* illustrate how it could be used both neutrally and pejoratively.

61. *Histrio-Mastix* (1633), p. 99.

62. See David Cressy, *Literacy and the Social Order* (Cambridge: Cambridge University Press, 1980).

63. See Samuel Schoenbaum, *Shakespeare's Lives*, 2nd edn (Oxford: Oxford University Press, 1991), pp. 66–68, 74–75, 101–104, 234, 279, 528–532; T.W. Baldwin, *William Shakspere's Small Latine and Lesse Greeke*, 2 vols (Urbana: Illinois University Press, 1944).

64. The lines come from Jonson's prefatory verses to the First Folio of Shakespeare's works (1623): quoted from Wells and Taylor, p. lxxii.

65. See Barish, *Antitheatrical Prejudice*, pp. 82–83.

66. *Histrio-Mastix*, in Pollard (ed.), *Shakespeare's Theater*, p. 286. Cf. Gager's comment that actors in the classical world did not come upon the stage 'of a devout mind toward their false gods . . . for [this] had been then in them thought commendable': *Letter to Dr. John Rainolds*, in Pollard (ed.), *Shakespeare's Theater*, p. 182.

67. Munday, *A Second and Third Blast of Retreat*, in Pollard (ed.), *Shakespeare's Theater*, p. 66; see Barish, *Antitheatrical Prejudice*, p. 180.

68. For an up-to-date overview of the literature on the term, see James Loxley, *Performativity* (London: Routledge, 2007). On how the Puritan demand for sincerity elicited attacks on ritual, see Barish, *Antitheatrical Prejudice*, pp. 95–96.

69. *Idolatrous Eye*, p. 33.

70. At this date, the terms 'atheist' and 'atheism' imply godlessness, impiety and disregard of moral obligation as well as (and arguably more than) disbelief in God (*OED*). Unless otherwise signalled, this study uses them in a similar sense.

71. I.e. 'family burial vault'.

72. See David A. Postles, *Social Geographies in England (1200–1640)* (Washington: New Academia Publishing, 2007).

73. John E. Booty (ed.), *The Book of Common Prayer, 1559* (Charlottesville/London: Folger Shakespeare Library/Virginia University Press, 1976, this edn, 2005), Morning Prayer, pp. 50–51, Holy Communion, pp. 259–260. On how one could do duty for many in the General Confession, see Ramie Targoff, *Common Prayer: The Language of Public Devotion in Early Modern England* (Chicago: Chicago University Press, 2001), pp. 28–34 (esp. p. 33).

74. Claire McEachern's Arden edition, from which the above transcription is taken, follows the quarto edition, assigning the reading of the epitaph to a

lord rather than (as often) Claudio. This has the effect of making Claudio
the stage-manager of the scene, while the lord acts on behalf of the male
community 'as the liturgical "I" of a ritualized, corporate, performative,
gendered identity' (McEachern here quotes a personal communication
from Phyllis Gorfain). See notes to this edition, pp. 306–307.

75. See below, pp. 55–56.
76. See McEachern (ed.), p. 307.
77. See my *Oral Culture and Catholicism in Early Modern England* (Cambridge:
Cambridge University Press, 2007), Ch. 2.
78. Proclamation 509, 16 May 1559: quoted from Pollard (ed.), *Shakespeare's
Theater*, p. 303.
79. 2 James I, Chapter 21, 27 May 1606: quoted from Pollard (ed.),
Shakespeare's Theater, p. 328.
80. *Licensing, Censorship and Authorship in Early Modern England* (Basingstoke:
Palgrave, 2000), pp. 51–52. Dutton comments that Sir Henry Herbert
(Master of the Revels from 1623) had a personal preference for whole-
some entertainment (pp. 46–47).
81. Janet Clare, *'Art Made Tongue-Tied By Authority': Elizabethan and Jacobean
Dramatic Censorship*, 2nd edn (Manchester: Manchester University Press,
1999), pp. 37, 124–125.
82. See Maurice Hunt, *Shakespeare's Religious Allusiveness: Its Play and Tolerance* (Aldershot: Ashgate, 2003).
83. On Biblical allusion, see Jonathan Bate, *Soul of the Age: The Life, Mind and
World of William Shakespeare* (London: Viking, 2008), pp. 63–64. In her
edition of *A Midsummer Night's Dream* (London: Penguin, 2005), Helen
Hackett reads the passage against Erasmus's allusions to the same Biblical
text in *The Praise of Folly* (pp. lvi–lviii). My thanks to Professor Hackett for
this reference.
84. *A Godly and Learned Exposition . . . Upon . . . Revelation* (1606: preached
1595), pp. 94, 120. On Perkins and images, see Frances Yates, *The Art of
Memory* (1966: this edn, London: Pimlico, 1992), Ch. 12, esp. p. 270. For a
reading of *The Winter's Tale* juxtaposing notions of idolatry and adultery,
see Julia Reinhard Lupton, *Afterlives of the Saints: Hagiography, Typology and
Renaissance Literature* (Stanford: Stanford University Press, 1996), pp.
185–196.
85. On medieval courtly love and the charge of idolatry, see Camille, *Gothic
Idol*, pp. 298–316.
86. See Richard A. McCabe's comments in his introduction to *Edmund Spenser:
The Shorter Poems* (London: Penguin, 1999), pp. xvii–xviii.
87. *Against Jerome Osorius . . . and . . . his Slaunderous Invectives* (1581), f. 321b.
88. The poem is from the sequence *Caelica*. See *Fulke Greville: Selected Poems*,
ed. Neil Powell (Manchester: Carcanet, 1990), p. 26.
89. See Margaret Aston, *England's Iconoclasts. Volume I. Laws Against Images*
(Oxford: Clarendon, 1988), and J.B. Phillips, *The Reformation of Images:
Destruction of Art in England, 1535–1660* (Berkeley: California University
Press, 1973), Fig. 19.
90. At this period the term 'sonnet' denotes not just the Petrarchan sonnet

and similar fourteen-line compositions, but poems for which the term 'lyric' would now seem more appropriate (*OED*).

91. Thomas Adams, *The Hapines of the Church* (1619 edition), p. 13.

92. An early draft of this material appears in my programme note to Nancy Meckler's production of *Romeo and Juliet* for the RSC (Stratford, 2006). See the analogous discussion of the passage in Gillian Woods, 'Catholic Semiotics in Shakespearean Drama', Oxford D. Phil. thesis, 2006, pp. 26–28. On the association of Romeo's name and character with pilgrims, see Levenson's notes to this passage (pp. 196–197).

93. Quoted in Aston, *England's Iconoclasts*, p. 467.

94. 'The Canonization', lines 35–45, quoted from John Donne, *The Complete English Poems*, ed. A.J. Smith (1971: this edn, London: Penguin, 1996), p. 48.

95. See Nigel Llewellyn, *Funeral Monuments in Post-Reformation England* (New York: Cambridge University Press, 2000).

96. See Paul Whitfield White, 'Theater and Religious Culture', Ch. 8 in John D. Cox and David Scott Kastan (eds), *A New History of Early English Drama* (New York: Columbia University Press, 1997).

97. See the edition of the *Dialogue* in *The Complete Works of St Thomas More*, Vol. 6, Part 1, ed. Thomas M.C. Lawler, Germain Marc'hadour and Richard C. Marius (New Haven/London: Yale University Press, 1981), Dialogue 4, Ch. 11 (reference p. 379).

98. Among recent studies, see Anne C. Parkinson, 'Religious Drama in Kendal: the Corpus Christi Play in the Reign of James I', *Recusant History*, 25: 4 (2001), pp. 604–612; and John Coldewey, 'Carnival's End: Puritan Ideology and the Decline of English Provincial Theatre', pp. 279–286 in Meg Twycross (ed.), *Festive Drama* (Cambridge: D.S. Brewer, 1996).

99. See David Cressy, *Bonfires and Bells: National Memory and the Protestant Calendar in Elizabethan and Stuart England* (Berkeley: California University Press, 1989); Ronald Hutton, *The Rise and Fall of Merry England: The Ritual Year, 1400–1700* (Oxford: Oxford University Press, 1994); Alison Chapman, 'The Politics of Time in Edmund Spenser's English Calendar', *Studies in English Literature, 1500–1900*, 42: 1 (2002), pp. 1–24; and, more controversially, Steve Sohmer, *Shakespeare's Mystery Play: The Opening of the Globe Theatre, 1599* (Manchester: Manchester University Press, 1999) (see the review of the latter study by Alison Chapman in *Shakespeare Quarterly*, 53: 1 (2002), pp. 137–140).

100. R. Chris Hassel, Jnr, *Renaissance Drama and the English Church Year* (Lincoln: Nebraska University Press, 1979).

101. Jensen's *Religion and Revelry* explores the link between festivity, drama and religious conservatism: see also her 'Singing Psalms to Horn-Pipes: Festivity, Iconoclasm and Catholicism in *The Winter's Tale*', *Shakespeare Quarterly*, 55: 3 (2004), pp. 279–306. The following studies take a more secular view of the topic: C.L. Barber, *Shakespeare's Festive Comedy: A Study of Dramatic Form and its Relation to Social Custom* (Princeton: Princeton University Press, 1959); Naomi Conn Leibler, *Shakespeare's Festive Tragedy: The Ritual Foundations of Genre* (London: Routledge, 1995); David Ruiter,

*Shakespeare's Festive History: Feasting, Festivity, Fasting and Lent in the
Second Henriad* (Aldershot: Ashgate, 2003); Michael D. Bristol, *Carnival and
Theater: Plebeian Culture and the Structure of Authority in Renaissance England*
(London: Methuen, 1985); François Laroque, *Shakespeare's Festive World*
(Cambridge: Cambridge University Press, 1993); Leah Marcus, *The Politics
of Mirth* (Chicago: Chicago University Press, 1984). On the relationship of
drama, misrule and the carnivalesque, see Steven Mullaney, *The Place of
the Stage* (Chicago: Chicago University Press, 1988); Louis Montrose, 'The
Purpose of Playing: Reflections of a Shakespearean Anthropology', *Helios*,
7 (1980), pp. 51–74; Peter Stallybrass and Allon White, *The Politics and
Poetics of Transgression* (London: Methuen, 1986); Douglas A. Bruster,
Drama and the Market in the Age of Shakespeare (Cambridge: Cambridge
University Press, 1992); and Chris Humphrey, *The Politics of Carnival:
Festive Misrule in Medieval England* (Manchester: Manchester University
Press, 2001).

102. On the effect of the professional theatre on earlier festive dramatic
traditions, see Meg Twycross, 'Some Approaches to Dramatic Festivity,
Especially Processions,' pp. 1–33 in Meg Twycross (ed.), *Festive Drama*
(Cambridge: D.S. Brewer, 1996). For some important qualifications to the
notion of medieval drama as a collective enterprise, see Sheila Linden-
baum, 'Rituals of Exclusion: Feasts and Plays of the English Religious
Fraternities', pp. 54–65 in the same volume.

103. For what is probably an example of the latter, see Appendix 1, 'A Court
Epilogue: Shrovetide 1599', in *As You Like It*, ed. Juliet Dusinberre (London:
Thomson, 2006), pp. 349–354.

104. 'Whose St Crispin's Day Is It? Shoemaking, Holiday Making and the
Politics of Memory in Early Modern England', *Renaissance Quarterly*, 54
(2001), pp. 1467–1494 (quotation p. 1471).

105. See David Bevington, 'Theatre as Holiday', in David L. Smith, Richard
Strier and David Bevington (eds), *The Theatrical City: Culture, Theatre and
Politics in London, 1576–1649* (Cambridge: Cambridge University Press,
1995), Ch. 3. It will be clear that my interpretation of the topic is slanted
differently from Bevington's valuable analysis. See also Robin Sowerby, *The
Classical Legacy in Renaissance Poetry* (New York: Longman, 1994), p. 293,
on how the epyllion could provide the Renaissance reader with a holiday
from morality.

106. See Chapter 3 below, esp. pp. 171–174.

107. The beginning of Act 5.1 was revised twice by Shakespeare: see Holland
(ed.), pp. 257–268. Holland's edition, from which this transcription is
taken, follows the Folio reading. Some Romantic commentators also use
the passage and its key-words to reflect on the moral ambivalence of fantasy (e.g. Ludwig Tieck, *Shakspeare's Treatment of the Marvellous* (1793),
excerpted in Jonathan Bate (ed.), *The Romantics on Shakespeare* (London:
Penguin, 1992), pp. 60–66).

108. This is one of the main themes in J.A. Bryant's *Hippolyta's View: Some
Christian Aspects of Shakespeare's Plays* (Lexington: Kentucky University
Press, 1961).

109. *Disce Vivere* (1604 edition), pp. 31–33, 37, 115 (irregular numbering).
110. Anonymous biography appended to Gouge, *Funerall Sermon*, p. 27: quoted and discussed in Pritchard, 'Puritans and the Blackfriars Theater', p. 93.
111. *The Poetry of Meditation* (New Haven: Yale University Press, 1954, rev. 1962), p. 14.
112. See Victor Houliston, 'Why Robert Persons Would Not Be Pacified: Edmund Bunny's Theft of *The Book of Resolution*', pp. 209–232 in *The Reckoned Expense: Edmund Campion and the Early English Jesuits*, ed. Thomas M. McCoog (1996: revised edition, Rome: Institutum Historicum Societatis Jesu, 2007).
113. *A Booke of Christian Exercise* (1584), pp. 8–9.
114. A relatively sympathetic view of antitheatricalism can be found in Jonathan V. Crewe, 'The Theater of the Idols: Theatrical and Antitheatrical Discourse' in *Staging the Renaissance*, ed. David Scott Kastan and Peter Stallybrass (London: Routledge, 1991), pp. 49–56.
115. *The Journal of Richard Norwood, Surveyor of Bermuda*, ed. Wesley Frank Craven and Walter B. Hayward (New York: Bermuda Historical Monuments Trust, 1945), pp. 6, 17, 42, 83. The last quotation is discussed in Owen C. Watkins, *The Puritan Experience* (London: Routledge and Kegan Paul, 1972), p. 76. See also the discussion of Norwood's theatregoing in Whitney, *Early Responses*, pp. 169–185.
116. On the Puritan objection to *adiaphora* (things indifferent), see Patrick Collinson, *The Elizabethan Puritan Movement* (London: Jonathan Cape, 1967), pp. 27–28, 71–72.
117. David Watkin, *Morality and Architecture Revisited* (London: John Murray, 2001) is an anti-modernist polemic which makes analogous points.
118. This refers to the opening words of two liturgical items suitable for victors giving thanks to God: of Psalm 115, *Non nobis Domine* ('Not unto us, Lord') and of the canticle *Te Deum laudamus* (We praise Thee, God). See *Henry V*, ed. Taylor, p. 258.
119. Cf. Ch. 3, p. 164.
120. The most sustained recent discussion of this is in Knapp, *Shakespeare's Tribe*, introduction.
121. This is the point of view advanced by Anthony B. Dawson in a book co-written with Paul Yachnin, *The Culture of Playgoing in Shakespeare's England: A Collaborative Debate* (Cambridge: Cambridge University Press, 2001), esp. Introduction. See also Crockett, *Play of Paradox*.
122. Knapp, *Shakespeare's Tribe*, p. 10; but see above, p. 38.
123. John Northbrooke, *Treatise Against Dicing, Dancing, Plays, and Interludes*, in Pollard (ed.), *Shakespeare's Theater*, p. 8; Knapp, *ibid.*
124. Prologue to *The Staple of News*, line 23: quoted and discussed in Knapp, *Shakespeare's Tribe*, pp. 38, 199.
125. See Adams's biography in *ODNB*.

NOTES TO CHAPTER TWO 253

2: SHAKESPEARE'S LIFE AND WORKS: CATHOLIC CRITIQUES

1. Quoted in Pierre Janelle, *Robert Southwell the Writer* (London: Sheed and Ward, 1935), p. 119. John R. Roberts and Lorraine Roberts, '"To Weave a New Webbe in Their Owne Loome": Robert Southwell and Counter-Reformation Poetics', Ch.5 in Helen Wilcox, Richard Todd and Alasdair MacDonald (eds), *Sacred and Profane: Secular and Devotional Interplay in Early Modern British Literature* (Amsterdam: VU University Press, 1996), discuss Jesuit literary theorists' influence on Southwell.

2. Janelle, *Robert Southwell*, esp. Ch. 6. Russell Fraser, *The War Against Poetry* (Princeton: Princeton University Press, 1970) gives an account of neo-platonic, utilitarian and moralistic attacks upon secular verse at this date; as he points out, humanist counters to these arguments typically concede that poetry ought to be useful.

3. On Puritanism and *adiaphora*, see Ch. 1, p. 75.

4. For a judicious recent survey, see John D. Cox, 'Was Shakespeare a Christian, And If So, What Kind of Christian Was He?', *Christianity and Literature*, 55: 4 (2006), pp. 539–566. On uses and abuses of the biographical approach to Shakespearean criticism, see Samuel Schoenbaum, *Shakespeare's Lives* (new edn, Oxford: Oxford University Press, 1991), e.g. pp. 526–528, 545–550. Recent biographies include Peter Ackroyd, *Shakespeare: The Biography* (London: Chatto and Windus, 2005); Katherine Duncan-Jones, *Ungentle Shakespeare: Scenes From His Life* (London: Thomson/Arden Shakespeare, 2001); Stephen Greenblatt, *Will in the World: How Shakespeare Became Shakespeare* (London: Jonathan Cape, 2004); Anthony Holden, *William Shakespeare: The Man Behind the Genius* (1st edn, London: Little, Brown, 1999); Park Honan, *Shakespeare: A Life* (Oxford: Oxford University Press, 1998); René Weis, *Shakespeare Revealed: A Biography* (London: John Murray, 2007); and Michael Wood, *In Search of Shakespeare* (London: BBC Books, 2003). Of these, Honan's biography will be drawn on most extensively; while it is not the most recent, it presents the most straightforward narrative of all the scholarly biographies in the above list.

5. Richard Wilson, *Secret Shakespeare: Studies in Theatre, Religion and Resistance* (Manchester: Manchester University Press, 2004); Clare Asquith, *Shadowplay* (New York: Public Affairs, 2005); John Finnis and Patrick Martin, 'Another Turn for the Turtle: Shakespeare's Intercession for Love's Martyr', *Times Literary Supplement*, 18 April 2003, pp. 12–14. See the discussion of the latter piece in *Shakespeare's Poems*, ed. Katherine Duncan-Jones and Henry Woudhuysen (London: Arden, 2007), pp. 93–94.

6. I have argued elsewhere that there was considerable theoretical support among Protestant Elizabethans for a less profane poetical praxis, but a practical reluctance to engage in it until Robert Southwell and Guillaume Salluste du Bartas offered acceptable models in the mid-1590s: Shell, *Catholicism, Controversy*, Ch. 2.

7. 'Forms of Opposition: Shakespeare and Middleton', *English Literary Renaissance*, 24 (1994), pp. 283–314. See Introduction, pp. 20–21.

8. It has sometimes been argued that the absence of Shakespeare's name from the communion token books of St Saviour's Southwark, his parish church in London, suggests that he was a non-communicant: see Eamon Duffy, 'Was Shakespeare a Catholic?', *The Tablet*, 27 April 1996, pp. 536–538, and Patrick Collinson, 'Willliam Shakespeare's Religious Inheritance and Environment', Ch. 8 in *Elizabethan Essays* (London: Hambledon, 1994), p. 231. However, only the heads of households were recorded, and since Shakespeare would have been lodging in the area, there remains no proof that he did not communicate. See Beatrice Groves, *Texts and Traditions: Religion in Shakespeare 1592–1604* (Oxford: Clarendon, 2007), pp. 31 and 34, quoting a personal communication from Jeremy Boulton.

9. See the edition of *King John* by R.L. Smallwood (New Penguin Shakespeare, 1974), appendix, and the discussion of the play in Jean-Christophe Mayer, *Shakespeare's Hybrid Faith: History, Religion and the Stage* (Basingstoke: Palgrave, 2006), Ch. 4.

10. See Gillian Woods, 'Catholic Semiotics in Shakespearean Drama', Oxford D. Phil. thesis, 2006, and David Bevington, *Shakespeare's Ideas* (Malden, MA: Wiley-Blackwell, 2008), Ch.5.

11. Quoted from *Shakespeare's Sonnets*, ed. Katherine Duncan-Jones (London: Arden, 1997, repr. 1998), p. 257.

12. See Eamon Duffy, 'Bare Ruined Choirs: Remembering Catholicism in Shakespeare's England', Ch. 2 in Richard Dutton, Alison Findlay and Richard Wilson (eds), *Theatre and Religion: Lancastrian Shakespeare* (Manchester: Manchester University Press, 2003), quotation p. 41. In *1599: A Year in the Life of William Shakespeare* (2005: this edn, London: Faber & Faber, 2006), James Shapiro brings this sonnet suggestively into dialogue with the whitewashing of religious paintings and the destruction of stained glass in Stratford-upon-Avon's Guild Chapel (pp. 164–167).

13. For one such attempt, see Thomas Carter, *Shakespeare Puritan and Recusant* (Edinburgh: Oliphant Anderson and Ferrier, 1897).

14. See above, p. 33.

15. *History of Great Britain* (1611), ix, 15: quoted from E.K. Chambers, *William Shakespeare: A Study of Facts and Problems*, 2 vols (Oxford: Clarendon, 1930), Vol. II, pp. 217–218. Persons is referred to under his pseudonym, 'N.D.' (Nicholas Doleman). On the Oldcastle controversy, see above, pp. 33, 83, 145–146.

16. See (e.g.) Michael Davies, 'The Transubstantiated Bard: Shakespeare and Catholicism', in Douglas Burnham and Enrico Giaccherini (eds), *The Poetics of Transubstantiation: From Theology to Metaphor* (Aldershot: Ashgate, 2005), Ch. 3.

17. Alexandra Walsham, *Church-Papists: Catholicism, Conformity and Confessional Polemic in Early Modern England* (1st ed. 1993: Woodbridge: Boydell, 1999). On Counter-Reformation rigorism across Europe at a parochial level, see Lake, 'Religious Identities in Shakespeare's England', Part 3, Ch. 5

in David Scott Kastan (ed.), *A Companion to Shakespeare* (Oxford: Blackwell, 1999), p. 70.

18. See *OED*.

19. The debates surrounding John Shakespeare's non-attendance at church afford a good way into the scholarly complexities of the issue: see note 28 below.

20. See below, pp. 101–102. In 'Lodge's *Glaucus and Scilla* and the Conditions of Catholic Authorship in Elizabethan England', *EnterText* (e-journal), 3:1 (2003), pp. 59–100, R.W. Maslen makes a convincing case for Lodge's early poetic stance being informed by religious alienation.

21. Donna B. Hamilton, *Anthony Munday and the Catholics, 1560–1633* (Aldershot: Ashgate, 2005).

22. On recusancy in Shakespeare's Warwickshire, see Honan, *Shakespeare*, p. 79. On this topic and others, Weis, *Shakespeare Revealed*, gives an especially full picture of the Catholic context to Shakespeare's life and work.

23. Honan, *Shakespeare*, pp. 63–64.

24. Honan, *Shakespeare*, p. 51. Robert Persons petitioned for Hunt and Southwell to be sent together on the English mission: see Christopher Devlin, *The Life of Robert Southwell* (London: Longmans, Green and Co., 1956), pp. 40, 71.

25. Honan, *Shakespeare*, pp. 51–52. On the Cottoms, see E.A.J. Honigmann, *Shakespeare: The 'Lost Years'* (1985; this edn, Manchester: Manchester University Press, 1998), Ch. 4.

26. Mark Eccles, *Shakespeare in Warwickshire* (Madison: Wisconsin University Press, 1963), p. 66.

27. Honan, *Shakespeare*, pp. 354–356.

28. See Robert Bearman, 'John Shakespeare: A Papist or just Penniless?', *Shakespeare Quarterly*, 56: 4 (2005), pp. 411–433. I confess myself moving away from the position I took in 'Why Didn't Shakespeare Write Religious Verse?', Ch. 6 in Takashi Kozuka and J.R. Mulryne (eds), *Shakespeare, Marlowe, Jonson: New Directions in Biography* (Aldershot: Ashgate, 2006), an article which went to press before Bearman's appeared. While Bearman plays down the religious argument, Park Honan (*Shakespeare*, pp. 38–39) hedges his bets more, suggesting that any religious reasons for John Shakespeare to absent himself from church could only have been exacerbated by debt.

29. For the circumstances of its discovery, and the possibly suspicious resurfacing of the document's first leaf, see Samuel Schoenbaum, *William Shakespeare: A Compact Documentary Life* (rev. edn, New York: Oxford University Press, 1987), pp. 45–54 (text pp. 46–49). The 'Spiritual Testament' was first printed by Edmond Malone in *The Plays and Poems of William Shakespeare* (1790), Vol. I, Part 2, in the 'Emendations and Additions' section (pp. 330–331). This volume has two sequences of pagination; the 'Emendations . . . ' are at the end of the first sequence.

30. Peter Davidson and Thomas M. McCoog S.J., 'Unreconciled: What Evidence Links Shakespeare and the Jesuits?' *Times Literary Supplement*, 16 March 2007, p. 12. See also Herbert Thurston S.J., 'A Controverted

Shakespeare Document', *Dublin Review*, 173 (1923), pp. 161–176 (ref. p. 165). Bearman, 'John Shakespeare's "Spiritual Testament"', has claimed that no copies of the document appear to have existed in any language before the 1630s.

31. In *An Inquiry Into the Authenticity of Certain Miscellaneous Papers and Legal Instruments* (1796), Malone tantalisingly remarked 'I have since obtained documents that clearly prove it could not have been the composition of any one of our poet's family; as will be fully shewn in his Life' (pp. 198–199); this fuller elucidation never took place. See also Robert Bearman, 'John Shakespeare's "Spiritual Testament": A Reappraisal', *Shakespeare Survey*, 56 (2003), pp. 184–202.

32. Thomas M. McCoog S.J., and Peter Davidson, 'Edmund Campion and William Shakespeare: *Much Ado About Nothing*', pp. 165–185 in Thomas M. McCoog S.J. (ed.), *The Reckoned Expense: Edmund Campion and the Early English Jesuits*, revised and expanded edition (Rome: Institutum Historicum Societatis Jesu, 2007). This expands the author's *TLS* article (see note 30 above). Responding to assertions made by earlier scholars (particularly Richard Wilson), Davidson and McCoog argue that the allusions in letters between Catholics written in 1581–2 to the 'Testaments' wanted on the English mission refer not to Borromeo's Testament, but to the translation of the New Testament being undertaken at the English College in Rheims, which was published in 1582. I am grateful to the authors for letting me see a draft of their work in its early stages, and would wish only to add that the lack of a link between John Shakespeare's 'Spiritual Testament' and these letters does not, of course, necessarily prove that the document itself is inauthentic.

33. For the relationship, see Devlin, *The Life of Robert Southwell*, Ch. 18. It has sometimes been argued that Shakespeare's work was influenced by Southwell's: for two recent arguments along these lines, see Anna Swärdh, *Rape and Religion in English Renaissance Literature: A Topical Study of Four Texts by Shakespeare, Drayton and Middleton*, Studia Anglistica Upsaliensia 124 (Uppsala: Acta Universitatis Uppsaliensis, 2003), and John Klause, *Shakespeare, the Earl and the Jesuit* (Madison, NJ: Fairleigh Dickinson University Press, 2008). In my view, critics who have taken this line have only succeeded in proving that Shakespeare and Southwell both drew extensively on contemporary commonplaces. In *The Poetry of Religious Sorrow in Early Modern England* (Cambridge: Cambridge University Press, 2008), Ch. 1, Gary Kuchar argues that Shakespeare attempts a 'parodic inversion of the literature of tears' (p. 49) in *Richard II*.

34. See my *Catholicism, Controversy*, Ch. 2. Roberts and Roberts, ' "To Weave a New Webbe . . ." ', follow Martz, *Poetry of Meditation*, in confirming Southwell's wide influence. Southwell has been the subject of two more recent monographs: Scott R. Pilarz S.J., *Robert Southwell and the Mission of Literature, 1561–1595: Writing Reconciliation* (Aldershot: Ashgate, 2004) and Anne R. Sweeney, *Robert Southwell: Snow in Arcadia: Redrawing the English Lyric Landscape* (Manchester: Manchester University Press, 2006).

See also the recent edition of his verse, ed. Peter Davidson and Anne Sweeney (Manchester: Carcanet, 2007).

35. Ralph Buckland, *An Embassage from Heaven* (1611), p. 7.

36. Sasha Roberts, *Reading Shakespeare's Poems in Early Modern England* (Basingstoke: Palgrave Macmillan, 2003). An anecdote relating how, in the 1580s, a Jesuit priest smashed a painted window depicting Mars and Venus is discussed in the introduction to *Shakespeare's Poems*, ed. Katherine Duncan-Jones and Henry Woudhuysen (London: Arden, 2007), p. 35.

37. Quoted from *St Robert Southwell: Collected Poems*, ed. Peter Davidson and Anne Sweeney (Manchester: Carcanet, 2007), pp. 1, 63. This is largely based around a single copytext, Stonyhurst MS A.v.4; for details of how the verse and prose epistles are distributed within all surviving early manuscript and printed collections, see *The Poems of Robert Southwell, S.J.*, ed. James H. Macdonald and Nancy Pollard Brown (Oxford: Clarendon, 1967), pp. 1–2, 75.

38. Listed as no. 719 in *ARCR*. If the publishers, as opposed to someone annotating a book for private use, intended a reference to Shakespeare, it would be odd – given the tone of the comments on Shakespeare in Gennings' *Life*, discussed below and published only two years earlier – that so little is made of it. In any case, it is almost certainly a coincidence that the volume appears in the year of Shakespeare's death.

39. This follows the account given by Macdonald and Pollard Brown.

40. For a more detailed discussion of the question, see my article 'Why Didn't Shakespeare Write Religious Verse?' in Kozuka and Mulryne (eds), *Shakespeare, Marlowe, Jonson.*

41. This reference appears in C. M. Ingleby *et al.*, *The Shakspere Allusion-Book*, 2 vols (London: Humphrey Milford/Oxford University Press, 1932), Vol. I, p. 125, but has attracted surprisingly little attention from commentators. An exception to this rule is Wood, *in Search of Shakespeare*, p. 174, drawing (with my permission) on an early, unpublished version of 'Why Didn't Shakespeare . . . ?' I am grateful to Michael Wood for a stimulating discussion on this topic.

42. John Trussell, *Raptus I Helenae* (1595); Giles Fletcher, *Licia . . . whereunto is added the rising to the crowne of Richard III* (1593). I am grateful to Katherine Duncan-Jones for these suggestions.

43. If one is to take at face value the highly specific comments in I.C.'s epistle to the reader, *Saint Marie Magdalens Conversion* must be dated to the early seventeenth century (see following note), at a time when *Richard III*, *The Rape of Lucrece* and *Troilus and Cressida* had all been written.

44. On the 1603 plague, see J. Leeds Barroll, *Politics, Plague and Shakespeare's Theater* (Ithaca: Cornell University Press, 1995), esp. Ch. 2 and Appendix 2. A date of 1603/4 seems more likely than 1602/3.

45. *Palladis Tamia* (1598), f. Oo1b.

46. Alison Goddard Elliott, 'Ovid and the Critics: Seneca, Quintilian, and "Seriousness"', *Helios*, n.s. 12: 1 (1985), pp. 9–20.

47. *Ovid's Metamorphosis Englished* (1626), ff. b3b–c2a. See Christopher Martin (ed.), *Ovid in English* (London: Penguin, 1998), p. xxv.

48. Raphael Lyne, *Ovid's Changing Worlds: English Metamorphoses, 1567–1632* (Oxford: Oxford University Press, 2001), Ch. 1.

49. On the continued tradition of moralising Ovid in the Renaissance, see Lyne, *Ovid's Changing Worlds*, Ch. 1 (on Arthur Golding's translation of the Metamorphoses).

50. On scholarly speculation over whether Southwell's line 'Still finest wits are stilling Venus' rose' refers to 'Venus and Adonis', see Shell, 'Why Didn't Shakespeare . . . ?' My own view is that the reflection is deliberately general but lends itself to being read as an attack on Shakespeare's poem, both by contemporaries and subsequently.

51. *Shakespeare and Ovid* (Oxford: Clarendon, 1993), pp. 3–4, commenting primarily on Thomas M. Greene, 'The Flexibility of the Self in Renaissance Literature', in Peter Demetz, Thomas M. Greene and Lowry Nelson Jnr, *The Disciplines of Criticism: Essays in Literary Theory, Interpretation and History* (New Haven: Yale University Press, 1968), pp. 241–264. On contemporary perceptions of Marlowe as an Ovidian poet-playwright, see Patrick Cheney, 'Biographical Representations: Marlowe's Life of the Author', Ch. 12 in Kozuka and Mulryne (eds), *Shakespeare, Marlowe, Jonson*.

52. See Raphael Lyne, 'Love and Exile After Ovid', Ch. 17 in Philip Hardie (ed.), *The Cambridge Companion to Ovid* (Cambridge: Cambridge University Press, 2002).

53. See Introduction, p. 3.

54. E.g. the Latin drama *Psyche et Filii Eius* (*c.* 1615: see my *Catholicism, Controversy*, p. 286). There may be some merit in distinguishing between the 'recusant' writing undertaken in Britain and the poetry and drama written at the British Catholic colleges overseas, where educational concerns would have figured more largely.

55. Bod MS Eng. poet. e. 122, ff. 46a–74a (quotation f. 46a). The volume is dated 1641, but the poem's style indicates an earlier date; it is written in poulter's measure, popular in Elizabethan England but unfashionable thereafter. For similar Catholic repudiations of classicism, see Richard Verstegan, *Odes* (1601), f. A4b, and the anonymously compiled anthology *Epitaphs* (1604), f. A4a.

56. On printed material, see *ARCR*.

57. In *ARCR*, p. 250, A.F. Allison and D.M. Rogers raise doubts about John Gennings's authorship of the earlier tract, though the new biographical information given in *ODNB*'s entries for the Gennings brothers re-establishes him as the likely author. Both this and the 1614 *Life* pose complex attribution issues: for a discussion of these, see my article 'The Sixteenth- and Seventeenth-Century *Lives* of Edmund Gennings' forthcoming in *Recusant History*. Frank W. Brownlow's 'A Jesuit Allusion to *King Lear*', *Recusant History*, 28: 3 (2007), pp. 416–423, came to my notice when the bulk of this section was written; even though our conclusions are different, my account benefits greatly from it. The reference to the King Lear story was first brought to my attention by a footnote in Susannah Brietz Monta, *Martyrdom and Literature in Early Modern England* (Cambridge: Cambridge University Press, 2005), p. 126.

58. Katherine Duncan-Jones has suggested to me that this may refer to the information that the play was performed at court, given on the title-page of the 1608 *King Lear* quarto.

59. See *A Critical Edition of the True Chronicle History of King Leir and his Three Daughters*, ed. Donald M. Michie (New York: Garland, 1991), Introduction; and *King Lear*, ed. R.A. Foakes (London: Thomson, 1997), p. 90. The reference to 'goodman Jennings' in Michie's edition (scene xxvii, line 13) is a mistranscription of 'Genitings' (i.e. 'Jennetings', a variety of apple) on f. I2a of the original.

60. This serves to qualify Huston Diehl's comment that 'Cordelia's plain speaking aligns [her] with early Protestantism, for plain speaking is a Protestant ideal': 'Religion in Shakespearean Tragedy', Ch. 5 in Claire McEachern (ed.), *The Cambridge Companion to Shakespearean Tragedy* (Cambridge: Cambridge University Press, 2002), quotation p. 100.

61. Cf. one recent interpretation of *Lear*, Kristian Levring's *The King Is Alive* (2000), which sets it against the sand dunes of the Namibian desert: see the review by Carolyn Jess, *Early Modern Literary Studies*, 10: 1 (2004), e-journal.

62. Maynard Mack, King Lear *in Our Time* (Berkeley: California University Press, this edn 1972), p. 97; *Lear*, ed. Foakes, p. 1.

63. See his entry in *ODNB*. I am grateful to Bro. Ninian Arbuckle for advice on Franciscan issues relating to his biography.

64. Quarto, 5: 3 (Scene 24), 302–303.

65. The word 'tragedy' occurs on p. 65.

66. On martyr-narratives, see Sarah Covington, *The Trail of Martyrdom: Persecution and Resistance in 16th-Century England* (Notre Dame: Notre Dame University Press, 2003); Anne Dillon, *The Construction of Martyrdom in the English Catholic Community, 1535–1603* (Aldershot: Ashgate, 2002); Brad S. Gregory, *Salvation at Stake: Christian Martyrdom in Early Modern Europe* (Cambridge, Mass./London: Harvard University Press, 1999); Monta, *Martyrdom*.

67. See Chambers, *Shakespeare: Facts and Problems*, Vol. II, p. 257. This may mean that he was reported to have been given the sacrament of extreme unction; see Peter Ackroyd, *Shakespeare: The Biography* (London: Chatto and Windus, 2005), p. 447, for the implications of this.

68. I find the arguments for specific verbal parallels between Shakespeare and Southwell inconclusive: 'Why Didn't Shakespeare . . . ?', p. 109 (note 34). See note 33 above.

69. Lodge refers to 'Peter his apostasie, Marie her losse and misse of Christ': *Prosopopoeia*, f. A5b. Two editions of the book appeared in 1596: all transcriptions are taken from STC 16662a. Helen Hackett has pointed out to me that *A Margarite of America*, highly profane in content, appeared the same year; the dedicatory epistle to this is dated 4 May 1596, while neither edition of *Prosopopoeia* indicates the exact time of composition. Two other works by Lodge also came out in 1596, *The Divel Conjured* and *Wits Miserie*: the former sedate and moralistic in character, the latter satirical and Rabelaisian but in line with post-Tridentine sensitivities, opposing plays which dealt with scriptural material (on this, see Patrick

Collinson, *From Iconoclasm to Iconophobia: The Cultural Impact of the Second English Reformation* (1st edn [Reading]: Reading University Press, 1986), p. 14; and Donna Hamilton, *Anthony Munday and the Catholics, 1560–1633* (Aldershot: Ashgate, 2005), p. 18). Whatever order these four items appeared in, the fact that Lodge published no imaginative writing after 1596 is consistent with the conversion experience he describes in *Prosopopeia*. On Lodge's biography, see Alexandra Halasz's life in *ODNB*; on his later work as a translator, see Erin Kelly, 'Jewish History, Catholic Argument: Thomas Lodge's *Workes of Josephus* as a Catholic Text', *Sixteenth-Century Journal*, 34: 4 (2003), pp. 993–1010, and Arthur F. Kinney, *Humanist Poetics: Thought, Rhetoric, and Fiction in 16th-Century England* (Amherst: Massachusetts University Press, 1986), pp. 418–419.

70. Anne Barton (Righter), *Shakespeare and the Idea of the Play* (this edn, Harmondsworth: Penguin, 1967), p. 26.

71. See Thomas M. McCoog, *The Society of Jesus in Ireland, Scotland and England 1541–1588*, Studies in Medieval and Renaissance Thought, Vol. 60 (Leiden: E.J. Brill, 1996), Ch. 4, esp. pp. 174–177.

72. BL, Add. MS 5541, f. 98, also transcribed in *Ben Jonson*, ed. C.H. Herford, Percy Simpson and Evelyn Simpson, 11 vols (Oxford: Clarendon, 1925–1952), Vol. XI, pp. 493–494. For evidence of Willford's Catholic sympathies, see the material on (e.g.), ff. 98b–99a, 118a. The poem is commented on by Ian Donaldson in *Jonson's Magic Houses: Essays in Interpretation* (Oxford: Clarendon, 1997), pp. 64–65.

73. *Sonnets*, ed. Duncan-Jones, pp. 343, 465; Duncan-Jones identifies it as developing a 'sectarian religious metaphor' (p. 459). I discuss this and the next text in more detail in 'Why Didn't Shakespeare . . . ?'

74. John Weever, 'Epig. 22. . . . *Ad Gulielmum Shakespeare*', in *Epigrammes*, ed. R.B. McKerrow (London: Sidgwick and Jackson, 1911), p. 75.

75. See Martin Wiggins, 'Shakespeare Jesuited: The Plagiarisms of "Pater Clarcus"', *The Seventeenth Century*, 20: 1 (2005), pp. 1–21. On medieval and post-medieval campaigns for Henry VI's canonisation, see R.A. Griffiths's article on the king in *ODNB*.

76. On the reading of Shakespeare in English Catholic educational institutions, see Wiggins, *op.cit.*; G. Blakemore Evans, 'The Douai Manuscript: Six Shakespearean Transcripts (1694–5)', *Philological Quarterly*, 41 (1962), pp. 158–172; 'The Roman Catholic Censorship of Shakespeare: 1641–1651', appendix to Roland Mushat Frye, *Shakespeare and Christian Doctrine* (1963: this edn, Princeton: Princeton University Press, 1975). On the reading of Shakespeare among Jesuits, see Willem Schrickx, '*Pericles* in a Book-List of 1619 from the English Jesuit Mission and Some of the Play's Special Problems', *Shakespeare Survey*, 29 (1976), pp. 21–32. I am grateful to David Scott Kastan for letting me see his work on the Valladolid folio in advance of publication.

77. 'William Shakeshafte', in *Shakespearean Gleanings* (London: Oxford University Press, 1944), pp. 52–56, and *The Elizabethan Stage* (Oxford: Clarendon, 1923), Vol. I, p. 280. More recently, see David George (ed.), *Records*

of *Early English Drama: Lancashire* (Toronto: Toronto University Press, 1991) (hereafter *REEDS*), pp. 156–158, 350 (Alexander Hoghton's will), 180 and 354 (evidence for Hesketh's papers).

78. For the case in favour see, among other sources, Oliver Baker, *In Shakespeare's Warwickshire and the Unknown Years* (London: Simpkin Marshall, 1937), pp. 297–319; Peter Milward, *Shakespeare's Religious Background* (Bloomington: Indiana University Press, 1973); Honigmann, *Shakespeare: The 'Lost Years'*, and 'The Shakespeare/Shakeshafte Question, Continued', *Shakespeare Quarterly*, 54: 1 (2003), pp. 83–86. For the case against, see Douglas Hamer, 'Was William Shakespeare William Shakeshafte?', *Review of English Studies*, n.s. 21: 81 (1970), pp. 41–48; and Robert Bearman, '"Was William Shakespeare William Shakeshafte?" Revisited', *Shakespeare Quarterly*, 53: 1 (2002), pp. 83–94. While hedging their bets, several recent biographers (especially Greenblatt and Wood) are broadly in favour of the idea. While the name's spelling varies among commentators, the present account follows *REEDS* in using 'Shakshafte'.

79. Recent accounts of the Simpsons' activities can be found in Paul Whitfield White, *Drama and Religion in English Provincial Society, 1485–1660* (Cambridge: Cambridge University Press, 2008), Ch. 5; Phebe Jensen, 'Recusancy, Festivity and Community: The Simpsons at Gowlthwaite Hall', Ch. 6 in Richard Dutton, Alison Findlay and Richard Wilson (eds), *Region, Religion and Patronage: Lancastrian Shakespeare* (Manchester: Manchester University Press, 2003) and Jensen's *Religion and Revelry*, pp. 49–52. For what appears to be a late (i.e. early 17th-century) cycle of Old Testament dramas written by a Catholic and intended for the stage, see Carleton Brown (ed.), *The Stonyhurst Pageants*, *Hesperia*, supplement, no. 7 (Göttingen/Baltimore: Vandenhoeck and Ruprecht/Johns Hopkins University Press, 1920). On these, see Rowland Wymer, 'Shakespeare and the Mystery Cycles', *English Literary Renaissance*, 34: 3 (2004), pp. 265–285.

80. BL Add.MS 11427, item 7. The ascription 'per Robertu[m] Owen Gent' comes at the end of the play, just after the epilogue, and could refer either to the epilogue or to the play as a whole. Owen describes himself as compiling item 1 in the MS, as authoring item 2 and as copying (possibly also translating) item 3. Where dated, the other items in the MS range between 1600 and 1629, with the heaviest concentration between 1600 and 1602; hence, a 1600–2 date has been tentatively postulated for *The History of Purgatory*. The play would repay sustained editorial attention. Its literary roughness and consciously archaic style both render dating problematic, and while its frequent allusions to Southwell's verse would support an early seventeenth-century date for a text produced within mainstream literary culture, an author from an obviously 'recusant' background might well have been familiar with Southwell earlier or later.

81. For Caxton's 1483 translation of this text, see Katherine Isabella Cust (ed.) *The Booke of the Pylgremage of the Sowle* (London: Basil Montagu Pickering, 1859). On post-medieval receptions and appropriations of de

Guileville in England, see Kathryn Walls and Marguerite Stobo (eds), *The Pilgrime* (Tempe, AZ: Arizona Center for Medieval and Renaissance Studies, 2008), introduction.

82. The numbering is irregular at this point in the MS, due in part to a change from foliation to pagination: two pages are numbered 5, with five unnumbered pages between them. These quotations come from the second and third of these pages.

83. The Douai Old Testament was not available till 1609.

84. However, as Helen Hackett has pointed out to me, one must be alert to the potential pun on 'parson/person'. On this, see Jensen, *Religion and Revelry*, pp. 163–164.

85. This is one of the key arguments in Barton (Righter), *Shakespeare and the Idea of the Play*.

86. Though the manuscript is not clear at this point, the speaker appears to be the soul voicing an epilogue.

87. See my *Oral Culture and Catholicism in Early Modern England* (Cambridge: Cambridge University Press, 2007), Conclusion.

88. The text quoted within the following discussion is the second quarto (ed. Ann Thompson and Neil Taylor, Arden Shakespeare, Third Series), which is likely to be of a very similar date to *The History of Purgatory* (see note 78 above).

89. I.e. 'gape with surprise' (Thompson and Taylor); F's reading of 'ayme' (aim, guess, conjecture), while equally satisfying in some ways, underplays the element of surprise which might have accompanied the introduction of Catholic matter on stage.

90. This speech is assigned to 'a Gentleman' in Q2 and Horatio in F.

91. For a recent reading of *Hamlet* that relates its hero's dilemmas to the conflicting psychological pressures brought about by Protestantism's relocating of authority, see Huston Diehl, 'Religion and Shakespearean Tragedy', Ch. 5 in Claire McEachern (ed.), *The Cambridge Companion to Shakespearean Tragedy* (Cambridge: Cambridge University Press, 2002).

92. *Hamlet in Purgatory* (Princeton: Princeton University Press, 2001). For a critique of the book which makes analogous points to what follows, see Sarah Beckwith, 'Stephen Greenblatt's *Hamlet* and the Forms of Oblivion', *Journal of Medieval and Early Modern Studies*, 33: 2 (2003), pp. 261–280. However, I believe Greenblatt's study to be an excellent literary introduction to the topic, and my debt to it in what follows is much greater than my differences from it.

93. See above, note 80.

94. For a recent reading of *Hamlet* in relation to contemporary religious controversy, see Jesse M. Lander, *Inventing Polemic: Religion, Print and Literary Culture in Early Modern England* (Cambridge: Cambridge University Press, 2006), Ch. 3.

95. See, most recently, Peter Marshall, *Beliefs and the Dead in Reformation England* (Oxford: Oxford University Press, 2002), esp. Ch. 6 (quotation p. 249); and John Newton, 'An Examination of Interpretations of Ghosts

from the Reformation to the Close of the 17th Century', PhD thesis, University of Durham, 2004.

96. F's 'enurn'd', with its overtones of pagan burial, could be seen as working against the allusion to mystery-play staging suggested below.

97. See Groves, *Texts and Traditions*, pp. 77–83.

98. This is more in keeping with the theme of the passage than the 'remote allusion' to the story of Jonah and the whale which Thompson and Taylor suggest (pp. 206–207).

99. See *OED*.

100. It first appears within Greenblatt's famous essay, 'Shakespeare and the Exorcists': Ch. 4 in *Shakespearean Negotiations: The Circulation of Social Energy in Renaissance England* (Berkeley: California University Press, 1988), p. 127.

101. *Shakespearean Negotiations*, p. 125.

102. Cf. Jesse Lander's contrast of Q1 and Q2 in his discussion of *Hamlet*: 'Q1 comfortably inhabits a conventional eschatology . . . Q2 spends considerably more time on the problems of providence, . . . [achieving] a specific, aesthetic distance from the world of religious controversy. This disposition must not be construed as one of disinterest or indifference; by aestheticising curious considerations, Q2 addresses the unperturbed, literate gentleman, one who can stand above, or rather sit quietly at a remove from, the fray, taking pleasure in speculation and drawing edification from the undermining of dogmatic positions' (*Inventing Polemic*, p. 139).

103. Mary Renault, letter to Colin Spencer, quoted in Caroline Zilboorg, *The Masks of Mary Renault* (Columbia/London: Missouri University Press, 2001), p. 193.

104. Sermon preached at Whitehall, the first Friday in Lent [1622/3], on John 11:35: 'Jesus wept.' Quoted from George R. Potter and Evelyn M. Simpson (eds), *The Sermons of John Donne*, Vol. IV (Berkeley: California University Press, 1959), p. 324.

105. See notes 4–5 above.

106. 'The Virtues of Disloyalty', in *Stiftung F.V.S. zu Hamburg, Verleihung der Shakespeare-Preise 1968 und 1969 durch die Universität Hamburg an die Herren Graham Greene . . . und Professor Roy Pascal* (Hamburg: Conti Press, 1969), pp. 49–52 (quotations on pp. 52, 51, 50). Greene's address was later reprinted in *The Virtue of Disloyalty* (London: Bodley Head, 1972); he comments in the preface, 'The attack should be taken with a grain of salt; it masks a different offensive, and yet it does represent a genuine suspicion which has qualified my admiration of Shakespeare – the suspicion of something cold and prudent in the poet's nature . . . ' (p. 2).

107. See Norman Sherry, *The Life of Graham Greene, Volume One: 1904–1939* (London: Jonathan Cape, 1989), pp. 316, 700; and Marie-Françoise Allain, *The Other Man: Conversations with Graham Greene*, trans. Guido Waldmann (London: Bodley Head, 1983), p. 159.

3: GOOD WORKS: SHAKESPEARE'S USE
OF RELIGIOUS MORALISM

1. Quoted from the edition of *Everyman* in G.A. Lester (ed.), *Three Late Medieval Morality Plays* (1981: repr. London: A. and C. Black, 2002), p. 102.

2. [Robert Chamberlain], *Conceits, Clinches, Flashes, and Whimzies* (1639), f. E4a. The fact that Shakespeare's literary productions are identified as valuable implies that the speaker is not poking fun simply at the idea of a playwright's collected works being published: on which, however, see Jennifer Brady and W.H. Herendeen (eds), *Ben Jonson's 1616 Folio* (Newark: Delaware University Press/London: Associated University Presses, 1991).

3. *The Practise of Pietie* (1613 edition), p. 78; M.K. (trans.), *A Breefe Treatise Exhorting Sinners to Repentance, Commonly Called, The Conversion of a Sinner* [1580], f. 8a.

4. Ian Green, *Print and Protestantism in Early Modern England* (Cambridge: Cambridge University Press, 2000), Preface.

5. See Heidi Brayman Heckel, '"Rowme" of Its Own: Printed Drama and Early Libraries', Ch. 7 in John D. Cox and David Scott Kastan (eds), *A New History of Early English Drama* (New York: Columbia University Press, 1997).

6. *Conversion of a Sinner*, f. 86b.

7. *Practise of Pietie*, p. 162, alluding to Song of Songs 2: 11–12.

8. 'Sweet and useful.' This is adapted from *Ars Poetica*, lines 343–344: *omne tulit punctum qui miscuit utile dulci / lectorem delectando pariterque monendo.* Quoted from Q. Horatii Flacci, *Opera*, ed. Edward C. Wickham, rev. H.W. Garrod (Oxford: Clarendon, 1901).

9. On declamations and disputative orations, see T.W. Baldwin, *William Shakspere's Small Latine and Lesse Greeke*, 2 vols (Urbana: Illinois University Press, 1944), Vol. 2, Ch. 40; on the relationship between drama and rhetorical education, see Joel B. Altman, *The Tudor Play of Mind: Rhetorical Inquiry and the Development of Elizabethan Drama* (Berkeley: California University Press, 1978). For a recent assessment of how this element of the grammar-school curriculum would have affected Shakespeare, see Peter Ackroyd, *Shakespeare: The Biography* (London: Chatto and Windus, 2005), pp. 58–59.

10. See the entry for 'sin' in the *Catholic Encyclopaedia* (online).

11. 'Heaven' is substituted for 'God' in the Folio text.

12. *A Refutation of the Apology for Actors*, in Pollard (ed.), *Shakespeare's Theater*, p. 268.

13. *Doctor Faustus*, Epilogue, 4–8 (quotation taken from B-text). From Christopher Marlowe, *Doctor Faustus and Other Plays*, ed. David Bevington and Eric Rasmussen (1995: this edn, Oxford: Oxford University Press, 1998). See above, p. 52.

14. www.britishdebate.com/schools/shakespeare (accessed 24 July 2007).

15. Cf. Joel B. Altman's identification of the difference between declarative and

interrogative drama, the 'intellectual energies' of the latter being 'devoted to discovery, not explanation': *Tudor Play of Mind*, p. 24. John Edward Price, 'Anti-Moralistic Moralism in *All's Well That Ends Well*', *Shakespeare Studies*, 12 (1979), pp. 95–111, distinguishes between platitudinous moralism and other kinds.

16. See (e.g.) the amount of space devoted to Shakespeare in *The Oxford Dictionary of Quotations*, 6th edn, ed. Elizabeth Knowles (Oxford: Oxford University Press, 2004), pp. 678–724. On Shakespeare's use of pre-existent proverbs and the stylistic inspiration he drew from them, see Morris Palmer Tilley, *A Dictionary of the Proverbs in England in the Sixteenth and Seventeenth Centuries* (1950; this edn, Ann Arbor: Michigan University Press, 1966), pp. vii–viii, and R.W. Dent, *Shakespeare's Proverbial Language: An Index* (Berkeley: California University Press, 1981), introduction. On collecting proverbs and *sententiae* in the Renaissance, see Ann Moss, *Commonplace-Books and the Structuring of Renaissance Thought* (Oxford: Clarendon, 1996), esp. index under 'Commonplace-Books: Constituents'.

17. Gabriel Egan, *Green Shakespeare: From Ecopolitics to Ecocriticism* (London/New York: Routledge, 2006), pp. 100–102; and, on the anti-hunt lobby in the sixteenth century, *As You Like It*, ed. Juliet Dusinberre (London: Thomson, 2006), p. 53.

18. See Michael Bath, 'Weeping Stags and Melancholy Lovers: The Iconography of *As You Like It*, II i', *Emblematica*, I (1986), pp. 13–52.

19. See Patricia Meyer Spacks, *Gossip* (1st edn, Chicago: Chicago University Press, 1985), esp Ch. 2; Jörg R. Bergmann, trans. John Bednarz, Jnr, with Eva Kafka Barron, *Discreet Indiscretions: The Social Organisation of Gossip* (New York: Aldine de Gruyter, 1993); M. Lindsay Kaplan, *The Culture of Slander in Early Modern England* (Cambridge: Cambridge University Press, 1997); Adam Fox, *Oral and Literate Culture in England, 1500–1700* (Oxford: Clarendon, 2000), pp. 85–86, 177–178, 340–343.

20. Cf. Gabriele Taylor's comments on soap opera: 'Vicarious living has the . . . attraction of presenting a story the development of which one can take an interest in and speculate about, secure in the knowledge that it cannot adversely affect oneself. Hence gossipers appear to be in the position of having their cake and eating it' ('Gossip as Moral Talk', Ch. 3 in *Good Gossip*, ed. Robert F. Goodman and Aaron Ben-Ze-ev (Lawrence: Kansas University Press, 1994), quotation p. 41).

21. Quoted from Dave Postles, 'Penance and the Market-Place: A Reformation Dialogue with the Medieval Church, *c.* 1250–*c.* 1600', *Journal of Ecclesiastical History*, 54: 3 (2003), pp. 441–468, quotation pp. 467–468.

22. See, most recently, Alexandra Walsham, *Charitable Hatred: Tolerance and Intolerance in England, 1500–1700* (Manchester: Manchester University Press, 2006).

23. *Censorship and Interpretation: The Conditions of Writing and Reading in Early Modern England* (Madison: Wisconsin University Press, 1984).

24. J.A. Sharpe, ' "Last Dying Speeches": Religion, Ideology and Public Execution in Seventeenth-Century England', *Past and Present*, 107 (1985), pp. 144–167; Frances Dolan, ' "Gentlemen, I Have One Thing More To Say":

Women on Scaffolds in England, 1563–1680', *Modern Philology*, 92: 2 (1994), pp. 157–178; Peter Lake with Michael C. Questier, *The Antichrist's Lewd Hat: Protestants, Papists and Players in Post-Reformation England* (New Haven: Yale University Press, 2002), Ch. 7; Karl S. Guthke, *Last Words: Variations on a Theme in Cultural History* (Princeton: Princeton University Press, 1992).

25. *The Manner of the Death and Execution of A. Cosbie* (1591); the poem is quoted from this text. See also W.R., *The Most Horrible and Tragicall Murther of . . . John Lord Bourgh* (1591), Henry Carey, *The Araignment, Examination, Confession and Judgement of A. Cosbye* (1591), and L.E. Semler, 'Robert Dallington's *Hypnerotomachia* and the Protestant Antiquity of Elizabethan England', *Studies in Philology*, 103: 2 (2006), pp. 208–241.

26. On exemplary behaviour in prison, see Lake and Questier, *Antichrist's Lewd Hat*, Ch. 6. A well-known near-contemporary prison verse is Chideock Tichborne's 'My prime of youth is but a frost of cares', first printed in *Verses of Prayse and Joye Writen Upon her Majesties Preservation. Whereunto is Annexed Tychbornes Lamentation, Written in the Tow re [sic] With His Owne Hand, and an Aunswere to the Same* (1586), f. A2b. See Richard S. M. Hirsch, 'The Works of Chideock Tichborne', *English Literary Renaissance*, 16:2 (1986), pp. 303–318, and 'The Text of "Tichborne's Lament" Reconsidered', *English Literary Renaissance*, 17:3 (1987), p. 277.

27. Paul Budra, *A Mirror for Magistrates and the 'De Casibus' Tradition* (Toronto: Toronto University Press, 2000).

28. *Richard II: The Critical Tradition*, ed. Charles R. Forker (New Jersey: Athlone, 1988), pp. 35, 40. Gary Kuchar reads this scene as parodying the tradition of tears-poetry: see Ch. 2, note 33.

29. Respectively Matthew 19:14 (quoted)/Mark 10.14; Matthew 19:24 (quoted)/ Mark 10:25 / Luke 18:25 (Shaheen, *Biblical References*, pp. 387–388).

30. See Ch. 4, esp. pp. 180–181.

31. 1630 edition, pp. 305–306.

32. David Bevington and Eric Rasmussen date Marlowe's play to around 1588–1589 (*Dr Faustus and Other Plays* (Oxford: Oxford University Press, 1995), p. xii); Stanley Wells *et al.* date *Richard II* to 'probably . . . no earlier than 1595' (*Oxford Shakespeare*, introduction to the play). In a thorough recent discussion of the date of *Richard II*, Charles R. Forker suggests that the play's first performance may have been in the autumn of 1595: Forker (ed.), *Richard II* (London: Arden, 2002), p. 120.

33. Some editors' punctuation, e.g. Forker's 'Forgiveness, horse', brings out the line's parodic quality even more strongly.

34. On martyrs, see Anne Dillon, *The Construction of Martyrdom in the English Catholic Community, 1535–1603* (Aldershot: Ashgate, 2002); Brad S. Gregory, *Salvation at Stake* (Cambridge, Mass.: Harvard University Press, 1999); Susannah Breitz Monta, *Martyrdom and Literature in Early Modern England* (Cambridge: Cambridge University Press, 2005). On exemplary deathbeds, see Ralph Houlbrooke, *Death, Religion and the Family in England, 1480–1750* (Oxford: Clarendon, 1998).

35. Katherine's deathbed in *King Henry VIII* would be a striking exception to

this rule if written by Shakespeare, but is a scene which critics usually assign to Fletcher: see the edition by Jay L. Halio (Oxford: Oxford University Press, 1999), pp. 19–22.

36. Quoted from 1605 edn, ff. *2b–3a.

37. Samuel Rowlands and M. Sparke(?), *A Most Excellent Treatise Containing the Way to Seek Heavens Glory* (3rd edn, 1639: frontispiece dated 1638). For previous editions of 1601 (Rowlands's portion only) and 1628, see STC 13048.5 and 21383.

38. On the figure of the bellman in popular literature, see Tessa Watt, *Cheap Print and Popular Piety, 1550–1640* (Cambridge: Cambridge University Press, 1991), pp. 97, 113–114. On the common imaginative stock shared by writers of underworld tracts, see Edwin Haviland Miller, *The Professional Writer in Elizabethan England: A Study of Non-Dramatic Literature* (Cambridge, Mass.: Harvard University Press, 1959), Ch. 7.

39. Quoted from *Henry IV: Part II*, ed. René Weis (Oxford: Oxford University Press, 1997, this edn 1998).

40. This is a commonplace, but Shaheen, *Biblical References*, p. 441, suggests Psalm 89.47 as the closest passage.

41. I.e. 'What price is . . . ?'

42. On the differences between early editions of the play brought about by this Act, see Weis (ed.), pp. 93, 98.

43. Again, 'Jesus' is altered to 'Oh' in Folio editions.

44. Lester (ed.), *Three Late Medieval Morality Plays*, p. 75, lines 272–274.

45. Quoted from *Henry V*, ed. Gary Taylor (1982: repr. Oxford: Oxford University Press, 1998). *Falstaff*, ed. Harold Bloom (New York: Chelsea House, 1992) includes two recent essays on this scene: Michael Platt, 'Falstaff in the Valley of the Shadow of Death', pp. 171–202, and Paul M. Cubeta, 'Falstaff and the Art of Dying', pp. 246–257. While intimations of a happy death are common to all editions of the plays, the scene poses notorious textual difficulties, and the phrase 'a babbled of green fields' is an emendation from 'a table of green fields'. See Taylor (ed.) *Henry V*, Appendix B, and Michael Dobson's review of the RSC Shakespeare, ed. Jonathan Bate and Eric Rasmussen, *London Review of Books*, 29: 9 (10 May 2007), pp. 3–8. Platt, however, suggests that 'a table of green fields' may be an intentional representation of Hostess Quickly mimicking Falstaff's delirious utterances (pp. 175–176, 194–195).

46. Cubeta, ' . . . Art of Dying', pp. 253–255 (quotation p. 255); Platt, ' . . . Shadow of Death', p. 176. Platt's reading opposes earlier arguments that Falstaff achieved a good death (especially Roy Battenhouse's 'Falstaff as Parodist and Perhaps Holy Fool', *Proceedings of the Modern Language Association*, 90: 1 (1975), pp. 32–52) but he still calls it 'Christ-like'.

47. On other echoes of Psalm 23, see note 43 above. However, on green fields as a way that the scripturally illiterate thought of heaven, cf. William Pemble, *Workes* (3rd edn 1635), p. 559.

48. Ephesians 4:22, 24.

49. For a discussion of the occasions on which Falstaff plays at penitence, see Cubeta, ' . . . Art of Dying', pp. 248, 251.

50. On Lollards' apocalypticism, see Katharine R. Firth, *the Apocalyptic Tradition in Reformation Britain, 1530–1645* (Oxford: Oxford University Press, 1979), pp. 7, 41, 48, 50.

51. See comments in Ch. 1, p. 33, and Ch. 2, p. 83; Kristen Poole, *Radical Religion from Shakespeare to Milton* (Cambridge: Cambridge University Press, 2000), pp. 18–19; Gary Taylor, 'The Fortunes of Oldcastle', *Shakespeare Studies*, 38 (1985), pp. 85–100; and Ch. 1, note 10.

52. Poole, *Radical Religion*, Ch. 1.

53. On audience response to Falstaff, see Whitney, *Early Responses*, Ch. 2.

54. See Ch. 4, pp. 210–211.

55. See Hunt, *Art of Hearing*, pp. 299–300.

56. *The Defence of Poesy*, p. 230: quoted from the edition in *Sir Philip Sidney*, ed. Katherine Duncan-Jones (Oxford: Oxford University Press, 1989). The anecdote was most often cited from Plutarch's *Lives* (293f) and his *Morals* (334A). The fact that it was the sorrows of Hecuba that moved him may have inspired the allusion to Hecuba in *Hamlet*: see William A. Ringler, Jnr, 'Hamlet's Defense of the Players', in Richard Hosley (ed.), *Essays on Shakespeare and Elizabethan Drama in Honour of Hardin Craig* (London: Routledge and Kegan Paul, 1963), pp. 201–211.

57. Thomas Heywood, *An Apology for Actors*, p. 243, paraphrasing a comment in Harington's 'An Apologie for Poetry', prefixed to his *Orlando Furioso*, f. ¶6a (reference taken from 1607 edn). There appears to be slippage here between Alexander of Pherae and the Sicilian tyrant Phalaris. This and all subsequent quotations are taken from the edition of Heywood's *Apology* in *Shakespeare's Theater*, ed. Tanya Pollard (Malden, MA/Oxford: Blackwell, 2004). On versions of the anecdote known in Renaissance England, see Richard Proudfoot, ' "The Play's the Thing": Hamlet and the Conscience of the Queen', Ch. 9 in John W. Mahon and Thomas A. Pendleton (eds), *'Fanned and Winnowed Opinions': Shakespearean Essays Presented to Harold Jenkins* (London/New York: Methuen, 1987), pp. 160–162.

58. On archival support for the story, see Proudfoot, ' "The Play's the Thing"', pp. 164–165.

59. *A Warning for Fair Women: A Critical Edition*, ed. Charles Dale Cannon (The Hague and Paris: Mouton, 1975), lines 2043, 2046–2048, and the commentary on pp. 188–189. See also *Hamlet*, ed. Harold Jenkins (Arden, 2nd series), p. 482; Proudfoot, ' "The Play's the Thing"'; Bullough, *Sources*, 7: 38).

60. On the question of whether Hamlet's contribution can be identified, see *Hamlet*, ed. Thompson and Taylor, pp. 273–274.

61. In a German version of *Hamlet*, *Der Bestrafte Brudermord*, this passage is altered to include an account of an episode in Strasbourg where a murderess confesses guilt at a performance of a tragedy where a murder is staged: see Albert Cohn, *Shakespeare in Germany in the Sixteenth and Seventeenth Centuries*, trans. Georgina Simpson (London: Asher and Co., 1865), pp. cxxii–cxxiii, 268. The story is rewritten to take place in Strasbourg, possibly because the company had come from there.

62. Given the likely Elizabethan pronunciation, 'trapically', there would also have been a pun on 'trap'. See John Doebler, 'The Play Within the Play: The *Muscipula Diaboli* in Hamlet', *Shakespeare Quarterly*, 23: 2 (1972), pp. 161–169, reference p. 161; and John Dover Wilson, *What Happens in Hamlet* (1935: this edn, Cambridge: Cambridge University Press, 1951), p. 191.

63. See Doebler, 'The Play within the Play', and Ch. 4 in his *Shakespeare's Speaking Pictures: Studies in Iconic Imagery* (Albuquerque: New Mexico University Press, 1974). On the Augustinian background, see Linda Maule, *The Devil's Mousetrap: Redemption and Colonial American Literature* (New York/Oxford: Oxford University Press, 1997), Ch. 1.

64. Ringler, 'Hamlet's Defense of the Players', p. 211.

65. The play does, in fact, rewrite *Hamlet*, including a reconstruction of a crime staged by the murderer. See *The Mousetrap and Other Plays* (London: HarperCollins, 1993), and Hubert Gregg, *Agatha Christie and All That Mousetrap* (London: William Kimber, 1980), Ch. 7.

66. On the extent to which the play is intended to affect Gertrude, see Proudfoot, '"The Play's the Thing"'. As he points out, memories of the King's Lynn incident, where a remarried widow admits to her husband's murder, may have fleshed out what is otherwise a 'curious lack of reference' to Gertrude (p. 165).

67. *Histrio-Mastix* (1633), Part 1, pp. 344–345.

68. Cf. Richard Brathwaite's religious dialogue *The Last Trumpet* (1635), where the Devil addresses the World as 'My matchlesse Mouse-trap' (p. 38), and T.G., *The Rich Cabinet* (1616), where woman is described as 'the mouse-trap of a mans soule' (f. 162v).

69. See Robert S. Miola, 'Jesuit Drama in Early Modern England', Ch. 4 in Richard Dutton, Alison Findlay and Richard Wilson (eds), *Theatre and Religion: Lancastrian Shakespeare* (Manchester: Manchester University Press, 2003).

70. See Jacob Bidermann, *Ludi Theatrales Sacri* (Monachii [Munich], 1666), preface (esp. †8b–††1a); and *Cenodoxus*, ed. D.G. Dyer, trans. Dyer and Cecily Longrigg (Edinburgh: Edinburgh University Press, 1975), pp. 1–2.

71. As Warren Chernaik suggests, these titles 'probably capitalise on the play's popularity, rather than suggesting any closer association with Shakespeare' (*ODNB*, s.v. Parrot, Henry). The reference in the subtitle of *Laquei Ridiculosi* is to Polonius's 'Ay, springes to catch woodcocks' (*Hamlet*, 1.3.115).

72. This *envoi* is repeated in *Laquei Ridiculosi*, f. Q7a. There were two editions in 1613; this reference comes from STC 19332.

73. See Ben Weinreb and Christopher Hibbert (eds), *The London Encyclopaedia* (London: PaperMac, 1993), p. 68.

74. For (e.g.) his attacks on Jonson, see Chernaik, *ODNB*.

75. Cf. Luke Wilson, 'Ben Jonson and the Law of Contract', Ch. 6 in Victoria Kahn and Lorna Hutson (eds), *Rhetoric and Law in Early Modern Europe* (New Haven: Yale University Press, 2001).

76. On contemporary professional writers, see Alexandra Halasz, *The Marketplace of Print: Pamphlets and the Public Sphere in Early Modern England* (Cambridge: Cambridge University Press, 1997), esp. Ch. 3.

77. On the salaried lecturers financed by Puritan congregations, see Patrick Collinson, *The Elizabethan Puritan Movement* (London: Jonathan Cape, 1967), Ch. 3.

78. Lines 79–81: from *John Donne: The Complete English Poems*, ed. A.J. Smith (1971: this edn, London: Penguin, 1996), p. 163.

79. E.g. John Carey, *John Donne: Life, Mind and Art* (1st edn, London: Faber and Faber, 1981).

80. 'Satire III' was probably written around 1593–1598 (Smith (ed.), p. 469); *As You Like It* may have first been performed in early 1599 (Dusinberre (ed.), p. 6). There is no reason to suppose that Jaques is based on Donne, but they have features in common: see Douglas Trevor, 'John Donne and Scholarly Melancholy', *Studies in English Literature 1500–1900*, 40: 1 (2000), pp. 81–102. On Jaques and satire, see Jensen, *Religion and Revelry*, pp. 146–148.

81. 'I was converted in trouble.'

82. 'Of Repentance', sermon 4 in *XCVI. Sermons* (1629), quotation p. 207.

83. On the poetic last will and testament, see Edward Wilson, 'The Testament of the Buck and the Sociology of the Text', *Review of English Studies*, n.s. 45, no. 178 (1994), pp. 157–184, esp. pp. 159, 164–165. Wilson cites *As You Like It*, 2.1.47–49: ' "Poor deer", quoth he, "thou mak'st a testament / As worldlings do, giving thy sum of more / To that which had too much". Though this is not a point that he makes, the theme of mock-bequest is picked up in this final scene.

84. See *OED*.

85. If the play was performed at Court during the Shrovetide festivities of 1599, the pre-Lenten overtones of repentance would have been even more appropriate (*As You Like It*, ed. Dusinberre, App. 1).

86. *Lasciva est nobis pagina, vita proba* (Epigram 1: 4, lines 7–8): quoted from Edwin Post (trans. and ed.), *Selected Epigrams of Martial* (Boston: Ginn and Co., 1908).

87. On the date of *As You Like It*, see note 77. Richard A. McCabe, 'Elizabethan Satire and the Bishops' Ban of 1599', *Yearbook of English Studies*, 11 (1981), pp. 188–193; James Shapiro, *1599: A Year in the Life of William Shakespeare* (London: Faber and Faber, 2005), pp. 153 ff.

88. Colin Burrow comments that, uniquely in this period, none of the work printed by Elizabethan satirists has a dedication to a patron: 'Roman Satire in the Sixteenth Century', Ch. 14 in Kirk Freudenberg (ed.), *The Cambridge Companion to Roman Satire* (Cambridge: Cambridge University Press, 2005), p. 251. If so, this would be an additional reason to placate the reading public.

89. On the distinction between natural and artificial fools, see John Southworth, *Fools and Jesters at the English Court* (1998: this edn, Stroud: Sutton, 2003), esp. Ch. 6.

90. C. John Sommerville, *The Secularisation of Early Modern England: From Religious Culture to Religious Faith* (New York: Oxford University Press, 1992).

91. However, for the ways in which classical ideas of virtue and Reformed ideas of grace could come into conflict, see Paul Cefalu, *Moral Identity in*

Early Modern English Literature (Cambridge: Cambridge University Press, 2004), esp. Introduction.

92. Debora Kuller Shuger, 'Subversive Fathers and Suffering Subjects: Shakespeare and Christianity', Ch. 3 in Donna B. Hamilton and Richard Strier (eds), *Religion, Literature and Politics in Post-Reformation England, 1540–1688* (Cambridge: Cambridge University Press, 1996), quotation p. 46. See also Roland Mushat Frye, *Shakespeare and Christian Doctrine* (Princeton: Princeton University Press, 1963).

93. Green, *Print and Protestantism*, pp. 502 (quotation), 565, 582.

94. While the texts that Green's *Print and Protestantism* discusses are for the most part firmly within Protestant literary culture, any suspicion of Pelagian tendencies in drama would have strengthened the already strong polemical link between the theatre and popery, given that Protestants frequently accused Catholics of tending towards Pelagianism because of their stress on human free will. An impressionistic keyword-search for 'Pelagian' on *EEBO* confirms that Catholics were often accused of being Pelagians.

95. Matthew 7:1–2, cf. Luke 6:37, 41–42.

96. *Political Theologies in Shakespeare's England: The Sacred and the State in Measure for Measure* (Basingstoke: Palgrave, 2001).

97. Of this scene, Brian Gibbons has commented that 'The difficulty is in finding any trace of Christian, rather than Stoic, advice in what the Duke-as-friar has said . . . it is as if Claudio is responding to what a friar ought to have said, not what has actually been said here': *Measure for Measure* (Cambridge: Cambridge University Press, 1991), footnote to 3.1.42–43.

98. J.W. Lever has written, 'As with some Elizabethan mansion built from the stones of a ruined abbey, *Measure for Measure* abounds in instances of morality and interlude devices made to serve new ends' (*Measure for Measure* (London: Arden, 1st edn 1963, repr. 1993), introduction, p. xciii). On the often problematic allegorical readings the play as a whole has attracted, see pp. lviii ff.

99. 'We have offended against thy holy laws. We have left undone those things which we ought to have done, and we have done those things which we ought not to have done . . . ' *The Elizabethan Prayer Book*, ed. Booty, p. 50.

100. Lorna Hutson, 'From Penitent to Suspect: Law, Purgatory, and Renaissance Drama', *Huntington Library Quarterly*, 65 (2002), pp. 295–319 (quotation p. 313).

101. Ruth Lunney, 'Rewriting the Narrative of Dramatic Character', *Medieval and Renaissance Drama in England*, 14 (2001), pp. 66–85.

102. *A Chaine of Graces* (1622), p. 10: quoted in Arnold Hunt, *The Art of Hearing: English Preachers and their Audiences, 1590–1640* (forthcoming, Cambridge University Press), Ch. 5. Nevertheless, as Hunt points out, Burges is ambiguous and contradictory in his advice on personal application, suggesting how difficult an issue this could be even for preachers.

103. See Janet Clare, *'Art Made Tongue-Tied by Authority': Elizabethan and Jacobean Dramatic Censorship* (1990; 2nd edn, Manchester: Manchester University Press, 1999); Richard Dutton, *Mastering the Revels: The Regulation*

and Censorship of Elizabethan Drama (London: Macmillan, 1991); Kevin Sharpe, *Criticism and Compliment: The Politics of Literature in the England of Charles I* (Cambridge: Cambridge University Press, 1987).

104. See Barton (Righter), *Shakespeare and the Idea of the Play*, pp. 24–31.
105. *The Conflict of Conscience*, ed. Herbert Davis and F.P. Wilson (Oxford: Malone Society, 1952), f. Aijb (facsimile). The quotation is taken from the prologue in the first issue; in the second, 'Frauncis Spera' was deleted from the title-page and specific references to him were removed from the prologue. As revised, the passage reads: 'Againe, nowe shall it stirre them more, who shall it heare or see, / For if this worldling had ben namde, we wold straight deeme in minde, / That all by him then spoken were, our selves we would not finde' (f. Aijb, facsimile, second sequence). This passage is discussed in David Bevington, 'Christopher Marlowe's *Dr Faustus* and Nathaniel Woodes', Ch. 42 in Mike Pincombe and Cathy Shrank (eds), *The Oxford Handbook of Tudor Literature, 1485–1603* (Oxford: Oxford University Press, 2009), on p. 705. See also M.A. Overell, 'Recantation and Retribution: Remembering Francis Spira, 1548–1638', pp. 154–168 in Kate Cooper and Jeremy Gregory (eds), *Retribution, Repentance and Reconciliation, Studies in Church History*, Vol. 40 (Woodbridge: Boydell/ Ecclesiastical History Society, 2004).
106. Timothy Hampton, *Writing from History: The Rhetoric of Exemplarity in Renaissance Literature* (Ithaca: Cornell University Press, 1990).
107. See (e.g.) Nussbaum's *Poetic Justice: The Literary Imagination and Public Life* (Boston: Beacon, 1995).
108. Matthew 7:5.

4: PROVIDENCE, FATE AND PREDESTINATION: FROM TRAGEDY TO TRAGICOMEDY

1. 'The Lord's mercy between the bridge and the water.'
2. William Camden, *Remaines* (1605), Part 2, p. 55.
3. Graham Greene – already invoked more than once in this study – alludes to the phrase several times in *Brighton Rock* (1st edn, 1938).
4. Antonino Poppi, 'Fate, Fortune, Providence and Human Freedom', Ch. 17 in Charles B. Schmitt *et al.* (eds), *The Cambridge History of Renaissance Philosophy* (Cambridge: Cambridge University Press, 1988), p. 641.
5. On the doctrine of predestination, see Richard A. Muller, *Christ and the Decree: Christology and Predestination in Reformed Theology from Calvin to Perkins* (Durham, NC: Labyrinth Press, 1986), and William Lane Craig, *The Problem of Divine Foreknowledge and Future Contingents from Aristotle to Suarez* (Leiden: E.J. Brill, 1988). The succeeding discussion of early modern controversies on the topic draws on the scholars cited in the Introduction, footnotes 25–27.
6. Epicurean thought was inimical to oracles: see James A. Francis, *Subversive Virtue: Asceticism and Authority in the 2nd-Century Pagan World*

(Philadelphia: Penn State University Press, 1995). On the interplay in the English Renaissance between the Stoic emphasis on fate and the Epicurean advocacy of free will, see Reid Barbour, *English Epicures and Stoics: Ancient Legacies in Early Stuart Culture* (Amherst: Massachussetts University Press, 1998), pp. 95–96.

7. *Hamlet* 1.1.111–124.

8. See Maurice Hunt, 'Malvolio, Viola, and the Question of Instrumentality: Defining Providence in *Twelfth Night*', *Studies in Philology*, 90 (1993), pp. 277–297.

9. R.A.D. Grant, 'Providence, Authority, and the Moral Life in *The Tempest*', *Shakespeare Studies*, 16 (1983), pp. 235–263 (quotation p. 238).

10. Cf. Raphael Lyne's comment that 'while Shakespeare's romances are to some extent based on a positive providential structure, it is always worth remarking that this apparently benign way of seeing the world harboured some sharp and brutal possibilities': *Shakespeare's Late Work* (Oxford: Oxford University Press, 2007), p. 69.

11. *Theodicy*, ed. Austin Farrer and trans. E.M. Huggard, from C.J. Gehardt's edition of Leibniz's collected philosophical works, 1875–90 (1951: repr. LaSalle, Indiana, 1988). See also Elmer J. Kremer and Michael J. Latzer (eds), *The Problem of Evil in Early Modern Philosophy* (Toronto: Toronto University Press, 2001).

12. Gareth B. Matthews, *Augustine* (Maden, MA: Blackwell, 2005), Ch. 12, discussing Augustine's *City of God*, Book 11.

13. R.A. Foakes has charted the shift from the 1950s onwards towards regarding *Lear*, rather than *Hamlet*, as Shakespeare's greatest achievement: *Hamlet Versus Lear: Cultural Politics and Shakespeare's Art* (Cambridge: Cambridge University Press, 1993).

14. See William M. Hamlin, *Tragedy and Scepticism in Shakespeare's England* (Basingstoke: Palgrave Macmillan, 2005).

15. On the reception of the doctrine of predestination in England, see Peter Lake, *Moderate Puritans and the Elizabethan Church* (Cambridge: Cambridge University Press, 1982) and Nicholas Tyacke, *Anti-Calvinists: The Rise of English Arminianism, c. 1590–1640* (Oxford: Clarendon, 1987).

16. Arnold Hunt, *The Art of Hearing: English Preachers and Their Audiences, 1590–1640* (forthcoming, Cambridge University Press).

17. Nor was the cult of Fortune universal amongst pagans: see Frederick Keifer, *Fortune and Elizabethan Tragedy* (San Marino: Huntington Library, 1983), pp. 1–2.

18. Keifer, *Fortune*, Ch. 1; Don Cameron Allan, 'Renaissance Remedies for Fortune: Marlowe and the *Fortunati*', *Studies in Philology*, 38: 2 (1941), pp. 188–197.

19. T.W. Baldwin, *William Shakspere's Small Latine and Lesse Greeke*, 2 vols (Urbana: Illinois University Press, 1944), Vol. I, pp. 310, 312 and 450; Vol. II, p. 590.

20. Claude M. Simpson, *The British Broadside Ballad and its Music* (New Brunswick: Rutgers University Press, 1966), pp. 225–231.

21. See Paul Budra, The Mirror for Magistrates *and the De Casibus Tradition* (Toronto: Toronto University Press, 2000), and Keifer, *Fortune*, Ch. 2.

22. As Leo Salingar comments, fortune's wheel 'suggests the very opposite of caprice or unpredictability; it is the very image of regularity': *Shakespeare and the Traditions of Comedy* (London: Cambridge University Press, 1978), p. 131 (see also pp. 129–134, 155).

23. Anthony Grafton, 'The Availability of Ancient Works', Ch. 22 in Schmitt *et al.* (eds), *Renaissance Philosophy*, p. 790.

24. On Boethius, see Keifer, *Fortune*, pp. 5–10. On the *Consolations* in Shakespeare's England, see John Bracegirdle's *Psychopharmacon: A Translation of Boethius's 'De Consolatione Philosophiae'*, ed. Noel Harold Kaylor Jnr and Jason Edward Streed (Tempe: Arizona Center for Medieval and Renaissance Studies, 1999), Introduction.

25. See Keifer, *Fortune*.

26. Thomas Becon, *The Demaundes of Holy Scripture* (1577), f. D2a. Though common, this mental habit illustrates a practical divergence from the classic Reformed dislike of intermediaries between man and God, on which see Keifer, *Fortune*, pp. 16–23.

27. *A Second Parallel* (1626), f. C3a.

28. *Of the Nature and Use of Lots* (1619), p. 21. Gataker is quoting Philippe de Mornay's *De Veritate Christianae Religionis*. On the friendship of Featley and Gataker, see *ODNB*.

29. Vittorio Gabrieli and Giorgio Melchiori (eds), *Sir Thomas More* (Manchester: Manchester University Press, 1990), 3.1.1–5.

30. While the exact nature of the link between Calvinism and tragedy in England has been much debated, the recognition of a relationship between the two is a critical commonplace. Dennis R. Klinck was one of the first critics to distinguish Calvinist fears about predestination from the religiously inflected gloom so characteristic of tragedy at this date: 'Calvinism and Jacobean Tragedy', *Genre*, 11: 3 (1978), pp. 333–358. On the relationship of fortune and nemesis, see Keifer, *Fortune*, pp. 30–38; on Calvinism and 'therapeutic despair', see Peter Iver Kaufman, *Prayer, Despair and Drama* (Urbana: Illinois University Press, 1996).

31. The term *de casibus* abbreviates the title of Giovanni Boccaccio's popular fourteenth-century work *De Casibus Virorum Illustrium* [On the fates of famous men], a collection of biographies chronicling the falls of famous people. On *The Mirror for Magistrates*, an English continuation, see Budra, Mirror for Magistrates *and the De Casibus Tradition*. On Judas, see Friedrich Ohly, trans. Linda Archibald, *The Damned and the Elect: Guilt in Western Culture* (Cambridge: Cambridge University Press, 1992).

32. However, cf. E.R. Dodds's discussion of fate in *Oedipus Rex* as compared to Peter denying Christ in the Gospels, 'The Evangelists clearly did not intend to imply that Peter's . . . action was 'fate-bound' in the sense that he could not have chosen otherwise; Peter fulfilled the prediction, but he did so by an act of free choice': 'On Misunderstanding the *Oedipus Rex*', in Erich Segal (ed.), *Oxford Readings in Greek Tragedy* (Oxford: Oxford University Press, 1983), pp. 177–188, quotation p. 182.

33. See George C. Herndl, *The High Design: English Renaissance Tragedy and the Natural Law* (Lexington: Kentucky University Press, 1970); Robert G. Hunter, *Shakespeare and the Mystery of God's Judgements* (Athens: Georgia University Press, 1976); Martha Tuck Rozett, *The Doctrine of Election and the Emergence of Elizabethan Tragedy* (New York: Princeton University Press, 1984); and John E. Curran, Jnr, Hamlet, *Protestantism and the Mourning of Contingency* (Aldershot: Ashgate, 2006).

34. Thomas Pierce, *The Christians Rescue from the Grand Error of the Heathen, (Touching the Fatal Necessity of all Events) and the Dismal Consequences Thereof, Which have Slily Crept Into the Church* (1658), p. 15.

35. References, unless otherwise specified, are from Jay L. Halio's edition of the Folio edition of *King Lear*, which contains an appendix listing passages unique to the Quarto edition; significant differences between Q and F will be noticed where appropriate.

36. Susan Snyder, '*King Lear* and the Psychology of Dying', *Shakespeare Quarterly*, 33: 4 (1982), pp. 449–460.

37. Q's reading for line 56, 'concealèd centres', similarly plays up the scene's apocalyptic overtones.

38. Alexandra Walsham, *Providence in Early Modern England* (Oxford: Oxford University Press, 1999) is the standard account.

39. *A Contemplation of Mysteries* [1574?], p. 48.

40. Cf. Frank Palmer's comment that 'What we learn from . . . *King Lear* . . . would not be possible were we . . . to blind ourselves to the self-pity of Lear's attempt to blame the gods for his suffering': *Literature and Moral Understanding: A Philosophical Essay on Aesthetics, Education and Culture* (Oxford: Clarendon, 1992), pp. 222–223.

41. For the connection between storms and madness, see (e.g.) Abraham Fleming, *A Straunge, and Terrible Wunder Wrought . . . in the Parish Church of Bongay* [1577], f. A4b.

42. Leslie Thomson, 'The Meaning of Thunder and Lightning: Stage Directions and Audience Response', *Early Theatre*, 2 (1999), pp. 11–24.

43. Thomas Hill, *A Contemplation of Mysteries*, Preface.

44. Walsham, *Providence*, Ch. 4.

45. See Bernard Capp, *Astrology and the Popular Press: English Almanacks, 1500–1800* (London: Faber, 1979).

46. Q: 'spiritual'.

47. *King Lear*, 1.2, 125–126, and Appendix, p. 293.

48. See the entry for the term in *OED*.

49. Keith Thomas, *Religion and the Decline of Magic* (1971: this edn, Harmondsworth: Penguin, 1984), Ch. 12. Subha Mukherji has commented that 'there was a well-established antinomy between astrology and Protestant Christianity, especially Calvinism': *Law and Representation in Early Modern Drama* (Cambridge: Cambridge University Press, 2006), p. 119. See also Alec Ryrie, *The Sorcerer's Tale: Faith and Fraud in Tudor England* (Oxford: Oxford University Press, 2008), Ch.5, esp. p.158.

50. However, the question of whether the passage was actively censored or not poses more problems than this study can answer. See Gary Taylor,

'Monopolies, Show Trials, Disaster and Invasion: *King Lear* and Censorship', pp. 76–119 in Gary Taylor and Michael Warren (eds), *The Division of the Kingdoms: Shakespeare's Two Versions of King Lear* (1983: this edn, Oxford: Clarendon, 1986). On other anti-Puritan material in Shakespeare's plays, see Ch. 1, pp. 33–34.

51. Donald M. Michie (ed.), *A Critical Edition of the True Chronicle History of King Leir and his Three Daughters . . .* (New York: Garland, 1991); see also Ch. 2 of this study, p. 95. On Tate, see *King Lear: A Parallel Text Edition*, ed. René Weis (London: Longman, 1993), pp. 2–3.

52. See Elizabeth Clarke, ' "A Heart Terrifying Sorrow": The Deaths of Children in Seventeenth-Century Women's Manuscript Journals', Ch. 4 in Gillian Avery and Kimberley Reynolds (eds), *Representations of Childhood Death* (Basingstoke: Macmillan, 2000).

53. *Philip Mornay, Lord of Plessis his Teares for the Death of his Sonne*, trans. John Healey (1609), ff. B5b–6a.

54. The allusion is to Job 9:3. De Mornay's tract is discussed by Patricia Phillippy in *Women, Death and Literature in Post-Reformation England* (Cambridge: Cambridge University Press, 2002), Ch. 5; relevant here is her comment that 'This wavering between the venting of excessive sorrow and its attempted restraint continues until the speaker is able definitively to bridle his blasphemous speech' (p. 163).

55. This line is transferred to Kent in F (*Lear*, ed. Halio, p. 262).

56. Erasmus's remark, which comes in the colloquy *Convivium Religiosum* (1522), is quoted and discussed in the context of St Cyprian's maxim 'There is no safety outside the church' (*Salus extra ecclesiam non est*) in Craig R. Thompson's edition of Erasmus's *Inquisitio De Fide: A Colloquy* (New Haven: Yale University Press, 1950), p. 115. On the broader question, see Cindy L. Vitto, 'The Virtuous Pagan in Middle English Literature', *Transactions of the American Philosophical Society*, 79: 5 (1989), pp. 1–100, and James Hankins, 'Socrates in the Italian Renaissance', Ch. 21 in Sara Ahbel-Rappe and Rachana Kamtekar (eds), *A Companion to Socrates* (Malden, MA/Oxford: Blackwell, 2006), esp. pp. 340–341.

57. On the image of the wheel of fire, see Stanley Wells and Gary Taylor (eds.), *King Lear* (Oxford: Oxford University Press, 2000), p. 54; *Lear*, ed. Weis, pp. 270–271; and R.A. Foakes (ed.), *King Lear*, Arden Shakespeare, 3rd series (London: Thomson, 1997), p. 353; and William R. Elton, *King Lear and the Gods* (San Marino: Huntington Library, 1966), pp. 236–238.

58. See Michael H. Keefer, 'Accommodation and Synecdoche: Calvin's God in *King Lear*', *Shakespeare Studies*, 20 (1988), pp. 147–168.

59. The redemptive reading of *Lear* in Maynard Mack, *King Lear in Our Time* (Berkeley: California University Press, 1965) and the atheistic reading in Elton, *King Lear and the Gods*, epitomise the opposite poles of interpretation that the play has invited. On the different interpretations engendered by the balance of biblical and non-Christian material in the play, see *The Tragedy of King Lear*, ed. Halio, pp. 12–15; for a recent reading of the play which links it to the emotional impact of Protestantism, see Huston Diehl,

'Religion and Shakespearean Tragedy', Ch. 5 in Claire McEachern (ed.), *The Cambridge Companion to Shakespearean Tragedy* (Cambridge: Cambridge University Press, 2002). The redemptive elements in *The Winter's Tale* are less controversial, and occur in most discussions of the play: see, for instance, S.L. Bethell, *The Winter's Tale: A Study* (New York: Staples, [1947]); Daryll Grantley, '*The Winter's Tale* and Early Religious Drama', *Comparative Drama*, 20: 1 (1986), pp. 17–34; Battenhouse (ed.), *Shakespeare's Christian Dimension*, p. 232; and Peter Milward, 'The Theology of Grace in *The Winter's Tale*', in *Shakespeare's Other Dimension* (Sophia University: Tokyo, 1989). On related pedagogical questions, see David Bevington, 'Shakespeare and Recent Criticism: Issues for a Christian Approach to Teaching', Ch.1 in Beatrice Batson (ed.), *Shakespeare and the Christian Tradition* (Lewiston: Edwin Mellen Press, 1994).

60. Foakes discusses the trend in his edition of *Lear*, pp. 2, 26, 32–33.

61. *Lear*, ed. Foakes, p. 84.

62. The term 'tragicomedy' will be used throughout in preference to 'romance'. For a recent account of the varying generic labels that Shakespeare's tragicomic plays have attracted, see Gordon McMullan, '"The Neutral Term"?: Shakespearean Tragicomedy and the Idea of the "Late Play"', Ch. 8 in Subha Mukherji and Raphael Lyne (eds), *Early Modern Tragicomedy* (Cambridge: D.S. Brewer, 2007).

63. See above, pp. 180–181.

64. The phrase 'corrupt lumpe' occurs in John Donne's *Essays in Divinity*: for a discussion of the passage, and of the infralapsarian position, see Alison Shell and Arnold Hunt, 'Donne's Religious World', Ch.5 in Achsah Guibbory (ed.), *The Cambridge Companion to John Donne* (Cambridge: Cambridge University Press, 2006), pp.77-78.

65. On Protestant despair, see Jan Stachniewski, *The Persecutory Imagination: English Puritanism and the Literature of Religious Despair* (Oxford: Clarendon, 1991), and Debora Kuller Shuger, *Habits of Thought in the English Renaissance: Religion, Politics and the Dominant Culture* (1990: this edn, Toronto: Toronto University Press/Renaissance Society of America, 1997), Ch. 2.

66. Arminian trends are discernible from the early 1590s, but books on the topic became widely available from 1610, the year of the Remonstrance and Counter-Remonstrance in the Netherlands: Tyacke, *Anti-Calvinists*, pp. 29–38. On the expression of anti-predestinarian views before the 1590s, see Kenneth Fincham and Nicholas Tyacke, *Altars Restored: The Changing Face of English Religious Worship, 1547–c. 1700* (Oxford: Oxford University Press, 2007), Ch. 3.

67. See Anthony Milton, *Catholic and Reformed: The Roman and Protestant Churches in English Protestant Thought, 1600–1640* (Cambridge: Cambridge University Press, 1995), pp. 414–416.

68. See (e.g.) Glynne Wickham, *Early English Stages, 1300–1600*, Vol. 3 (London: Routledge and Kegan Paul, 1981); Verna A. Foster, *The Name and Nature of Tragicomedy* (Aldershot: Ashgate, 2004), pp. 9, 35–51; Mimi Still

Dixon, 'Tragicomic Recognitions: Medieval Miracles and Shakespearean Romance', pp. 56–79 in Nancy Klein Maguire (ed.), *Renaissance Tragicomedy: Explorations in Drama and Politics* (New York: AMS, 1987).

69. See above, note 31.

70. *The Poetics*, trans. and ed. Malcolm Heath (London: Penguin, this edn, 1996), p. 22. See Sarah Dewar-Watson, 'Aristotle and Tragicomedy', Ch. 1 in Mukherji and Lyne (eds), *Early Modern Tragicomedy*.

71. 'The Defence of Poesy' in *Sir Philip Sidney: A Critical Edition of the Major Works*, ed. Katherine Duncan-Jones (Oxford: Oxford University Press, 1989), p. 244.

72. The broadest survey of Renaissance tragicomedy in a European context remains Marvin T. Herrick, *Tragicomedy: Its Origin and Development in Italy, France and England* (1955: this edn, Urbana: Illinois University Press, 1962). The terminology used below is indebted to Herrick's work. See also Frank Humphry Ristine, *English Tragicomedy: Its Origin and History* (New York: Columbia University Press, 1910).

73. Quoted from the partial translation of Guarini's *Compendio della Poesia Tragicomica* in A.H. Gilbert (ed.), *Literary Criticism: Plato to Dryden* (1940: this edn, Detroit: Wayne State University Press, 1962), p. 523. For the quotation in its original Italian, see *Il Pastor Fido e Il Compendio della Poesia Tragicomica*, ed. Gioachino Brognoligo, Scrittore d'Italia, 61 (1914), p. 245; see also the recent translation into French by Laurence Giavarini (Paris: Honoré Champion, 2008), and Matthew Treherne, 'The Difficult Emergence of Pastoral Tragicomedy: Guarini's *Il Pastor Fido* and its Critical Reception in Italy, 1586–1601', Ch. 2 in Mukherji and Lyne (eds), *Early Modern Tragicomedy*.

74. Cf. Treherne, 'Difficult Emergence', pp. 40–41.

75. Translation from Louise George Clubb, *Italian Drama in Shakespeare's Time* (New Haven: Yale University Press, 1989), p. 231.

76. See Elizabeth Story Donno (ed.), *Three Renaissance Pastorals: Tasso, Guarini, Daniel* (Binghamton, New York: Medieval and Renaissance Texts and Studies, 1993), p. xx, and W.W. Greg, *Pastoral Poetry and Pastoral Drama* (London: A.H. Bullen, 1906), p. 203.

77. See Robert Henke, *Pastoral Transformations: Italian Tragicomedy and Shakespeare's Late Plays* (Newark: Delaware University Press, 1997), p. 20.

78. Cf. Robert Henke's comment that the comparison between Italian tragicomedy and Shakespeare's last plays is most sustainable when it is 'not primarily based on the assumption of direct Italian-English "influence" but on the presence of independent, yet parallel historical, cultural and theatrical developments': *Pastoral Transformations*, p. 18. See also Maguire (ed.), *Renaissance Tragicomedy. Il Pastor Fido* was available in an English printing from 1591, with a translation appearing in 1602 (*STC* 12415). See Donno (ed.), introduction, and G.K. Hunter, 'Italian Tragicomedy on the English Stage', Ch. 5 in *Dramatic Identities and Cultural Traditions* (Liverpool: Liverpool University Press, 1978). Shakespeare's collaborator John Fletcher pioneered Guarinian theory and practice in England in his

tragicomedy *The Faithful Shepherdess*, which was given a prologue drawing heavily on the *Compendio* when printed around 1610. As Gordon McMullan has commented in his *ODNB* entry on Fletcher, this preface 'must be understood as a response to a particular theatrical moment' – in particular, to the dusty reception of Fletcher's own play when it was first performed in 1607/8. See also McMullan's *The Politics of Unease in the Plays of John Fletcher* (Amherst: Massachussetts University Press, 1994), pp. 55–70, 289. For a general account of the relationship between English and Italian theatre in this era, see Leo Salingar, 'Elizabethan Dramatists and Italy: A Postscript', in *Theatre of the English and Italian Renaissance*, ed. J.R. Mulryne and Margaret Shewring (New York: St Martin's Press, 1991), pp. 221–237.

79. As John Cairncross comments, even Corneille's rewriting of that most fatalistic of Greek tragedies, *Oedipus Rex*, is permeated by a stress on free will: *The Cid/Cinna/The Theatrical Illusion*, ed. Cairncross (London: Penguin, this edn 1975), p. 13.

80. Cinthio, however, disliked the term 'tragicomedy': see Herrick, *Tragicomedy*, p. 135, and Dewar-Watson, 'Aristotle', in Mukherji and Lyne (eds), *Early Modern Tragicomedy*, p. 16. His theoretical writing can be found in *Scritti Critici*, ed. Camillo Guerrieri Crocetti (Milan: Marzorati, 1973), pp. 169–224.

81. For Shakespeare's level of indebtedness to continental tragicomedy, see Barbara A. Mowat, 'Shakespearian Tragicomedy', pp. 80–96 in Maguire (ed.), *Renaissance Tragicomedy*, and Clubb, *Italian Drama*.

82. See Michael Neill's suggestive 'Turn and Counterturn: Merchanting, Apostasy and Dramatic Form in Massinger's *The Renegado*', Ch. 10 in Mukherji and Lyne (eds), *Early Modern Tragicomedy*, and the tables for the years in question in Alfred Harbage, *Annals of English Drama, 975–1700*, 3rd edn, rev. Sylvia Stoler Wagonheim (London: Routledge, 1989).

83. See Erica Veevers, *Images of Love and Religion: Queen Henrietta Maria and Court Entertainments* (Cambridge: Cambridge University Press, 1989), Ch. 2, and Karen Britland, *Drama at the Courts of Queen Henrietta Maria* (Cambridge: Cambridge University Press, 2006).

84. See Battenhouse (ed.), *Shakespeare's Christian Dimension*, p. 232.

85. *The Winter's Tale*, ed. Susan Snyder and Deborah T. Curren-Aquino (Cambridge: Cambridge University Press, 2007), p. 48.

86. On the notion of inexact analogy and its usefulness within drama, see Annabel Patterson, *Censorship and Interpretation: The Conditions of Writing and Reading in Early Modern England* (Madison: Wisconsin University Press, 1984). On the treatment of predestination in English Reformation drama, see Paul Whitfield White, *Theatre and Reformation: Protestantism, Patronage and Playing in Tudor England* (Cambridge: Cambridge University Press, 1993), pp. 98–99, 114–123, 186–188.

87. Cf. Peter Lake, 'Religious Identities in Shakespeare's England', Part 3, Ch. 5 in David Scott Kastan (ed.), *A Companion to Shakespeare* (Oxford: Blackwell, 1999), p. 79: 'the religious scene of Elizabeth's reign is best

seen as a number of attempts, conducted at very different levels of self-consciousness and coherence, at creative bricolage, mixing and matching, as a variety of cases and pitches were made for popular support . . . '

88. As Stanley Wells and Gary Taylor have commented of *King Lear*, 'the play . . . [promulgates] Christian values [and draws] on the language and associations of Christianity . . . in, especially, the portrayal of Cordelia; but Shakespeare was clearly anxious not to place the action within a specific philosophical or religious context': Wells and Taylor (eds), *The History of King Lear* (Clarendon: Oxford, 2000), pp. 34–35.

89. The scene has been much commented on: see Snyder and Curran-Aquino (eds), pp. 30–33. Commentators have tended to focus on the question of whether one is to read the bear as comic, tragic or simply awesome. I would read the bear not as undercutting but as consummating the tragic nature of Antigonus's death, echoing the fate of those who foolishly mocked at the prophet Elisha (2 Kings 2:24): see Roy Battenhouse (ed.), *Shakespeare's Christian Dimension: An Anthology of Commentary* (Bloomington: Indiana University Press, 1994), pp. 233–234. Critics tend to be more concerned with the bear than with his prey, but an extended discussion of Antigonus' fate can be found in Denis Biggins, ' "Exit pursued by a Beare": A Problem in *The Winter's Tale*', *Shakespeare Quarterly*, 13: 1 (1962), pp. 3–13.

90. 'That Paulina has agreed to marry a suitor chosen by Leontes . . . is new information' (Snyder and Curren-Aquino (eds), p. 249); as in *Measure for Measure*, the disposer's speech is not ratified by the potential bride.

91. Stephen Orgel underestimates the force of this when he states: 'Paulina essentially writes [Antigonus] off as soon as he leaves . . . and when, at the play's end, Camillo is offered as a replacement, there is no question of her remaining true to her husband's memory' (Orgel (ed.), *The Winter's Tale* (Oxford: Clarendon, 1996), pp. 39–40).

92. However, for the structural importance of Mamilius, see Stanley Cavell, *Disowning Knowledge in Six Plays of Shakespeare* (Cambridge: Cambridge University Press, 1st edn 1987), Ch. 6. Both characters are sometimes brought back onto stage by directors: see Snyder and Curren-Aquino (eds), p. 60.

93. See Orgel (ed.), *The Winter's Tale*, pp. 12–16.

94. See above, note 89.

95. See Walsham, *Providence*, pp. 103–104; and Richard Wunderli and Gerald Broce, 'The Final Moment Before Death in Early Modern England', *Sixteenth Century Journal*, 20: 2 (1989), pp. 259–275.

96. *Name and Nature of Tragicomedy*, p. 36.

97. Cf. Robert G. Hunter's comment that '*Macbeth* should be apprehended simultaneously as the providential tragicomedy of a society and as the psychological tragedy of a villain protagonist . . . what the play shows us is that, experienced from within, by its victim and instrument, the providential pattern signifies nothing': *Shakespeare and the Mystery of God's Judgements*, p. 182.

98. Walsham, *Providence*, p. 104.

99. *Winter's Tale*, ed. Orgel, p. 7.

100. Daryll Grantley, '*The Winter's Tale* and Early Religious Drama', *Comparative Drama*, 20 (1986), pp. 17–34.

101. Cf. Orgel (ed.), *Winter's Tale*, Introduction, p. 35; and Raymond Williams, *Modern Tragedy* (this edn, Stanford: Stanford University Press, 1966), p. 49.

102. A high-profile instance of a typical phenomenon can be found in Charles I's annotations to the Second Folio of Shakespeare, described by T.A. Birrell in *English Monarchs and Their Books: From Henry VII to Charles II* (London: British Library, 1987), pp. 44–45.

103. See Battenhouse (ed.), *Shakespeare's Christian Dimension*, under title of play.

104. Cf. Keifer's contention that ideas of fortune gain in importance to the dramatist as the sixteenth century progresses: *Fortune*, p. xvii.

105. However, for antitheatricalist objections, see Ch. 1, pp. 49–51.

106. On the influence of Elizabethan translations of Seneca's tragedies on conceptions of fate and fortune, see Keifer, *Fortune*, Ch. 3.

107. Anthony Milton, *Catholic and Reformed: The Roman and Protestant Churches in English Protestant Thought, 1600–1640* (Cambridge: Cambridge University Press, 1995). On the question of dating, see Jay L. Halio (ed.), *The Tragedy of King Lear* (Cambridge: Cambridge University Press, 1992), pp. 1–2.

108. Arnold Hunt, *The Art of Hearing: English Preachers and their Audiences, 1590–1640* (Cambridge: Cambridge University Press, forthcoming), discusses the tightening of regulations on the preaching of predestination in the 1620s and 1630s.

109. Brian Cummings, *The Literary Culture of the Reformation: Grammar and Grace* (Oxford: Oxford University Press, 2002), Ch. 7, Section 3.

110. *Video meliora proboque / Deteriora sequor* (*Metamorphoses*, 7: 20–21). See Norman Fiering, *Moral Philosophy at Seventeenth-Century Harvard* (Chapel Hill: North Carolina University Press, 1981), pp. 115–116. I am grateful to Arnold Hunt for this reference.

111. Hamlin, *Scepticism*, p. 3.

112. On ineffectual repentance, see Richard A. Muller, 'Perkins' *A Golden Chaine*: Predestinarian System or Schematised *Ordo Salutis*?', *Sixteenth-Century Journal*, 9:1 (1978), pp. 66–81; Baird Tipson, 'A Dark Side of Seventeenth-Century English Protestantism: The Sin Against the Holy Spirit', *Harvard Theological Review*, 77: 3/4 (1984), pp. 301–330.

113. The material discussed below comes largely from Act 5 of *The Two Noble Kinsmen*, which critics have usually attributed to Shakespeare himself; however, perhaps one need not be overly concerned about detailed questions of attribution where the issues, as here, are thematic rather than stylistic. On Fletcher and tragicomedy, see footnote 78 above; Gordon McMullan's entry for the playwright in *ODNB*; Henke, *Pastoral Transformations*, Chs 2–3; and Eugene M. Waith, *The Pattern of Tragicomedy in Beaumont and Fletcher* (New Haven: Yale University Press, 1952).

114. For an account of how the play alters 'The Knight's Tale', see Paula S. Berggren, ' "For what we lack, / We laugh": Incompletion and *The Two Noble Kinsmen*', *Modern Language Studies*, 14: 4 (1984), pp. 3–17.

115. Introduction to Waith's edition of *The Two Noble Kinsmen* (Oxford: Clarendon Press, 1989), p. 58. On the gods in the play, see also Kenneth Muir, *Shakespeare as Collaborator* (London: Methuen, 1960), pp. 129–130, 144–146.

116. Potter (p. 327) glosses this as 'refrain from disputing with beings too high to argue with'.

117. *The Knight's Tale*, ed. A.C. Spearing (Cambridge: Cambridge University Press, 1966), pp. 77–78.

118. See Shell and Hunt, 'Donne's Religious World'.

119. Cf. *Two Noble Kinsmen*, ed. Potter, p. 209. Potter also detects an allusion to contemporary Arminian–Calvinist debates in the oblique references to 'faith' in 1.2 (*Two Noble Kinsmen*, pp. 38, 162).

120. E.g. Thomas Rogers's use of this text to reinforce a supralapsarian position in *The English Creede* (1585), ff. G3b–4b.

CONCLUSION

1. 'Whatever may be said against the divine hybrids, the curious cross-breeds that people the Orphic pantheon, they express the Orphic spirit at its fullest, and it is remarkable with what persistence and shrewdness the Renaissance antiquarians justified a predilection for them': Edgar Wind, *Pagan Mysteries in the Renaissance* (London: Faber and Faber, 1958), p. 164.

2. The discussion below draws extensively on Barbara C. Bowen, 'Mercury at the Crossroads in Renaissance Emblems', *Journal of the Warburg and Courtauld Institutes*, 48 (1985), pp. 222–229, and Simon Hornblower and Antony Spawforth (eds), *The Oxford Classical Dictionary*, 3rd edn (Oxford: Oxford University Press, 1996), entry for 'Terminus'. On 'herm/herma' and 'term' as alternatives, see *OED*.

3. See the definitions of 'Hermeracles', 'Hermeros' and 'Hermathena' in Lewis and Short.

4. For a recent account of the collaboration between Shakespeare and Fletcher in the play, see Lois Potter's edition of the play in the Arden series (Walton-on-Thames: Thomas Nelson, 1997), pp. 24–34. Potter describes the succeeding portion of Act 5.1 as 'probably the most obviously Shakespearean scene of the play'. As Potter further points out, the term 'heavenly limiter' may mean either Jove or Terminus; I would wish to stress the way in which gods could be conflated with Terminus (see above, note 1). Steve Sohmer has argued that *King Lear* was written or revised to include a number of allusions to the festival of Terminalia in the primitive Roman calendar, appropriate to the date of *Lear*'s performance before James I: 'The Lunar Calendar of Shakespeare's *King Lear*', *Early Modern Literary Studies*, 55: 2 (1999), p. 1–17.

5. Several other names in the play were also changed to play up mythological allusion: *The Winter's Tale*, ed. Susan Snyder and Deborah T. Curren-Aquino (Cambridge: Cambridge University Press, 2007), pp. 79–81. Giulio Romano's role in the development of Renaissance herm-

iconography would be worth fuller investigation in this light, given the attribution of the statue to him within the play (5.2.83): see Bette Talvacchia, 'The Rare Italian Master and the Posture of Hermione in *The Winter's Tale*', *Literature, Interpretation, Theory*, 3: 3 (1992), pp. 163–174.

6. On the Hermione / herm pun, see Julia Gasper and Carolyn Williams, 'The Meaning of the Name "Hermione"', *Notes and Queries*, 231 (1986), p. 367, and Mitsuru Kamachi, 'What's in a Name?: Hermione and the Hermetic Tradition in *The Winter's Tale*', *Shakespeare Studies* (Shakespeare Society of Japan), 29 (1991), pp. 21–36.

7. E.g. John Foxe, *Actes and Monuments* (1583), p. 856 (footnote), cited in *OED*. Three recent commentators on the play's appropriation of Catholic religious models are Walter S.H. Limn, 'Knowledge and Belief in *The Winter's Tale*', *Studies in English Literature, 1500–1900*, 41: 2 (2001), pp. 317–334, Alice Dailey, 'Easter Scenes from an Unholy Tomb: Christian Parody in *The Widow's Tears*', Ch. 7 in Regina Buccola and Lisa Hopkins (eds), *Marian Moments in Early Modern British Drama* (Aldershot: Ashgate, 2007) and Jensen, *Religion and Revelry*, pp.196–197, 224–229.

8. See (most recently) Margaret Jones-Davies, '*Cymbeline* and the Sleep of Faith', Ch. 12 in Richard Dutton, Alison Findlay and Richard Wilson (eds), *Theatre and Religion: Lancastrian Shakespeare* (Manchester: Manchester University Press, 2003). Though the scene does raise questions about interpretive processes, the earliest examples of 'hermeneutic/al' in *OED* post-date *The Winter's Tale* by several years.

9. Though directors have not always chosen to depict Hermione's statue as upright, this seems the most obvious reading of the text: see Snyder and Curren-Aquino (eds), footnote to 5.3.20 and succeeding stage direction.

10. E.g. in John Merbecke, *A Booke of Notes and Common Places . . . Necessarie To Those That Desire the True Understanding and Meaning of Scripture* (1581), f. Iii1a.

11. 'Hermione' is a man's name in the romance *The Rare Triumphs of Love and Fortune* (1582), which may have been among Shakespeare's sources for *Cymbeline*: see Butler (ed.), *Cymbeline*, p. 14.

12. *Minerva Britanna* (1612), Part 2, p. 193.

13. *Ovid's Fasti: Roman Holidays*, trans. and ed. Betty Rose Nagle (Bloomington: Indiana University Press, 1995), Book 2, pp. 637–677. See also Livy, *Ab Urbe Condita*, ed. Robert Maxwell Ogilvie (Oxford: Clarendon, 1974), Book 1, Section 55, pp. 1–4.

14. Cf. Maurice Hunt, *Shakespeare's Religious Allusiveness: Its Play and Tolerance* (Aldershot: Ashgate, 2004), Ch. 5.

15. *Winter's Tale*, ed. Snyder and Curren-Aquino, p. 56.

16. While to my knowledge this has not been discussed before, *Cymbeline* has often been recognized as one of Shakespeare's most mythologically allusive plays: see (e.g.) Ann Thompson, 'Philomel in *Titus Andronicus* and *Cymbeline*', *Shakespeare Survey*, 31, ed. Kenneth Muir (1978), pp. 23–32, esp. p. 29.

17. However, cf. F.D. Hoeniger's comment on the episode where Innogen mistakes Cloten's dead body dressed in Posthumus's clothes for Post-

humus: 'The complex incongruity of this incident makes one wonder whether in the world of this play some Hardyish god is at work' ('Irony and Romance in *Cymbeline*', *Studies in English Literature, 1500–1900*, 2: 2 (1962), pp. 219–228, quotation p. 233).

18. On Posthumus's repentance, see (most recently) Ros King, *Cymbeline: Constructions of Britain* (Aldershot: Ashgate, 2005), pp. 135–141. It may be relevant that the Terminalia, marking the end of the old Roman year, were celebrated in February, traditionally the month of purging.

19. See the Introduction to Butler's edition of *Cymbeline*, p. 17.

20. Tom Rist is one critic to have argued for this act's technical virtuosity: *Shakespeare's Romances and the Politics of Counter-Reformation* (Lewiston: Edwin Mellen Press, 1999), p. 100.

21. Willy Maley sees this as 'a covert reintroduction of Catholicism by the back door' in the cause of Eurocentric religious toleration: 'Postcolonial Shakespeare: British Identity Formation and *Cymbeline*', in Jennifer Richards and James Knowles (eds), *Shakespeare's Late Plays: New Readings* (Edinburgh: Edinburgh University Press, 1999), pp. 145–157, quotation p. 149. In '*Cymbeline* and the Sleep of Faith' (Dutton, Findlay and Wilson (eds), *Theatre and Religion*) Jones-Davies similarly reads it as a transconfessional plea for religious toleration; cf. also the discussion in 'Shakespeare's Ecumenical Britain', Ch. 10 in Andrew Hadfield, *Shakespeare, Spenser and the Matter of Britain* (Basingstoke: Palgrave, 2004). For how *Cymbeline* acts as a commentary on the *Romanitas* of Britain, see Adrian Hastings, *The Constructions of Nationhood: Ethnicity, Religion and Nationalism* (Cambridge: Cambridge University Press, 1997), pp. 207–208. Miola, 'An Alien People', argues that England is paying tribute to classical, not Catholic Rome in distinguishing between its virtuous ancient self and the modern, Machiavellian corruption of Iachimo (p. 44). There is also a tradition of reading James VI/I as a Caesar, and the play as reinforcing royal authority: see King, *Cymbeline*, pp. 143, 149, who argues that its language is too 'uncomfortable' to allow this interpretation to be fully endorsed.

22. Book 2 (23 February), 683–684. Translation from *Fasti*, trans. and ed. Nagle, p. 75.

23. *City of God*, trans. Henry Bettenson, intro. G.R. Evans (London: Penguin, 2003), Book VII, chs 7–15. Augustine is attacking a related but different mythological contention that Janus should take precedence of Jupiter (p. 265).

24. *The Worthy Tract of Paulus Jovius, Contayning a Discourse of Rare Inventions . . . Called Imprese* (1585), f. G7a. See also Edgar Wind, 'Ænigma Termini: The Emblem of Erasmus', *Journal of the Warburg Institute*, 1 (1937–8), pp. 66–69; Jeanne Guillaume, 'Hic Terminus Haeret: Du Terme d'Erasme à la Device de Claude Gouffier: La Fortune d'un Emblème à la Renaissance', *Journal of the Warburg and Courtauld Institutes*, 44 (1981), pp. 186–192; and Matthias Winner, 'The Terminus as a Rebus in Holbein's Portraits of Erasmus', pp. 96–109 in *Hans Holbein the Younger: The Basel Years, 1515–1532* (Munich: Prestel, [2006]), and the catalogue entry for the design for a stained-glass window, no. 111 (pp. 342–345) in the same volume.

The motto is sometimes adapted as *Concedo nulli*: see James K. McConica, 'The Riddle of "Terminus"', *Erasmus in English*, 2 (1971), pp. 2–7.

25. A.W. von Schlegel, *A Course of Lectures on Dramatic Art and Literature*, trans. John Black, 2 vols (1815), Vol. 2, pp. 94–95. See Thomas G. Sauer, *A. W. Schlegel's Shakespearean Criticism in England, 1811–1846* (Bonn: Bouvier, 1981), esp. Ch. 1. Jonathan Bate, *Shakespeare and the English Romantic Imagination* (1986: this edn, Oxford: Clarendon, 1989), discusses this passage in relation to Coleridge's thought (pp. 12–13).

26. Schlegel, *Lectures*, Vol. 2, p. 153. Bate discusses the remarks in *Shakespeare and the English Romantic Imagination*, pp. 14–15.

27. See Ch. 1, p. 75.

28. Claude Paradin, *Devises Heroïques* (1557), p. 103.

29. On teleology, see Alasdair MacIntyre, *After Virtue: A Study in Moral Theory* (2nd edn, London: Duckworth, 1985). While the notion of *telos* dates back to Aristotle, the word 'teleology' was not apparently current in Shakespeare's time: the earliest examples on *EEBO* (accessed July 2007) date from the 1690s, predating those in the *OED*.

30. See *Hans Holbein: The Basel Years*, p. 342. However, some were not convinced: Wind, 'Ænigma Termini', p. 66; McConica, 'Riddle', p. 7, note 17.

31. *Oxford Classical Dictionary*, ed. Hornblower and Spawforth, entries for 'Mercurius' and 'Hermes'.

32. Bowen, 'Mercury', p. 222. For a twentieth-century qualification of this theory, see Hetty Goldman, 'The Origin of the Greek Herm', *American Journal of Archaeology*, 46: 1 (1942), pp. 58–68.

33. Stanley Wells has commented: '[Shakespeare] lies not merely in the chancel but as close to the altar as it is possible to get. . . . It is surely inconceivable that [the gravestones of Shakespeare and his family] occupy their original positions. Is it not likely that at some point the Stratford chancel floor was relaid . . . [and] that at the same time some or all of the gravestones most worthy of note were preserved and replaced in the star spots?' ('Flyleaf', *Daily Telegraph*, 22 April 1995, A8). According to J.O. Halliwell-Phillipps, the present gravestone is a replacement, installed in the eighteenth century: *Outlines of the Life of Shakespeare*, sixth edition (London: Longmans, Green and Co., 1886), Vol. I, p. 246. On issues relating to the gravestone's original position, see Val Horsler with Martin Gorick and Paul Edmondson, *Shakespeare's Church: A Parish for the World* (London: Third Millennium, 2010), pp.114–116. The publication of this book coincided with my own study being prepared for the press, so I was unable to exploit it as fully as I would have liked; however, it also valuably supplements the comments on Holy Trinity Church in the introduction.

34. The gravestone is described as on the north side of the chancel, underneath the monument, in Nicholas Rowe's early-eighteenth-century biography of Shakespeare: *The Works of Mr. William Shakespear* (1709), Vol. 1, pp. xxxvi–vii.

35. 'It should be remembered that the transfer of bones from graves to the charnel-house was then an ordinary practice at Stratford-on-Avon': Halliwell-Phillipps, *Outlines*, Vol. I, p. 244.

36. On this attribution, see Samuel Schoenbaum, *William Shakespeare: A Compact Documentary Life* (revised edition, New York: Oxford University Press, 1987), p. 306 (this transcription has been followed above and below, for the monument inscription). Susan Brigden and Susan Doran have suggested to me that the rhyme may reflect contemporary anxieties about the reassemblage of bodily parts at the Resurrection.

37. 'Reconsidering Shakespeare's Monument', *Review of English Studies*, 48: 190 (1997), pp. 168–182 (esp. pp. 180–181). Patrick Cheney, *Shakespeare, National Poet-Playwright* (Cambridge: Cambridge University Press, 2004), pp. 267–270, 280–281, considers the pagan allusions in the monument's inscription.

38. Configurations are various, with bust-monuments – despite the fact that they usually have arms – showing a particular similarity to classical herms. However, Nigel Llewellyn has identified contemporary terminological uncertainty with regard to these: *Funeral Monuments in Post-Reformation England* (Cambridge: Cambridge University Press, 2000), pp. 110–114, 223. Price, 'Reconsidering Shakespeare's Monument', argues that this was designed as part of a two-tiered sepulchre.

39. *Judicio Pylium, genio Socratem, arte Maronem:* / *Terra tegit, populus mæret, Olympus habet.* 'Pylus' refers to Nestor, King of Pylus; 'Maro' refers to Vergil. Translation from Jonathan Bate's introduction to Horsler et al., *Shakespeare's Church*, p.9.

40. Jonson's poem responds at several points to William Basse's tribute in the same volume, and its classicizing agenda can be seen as a riposte to Basse's evocation of Shakespeare's burial in Christian terms: 'Renownèd Spenser, lie a thought more nigh / To learnèd Chaucer; and rare Beaumont, lie / A little nearer Spenser, to make room / For Shakespeare in your threefold, four-fold tomb. / To lodge all four in one bed make a shift / Till doomsday . . . '. Both poems are quoted from *The Complete Works*, ed. Wells and Taylor, pp. xliv–xlv.

41. Schoenbaum, *William Shakespeare*, Ch. 15. Schoenbaum comments on the page from which this transcription is taken: 'To find here a confession of personal faith is to consider the matter too curiously. The preamble is formulaic . . . ' (p. 298).

42. This is not an attempt to topple Shakespeare's bust from its hermetic pedestal. R.A. Foakes's caveat on the topic of iconoclastic criticism is relevant here: 'the effect such attacks . . . seek to achieve is to substitute the critic for the author at the centre of power in the academy, and power corrupts the critic too': *Hamlet Versus Lear: Cultural Politics and Shakespeare's Art* (Cambridge: Cambridge University Press, 1993), p. 10. Foakes is responding to Gary Taylor's *Reinventing Shakespeare: A Cultural History from the Restoration to the Present* (New York: Weidenfeld and Nicolson, 1989); my intention is not to second this specific criticism but to point to the general danger he identifies. See also Peter Conrad, *Creation: Artists, Gods and Origins* (London: Thames and Hudson, 2007) for a recent meditation on the claim, familiar within secular humanism, that creative artists have unseated God.

SELECT BIBLIOGRAPHY

Ackroyd, Peter. *Shakespeare: The Biography*. London: Chatto and Windus, 2005.

Altman, Joel B. *The Tudor Play of Mind: Rhetorical Inquiry and the Development of Elizabethan Drama*. Berkeley: California University Press, 1978.

Anon. *The Manner of the Death and Execution of A. Cosbie*. London, 1591.

—— *Epitaphs*. 'Roan' [i.e. English secret press], 1604.

—— *A Warning for Fair Women: A Critical Edition*. Ed. Charles Dale Cannon. The Hague/Paris: Mouton, 1975.

—— *A Critical Edition of the True Chronicle History of King Leir and his Three Daughters*. Ed. Donald M. Michie. New York: Garland, 1991.

Aston, Margaret. *England's Iconoclasts. Vol. I. Laws Against Images*. Oxford: Clarendon, 1988.

Baldwin, T.W. *William Shakspere's Small Latine and Lesse Greeke*. 2 vols. Urbana: Illinois University Press, 1944.

Barber, C.L. *Shakespeare's Festive Comedy: A Study of Dramatic Form and its Relation to Social Custom*. Princeton: Princeton University Press, 1959.

Barish, Jonas. *The Antitheatrical Prejudice*. Berkeley: California University Press, 1981.

Barroll, J. Leeds. *Politics, Plague and Shakespeare's Theater*. Ithaca: Cornell University Press, 1995.

Barton (Righter), Anne. *Shakespeare and the Idea of the Play*. 1962. This edn, Harmondsworth: Penguin, 1977.

Baspole, William. *The Pilgrime*. Ed. Kathryn Walls with Marguerite Stobo. Medieval and Renaissance Texts and Studies, vol. 337. Tempe, Arizona: Arizona Center for Medieval and Renaissance Studies, 2008.

Bate, Jonathan. *Shakespeare and Ovid*. Oxford: Clarendon, 1993.

—— ed. *Shakespeare and the Romantics*. London: Penguin, 1992.

Batson, E. Beatrice, ed. *Shakespeare and the Christian Tradition*. Lewiston, NY/Lampeter: Edwin Mellen Press, 1994.

Battenhouse, Roy. 'Falstaff as Parodist and Perhaps Holy Fool.' *Proceedings of the Modern Language Association*, 90: 1 (1975), pp. 32–52.

—— ed. *Shakespeare's Christian Dimension: An Anthology of Commentary*. Bloomington: Indiana University Press, 1994.

Bearman, Robert. '"Was William Shakespeare William Shakeshafte?" Revisited.' *Shakespeare Quarterly*, 53: 1 (2002), pp. 83–94.

—— 'John Shakespeare's "Spiritual Testament": A Reappraisal.' *Shakespeare Survey*, 56 (2003), pp. 184–202.

—— 'John Shakespeare: A Papist or just Penniless?' *Shakespeare Quarterly*, 56: 4 (2005), pp. 411–433.

Beauregard, David N. *Catholic Theology in Shakespeare's Plays*. Newark: Delaware University Press, 2008.

Beckett, Lucy. *In the Light of Christ: Writings in the Western Tradition*. San Francisco: Ignatius Press, 2006.

Bell, Millicent. *Shakespeare's Tragic Skepticism*. New Haven/London: Yale University Press, 2002.

Berggren, Paula S. ' "For what we lack, / We laugh": Incompletion and *The Two Noble Kinsmen*.' *Modern Language Studies*, 14: 4 (1984), pp. 3–17.

Bevington, David. 'Theatre as Holiday.' In David L. Smith, Richard Strier and David Bevington (eds), *The Theatrical City: Culture, Theatre and Politics in London, 1576–1649* (Cambridge: Cambridge University Press, 1995), pp. 101–116.

—— *Cenodoxus*. Ed. D.G. Dyer. Trans. D.G. Dyer and Cecily Longrigg. Edinburgh: Edinburgh University Press, 1975.

Biggins, Denis. '"Exit pursued by a Beare": A Problem in *The Winter's Tale*.' *Shakespeare Quarterly*, 13: 1 (1962), pp. 3–13.

Bloom, Harold, ed. *Falstaff*. New York: Chelsea House, 1992.

Bossy, John. *The English Catholic Community, 1570–1850*. London: Darton, Longman and Todd, 1975.

Bowen, Barbara C. 'Mercury at the Crossroads in Renaissance Emblems.' *Journal of the Warburg and Courtauld Institutes*, 48 (1985), pp. 222–229.

Bradshaw, Graham. *Shakespeare's Scepticism*. Ithaca, NY: Cornell University Press, 1987.

Bristol, Michael D. *Carnival and Theater: Plebeian Culture and the Structure of Authority in Renaissance England*. New York/London: Methuen, 1985.

Brownlow, Frank W. *Shakespeare, Harsnett and the Devils of Denham*. Newark/London: Delaware University Press/Associated University Presses, 1993.

—— 'A Jesuit Allusion to *King Lear*.' *Recusant History*, 28: 3 (2007), pp. 416–423.

Bruster, Douglas A. *Drama and the Market in the Age of Shakespeare*. Cambridge: Cambridge University Press, 1992.

Buccola, Regina. *Fairies, Fractious Women and the Old Faith*. Selinsgrove: Susquehanna University Press, 2006.

—— and Lisa Hopkins, eds. *Marian Moments in Early Modern British Drama*. Aldershot: Ashgate, 2007.

Budra, Paul. The Mirror for Magistrates *and the De Casibus Tradition*. Toronto: Toronto University Press, 2000.

Bullough, Geoffrey. *Narrative and Dramatic Sources of Shakespeare*. 8 vols, London/New York: Routledge and Kegan Paul/Columbia University Press, 1957–75.

Burns, William E. ' "A Proverb of Versatile Mutability": Proteus and Natural Knowledge in Early Modern Britain.' *Sixteenth-Century Journal*, 32: 4 (2001), pp. 969–980.

Burrow, Colin. 'Roman Satire in the Sixteenth Century.' Ch. 14 in Kirk Freudenberg (ed.), *The Cambridge Companion to Roman Satire*. Cambridge: Cambridge University Press, 2005.

Callaghan, Dympna. 'Shakespeare and Religion.' *Textual Practice*, 15: 1 (2001), pp. 1–4.

Cavell, Stanley. *Disowning Knowledge in Six Plays of Shakespeare*. Cambridge: Cambridge University Press, 1st edn, 1987.

Chambers, E.K. *William Shakespeare: A Study of Facts and Problems*. 2 vols. Oxford: Clarendon, 1930.

—— *The Elizabethan Stage*. 5 vols. Oxford: Clarendon, 1923.

—— *Shakespearean Gleanings*. London: Oxford University Press, 1944.

Chapman, Alison. 'Whose St Crispin's Day Is It? Shoemaking, Holiday Making and the Politics of Memory in Early Modern England.' *Renaissance Quarterly*, 54 (2001), 1467–1494.

—— 'The Politics of Time in Edmund Spenser's English Calendar.' *Studies in English Literature*, 42: 1 (2002), pp. 1–24.

Cheney, Patrick. *Shakespeare, National Poet-Playwright*. Cambridge: Cambridge University Press, 2004.

Church of England, *Certain Sermons or Homilies Appointed to be Read in Churches*. Oxford: Oxford University Press, 1844.

—— *The Book of Common Prayer, 1559. The Elizabethan Prayer Book*. Ed. John E. Booty. Washington: Folger Shakespeare Library, 1976.

Cinthio, Giovanni Battista Giraldi. *Scritti Critici*. Ed. Camillo Guerrieri Crocetti. Milan: Marzorati, 1973.

Clare, Janet. *'Art Made Tongue-Tied By Authority': Elizabethan and Jacobean Dramatic Censorship*. 1990. 2nd edn, Manchester: Manchester University Press, 1999.

Clarke, Elizabeth. ' "A Heart Terrifying Sorrow": The Deaths of Children in Seventeenth-Century Women's Manuscript Journals.' Ch. 4 in Gillian Avery and Kimberley Reynolds (eds), *Representations of Childhood Death*. Basingstoke: Macmillan, 2000.

Clubb, Louise George. *Italian Drama in Shakespeare's Time*. New Haven: Yale University Press, 1989.

Coatalen, Guillaume. 'Shakespeare and Other "Tragicall Discourses" in an Early Seventeenth-Century Commonplace-Book from Oriel College, Oxford.' *English Manuscript Studies 1100–1700*, 13 (2007), pp. 120–164.

Cody, Richard. *The Landscape of the Mind: Pastoralism and Platonic Theory in Tasso's* Aminta *and Shakespeare's Early Comedies*. Oxford: Clarendon, 1969.

Cohen, Walter. 'The Reformation and Elizabethan Drama.' *Shakespeare-Jahrbuch*, 120 (1984), pp. 45–52.

Coldewey, John. 'Carnival's End: Puritan Ideology and the Decline of English Provincial Theatre.' In Meg Twycross (ed.), *Festive Drama* (Cambridge: D.S. Brewer, 1996), pp. 279–286.

Collinson, Patrick. *From Iconoclasm to Iconophobia: The Cultural Impact of the Second English Reformation* [Reading]: Reading University Press, 1988.

—— *The Birthpangs of Protestant England: Religious and Cultural Change in the Sixteenth and Seventeenth Centuries*. Basingstoke: Macmillan, 1988.

—— *Elizabethan Essays*. London: Hambledon, 1994.

—— 'The Theatre Constructs Puritanism.' In David L. Smith, Richard Strier and David Bevington (eds), *The Theatrical City: Culture, Theatre and Politics in London, 1576–1649* (Cambridge: Cambridge University Press, 1995), pp. 157–169.

—— Arnold Hunt and Alexandra Walsham, 'Religious Publishing in England, 1557–1640.' Ch. 1 in John Barnard and D.F. McKenzie with Maureen Bell (eds), *The Cambridge History of the Book in Britain, Volume 4, 1557–1695*. Cambridge: Cambridge University Press, 2002.

Corbin, Peter, and Douglas Sedge, eds. *The Oldcastle Controversy: Sir John Oldcastle, Part I and The Famous Victories of Henry V*. Manchester: Manchester University Press, 1991.

Coster, Will, and Andrew Spicer, eds. *Sacred Space in Early Modern Europe*. Cambridge: Cambridge University Press, 2005.

Covington, Sarah. *The Trail of Martyrdom: Persecution and Resistance in 16th-Century England*. Notre Dame: Notre Dame University Press, 2003.

Cox, John D. 'Was Shakespeare a Christian, And If So, What Kind of Christian Was He?' *Christianity and Literature*, 55: 4 (2006), pp. 539–566.

—— and David Scott Kastan, eds. *A New History of Early English Drama*. New York: Columbia University Press, 1997.

Craig, John. 'Psalms, Groans and Dogwhippers: The Soundscape of Worship in the English Parish Church, 1547–1642.' Ch. 6 in Will Coster and Andrew Spicer (eds), *Sacred Space in Early Modern Europe*. Cambridge: Cambridge University Press, 2005.

Craig, William Lane. *The Problem of Divine Foreknowledge and Future Contingents from Aristotle to Suarez*. Leiden: E.J. Brill, 1988.

Cressy, David. *Literacy and the Social Order*. Cambridge: Cambridge University Press, 1980.

—— *Bonfires and Bells: National Memory and the Protestant Calendar in Elizabethan and Stuart England*. Berkeley: California University Press, 1989.

—— *Birth, Marriage and Death: Ritual, Religion and the Life-Cycle in Tudor and Stuart England*. Oxford: Oxford University Press, 1997.

Crewe, Jonathan V. 'The Theater of the Idols: Theatrical and Antitheatrical Discourse.' Ch. 5 in David Scott Kastan and Peter Stallybrass (eds), *Staging the Renaissance*. London: Routledge, 1991.

Crockett, Bryan. *The Play of Paradox: Stage and Sermon in Renaissance England*. Philadelphia: Pennsylvania University Press, 1995.

Cubeta, Paul M. 'Falstaff and the Art of Dying.' In Harold Bloom (ed.), *Falstaff* (New York: Chelsea House, 1992), pp. 246–257.

Cummings, Brian. *The Literary Culture of the Reformation: Grammar and Grace*. Oxford: Oxford University Press, 2002.

Dailey, Alice. 'Easter Scenes from an Unholy Tomb: Christian Parody in *The Widow's Tears*.' Ch. 7 in Regina Buccola and Lisa Hopkins (eds), *Marian Moments in Early Modern British Drama*. Aldershot: Ashgate, 2007.

Dawson, Anthony B., and Paul Yachnin. *The Culture of Playgoing in Shakespeare's England: A Collaborative Debate*. Cambridge: Cambridge University Press, 2001.

Demetz, Peter, Thomas Greene and Lowry Nelson Jnr, eds. *Essays in Literary Theory, Interpretation and History*. New Haven: Yale University Press, 1968.

Dent, R.W. *Shakespeare's Proverbial Language: An Index*. Berkeley: California University Press, 1981.

Devlin, Christopher. *The Life of Robert Southwell*. London: Longmans, Green and Co., 1956.

Dewar-Watson, Sarah. 'Aristotle and Tragicomedy.' Ch. 1 in Subha Mukherji and Raphael Lyne (eds), *Early Modern Tragicomedy*. Woodbridge: D.S. Brewer, 2007.

Diehl, Huston. 'Religion in Shakespearean Tragedy.' Ch. 5 in Claire McEachern (ed.), *The Cambridge Companion to Shakespearean Tragedy*. Cambridge: Cambridge University Press, 2002.

Dillon, Anne. *The Construction of Martyrdom in the English Catholic Community, 1535–1603*. Aldershot: Ashgate, 2002.

Dixon, Mimi Still. 'Tragicomic Recognitions: Medieval Miracles and Shake-spearean Romance.' In Nancy Klein Maguire (ed.), *Renaissance Tragicomedy: Explorations in Drama and Politics* (New York: AMS, 1987), pp. 56–79.

Doebler, John. 'The Play within the Play: The *Muscipula Diaboli* in *Hamlet*.' *Shakespeare Quarterly*, 23: 2 (1972), pp. 161–169.

—— *Shakespeare's Speaking Pictures: Studies in Iconic Imagery*. Albuquerque: New Mexico University Press, 1974.

Donaldson, Ian. *Jonson's Magic Houses: Essays in Interpretation*. Oxford: Clarendon, 1997.

Donne, John. *The Complete English Poems*. Ed. A.J. Smith. 1971, This edn, London: Penguin, 1996.

—— *The Sermons of John Donne*. Ed. George R. Potter and Evelyn M. Simpson. 10 vols. Berkeley: California University Press, 1953–1962.

Donno, Elizabeth Story, ed. *Three Renaissance Pastorals: Tasso, Guarini, Daniel.* Binghamton, New York: Medieval and Renaissance Texts and Studies, 1993.

Duncan-Jones, Katherine. *Ungentle Shakespeare: Scenes From His Life.* London: Thomson/Arden Shakespeare, 2001.

Duffy, Eamon. 'Was Shakespeare a Catholic?' *The Tablet,* 27 April 1996, pp. 536–538.

—— 'Bare Ruined Choirs: Remembering Catholicism in Shakespeare's England.' Ch. 2 in Richard Dutton, Alison Findlay and Richard Wilson (eds), *Theatre and Religion: Lancastrian Shakespeare.* Manchester: Manchester University Press, 2003.

Dutton, Richard. *Mastering the Revels: The Regulation and Censorship of Elizabethan Drama.* London: Macmillan, 1991.

—— *Licensing, Censorship and Authorship in Early Modern England.* Basingstoke: Palgrave, 2000.

—— Alison Findlay and Richard Wilson, eds. *Theatre and Religion: Lancastrian Shakespeare.* Manchester: Manchester University Press, 2003.

Elliott, Alison Goddard. 'Ovid and the Critics: Seneca, Quintilian, and "Seriousness".' *Helios,* n.s. 12: 1 (1985), pp. 9–20.

Elton, William R. *King Lear and the Gods.* Los Angeles: Huntington Library, 1966.

Evans, G. Blakemore. 'The Douai Manuscript: Six Shakespearean Transcripts (1694–5).' *Philological Quarterly,* 41 (1962), pp. 158–172.

Fincham, Kenneth, and Nicholas Tyacke. *Altars Restored: The Changing Face of English Religious Worship, 1547–c. 1700.* Oxford: Oxford University Press, 2007.

Foakes, R.A. *Hamlet Versus Lear: Cultural Politics and Shakespeare's Art.* Cambridge: Cambridge University Press, 1993.

Forker, Charles R., ed. *Richard II: The Critical Tradition.* New Jersey: Athlone, 1988.

Foster, Verna A. *The Name and Nature of Tragicomedy.* Aldershot: Ashgate, 2004.

Fox, Adam. *Oral and Literate Culture in England, 1500–1700.* Oxford: Clarendon, 2000.

Fraser, Russell. *The War Against Poetry.* Princeton: Princeton University Press, 1970.

Friedman, Michael D. *"The World Must Be Peopled": Shakespeare's Comedies of Forgiveness.* Madison/London: Fairleigh Dickinson University Press/Associated University Presses, 2002.

Gennings, John, and John Wilson, attrib. *The Life and Death of Mr. Edmund Geninges Priest.* St Omer, 1614.

Giamatti, A. Bartlett. *Exile and Change in Renaissance Literature.* New Haven: Yale University Press, 1984.

Gilbert, Allan H., ed. *Literary Criticism: Plato to Dryden.* 1940. This edn, Detroit: Wayne State University Press, 1962.

Goldman, Hetty. 'The Origin of the Greek Herm.' *American Journal of Archaeology*, 46: 1 (1942), pp. 58–68.

Grant, R.A.D. 'Providence, Authority, and the Moral Life in *The Tempest*.' *Shakespeare Studies*, 16 (1983), pp. 235–263.

Grantley, Daryll. '*The Winter's Tale* and Early Religious Drama.' *Comparative Drama*, 20: 1 (1986), pp. 17–34.

Green, Ian. *Print and Protestantism in Early Modern England*. Cambridge: Cambridge University Press, 2000.

—— and Kate Peters. 'Religious Publishing in England, 1640–1695.' Ch. 2 in John Barnard and D.F. McKenzie with Maureen Bell (eds), *The Cambridge History of the Book in Britain, Volume 4, 1557–1695*. Cambridge: Cambridge University Press, 2002.

Greenblatt, Stephen. *Shakespearean Negotiations: The Circulation of Social Energy in Renaissance England*. Berkeley: California University Press, 1988.

—— *Hamlet in Purgatory*. Princeton: Princeton University Press, 2001.

—— *Will in the World: How Shakespeare Became Shakespeare*. New York: W.W. Norton, 2004.

Greene, Thomas M. 'The Flexibility of the Self in Renaissance Literature.' In Peter Demetz, Thomas M. Greene and Lowry Nelson Jnr (eds), *The Disciplines of Criticism: Essays in Literary Theory, Interpretation and History* (New Haven: Yale University Press, 1968), pp. 241–264.

Groves, Beatrice. *Texts and Traditions: Religion in Shakespeare 1592–1604*. Oxford: Clarendon, 2007.

Guarini, Giovanni Battista. *Il Compendio della Poesia Tragicomica = De la Poésie Tragi-comique*. Ed. Laurence Giavarini. Paris: Honoré Champion, 2008.

—— *Il Pastor Fido e Il Compendio della Poesia Tragicomica*. Ed. Gioachino Brognoligo. [N.p.]: Scrittore d'Italia, 61 (1914).

Guileville, Guillaume de. *The Booke of the Pylgremage of the Sowle*. Ed. Katherine Isabella Cust. London: Basil Montagu Pickering, 1859.

Guillaume, Jeanne. 'Hic Terminus Haeret: Du Terme d'Erasme à la Device de Claude Gouffier: La Fortune d'un Emblème à la Renaissance.' *Journal of the Warburg and Courtauld Institutes*, 44 (1981), pp. 186–192.

Hadfield, Andrew. *Shakespeare, Spenser and the Matter of Britain*. Basingstoke: Palgrave, 2004.

Hamilton, Donna B. 'Shakespeare and Religion.' Ch. 11 in *The Shakespeare International Yearbook*, vol. 1, ed. W.R. Elton and John M. Mucciolo. Aldershot: Ashgate, 1999.

Hamlin, William M. *Tragedy and Scepticism in Shakespeare's England*. Basingstoke: Palgrave Macmillan, 2005.

Hampton, Timothy. *Writing from History: The Rhetoric of Exemplarity in Renaissance Literature*. Ithaca: Cornell University Press, 1990.

Harbage, Alfred. *Annals of English Drama, 975–1700*. 3rd edn., rev. Sylvia Stoler Wagonheim. London: Routledge, 1989.

Hassel, R. Chris, Jnr. *Renaissance Drama and the English Church Year*. Lincoln: Nebraska University Press, 1979.

—— *Shakespeare's Religious Language: A Dictionary*. London/New York: Thoemmes Continuum, 2005.

Henke, Robert. *Pastoral Transformations: Italian Tragicomedy and Shakespeare's Late Plays*. Newark: Delaware University Press, 1997.

Herndl, George C. *The High Design: English Renaissance Tragedy and the Natural Law*. Lexington: Kentucky University Press, 1970.

Herrick, Marvin T. *Tragicomedy: Its Origin and Development in Italy, France and England*. 1955. This edn, Urbana: Illinois University Press, 1962.

Hill, Tracey. ' "He Hath Changed His Coppy": Anti-Theatrical Writing and the Turncoat Player.' *Critical Survey*, 9: 3 (1997), pp. 59–77.

—— *Anthony Munday and Civic Culture: Theatre, History and Power in Early Modern England*. Manchester: Manchester University Press, 2004.

Hoeniger, F.D. 'Irony and Romance in *Cymbeline*.' *Studies in English Literature, 1500–1900*, 2: 2 (1962), pp. 219–228.

Honan, Park. *Shakespeare: A Life*. Oxford: Oxford University Press, 1998.

Honigmann, E.A.J. *Shakespeare: The 'Lost Years'*. 1985. This edn, Manchester: Manchester University Press, 1998.

—— 'The Shakespeare/Shakeshafte Question, Continued.' *Shakespeare Quarterly*, 54: 1 (2003), pp. 83–86.

Hunt, Maurice. 'Malvolio, Viola, and the Question of Instrumentality: Defining Providence in *Twelfth Night*.' *Studies in Philology*, 90 (1993), pp. 277–297.

—— *Shakespeare's Religious Allusiveness: Its Play and Tolerance*. Aldershot: Ashgate, 2004.

Hunter, Robert G. *Shakespeare and the Mystery of God's Judgements*. Athens: Georgia University Press, 1976.

Hutson, Lorna. 'From Penitent to Suspect: Law, Purgatory, and Renaissance Drama.' *Huntington Library Quarterly*, 65: 3/4 (2002), pp. 295–319.

Ingleby, C. M., *et al.*, *The Shakspere Allusion-Book*. 2 vols. London: Humphrey Milford/Oxford University Press, 1932.

Jensen, Phebe. 'Recusancy, Festivity and Community: The Simpsons at Gowlthwaite Hall.' Ch. 6 in Richard Dutton, Alison Findlay and Richard Wilson (eds), *Region, Religion and Patronage: Lancastrian Shakespeare*. Manchester: Manchester University Press, 2003.

—— *Religion and Revelry in Shakespeare's Festive World*. Cambridge: Cambridge University Press, 2008.

Jones-Davies, Margaret. '*Cymbeline* and the Sleep of Faith.' Ch. 12 in *Theatre and Religion: Lancastrian Shakespeare*, ed. Richard Dutton, Alison Findlay and Richard Wilson. Manchester: Manchester University Press, 2003.

Jonson, Ben. *Works*. Ed. C.H. Herford, Percy Simpson and Evelyn Simpson. 11 vols. Oxford: Clarendon, 1925–1952.

Kahn, Victoria, and Lorna Hutson, eds. *Rhetoric and Law in Early Modern Europe*. New Haven: Yale University Press, 2001.

Kastan, David Scott, and Peter Stallybrass, eds. *Staging the Renaissance*. London: Routledge, 1991.

Keefer, Michael H. 'Accommodation and Synecdoche: Calvin's God in *King Lear*.' *Shakespeare Studies*, 20 (1988), pp. 147–168.

Keifer, Frederick. *Fortune and Elizabethan Tragedy*. San Marino: Huntington Library, 1983.

Kelly, Erin. 'Jewish History, Catholic Argument: Thomas Lodge's *Workes of Josephus* as a Catholic Text.' *Sixteenth-Century Journal*, 34: 4 (2003), pp. 993–1010.

Kerrigan, William. *Shakespeare's Promises*. Baltimore: Johns Hopkins University Press, 1999.

King, Ros. *Cymbeline: Constructions of Britain*. Aldershot: Ashgate, 2005.

Kinney, Arthur F. *Markets of Bawdrie: The Dramatic Criticism of Stephen Gosson*. Salzburg: Salzburg Studies in English Literature, 1974.

—— *Humanist Poetics: Thought, Rhetoric, and Fiction in 16th-Century England*. Amherst: Massachusetts University Press, 1986.

Kirsch, Arthur S. 'A Caroline Commentary on the Drama.' *Modern Philology*, 66: 3 (1969), pp. 256–261.

Klause, John. 'Politics, Heresy and Martyrdom in Shakespeare's Sonnet 124 and *Titus Andronicus*.' In James Schiffer (ed.), *Shakespeare's Sonnets: Critical Essays*. New York: Garland, 1999, pp. 219–240.

—— *Shakespeare, the Earl and the Jesuit*. Madison: Fairleigh Dickinson University Press, 2008.

Klinck, Dennis R. 'Calvinism and Jacobean Tragedy.' *Genre*, 11: 3 (1978), pp. 333–358.

Knapp, Jeffrey. *Shakespeare's Tribe: Church, Nation and Theater in Early Modern England*. Chicago: Chicago University Press, 2002.

Lake, Peter. *Moderate Puritans and the Elizabethan Church*. Cambridge: Cambridge University Press, 1982.

—— *Anglicans and Puritans? Presbyterianism and English Conformist Thought from Whitgift to Hooker*. London: Allen and Unwin, 1988.

—— 'Religious Identities in Shakespeare's England.' Part 3, Ch. 5 in David Scott Kastan (ed.), *A Companion to Shakespeare*. Oxford: Blackwell, 1999.

——, with Michael C. Questier. *The Antichrist's Lewd Hat: Protestants, Papists and Players in Post-Reformation England*. New Haven: Yale University Press, 2002.

Lander, Jesse M. *Inventing Polemic: Religion, Print and Literary Culture in Early Modern England*. Cambridge: Cambridge University Press, 2006.

Laroque, François. *Shakespeare's Festive World*. Cambridge: Cambridge University Press, 1993.

Leibler, Naomi Conn. *Shakespeare's Festive Tragedy: The Ritual Foundations of Genre*. London: Routledge, 1995.

Limn, Walter S.H. 'Knowledge and Belief in *The Winter's Tale*.' *Studies in English Literature, 1500–1900*, 41: 2 (2001), pp. 317–334.

Llewellyn, Nigel. *Funeral Monuments in Post-Reformation England*. Cambridge: Cambridge University Press, 2000.

Low, Anthony. '*Hamlet* and the Ghost of Purgatory: Intimations of Killing the Father.' *English Literary Renaissance*, 29: 3 (1999), pp. 443–467.

Lunney, Ruth. 'Rewriting the Narrative of Dramatic Character.' *Medieval and Renaissance Drama in England*, 14 (2001), pp. 66–85.

Lyne, Raphael. *Ovid's Changing Worlds: English Metamorphoses, 1567–1632*. Oxford: Oxford University Press, 2001.

—— 'Love and Exile after Ovid.' Ch. 17 in Philip Hardie (ed.), *The Cambridge Companion to Ovid*. Cambridge: Cambridge University Press, 2002.

—— *Shakespeare's Late Work*. Oxford: Oxford University Press, 2007.

Mack, Maynard. King Lear *in Our Time*. Berkeley: California University Press, 1965.

Maguire, Nancy Klein, ed. *Renaissance Tragicomedy: Explorations in Genre and Politics*. New York: AMS, 1987.

Maley, Willy. 'Postcolonial Shakespeare: British Identity Formation and *Cymbeline*.' In Jennifer Richards and James Knowles (eds), *Shakespeare's Late Plays: New Readings*. Edinburgh: Edinburgh University Press, 1999, pp. 145–157.

Maltby, Judith. *Prayer Book and People in Elizabethan and Early Stuart England*. Cambridge: Cambridge University Press, 1998.

Marcus, Leah. *The Politics of Mirth: Jonson, Herrick, Milton, Marvell, and the Defense of Old Holiday Pastimes*. Chicago: Chicago University Press, 1986.

Marlowe, Christopher. *Doctor Faustus and Other Plays*. Ed. David Bevington and Eric Rasmussen. 1995. This edn, Oxford: Oxford University Press, 1998.

Marotti, Arthur F. *Religious Ideology and Cultural Fantasy: Catholic and Anti-Catholic Discourse in Early Modern England*. Notre Dame: Notre Dame University Press, 2005.

Marshall, Peter. *Beliefs and the Dead in Reformation England*. Oxford: Oxford University Press, 2002.

Martin, Christopher, ed. *Ovid in English*. London: Penguin, 1998.

Martz, Louis L. *The Poetry of Meditation*. 1954. Rev. edn, New Haven: Yale University Press, 1962.

Marx, Steven. *Shakespeare and the Bible*. Oxford: Oxford University Press, 2000.

Maslen, R.W. 'Lodge's *Glaucus and Scilla* and the Conditions of Catholic Authorship in Elizabethan England.' *EnterText* (e-journal), 3: 1 (2003), pp. 59–100.

Maule, Linda. *The Devil's Mousetrap: Redemption and Colonial American Literature.* New York/Oxford: Oxford University Press, 1997.

Mayer, Jean-Christophe. *Shakespeare's Hybrid Faith: History, Religion and the Stage.* Basingstoke: Palgrave, 2006.

McAlindon, Tom. 'Perfect Answers: Religious Inquisition, Falstaffian Wit.' In *Shakespeare Survey*, 54, ed. Peter Holland (2001), pp. 100–107.

McCabe, Richard A. 'Elizabethan Satire and the Bishops' Ban of 1599.' *Yearbook of English Studies*, 11 (1981), pp. 188–193.

McCabe, William H. *An Introduction to the Jesuit Theater.* Ed. Louis J. Oldani. St Louis: Institute of Jesuit Sources, 1983.

McConica, James K. 'The Riddle of "Terminus".' *Erasmus in English*, 2 (1971), pp. 2–7.

McCoog, Thomas M., S.J. *The Society of Jesus in Ireland, Scotland and England 1541–1588.* Studies in Medieval and Renaissance Thought, Vol. 60. Leiden: E.J. Brill, 1996.

—— and Peter Davidson, 'Edmund Campion and William Shakespeare: *Much Ado About Nothing*.' In Thomas M. McCoog S.J. (ed.), *The Reckoned Expense: Edmund Campion and the Early English Jesuits* (1996; revised and expanded edition, Rome: Institutum Historicum Societatis Jesu, 2007), pp. 165–185.

McEachern, Claire, ed. *The Cambridge Companion to Shakespearean Tragedy.* Cambridge: Cambridge University Press, 2002.

McMullan, Gordon. '"The Neutral Term"?: Shakespearean Tragicomedy and the Idea of the "Late Play".' Ch. 8 in Subha Mukherji and Raphael Lyne (eds), *Early Modern Tragicomedy.* Cambridge: D.S. Brewer, 2007.

Miller, Edwin Haviland. *The Professional Writer in Elizabethan England: A Study of Non-Dramatic Literature.* Cambridge, Mass.: Harvard University Press, 1959.

Milton, Anthony. *Catholic and Reformed: The Roman and Protestant Churches in English Protestant Thought, 1600–1640.* Cambridge: Cambridge University Press, 1995.

Milward, Peter. *Shakespeare's Religious Background.* Bloomington: Indiana University Press, 1973.

—— *Biblical Themes in Shakespeare: Centring on King Lear.* Tokyo: Renaissance Institute, 1975.

—— *Shakespeare's Other Dimension.* Tokyo: Sophia University, 1989.

Miola, Robert S. 'Jesuit Drama in Early Modern England.' Ch. 4 in Richard Dutton, Alison Findlay and Richard Wilson (eds), *Theatre and Religion: Lancastrian Shakespeare.* Manchester: Manchester University Press, 2003.

—— 'An Alien People Clutching their Gods'? Shakespeare's Ancient Religions.' In *Shakespeare Survey 54: Shakespeare and Religions*, ed. Peter Holland (2001), pp. 31–45.

Monta, Susannah Breitz. *Martyrdom and Literature in Early Modern England*. Cambridge: Cambridge University Press, 2005.

Moschovakis, Nicholas. ' "Irreligious Piety" and Christian History: Persecution as Pagan Anachronism in *Titus Andronicus*.' *Shakespeare Quarterly*, 53: 4 (2002), pp. 460–486.

Moss, Ann. *Commonplace-Books and the Structuring of Renaissance Thought*. Oxford: Clarendon, 1996.

Mowat, Barbara A. 'Shakespearian Tragicomedy.' In Nancy Klein Maguire (ed.), *Renaissance Tragicomedy: Explorations in Genre and Politics*. New York: AMS, 1987, pp. 80–96.

Mukherji, Subha. *Law and Representation in Early Modern Drama*. Cambridge: Cambridge University Press, 2006.

—— and Raphael Lyne, eds. *Early Modern Tragicomedy*. Woodbridge: D.S. Brewer, 2007.

Mullaney, Steven. *The Place of the Stage: License, Play and Power in Renaissance England*. Chicago: Chicago University Press, 1988.

Muller, Richard A. 'Perkins' A Golden Chaine: Predestinarian System or Schematised Ordo Salutis?' *Sixteenth-Century Journal*, 9: 1 (1978), pp. 66–81.

—— *Christ and the Decree: Christology and Predestination in Reformed Theology from Calvin to Perkins*. Durham: Labyrinth Press, 1986.

Mullett, Michael A. *Catholics in Britain and Ireland, 1558–1829*. Basingstoke: Macmillan, 1998.

Mulryne, J.R., and Margaret Shewring, eds. *Theatre of the English and Italian Renaissance*. New York: St Martin's Press, 1991.

O'Connell, Michael. *The Idolatrous Eye: Iconoclasm and Theater in Early-Modern England*. New York: Oxford University Press, 2000.

Ohly, Friedrich. *The Damned and the Elect: Guilt in Western Culture*. Trans. Linda Archibald. Cambridge: Cambridge University Press, 1992.

Parkinson, Anne C. 'Religious Drama in Kendal: the Corpus Christi Play in the Reign of James I', *Recusant History*, 25: 4 (2001), pp. 604–612.

Patterson, Annabel. *Censorship and Interpretation: The Conditions of Writing and Reading in Early Modern England*. Madison: Wisconsin University Press, 1984.

Phillips, J.B. *The Reformation of Images: Destruction of Art in England, 1535–1660*. Berkeley: California University Press, 1973.

Pilarz, Scott R. *Robert Southwell and the Mission of Literature, 1561–1595: Writing Reconciliation*. Aldershot: Ashgate, 2004.

Platt, Michael. 'Falstaff in the Valley of the Shadow of Death.' In Harold Bloom
(ed.), *Falstaff*. New York: Chelsea House, 1992, pp. 171–202.

Pollard, Tanya, ed. *Shakespeare's Theater: A Sourcebook*. Malden: Blackwell, 2004.

Poole, Kristen. *Radical Religion from Shakespeare to Milton: Figures of Nonconformity in Early Modern England*. Cambridge: Cambridge University Press,
2000.

Popkin, Richard. *The History of Scepticism*. 1979: rev. and expanded edn, New
York: Oxford University Press, 2003.

Poppi, Antonino. 'Fate, Fortune, Providence and Human Freedom.' Ch. 17 in
Charles B. Schmitt et al. (eds), *The Cambridge History of Renaissance
Philosophy*. Cambridge: Cambridge University Press, 1988.

Postles, Dave. 'Penance and the Market-Place: A Reformation Dialogue with the
Medieval Church, c. 1250–c. 1600.' *Journal of Ecclesiastical History*, 54: 3
(2003), pp. 441–468.

Price, Diana. 'Reconsidering Shakespeare's Monument.' *Review of English
Studies*, 48: 190 (1997), pp. 168–182.

Price, John Edward. 'Anti-Moralistic Moralism in *All's Well That Ends Well*.'
Shakespeare Studies, 12 (1979), pp. 95–111.

Pritchard, Allan. 'Puritans and the Blackfriars Theater: The Cases of Mistresses
Duck and Drake.' *Shakespeare Quarterly*, 45: 1 (1994), pp. 92–95.

Proudfoot, Richard. '"The Play's the Thing": Hamlet and the Conscience of the
Queen.' Ch. 9 in John W. Mahon and Thomas A. Pendleton (eds),
*"Fanned and Winnowed Opinions": Shakespearean Essays Presented to
Harold Jenkins*. London/New York: Methuen, 1987.

Raffel, Burton. 'Shakespeare and the Catholic Question.' *Religion and Literature*,
30: 1 (1998), pp. 35–51.

Richards, Jennifer, and James Knowles, eds. *Shakespeare's Late Plays: New
Readings*. Edinburgh: Edinburgh University Press, 1999.

Richmond, Velma Bourgeois. *Shakespeare, Catholicism and Romance*. New York:
Continuum, 2000.

Ringler, William A., Jnr. 'Hamlet's Defense of the Players.' In Richard Hosley
(ed.), *Essays on Shakespeare and Elizabethan Drama in Honour of Hardin
Craig* (London: Routledge and Kegan Paul, 1963), pp. 201–211.

Rist, Tom. *Shakespeare's Romances and the Politics of Counter-Reformation*.
Lewiston: Edwin Mellen Press, 1999.

Robinson, Marsha S. *Writing the Reformation: Actes and Monuments and the
Jacobean History Play*. Aldershot: Ashgate, 2002.

Rosendale, Timothy. *Liturgy and Literature in the Making of Protestant England*.
Cambridge: Cambridge University Press, 2007.

Roston, Murray. *Biblical Drama in England from the Middle Ages to the Present
Day*. London: Faber and Faber, 1968.

Rozett, Martha Tuck. *The Doctrine of Election and the Emergence of Elizabethan Tragedy.* New York: Princeton University Press, 1984.

Ruiter, David. *Shakespeare's Festive History: Feasting, Festivity, Fasting and Lent in the Second Henriad.* Aldershot: Ashgate, 2003.

Salingar, Leo. 'Elizabethan Dramatists and Italy: A Postscript.' In J.R. Mulryne and Margaret Shewring (eds), *Theatre of the English and Italian Renaissance* (New York: St Martin's Press, 1991), pp. 221–237.

Schoenbaum, Samuel. *Shakespeare's Lives.* 1970. 2nd edn, Oxford: Oxford University Press, 1991.

—— *William Shakespeare: A Compact Documentary Life.* 1975. Rev. edn, New York: Oxford University Press, 1987.

Schrickx, Willem. '*Pericles* in a Book-List of 1619 from the English Jesuit Mission and Some of the Play's Special Problems.' *Shakespeare Survey,* 29 (1976), pp. 21–32.

Semper, I.J. 'The Jacobean Theater Through the Eyes of Catholic Clerics.' *Shakespeare Quarterly,* 3: 1 (1952), pp. 45–51.

Shaheen, Naseeb. *Biblical References in Shakespeare's Plays.* 1999. Revised edn. Newark: Delaware University Press/London: Associated University Presses, 2002.

Shell, Alison. 'Why Didn't Shakespeare Write Religious Verse?' Ch. 6 in Takashi Kozuka and J.R. Mulryne (eds), *Shakespeare, Marlowe, Jonson: New Directions in Biography.* Aldershot: Ashgate, 2006.

Shuger, Debora Kuller. 'Subversive Fathers and Suffering Subjects: Shakespeare and Christianity.' Ch. 3 in Donna B. Hamilton and Richard Strier (eds), *Religion, Literature and Politics in Post-Reformation England, 1540–1688.* Cambridge: Cambridge University Press, 1996.

—— *Habits of Thought in the English Renaissance: Religion, Politics and the Dominant Culture.* 1990. This edn, Toronto: Toronto University Press/Renaissance Society of America, 1997.

—— *Political Theologies in Shakespeare's England: The Sacred and the State in Measure for Measure.* Basingstoke: Palgrave, 2001.

Smith, David L., Richard Strier and David Bevington, eds. *The Theatrical City: Culture, Theatre and Politics in London, 1576–1649.* Cambridge: Cambridge University Press, 1995.

Snyder, Susan. '*King Lear* and the Psychology of Dying.' *Shakespeare Quarterly,* 33: 4 (1982), pp. 449–460.

Sommerville, C. John. *The Secularisation of Early Modern England: From Religious Culture to Religious Faith.* New York: Oxford University Press, 1992.

Southwell, Robert, S.J. *Collected Poems.* Ed. Peter Davidson and Anne Sweeney. Manchester: Carcanet, 2007.

Stachniewski, Jan. *The Persecutory Imagination: English Puritanism and the Literature of Religious Despair.* Oxford: Clarendon, 1991.

Strier, Richard, 'Shakespeare and the Sceptics.' *Religion and Literature*, 32:2 (2000), pp.171–196.

Sweeney, Anne R. *Robert Southwell: Snow in Arcadia: Redrawing the English Lyric Landscape.* Manchester: Manchester University Press, 2006.

Taylor, Dennis, and David N. Beauregard, eds. *Shakespeare and the Culture of Christianity in Early Modern England.* New York: Fordham University Press, 2004.

Taylor, Gary. 'The Fortunes of Oldcastle.' *Shakespeare Studies*, 38 (1985), pp. 85–100.

—— 'Monopolies, Show Trials, Disaster and Invasion: King Lear and Censorship.' In Gary Taylor and Michael Warren (eds), *The Division of the Kingdoms: Shakespeare's Two Versions of* King Lear (1983: this edn Oxford: Clarendon, 1986), pp. 76–119.

—— *Reinventing Shakespeare: A Cultural History from the Restoration to the Present.* New York: Weidenfeld and Nicolson, 1989.

—— 'Forms of Opposition: Shakespeare and Middleton.' *English Literary Renaissance*, 24 (1994), pp. 283–314.

Thomas, Keith. *Religion and the Decline of Magic.* 1971. This edn, Harmondsworth: Penguin, 1984.

Thomson, Leslie. 'The Meaning of Thunder and Lightning: Stage Directions and Audience Response.' *Early Theatre*, 2 (1999), pp. 11–24.

Tipson, Baird. 'A Dark Side of Seventeenth-Century English Protestantism: The Sin Against the Holy Spirit.' *Harvard Theological Review*, 77: 3/4 (1984), pp. 301–330.

Toon, Peter. 'The Articles and Homilies.' Ch. 2 in part IV of Stephen Sykes, John Booty and Jonathan Knight (eds), *The Study of Anglicanism.* London: SPCK/Fortress Press, 1998.

Treherne, Matthew. 'The Difficult Emergence of Pastoral Tragicomedy: Guarini's *Il Pastor Fido* and its Critical Reception in Italy, 1586–1601.' Ch. 2 in Subha Mukherji and Raphael Lyne (eds), *Early Modern Tragicomedy.* Woodbridge: D.S. Brewer, 2007.

Tyacke, Nicholas. *Anti-Calvinists: The Rise of English Arminianism, c. 1590–1640.* Oxford: Clarendon, 1987.

Veevers, Erica. *Images of Love and Religion: Queen Henrietta Maria and Court Entertainments.* Cambridge: Cambridge University Press, 1989.

Velz, John W. 'Shakespeare and the Geneva Bible: The Circumstances.' Ch. 7 in J.R. Mulryne and Takashi Kozuka (eds), *Shakespeare, Marlowe, Jonson: New Directions in Biography.* Aldershot: Ashgate, 2006.

Walsham, Alexandra. *Church-Papists: Catholicism, Conformity and Confessional Polemic in Early Modern England.* 1993. This edn, Woodbridge: Boydell, 1999.

—— *Providence in Early Modern England*. Oxford: Oxford University Press, 1999.

—— '"Domme Preachers": Post-Reformation English Catholicism and the Culture of Print.' *Past and Present*, 168: 1 (2000), pp. 72–123.

—— *Charitable Hatred: Tolerance and Intolerance in England, 1500–1700*. Manchester: Manchester University Press, 2006.

Waters, D. Douglas. *Christian Settings in Shakespeare's Tragedies*. Rutherford/London: Fairleigh Dickinson University Press/Associated University Presses, 1994.

Watt, Tessa. *Cheap Print and Popular Piety, 1550–1640*. Cambridge: Cambridge University Press, 1991.

Weis, René. *Shakespeare Revealed: A Biography*. London: John Murray, 2007.

Wells, Stanley. 'Flyleaf.' *Daily Telegraph*, 22 April 1995, A8.

White, Mary Frances. *Fifteenth Century Misericords in the Collegiate Church of Holy Trinity, Stratford-upon-Avon*. Stratford-upon-Avon: M.F. White, 1974.

White, Paul Whitfield. *Theatre and Reformation: Protestantism, Patronage and Playing in Tudor England*. Cambridge: Cambridge University Press, 1993.

—— 'Theater and Religious Culture.' Ch. 8 in John D. Cox and David Scott Kastan (eds), *A New History of Early English Drama*. New York: Columbia University Press, 1997.

—— *Drama and Religion in English Provincial Society, 1485–1660*. Cambridge: Cambridge University Press, 2008.

Whitney, Charles. *Early Responses to Renaissance Drama*. Cambridge: Cambridge University Press, 2006.

Wickham, Glynne. *Early English Stages, 1300 to 1600. Vol. 3. Plays and Their Makers*. London: Routledge and Kegan Paul, 1981.

Wiggins, Martin. 'Shakespeare Jesuited: The Plagiarisms of "Pater Clarcus".' *The Seventeenth Century*, 20: 1 (2005), pp. 1–21.

Wilson, Luke. 'Ben Jonson and the Law of Contract.' Ch. 6 in Victoria Kahn and Lorna Hutson (eds), *Rhetoric and Law in Early Modern Europe*. New Haven: Yale University Press, 2001.

Wind, Edgar. *Pagan Mysteries in the Renaissance*. London: Faber and Faber, 1958.

—— 'Ænigma Termini: The Emblem of Erasmus.' *Journal of the Warburg Institute*, 1 (1937–8), pp. 66–69.

Wood, Michael. *In Search of Shakespeare*. London: BBC Books, 2003.

Woods, Gillian. 'Catholic Semiotics in Shakespearean Drama.' Oxford D. Phil. thesis, 2006.

Wunderli, Richard, and Gerald Broce. 'The Final Moment Before Death in Early Modern England.' *Sixteenth-Century Journal*, 20: 2 (1989), pp. 259–275.

Zitner, Sheldon P. 'Gosson, Ovid and the Elizabethan Audience.' *Shakespeare Quarterly*, 9: 2 (1958), pp. 206–208.

INDEX